MW01025528

The Spirit of Torah

תורה ונפש

MOSAICA PRESS

The
Spirit
תורה
ונפש
# of Torah

Penetrating Insights
into the Chumash

Aaron Muller

Mosaica Press, Inc.

© 2018 by Aaron Muller

Designed and typeset by Brocha Mirel Strizower

ISBN-10: 1-946351-18-0

ISBN-13: 978-1-946351-18-0

All rights reserved. No part of this book may be used or reproduced or transmitted in any form or by any means, electronic or mechanical, including photocopying, recording, or by any information storage and retrieval system, without written permission from the publisher.

Published and distributed by:

Mosaica Press, Inc.

www.mosaicapress.com

info@mosaicapress.com

A Note to the Reader: When translating any work there's always a risk of not being faithful to the author's original intent. The objective in translating passages found in this book was to give the reader a loose translation, as a word-for-word translation could at times create confusion and difficulty in comprehending. Of course, it's always best to read the original Hebrew wording to get a genuine feel for what the original author has written.

אשא עיני אל ההרים אל תקרי אל ההרים אלא אל ההורים
(בראשית רבה סח)

ספר זה מוקדש לזכר ולעילוי נשמת

ר' אברהם חיים ב"ר אהרן אלעזר הכהן מיללער ז"ל
איש ישר ונאמן רודף צדקה וחסד
נלב"ע כ"ד טבת תשמ"ה

וזוגתו פיגא בת ר' אברהם משה ז"ל
בטח לב בעלה ויהללו בשערים מעשיה
נלב"ע י"ד שבט תשס"ד

לעילוי נשמת
ר' אהרן אלעזר ב"ר משה הכהן מיללער הי"ד
נלב"ע ער"ח חשון תש"ה

וזוגתו אידל בת יוסף ע"ה
נלב"ע כ"ז סיון תש"ד

לעילוי נשמת
ר' אברהם משה ב"ר צבי בורשטיין ז"ל
נלב"ע י"ב תשרי תשכ"ו

וזוגתו שרה טויבא בת ר' אברהם יוסף ע"ה
נלב"ע ט"ז אדר א' תשל"ג

ת.נ.צ.ב.ה.

In loving memory of

שמעון אלתר בן ר' **משה שטערן** ז"ל

Sigmund (Sigi) F. Stern

נפטר א' אייר תשנ"א

who was unable to benefit from a formal yeshiva
education due to the war. Upon retirement, he
participated in daily *shiurim* and enjoyed them
immensely. He would have had tremendous *nachas*
from the Torah in this inspiring *sefer*.

Dedicated by Barbara and Dovid Hurwitz

לעילוי נשמת

משה בן ר' **זאב שטערן** ז"ל

Moses Stern

נפטר ה' אלול תשכ"ח

וזוגתו **שרה מרים יוכבד** ב"ר **שמעון** ע"ה

Sara Stern

נפטרה ג' סיון תשכ"ז

לעילוי נשמת

חיים משולם בן ר' **משה שטערן** ז"ל

Charlie Stern

וזוגתו **גאלדי** בת ר' **אברהם דוד** ע"ה

Goldie Stern

לעילוי נשמת

הענטשא בת ר' **משה שטערן** ע"ה

Helene Kleiner

נפטרה ט"ז שבט תשע"ד

לעילוי נשמת
אהרן יחיאל אלתר בן ר' **שמעון ברוך וייס** ז"ל
Aaron Weiss
נפטר ו' אייר תשכ"ד

וזוגתו **לאה** בת ר' **שרגא פייוועל** ז"ל
Lillian Weiss
נפטרה ו' תשרי תשנ"ח

לעילוי נשמת
הרב **יוסף** בן **שמאי** ז"ל
Rabbi Joseph Levinson
נפטר כ"א חשון תש"ס

וזוגתו **גולדא העֶנדל** בת ר' **אהרן יחיאל אלתר** ז"ל
Goldie Levinson
נפטרה י"א סיון תשע"ו

In honor of
Ruth Stern
A devoted mother, grandmother,
and great grandmother

Your love, good humor, and care for your children
are your hallmark.
May Hashem grant you many more
years of good health and *nachas* from your children
and grandchildren.

לעילוי נשמת

ר' **משה יהושע**

ב"ר **מרדכי אליעזר דעמביצער** ז"ל

נלב"ע כ"ב תמוז תש"נ

L'ilui Nishmas

Dovid Mordechai **ben** Yecheskal *z"l*

Yecheskal **ben** Yosef *z"l*

Fruma **bas** Yaakov Yosef *a"h*

Reva **bas** Yecheskal *a"h*

Shmuel **ben** Avraham *z"l*

Zelda **bas** Binyomin *a"h*

Levi Yitzchok **ben** Shmuel *z"l*

Miriam **bas** Eliyahu *a"h*

Moshe **ben** Avigdor *z"l*

Fruma **bas** Eliyahu *a"h*

Eliyahu **ben** Moshe *z"l*

May their souls be bound to the Source of Life.

Dedicated by their children, grandchildren,
great grandchildren, nieces, nephews, great nieces,
and great nephews

In memory of
Menachem ben Moshe HaKohen
4 Elul 5776

To a man whose dedication to Judaism allowed
our family to grow to what it has become today

Dedicated by iKAHN Capital

לעילוי נשמות

מורינו ורבינו הרב **עמרם** בן הרב **שמואל דוד** זצוק"ל
ואשתו הרבנית **יוטא פייגע** בת הרב **יחיאל אלתר** זצוק"ל

הורינו ומורינו
ר' **יחזקאל** בן רב **יצחק אהרן**
ר' **חנניה** בן ר' **דוד**
ר' **יונה** בן ר' **יעקב** ואשתו מרת **חיה שרה** בת ר' **יוסף יעקב**
ר' **דניאל** בן ר' **יונה** ואשתו מרת **איטה מרים** בת ר' **דוד הכהן**
מרת **אלטא חוה העניטשא** בת ר' **יעקב צבי**

אחינו
רחמים יעקב שמעון בן ר' **חנניה**
דבורה דינה בת ר' **דניאל**
מרת **שרה גיטל** בת ר' **צבי**

ונכדנו
אלישע ברוך טוביה בן רב **אורי מנחם** יבלחט"א

וגם לזכות לתורה לחופה ולמעשים טובים לאמונה שלימה לתשובה שלימה
ולרפואה שלימה בתוך שאר חולי ישראל לפרנסה ברווח בעושר ובאושר
ולשמירה על הגוף והנפש לכל צאצאיהם ולכל משפחותיהם ובמיוחד
ל**יחזקאל** בן רב **גרשון לוי** נ"י
וגם לכל כלל ישראל עמו"ש

לעילוי נשמת
חיים צבי
בן זאב וואלף הלוי גנסלר ז"ל
Herman H. Gensler
כ"ה אדר תשס"ט

וזוגתו **רבקה מלכה** בת היימאן ז"ל
Rhoda M. Gensler
כ"ד אב תשע"ה

לעילוי נשמת
הרב צבי אביגדור ב"ר יעקב ברזיל ז"ל
נפ' כ"ג תמוז תשמ"ו

וזוגתו **אסתר עטל** בת ר' שמואל ע"ה
נפ' כ"ד שבט תשס"ד

לעילוי נשמת
אליהו בן שלמה הלוי הורביץ ז"ל
Allen Hurwitz
נפטר ג' מנחם אב תשד"מ

וזוגתו **רבקה** בת אברהם שלמה ע"ה
Regina Hurwitz
נפטרה כ"ז אדר ב' תשס"ג

לעילוי נשמת
רבקה בת יצחק הכהן ע"ה

לעילוי נשמות
משה לייב בן אברהם יוסף ז"ל
Morris Rosenbaum
נפטר ה' תשרי תשי"ב

וזוגתו **בלימא** בת ירחמיאל אליהו ע"ה
Bleema Rosenbaum
נפטרה ח' טבת תשי"א

שאול בן מרדכי ז"ל
Charlie Applebaum
נפטר כ' תמוז תשכ"ט

וזוגתו **פייגע** בת משה לייב ע"ה
Faye Applebaum
נפטרה כ"ט טבת תשמ"ח

ירחמיאל מרדכי בן שאול ז"ל
Dr. Reginald Alev
נפטר כ"ו אלול תשע"ה

שושנה בת שאול ע"ה
Joyce Applebaum
נפטרה ג' אדר ב' תשס"ח

ברוך ב"ר חיים ז"ל
Benjamin Bromberg
נפטר כ' שבט תשכ"ה

וזוגתו **חנה** בת ברוך ע"ה
Anna Bromberg
נפטרה ג' חשון תשנ"א

בס"ד

שמואל קמנצקי
Rabbi S. Kamenetsky

2018 Upland Way
Philadelphia, PA 19131

Home: 215-473-2798
Study: 215-473-1212

[Handwritten Hebrew letter]

I hereby commend [you] on [your] *sefer*, full of charm and grace. I am sure it will bring great benefit and *chizuk* to all who read it, especially in that [you] bring the words of the Acharonim in full, enabling the reader to look at the original source.

I am certain that the work will bring satisfaction to all who learn it, thereby bringing them great benefit, causing great satisfaction in the Heavens above, as every reader will find something in the *sefer* that speaks to him and helps him grow.

My blessings from the depths of my heart that [you] will be included among those who successfully bring merit to the public, whose "righteousness stands forever."

From the depths of my heart,
[Rav] Shmuel Kamenetsky

Yeshiva Zeev HaTorah

Rav Shmuel Brazil, Rosh HaYeshiva

Israel office:

ישיבת זיו התורה
רח' רמת הגולן 16ב
ירושלים 97704

Phone: (072)257-3593
Fax: (02)540-9388

From America Dial:

Phone: (732)730-9723
Fax: (732)719-2202

U.S Address:

Yeshiva Zeev Hatorah
1950 New Central Ave.,
Lakewood, NJ 08701

Online:

office@zeevhatorah.org
www.zeevhatorah.org

פרשת בהעלותך את הנרות תשע"ז

I have known Reb Ahron Muller נ"י for many years, and as time passes he continues to amaze me even more. His dedication and *mesiras nefesh* for servicing *Harbatzas Hatorah* is incredible. His weekly *Parsha Sheet* website posts for every Shabbos, a collection of nearly a hundred different *Divrei Torahs* on the *parsha* culled from mailings of outstanding and well known *Roshei Yeshivas, Tzadikkim, Rabbanin* and *Bnei Torah*, and are all available at your fingertips. The list is constantly growing to suit everyone's taste interest, and style.

This *Marbitz Torah* has presently authored a wonderful addition to the list by publishing his own book of stimulating insights and provoking thoughts on the *parsha* which inspire personal growth. His Torah thoughts are not presented merely as a condensed *gut vort* tailored for the "on the run" reader known for its brevity and conciseness. Rather, the intent of the author is to give the reader the opportunity to actually learn the text in the original *Lashon Hakodesh* form and is accompanied with its English translation, as he skillfully weaves and develops the thought to its conclusion. At the end, one is left with a new insight food for thought, that if incubated could shape one's future conduct and deepen his relationship with *Hashem*, his fellow *Yid*, and himself.

My *beracha* is that he continues his *avodas Hakodesh* for *Klal Yisrael* in breathing life and guidance into the *parshiyos* of the Torah so that our connection to them will open our minds and hearts to a higher spirit and a more meaningful daily living.

Beyedidus Rabba,

Rav Shmuel Brazil

MERCAZ HATORAH BELLE HARBOR

YESHIVA MERCAZ HATORAH BELLE HARBOR 505 BEACH 129TH STREET BELLE HARBOR, NY 11694 PH: 718-474-3064 FX: 718-634-4510
Rosh HaYeshiva
RAV SHMUEL ZEV DICKER

בס"ד

יום ד' תשע"ז   פרשת קרח

לכבוד תלמידי ר' אהרן מיללער שליט"א,

מאד שמחתי שמלא לבך להדפיס ספרך על פרשיות התורה ונהניתי מאד בראותי קטעים שהם מלאים
דברי תורה ויראת שמים.

יהי רצון שיהיה חפץ ה' בידך ותצליח לחזק הלומדים מספרך בתורה ויראת שמים ויהא חלקך עם מזכי
הרבים שאמרו חז"ל כל המזכה את הרבים אין חטא בא לידו.

ועל זה באתי על החתום,

שמואל זאב דיקער

רב שלום רוזנר
ק"ק נופי השמש
בית שמש, ת"ו

_____

דברי ברכה

I have had the זכות of seeing a few of the דברי תורה compiled by R' Aaron Muller. The author has worked hard
to deliver powerful דברי תורה that are both organized and
inspiring. He quotes the original sources to help with
deeper understanding, and he relates them to our lives
in a very real way. May 'ה bless the author's efforts, and
may we merit the complete fulfillment of נבואת ישיעהו —
כי מלאה הארץ דעה את ה' כמים לים מכסים.

בברכת התורה,
Shalom Rosner

Table of Contents

Shemos

Vayikra

Bamidbar

Devarim

Acknowledgments

אודה ה' מאד בפי ובתוך רבים אהללנו.
*With my mouth, I will greatly thank Hashem and amongst
the multitudes I will praise Him.* (Tehillim 109:30)

It is with a great sense of humility and responsibility that I approach the task of thanking those who assisted me in bringing this book to reality. What began as a small thought hidden away in the crevices of my brain developed into a project that was completed with the help and encouragement of many.

The great and legendary *mashgiach* Rav Shlomo Wolbe in his introduction to *Alei Shur* discusses the idea of *teshuvah* according to the Rambam and Rabbeinu Yonah, in which it has the unique quality and power to literally transform the sinner into a new person. What does it mean to become a new person, asks Rav Wolbe. Do the personality, intellect, and abilities of the person actually change and experience transformation? Is his name not still the same as it was prior to *teshuvah*?

Explains Rav Wolbe, this "new person" was always in existence but hidden away in the depth of the same old person that sinned. A person can be compared to a great multi-story building, that on each floor has more and more furnishings than that of the floor below. As we navigate life and hopefully climb from one level to the next, we can reveal and discover the many skills and aptitudes not known to us while on the floor below, thereby literally changing who we are as we amass and acquire new-found abilities — unknown to us beforehand — with which to serve Hashem.

With this thought in mind, I thank Hashem for giving me the strength and opportunity to develop the thoughts in this book while studying the weekly *parashah*. This journey was one which has allowed me to reveal particular inner traits, hidden away at different floors, a true self-discovery. I am thankful, as the *divrei Torah* within the forthcoming pages served as a platform for me to become inspired and deepen my relationship with Him.

It didn't take time for me to realize the unbelievable amount of effort on the part of a whole team of people that goes into publishing an actual book. Thank you, Rabbis Yaacov Haber and Doron Kornbluth, for agreeing to publish this work and for the guidance and insight throughout the publishing process. To Mrs. Sherie Gross and Rabbi Reuven Butler, thank you for your editing expertise and for prompting me to clarify abstract ideas into succinct wording. To Mrs. Rayzel Broyde and her team, thank you for creating a most beautiful cover and book design. To Mrs. Ilana Hiller and Mrs. Ester Becker, thanks for coordinating amongst the team and for your patience each step of the way. It was a true humbling experience to be working with individuals with a unique spectrum of talents. While it may be easy to become impassive to the needs and requests of an author after some time, you all treated this project with care from the very start, while showing real concern and taking all into consideration every step of the way.

Thank you to Rabbi Hillel Fendel for assisting in the translation of the many Hebrew sources referenced in the book, for reading the entire manuscript and contributing your many thoughts to enhance the presentation of the ideas. Your advice and suggestions throughout this project were professional, skilled, and invaluable.

To my dear parents, Mr. Heshy Muller and Dr. Dovid and Mrs. Barbara Hurwitz. Thank you for providing me with the necessary tools to have a chance at succeeding in this world. I may not have been aware of it at the time but from a very young age you served as strong role models, demonstrating a Torah way of life through actions and words. Your persistent and optimistic nature has brought me far and I am thankful to have had and continue to have the privilege of absorbing the rich personality traits you embody. May Hashem continue to give you good health and happiness for many more years to come.

To my dear children. Shimmy, Rachelli, Tzipora, Sarah, and Batsheva. Thank you for being the best children ever. Your smiles and irresistible personalities are a great source of happiness. I know I am truly fortunate to be your Father.

To my siblings, Moshe and Michal Muller, Sarit and Ari Dicker, and Avichai and Elisheva Muller. All have families but some have great ones. Your support, encouragement, and inspiration are priceless. Although our families grow and life gets busy at times limiting our once daily interactions; I will forever cherish our relationships and each of your unique personalities.

To my in-laws, Rav Shmuel and Rebbetzin Miriam Brazil and Mr. Yitzchak Gensler. It has been an honor to be welcomed into your family from the very beginning. Thank you for allowing me to marry your daughter and for always offering advice, encouragement, and support. Your commitment and dedication to Klal Yisrael continue to astound and inspire me.

I owe a great debt of gratitude to Yeshiva Merkaz HaTorah of Belle Harbor. During my time spent in the yeshiva I was *zocheh* to be in the company of the Rosh HaYeshiva Rav Levi Dicker, *zt"l*. Rav Levi was of a different generation, an *Ish Emes,* but most of all inspired his *talmidim* by allowing them to discover the sweetness of Torah, simply by teaching a few short lines of Gemara with ultimate precision and clarity. For this eye-opening opportunity, I am forever grateful. Thank you to the Rosh HaYeshiva Rav Shmuel Zev Dicker, *shlita*, for always offering a kind word and showing the ultimate concern for your *talmidim.* May Hashem continue to grant you success in teaching Torah and leading the yeshiva for many more years in good health.

To my *rebbi*, Rav Ezra Rodkin, *shlita*, of Yeshivas Peer HaTorah. Thank you for your sage advice throughout the years. Your intriguing *shiurim* introduced me to the world of *machshavah* with an always deeper and enriching thought in comprehending a seemingly simple *pasuk* of *Chumash*.

Living in New Hempstead, NY, I am privileged to be a part of a wonderful *shul*, Congregation Ohaiv Shalom, headed by Rav Yisrael Sapirstein, *shlita*. Not a Shabbos goes by in which I am not moved and enthused by your Shabbos morning *derashos*. I am very fortunate to be part of a *kehillah* with a humble human being such as yourself leading the community.

Thank you to Rabbi Shmuel Brazil and Yeshivas Zeev HaTorah for assisting in the coordination of bringing this *sefer* to publication.

To my dear wife Shaindy. For all your encouragement and advice offered throughout this project I cannot compensate you. But, rest assured that this book is a product of your work as much as it is mine. Many of the ideas presented in this book were conceived while observing your interactions with others and perceiving the sensitive and caring nature with which you conduct yourself. You continue to be a source from which I grow in *ruchniyus* and make my life a more meaningful one.

The Gemara in *Maseches Shabbos* 118b teaches:

אמר ר' יוסי מימי לא קראתי לאשתי אשתי אלא לאשתי ביתי.

Rav Yosi said: In all my days, I have never called my wife, my wife. Rather, I called my wife, my house.

I am astounded by the amount you accomplish during an average day. Your perseverance and determination are an inspiration while your integrity and kind-hearted nature are traits which are admired by all.

Aaron Muller
15 Sivan 5777

Introduction

Ever buy some new electronic gadget, bring it home, but then after you finally manage to tear open the thick, annoying plastic packaging you realize you forgot to purchase the AAA batteries? You finally get the batteries you need, insert them properly, but still nothing. It won't work. No lights, movement, or noise. You try inserting the batteries again carefully, yet still no sign of life. You reread the instructions and still no luck. Finally, you reach that of-course-it-won't-work moment and realize you forgot to switch the red button to the On position.

We are all created with quality parts, built strong, and even come with instructions — the Torah. We are generously created with batteries included, our holy *neshamos*. During the week we operate with one battery, and on Shabbos an extra one is added for an even greater experience and opportunity. But although the positive and negative charges are set up just right, we still need to remember to press the On switch to get things moving. While our *neshamah* is with us, it still needs to be inspired and fueled in order for it to provide us with its intended function and for us to elevate our existence in *Olam HaZeh*.

The *neshamah* is that battery that needs to be recharged from time to time, or it can't provide the desired effects and just sits idle in the battery chamber unused.

This book is a collection of essays on the weekly *parashah* intended to jump-start the *neshamah* facilitated by the lessons found in the

1

parashah. The ideas are targeted at awakening the soul by giving a deep-er meaning to, and looking beyond, the surface of the *pasuk*.

Besides for relating ideas that can help inspire and stimulate spiritual growth; it is my intention to fill a gap found with many of the English *divrei Torah seforim* published today. In many of the writings available on the *parashah*, authors will quote some of the earlier commentary on a *pasuk* but seldom does the reader actually see the text which is being referenced. While for some readers, references alone serve their purpose and are relied upon, while for others, seeing the actual text may enhance and enrich the idea presented. The words of our *Rishonim* and *Acharonim* were written with great measure and precision, worthy of each word being read and re-read. While translations are wonderful it is always at the risk of losing an essential concept that the author wished to convey.

This book is unique in that it attempts to introduce the reader to the Hebrew text with translation instead of simply referencing the thought. It is my hope that the richness of the original text will both make the thought more meaningful and allow one to receive an unadulterated version of what the author intentioned.

Rav Avraham Bornstein, *zt"l*, the first Sochatchover Rebbe, known as the *Avnei Nezer*, presents a beautiful idea in the introduction to his *sefer Eglei Tal* on the subject of *Torah lishmah*; Torah study for its own sake.

ומדי דברי זכור אזכור מה ששמעתי קצת בני אדם טועין מדרך השכל בעניין לימוד תורתינו הקדושה ואמרו כי הלומד ומחדש חידושים ושמח ומתענג בלימודו אין זה לימוד תורה כל כך לשמה כמו אם היה לומד בפשיטות שאין לו מהלימוד שום תענוג והוא רק לשם מצוה. אבל הלומד ומתענג בלימודו הוי מתערב בלימודו גם הנאת עצמו. ובאמת זה טעות מפורסם. ואדרבה, כי זה היא עיקר מצות לימוד התורה להיות שש ושמח ומתענג בלימודו ואז דברי תורה נבלעין בדמו. ומאחר שנהנה מדברי תורה הוא נעשה דבוק לתורה.

While on this topic, I would mention something illogical I have heard from some people about Torah study. They say that when one is happy as he learns, coming up with new insights and enjoying his studies — this is not the highest form of Torah learning. They believe that one who studies simply and without any personal enjoyment, this is the highest level of "Torah for its own sake," where-as one who combines his own enjoyment in his learning is no longer studying

Torah "for its own sake." In truth, this is a common mistake. But the fact is that the main aspect of Torah study is the joy and happiness one has from his learning. This helps the words of Torah to become a part of him, practically "absorbed in his blood." When one takes pleasure in his Torah learning, he becomes joined to and bonded with the Torah. (Introduction to Eglei Tal)

As the *Avnei Nezer* explains, enjoying and finding pleasure in Torah learning is not something to feel guilty of. The Torah is here to guide our lives and to inspire a spiritual existence. It's intended to infuse and inject us with life and vitality in our *avodas Hashem*. The pleasure we absorb when we learn is Hashem's way of allowing us to connect with Him and bring us closer to Him.

Perhaps when the reader experiences for themselves the holy words that were chosen and written by the earlier commentaries they will connect and feel an excitement as they develop their own feel and unique understanding of their inspiring thoughts and words.

Another feature added to this book is a short biographical sketch of each commentary referenced so that readers have the ability to connect with the author and understand in which time period they lived, where they originated, the town or city in which they served as Rav or leader, and a glimpse of their lifespan. This is intended to help readers attach themselves and develop a mental image of who it is they are reading about, making the *divrei Torah* more relatable, personable, and alive.

The decision to publish the ideas found in this book was a passage in the introduction to the *sefer Sharei Yosher*. The great *Rosh Yeshiva* Rav Shimon Shkop, *zt"l*, explains that with all wisdom endowed by Hashem to an individual, it is important for one to firmly plant in his heart that the acquisition of this wisdom was not given solely for the one who has it, but rather to be a watchman over it and dispense it accordingly, sharing that which was deposited with him.

On a similar note, when the Mishkan was erected and all the vessels were brought to Moshe, the Torah uses the phrase of *"vayitein, and he [Moshe] placed,"* to describe the placement of each vessel. In *Shemos* (40:20) which describes Moshe placing the *Luchos* inside the *Aron*, the words *"vayikach vayitein"* and he [Moshe] took and placed" are used.

Rav Moshe Midner, *zt"l*, the great *Mashgiach* of the Slonimer Yeshiva, explains the necessity of the extra word of *vayikach* in reference to the *Luchos*. Torah is given to us to share. When we take, as in *vayikach*, it must be paired with a *vayitein*, in which the receiver is ready to take the Torah which was given to him and pass it on, sharing it with others as well.

I am hopeful that the ideas and thoughts presented in the coming pages can generate within the reader food for thought and awaken within him a desire for a deeper and more meaningful relationship with Hashem thereby giving more meaning to one's existence.

הפעם אודה את ה' אשירה ואזמרה, אשר עד הנה עזרוני רחמיו
להוציא לאור ספר זה אשר להתלמד בו חברתיו, ולהועיל לשכמותי
לרבים נתתיו. אולי אזכה שיזכו אחרים על ידי, וייטב להם בעבורי,
ואעשה נחת רוח ליוצרי. כן יאמר ה' לתת חלקי בתורתו, ללמוד
וללמד לשמור ולעשות. וחפצו בידי יצליח אמן כן יהי רצון.

(מתוך סוף ספר מסילת ישרים)

Bereishis

Bereishis

וַיְהִי מִקֵּץ יָמִים וַיָּבֵא קַיִן מִפְּרִי הָאֲדָמָה מִנְחָה לַה': וְהֶבֶל הֵבִיא גַם הוּא
מִבְּכֹרוֹת צֹאנוֹ וּמֵחֶלְבֵהֶן וַיִּשַׁע ה' אֶל הֶבֶל וְאֶל מִנְחָתוֹ:
וַיֹּאמֶר קַיִן אֶל הֶבֶל אָחִיו וַיְהִי בִּהְיוֹתָם בַּשָּׂדֶה
וַיָּקָם קַיִן אֶל הֶבֶל אָחִיו וַיַּהַרְגֵהוּ:

Now it came to pass at the end of days, that Kayin brought
of the fruit of the soil — an offering to Hashem. And Hevel,
too, brought of the firstborn of his flocks and of their fats, and
Hashem turned to Hevel and to his offering. (Bereishis 4:3–4)

Kayin spoke to Hevel his brother, and it came to pass when
they were in the field, that Kayin rose up against Hevel his
brother and killed him. (4:8)

At first glance, the Torah seems to introduce us to the first episode of
sibling rivalry in history, including the disturbing outcome in which the
first human ever to die was murdered by his brother.

But was it really that simplistic?

The Brothers' Offerings

When describing Hevel's offering of the firstborn of his flocks,
the Torah uses the phrase *gam hu*, that Hevel, as well, brought...This

emphasis unlocks a whole new understanding of the incident that took place between Kayin and Hevel.

The *Kli Yakar*, Rav Shlomo Ephraim Luntschitz, offers a unique perspective based on this choice of words.

ומ"ש והבל הביא גם הוא. מהו גם, וראיתי בספר צרור המור שמאשים קצת את הבל שלא נתעורר מעצמו על הקרבן כי לא הביאו עד אחר שראה את קין הולך ומקריב וע"כ נאמר והבל הביא גם הוא במלת גם רמז שאיחר קרבנו והביא מצד הקנאה באחיו. ויכול להיות שעל העושה מצד הקנאה אמר שלמה (קהלת ד:ד) וראיתי אני את כל עמל ואת כל כשרון המעשה כי הוא קנאת איש מרעהו גם זה הבל ר"ל זהו הגם שהבל נכשל בו כמו שנאמר והבל הביא גם הוא. ונ"ל להביא כדמות ראיה לדבריו שנאמר ויהי בהיותם בשדה ויקם קין אל הבל אחיו ויהרגהו. הזכיר שדה לפי שהיה ויכוח ביניהם בענין הקרבנות וכל אחד מטיל דופי בקרבנו של חבירו כמנהג שני אנשים אשר להם הריב כי הבל מאשים את קין על אשר הביא מן הגרוע זרע פשתן. וקין מאשים את הבל על אשר לא נתעורר אל המעשה מעצמו כ"א עד אחר שראה את קרבנו של קין עבר עליו רוח קנאה ורצה להשוות אליו כ"א עד אחר שראה את קרבנו של קין עבר עליו רוח קנאה ורצה להשוות אליו גם הוא, ואמר לו יען כי אין אתה מתעורר אל מעשה הטוב מעצמך כ"א עד שאתה רואה אחרים עושים א"כ תינח בזמן שאתה יושב בתוך עמך אבל בהיותך בשדה במקום שאין איש מצוי שמה א"כ שם ודאי לעולם לא תעשה שום דבר טוב וא"כ אין אתה ראוי להיות בעולם כי אין חפץ ה' בכסילים והבלים רבים העושים מצד הקנאה ולא לשם שמים, ובזה נצחו קין להבל לכך נאמר ויהי בהיותם בשדה. כשהשיב לו תשובה נצחת מצד השדה אז ויקם קין אל הבל אחיו ויהרגהו, כי השדה מקום החטא ושם תהא קבורתו.

וז"ש שקרבנו של אדה"ר היה לו קרן אחת במצחו (חולין ס.), רצו בזה לפי שהיה אדה"ר יחיד בעולם קרן א' א"כ ודאי לא ראה המעשה משום אדם אלא מעצמו נתעורר אל המעשה על כן נתקבל קרבנו. לכך נאמר אדם כי יקריב קרבן לה'. כשיהיה כאדה"ר שנתעורר אל הקרבן מעצמו וזהו שאמר כי יקריב מכם ר"ל מכם ובכם יבוא לו ההתעוררות זהו קרבן לה' ולא קנאת איש מרעהו. ויתבאר זה עוד לקמן פרשת ויקרא א:ב בע"ה.

And regarding what it says here, "and Hevel also brought" — What is meant by "also"? I saw in the sefer Tzror HaMor that this word somewhat indicts Hevel because he was not self-motivated to bring the offering. He did not bring it until he saw Kayin go and offer a sacrifice. It therefore says, "Hevel also brought." The word "also" is an allusion that he delayed his offering and only brought it out of jealousy of his brother.

Perhaps, then, Shlomo [HaMelech] was referring to someone who acts out of jealousy when he wrote in Koheles, "I saw that all labor and every skill comes from man's envy of his neighbor; this also [gam] is vanity [Hevel]."[1] In other words, the "also" is intimating that in which Hevel "also" stumbled [i.e., envy], as it says, "Hevel 'also' brought."

1   *Koheles* 4:4.

And it seems to me that we can bring a semblance of proof to his words, because it says, "And it came to pass, when they were in the field, that Kayin rose up against his brother Hevel and killed him."[2] The reason it mentions the field [which seems unnecessary] is that they quarreled [there] about the offerings. Each one depre-cated the other's offering, in the manner of two men who have a grievance with each other. Hevel accused Kayin of bringing [his offering] from inferior flaxseed, and Kayin accused Hevel of not being self-motivated to do the deed [of bringing the offering] until after he saw Kayin's offering and was overcome by a spirit of jealousy urging him to equate himself with Kayin. [Kayin] said to him, "Since you were not self-motivated to do this good deed, but only did it after you saw another doing it, therefore [you only do good deeds] when you are among people, but when you are 'in the field'; a place where no one is usually around, certainly there you will never do anything good. Therefore, you are not fit to live in the world, for Hashem is not fond of fools nor of the vain majority who do things out of envy and not for the sake of Heaven."

With this [argument] Kayin prevailed over Hevel, and therefore it says, "And it came to pass, when they were in the field," mentioning the field — for when Kayin replied with this winning response concerning the field, then "Kayin rose up against his brother Hevel and killed him" specifically in the field, the place of Hevel's sin, and there should be his burial place.[3]

As for the [Sages'] statement that "Adam's sacrifice had just one horn in its forehead,"[4] they wished to teach us that since Adam was the only human in the world — "a single horn," so to speak — he certainly had not previously seen this deed [of bringing an offering to G-d] being done by anyone. Rather, he was self-motivated to do this deed, and therefore his sacrifice was accept-ed. For this reason, it states [in the pasuk from Vayikra cited above], "When a man [adam] from among you brings an offering to G-d" [using the term adam] — that is, when you shall be like Adam, who was self-motivated to bring an offering — then "you shall bring your offering." That is, an offering מכם — "from yourselves" — indicating that if the motivation to bring the offering comes from you, from within you, that is considered [as the pasuk states] "an offering to G-d" [without ulterior motives], and not [an offering that is brought] out of a man's envy of his friends. This idea will be explained further, with G-d's help, in Parashas Vayikra.[5]

---

2   *Bereishis* 4:8.
3   Based on Elihu Levine's translation of *Kli Yakar*, Menucha Publishers.
4   *Chullin* 60a.
5   See *Kli Yakar* to *Vayikra* 1:2.

The *Kli Yakar* teaches that what prompted Kayin to kill Hevel was Hevel's lack of self-motivation in offering a *korban* to Hashem. Kayin begins by offering flaxseed, an inferior-grade *korban*, to which Hevel responds by arriving on the scene and seeking to out-perform his brother with a *korban* of superior quality. When Kayin observes this behavior, he reacts by analyzing Hevel's motivation and decides that Hevel's offering was motivated by envy in an ef-fort to equate himself with his brother. Kayin then concludes that Hevel's offering brought with tainted intentions renders Hevel no longer worthy of living.

The Root of Tefillah

Earlier in the *parashah*, the Torah describes the scene prior to the creation of trees and plants:

וְכֹל שִׂיחַ הַשָּׂדֶה טֶרֶם יִהְיֶה בָאָרֶץ וְכָל עֵשֶׂב הַשָּׂדֶה טֶרֶם יִצְמָח כִּי לֹא הִמְטִיר ה' אֱלֹקִים עַל הָאָרֶץ וְאָדָם אַיִן לַעֲבֹד אֶת הָאֲדָמָה:

Now no tree of the field was yet on the earth, neither did any herb of the field yet grow, because the Lord G-d had not brought rain upon the earth, and there was no man to work the soil. (Bereishis 2:5)

כי לא המטיר: ומה טעם לא המטיר, לפי שאדם אין לעבוד את האדמה ואין מכיר בטובתם של גשמים, וכשבא אדם וידע שהם צורך לעולם התפלל עליהם וירדו, וצמחו האילנות והדשאים.

Because...not caused it to rain — Because there was no man to work the soil, and no one recognized the benefit of rain, but when man came and un-derstood that rains are essential to the world, he prayed for them, and they came, and the trees and the herbs grew. (Rashi)

Continuing with the idea of the *Kli Yakar*, perhaps this Rashi can be understood to mean that there was no man on the *adamah*, the earth, which represents a setting where one is alone without an audience to prompt an offering of *tefillah*, since nothing had yet existed, unlike with the episode of Kayin and Hevel. However, Hashem then created Adam and the first *tefillah* was performed in the purest of forms which took place in the field, a place where man recognized and understood the need for rain, and a *tefillah* was generated solely on this recognition and not as a result of any external motivations. Adam's *tefillah* occurred not because anyone was watching or driven by someone else who preceded his *tefillah*. Adam existed alone and saw the need; he appreciated what Hashem had done and through this acknowledgment a *tefillah* was offered.

It is well known that Yitzchak instituted the afternoon prayer, *Minchah*. As is written:

וַיֵּצֵא יִצְחָק לָשׂוּחַ בַּשָּׂדֶה לִפְנוֹת עָרֶב וַיִּשָּׂא עֵינָיו וַיַּרְא וְהִנֵּה גְמַלִּים בָּאִים:

And Yitzchak went forth to pray in the field toward evening, and he lifted his eyes and saw, and behold, camels were approaching. (Bereishis 24:63)

It was specifically "in the field" where Yitzchak instituted this prayer, because a field is an isolated environment, away from people and absent of the complications of jealousy and pride. He had no motive other than pure and sincere *tefillah*, which was offered while planting the roots of all future *tefillah*.

Tefillah without Heart

We are given the opportunity to stand before Hashem daily and beseech Him to grant us our needs, yet at times it's *tefillah* without intent or focus, a dangerous habitual exercise lacking purpose. We say in our *davening*:

הראינו ה' חסדך ...
אתה ה' לא תכלא רחמיך ממני ...
ותן בליבנו בינה להבין ולהשכיל ...
והאר עינינו בתורתך ודבק ליבנו במצוותיך ...
שים שלום טובה וברכה ...

Show us, Hashem, Your kindness...
You, Hashem, do not withhold Your mercy from me...
And instill in our hearts to understand and comprehend...
Enlighten our eyes in Your Torah, attach our hearts to Your commandments...
Grant peace, goodness, blessing...

While reciting *Bircas HaMazon* we speak to Hashem about matters which concern us and worry us daily. In the passage of *Racheim* in *Bircas Hamazon* we say:

רחם נא ה' אלקינו על ישראל עמך ועל ירושלים עירך ועל ציון משכן כבודך ועל מלכות
בית דוד משיחך ועל הבית הגדול והקדוש שנקרא שמך עליו: אלקינו אבינו, רענו זוננו
פרנסנו וכלכלנו והרויחנו, והרוח לנו ה' אלקינו מהרה מכל צרותינו. ונא אל תצריכנו ה'
אלקינו לא לידי מתנת בשר ודם ולא לידי הלואתם, כי אם לידך המלאה הפתוחה הקדושה
והרחבה, שלא נבוש ולא נכלם לעולם ועד.

Have mercy, Hashem our G-d, on Israel Your People; on Yerushalayim, Your city; on Tzion, the resting place of Your Glory...tend us, nourish us, sustain us, support us...Please, Hashem our G-d, do not make us dependent neither upon the gifts of flesh and blood nor upon their loans...

What typically follows after a request is made is where the supplicant waits eagerly and anxiously for a positive response.

Yet many of us don't even look for or await the response, as the request was made with mere lip service, an insincere offering of words and a distanced heart. Hashem is as if saying, "Come and take what you asked for. I am ready to grant you the mercy you ask for as well as your share in Torah. You want peace? Come and get it, I will make it accessible."

We were given the platform in *Bircas HaMazon* to ask for sustenance and self-reliance. The request asks that Hashem have mercy on *Yerushalayim* and the Beis HaMikdash, yet we leave the gifts behind like someone who is rewarded a prize and it goes unclaimed. Hashem wants and is prepared to give but wants us to ask for it sincerely with meaning and cognizance.

Purchasing a drink on a hot day in an amusement park for seven dollars causes one to cherish and savor every last drop, with an appreciation for the drink like never before — simply because it costs so much. In general, we don't appreciate that which is given for free.

Hashem puts a price on His "goods" so that we can appreciate what He gives us — and the price is "sincere *tefillah.*" The goods are for sale and ready to ship, but they must be paid for. *Tefillah* must be unadulterated, for the sole purpose of speaking with the One Who provides us with all our needs. It ought to be real, meaningful, and sincere, lest we descend to the level described in the words of the *Navi* (Prophet) Yeshayahu:

וַיֹּאמֶר אֲדֹנָי יַעַן כִּי נִגַּשׁ הָעָם הַזֶּה בְּפִיו וּבִשְׂפָתָיו כִּבְּדוּנִי וְלִבּוֹ רִחַק מִמֶּנִּי וַתְּהִי יִרְאָתָם אֹתִי מִצְוַת אֲנָשִׁים מְלֻמָּדָה:

Hashem said, "Because this people has come near, honoring Me with their mouth and lips, but drawing their heart far from Me, and their fear of Me has become the commandments of people learned by rote." (Yeshayahu 29:13)

Hashem's Request of Rabbi Yishmael Kohen Gadol

The Gemara in *Maseches Berachos* teaches:[6]

תניא: אמר רבי ישמעאל בן אלישע: פעם אחת נכנסתי להקטיר קטורת לפני ולפנים, וראיתי אכתריאל י-ה ה' צב-אות שהוא יושב על כיסא רם ונישא, ואמר לי: ישמעאל בני, ברכני. אמרתי לו: יהי רצון מלפניך שיכבשו רחמיך את כעסך, ויגולו רחמיך על מדותיך, ותתנהג עם בניך במדת הרחמים, ותכנס להם לפנים משורת הדין. ונענע לי בראשו.

It was learned: Rabbi Yishmael ben Elisha said, I once entered the innermost chamber to offer incense, and I saw Akasriel, Hashem, Master of Legions, as He was sitting on His throne, great and high. And He said to me, "Yishmael, My son, bless Me." I said to Him, "May it be Your Will before You that Your mercy extinguishes Your anger, and that Your mercy overcomes Your [other] traits, and that You behave merciful with Your children, and that You judge them favorably over and above the law." And He nodded His head [in agreement].

The *meforshim* (commentators) are perplexed by this passage in the Gemara. Does Hashem need our *berachos*? We would typically expect the opposite to occur, and that Hashem would provide us with *His* blessing!

Perhaps we need to adjust our preconceived notions. Many imagine Hashem to be a punitive superior force Who constantly monitors our spiritual standing and waits to catch us in sin. The opposite is true, however. Hashem loves us, His children, and desires that we speak with Him and beseech Him for our daily needs. He wants us to view Him as our Father and to speak to Him as a child asking for his needs from his parents. Hashem told Yishmael the *Kohen Gadol* (High Priest), "*Barcheini*, bless Me!" In other words, the greatest blessing we can offer Hashem is to view Him as our Father and speak with Him in a meaningful way as a child speaks with his father. Hashem began with *Barcheini*! Which was Yishmael's cue to ask for the needs of Klal Yisrael. To this Yishmael responded for Hashem's mercy to overpower His anger and to deal with His children in a merciful manner.

Hashem says, "Tell Me what you want and I will give it to you" — but the caveat is to ask earnestly and to be aware of Who it is we stand before in supplication, recognizing that He alone has the ability to grant us all our needs.

Hashem Awaits Us

Imagine the following:

> You finally agreed to it. It wasn't an easy decision to make, but all your son's friends were going; not sending him to sleep-away camp was simply no longer an option. It's the first time your son is spending a considerable amount of time away from home, and you wish he was home instead. The long summer days are spent imagining what he is doing in camp, thinking about the good times you had spending time together. As the summer progresses it does not get any easier and your desire to see and embrace him grows increasingly stronger. It's been too long already and the weekly phone conversations do not satisfy your inner yearning. It's finally now the last week of the camp season, and you pine for the day you will see him at the bus stop. The day has arrived and you leave the house with plenty of time to be there before the bus arrives. The excitement is palpable and you watch your son's face peeking from the window as the bus pulls up to the curb. You're at the door of the bus waiting with open hands to hug him — but as he steps down to the curb, he runs right past you to find his group of friends.

What a letdown! The parent is saddened and even shamed at the experience, realizing that the deep feelings he has for his son aren't mutual. Words cannot describe the disappointment and feelings of abandonment.

Perhaps this sounds unrealistic and far-fetched, but is it really so foreign to us? Hashem awaits our presence three times daily. With open hands, He seeks to speak with us and grant us the love and affection only a parent can share. But when we walk into shul, we go right past those open hands and find some other activity in which to take part.

Tefillah is that tool given to us as a way to speak with Hashem and pour our hearts out to Him. It's an opportunity for a serious and heartfelt talk three times daily. Wasting away such a privilege with thoughtless *tefillah* is a lost fortune.

It's an opportunity for a serious and heartfelt talk three times daily.

Rav Yitzchak Hutner is quoted as saying, "The purpose of *tefillah* is not to get us out of trouble. The purpose of trouble is to get us into *tefillah*."[7]

---

7   See *Sefer Chovas HaTalmidim* in chap. 9 where he uses the words: שלפעמים את הדאגות שולח ה' כדי שנתפלל אליו יתברך.

Noach

אֶת קַשְׁתִּי נָתַתִּי בֶּעָנָן וְהָיְתָה לְאוֹת בְּרִית בֵּינִי וּבֵין הָאָרֶץ:

My rainbow I have placed in the cloud, and it shall be a sign
of a covenant between Myself and the earth. (Bereishis 9:13)

After the Great Flood (*Mabul*) devastated the world and destroyed all
that existed before it, Hashem vowed never again to bring a *Mabul* to
cleanse the world of sin. Hashem used the sign of a rainbow to seal His
covenant with the earth.

The Ramban sheds light on the significance of a rainbow and the
message of its physical appearance.

ואמרו בטעם האות הזה כי הקשת לא עשאו שיהיו רגליו למעלה שיראה כאלו מן השמים
מורים בו וישלח חציו ויפיצם בארץ (תהלים יח טו) אבל עשאו בהפך מזה להראות שלא
יורו בו מן השמים וכן דרך הנלחמים להפוך אותו בידם ככה כאשר יקראו לשלום למי
שכנגדם ועוד שאין לקשת יתר לכונן חצים עליו.

Regarding the symbolic meaning of this sign, the commentators say that
Hashem did not make the rainbow with its ends pointing upwards and its
arched part pointing downwards, whereby it would appear as if it is being
used to shoot from heaven, to "send forth his arrows and scatter them in the
land" (Tehillim 18:16). Rather, He made the bow in the opposite manner,
indicating that it would not be used to shoot from heaven — for it is the
manner of warriors to invert the bows in their hands in this way when they

16

wish to declare their peaceful intentions toward their opponents. Moreover, on this bow, there is no string on which to place arrows. (Ramban pasuk 12, s.v. "zohs ohs habris")[8]

To better understand the idea brought in the Ramban, let us consider that following the *Mabul,* Noach and his family may have viewed Hashem as One Who uses strict and harsh judgment, leaving no room for mercy or forgiveness.[9] Hashem, in His infinite kindness, wanted to "set the record straight." He created the world with both *Midas HaRachamim* and *Midas HaDin.*[10] The world could not exist with strict judgment alone, but rather needed to be paired with His mercy and compassion. The rainbow, according to the Ramban, was Hashem's reassurance that His agenda was not about destroying the world: the arch was made to face the opposite way of the manner it would be held if used to shoot arrows. This was a sign that Hashem's Will was not to destroy, but rather to forgive and absolve mankind of their sins — on condition that they repent via the means of *teshuvah.*

A Rainbow and a Bow

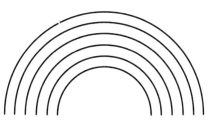

A parallel can be drawn between the rainbow shown to Noach following the *Mabul* and the momentous event that took place at *Yam Suf,* the Crossing of the Red Sea. As both the Rambam[11] and Tosafos[12] understand, the B'nei Yisrael did not actually cross the *Yam Suf* while fleeing the Egyptians.

---

8 Translation based on *Ramban al HaTorah,* Artscroll.
9 This may be further evident from the following *Chazal* found in the Zohar.
תנו רבנן, מה השיב הקב"ה לנח, כשיצא מן התיבה, וראה כל העולם חרב, והתחיל לבכות עליו, ואמר רבונו של עולם רחום, היה לך לרחם על בריותיך, השיבו הקב"ה רעיא שטיא, עתה תאמר זה, ולא בזמן שאמרתי לך בלשון רכה, שכתוב לך תבת עצי גופר וגו', ואני הני מביא את המבול וגו'... כל כך נתעכבתי עמך, ואמרתי לך, כדי שתבקש רחמים על העולם, ומאז ששמעת שאתה תנצל בתיבה, לא נכנס בלבך צער העולם, ועשית תיבה ונצלת, ועתה שנאבד העולם פתחת פיך לדבר לפני בקשות ותחנונים... (זהר חדש נח קיג).
10 The attributes of strict judgment and mercy. Rashi to *Bereishis* 1:1, s.v. "*Bara Elokim.*"
11 In his commentary to the Mishnah, quoted below.
12 *Maseches Arachin* 15a.

Rather, Hashem led them in a semi-circle, having them leave from one point of the coast and arriving at another without actually crossing from one side to the other.

The Rambam writes:

והחמישי שהוא נבקע לדרכים רבות כמספר השבטים קשת עגולה קשת עגולה בתוך קשת עגולה.

And the fifth miracle [of the ten at Yam Suf] included multiple crossing paths [for B'nei Yisrael] equal to the number of tribes. The [paths were designed] as rainbows, one within the other [with B'nei Yisrael entering and exiting on the same side of the sea]. (Rambam to Avos 5:4)

After leaving Mitzrayim, the B'nei Yisrael had seen it all. The nation of Mitzrayim was brought to its knees with the most horrific plagues and punishment as Hashem revealed His power and might. Perhaps Hashem desired to communicate to B'nei Yisrael a message similar to that conveyed to Noach and his family after the *Mabul* several centuries earlier, which is that although Hashem carries out strict judgment such as with the Egyptians for the years of suffering they caused His children, His attribute of *rachamim*/mercy was still at play vis-à-vis the B'nei Yisrael, and by splitting the waters in a manner which had the *shevatim* travel in a rainbow-like manner He communicated this to them.

Through this peculiar route at the *Yam Suf*, Hashem was giving them hope. While it may not have served a functional purpose of escaping the enemy and beating them to the other side, it was a journey of *emunah*, a route taken to impact them with a message of faith and the realization that Hashem cared for them and that they could rely on His compassion. Traveling from one side of the coast to the other was necessary so that they would recognize Hashem's love and compassion for them; if they would have simply crossed from one side to the other, they would have interpreted the event as merely a strategic move to flee the Egyptians.

Finding Color in Darkness

The *pasuk* with which we began communicates a similar message. Hashem tells us, "I have placed My rainbow, full of light, color, and hope, inside the dark clouds that at times cause life to seem bleak and miserable. Even in the darkest of times, I am with you; My bow is not pointed toward you to shoot, but is rather inverted as a sign of peace and kindness. The cloudy and gloomy moments in life are also good for you, even if they may be difficult to comprehend at the moment."

Yes, we are to trust in Hashem, and recognize that He is merciful and compassionate, and see that His interactions with us are full of kindness. As we read in *Tehillim:*

אהב צדקה ומשפט חסד ה' מלאה הארץ:

He loves righteousness and justice; the earth is full of the kindness of Hashem. (Tehillim 33:5)

A beautiful story that articulates this point is told in the book *Aleinu LeShabeach:*[13]

Yitzchak Slutzky was sixteen years old when his family was murdered by the Nazis. His family was one of the first in Poland to be gassed in Auschwitz, but he and his younger sister managed to escape, through a miraculous chain of events.

Yitzchak took upon himself the challenge of caring for his sister and protecting her from harm. For a long time, the two hid in a dark, cramped underground cellar. The non-Jews in his village knew that Yitzchak and his sister were hiding, but they remained silent and did not report them to the Nazis.

Yitzchak did not allow his sister to leave the cellar, and he found ways to provide for her. Several months passed, with the girl remaining in the cellar and Yitzchak leaving occasionally to bring whatever food, clothing, and other items they needed.

13   Vol. 2, pg. 500. Artscroll/Mesorah.

One day, when he was returning from one of these errands, he sensed that something was wrong. And indeed, his sister was not in the cellar.

Later, when Yitzchak recalled what had happened, he said, "Had I thought at the time about what I was going to do, I would never have done it. But I did not think about anything; all I thought about was how to save my sister."

He ran from the cellar and asked the people in the area whether anyone had seen his sister or knew where she was. They pointed to the Nazi headquarters in the center of the village, which confirmed his fears. Yitzchak ran to the building and burst inside, running right by the guards stationed outside. When he entered the building, he began to scream, "Bring me my sister, now!"

The Nazi officials, who were not accustomed to scenes like this, cocked their rifles and aimed at him, ready to shoot. But as they were about to shoot, their commander heard the strange screams. He poked his head out of his office, and summoned Yitzchak to enter.

Yitzchak would not be silent even in the commander's office. He continued to shout that his sister be returned to him immediately.

Amused by the scene, the commander decided to goad Yitzchak even further. "I'll give you back your sister," he said contemptuously, "on one condition: that you open your palm and show me that there is hair on it."

Yitzchak turned to the satanic commander and said, "If I show you that there is hair on my palm, you will give back my sister?"

"I already told you the answer," the commander said derisively.

Yitzchak held out his hand, and a commander nearly fainted.

There was hair growing on the palm of his hand! German culture depicts a satanic person as someone who has hair on the palm of his hand. "Give him his sister," the frightened commander shouted, "and get him out of here immediately!"

Yitzchak and his sister survived the war and immigrated to Eretz Yisrael. When he told the story of his sister's miraculous rescue, he showed people that he actually had hair growing on the palm of his hand.

He explained, "My father owned a large bakery in Poland. As a child, I loved to walk between the ovens and mixers. When I was seven years old, I put my hand into one of the mixers, and large pieces of skin were torn from the palm of my hand. My parents rushed me to the hospital, but the techniques used there were very primitive. To help my hand heal, the doctors cut a piece of skin from a different part of my body and grafted it onto my hand. The transplanted skin had hair growing from it, and the hair has continued to grow from my palm ever since.

"I remember that along with the feelings of gratitude that my parents had when my hand healed from the injury, my mother was distressed by the strange appearance of my palm. When we would go out, she would tell me to put my hand in my pocket so that people wouldn't see it. I was also very embarrassed by the strange sight, and my friends used to make fun of it, too.

"Only Hashem, Who sees from one end of the world till the other, knew what was going to happen to me during the war; only He knew that my sister would be taken by the Nazis, and that she would be saved by the miraculous sight of hair on the palm of my hand."

We must understand that we have but a microscopic view of our purpose in Hashem's infinite world.

While at times the predicament we find ourselves in causes us to feel upset and forsaken, we must try to remember that Hashem's Mercy is at work. We may not perceive it at the moment and it may even take several years but eventually all the pieces of the puzzle come together and complete the whole picture.

The bird's-eye view while up in an airplane always amazes me to see how highways connect together so effortlessly. Yet while traveling in the car below things look terribly planned and constructed poorly leading to endless traffic jams. We must understand that we have but a microscopic view of our purpose in Hashem's infinite world and will one day merit to perceive the intricacies of His master plan.

Lech Lecha

וַיֹּאמֶר ה' אֶל אַבְרָם לֶךְ לְךָ מֵאַרְצְךָ וּמִמּוֹלַדְתְּךָ וּמִבֵּית אָבִיךָ
אֶל הָאָרֶץ אֲשֶׁר אַרְאֶךָּ:

*Hashem said to Avram, "Go forth from your land
and from your birthplace and from your father's house,
to the land that I will show you." (Bereishis 12:1)*

Rav Naftali Tzvi Yehudah Berlin, the *Netziv*, in his *Ha'amek Davar* asks the question. Looking at the *pasuk* and its message, it would seem that the order of where *Avram* was to leave from is out of order. *Avram* should have been commanded to leave first his birthplace, then his father's home, and finally his land. If he was commanded to leave his land first, wasn't it obvious that it would entail leaving his birthplace and father's home as well?

מארצך וממולדתך ומבית אביך. להפך היה ראוי לכתוב, תחלה ילך מבית אביו ואח"כ
ממולדתו ואח"כ מארצו. אלא נתן לנו להבין בזה אזהרה על שכחת הלב, שיסיע דעתו מהם
ומהמונם, ותחלה נשכח ארצו ואח"כ מולדתו ואח"כ בית אביו. ולזה כוונו חז"ל במדרש
רבה במה שאמרו הדא הוא דכתיב שכחי עמך ובית אביך (תהלים מ"ה). זה מצאתי. ועיין
עוד להלן כ"ב ב'.

"Go from your land, and from your birthplace, and from your father's house..." — It would have been more appropriate for the Torah to write the

23

opposite: First he should be told to leave "your father's house," followed by "your birthplace," and finally "your land." But the explanation is that Avram was given a warning on the importance of forgetting and uprooting the memories of his homeland and the people there: He should first rid his heart of the memories of his land, then of his birthplace, and then of his father's house, thus severing all ties to the past in which he grew up. (Ha'amek Davar)

Avram was not commanded simply to move from one location to another in the physical sense, but also to uproot the emotional ties to his old life and to detach himself from the negative and false beliefs with which he grew up in that environment.

Shock and Surprise

Another question may be asked:

Avram was tested with the *Asarah Nisyonos*, the ten tests, with *Lech Lecha* being one of them. Was this so hard for Avram? If Hashem were to appear to an individual with the command to leave his home with the promise that it would be beneficial in the end, would it be so difficult to consent? What was the actual test and challenge for Avram, given that Hashem also promised a reward at the end?

Picture this scene. While at work one day, Mr. Goldberg suffers a major heart attack and is rushed to the ER. The severity of his situation is such that the doctors are unsure whether he will survive, and a team of specialists is called in to assist with his resuscitation. His wife is immediately called by the ER staff and the conversation begins:

"Mrs. Goldberg?"

"Yes, that's me."

"We're calling from the local hospital, how are you today?"

"I'm fine, thanks, why do you ask?"

"We'd like you to come to the hospital, as your husband was brought in because he wasn't feeling so well."

"Is his condition serious? What happened?"

"We hope he'll be OK, but you should come now. He suffered a heart attack but is being stabilized. He is being treated by the best medical staff with the most advanced cardiac care available."

"OK, I'll be right over."

Now, imagine if when Mrs. Goldberg received the call she had been told, "Come quickly, your husband suffered a major heart attack, is not responsive and may not survive." The shock would have scared her and made a bad situation even worse. Instead, the nursing staff broke the news in a delicate and sensitive manner so as to prepare her for a more serious situation. When Mrs. Goldberg will arrive at the hospital, she will already be conditioned to digest the severity of her husband's state of health.

Perhaps this was Avraham Avinu's test: He was given the entire directive at once, beginning with the hardest part, with no time to prepare himself emotionally! Hashem appears to him and says *lech lecha*, "Go! Leave your homeland!" Hashem didn't break the news slowly, but rather issued a command that was immediate and direct. Still, Avram managed to find the strengths to accept the command, even though it seemingly overturned his life at once.

Avram was given the entire directive at once beginning with the hardest part, with no time to prepare himself emotionally!

Throughout life, we find ourselves tested with situations that vary in intensity; some are easier to accept and deal with, while others are delivered with a bang, leaving us wondering why they could not have been given more gradually. The *nisayon* that Avram passed in this case is an example of accepting Hashem's decisions, no matter how abruptly or uncomfortably they are delivered.

Vayeira

וַיֵּרָא אֵלָיו ה' בְּאֵלֹנֵי מַמְרֵא וְהוּא יֹשֵׁב פֶּתַח הָאֹהֶל כְּחֹם הַיּוֹם:

Hashem appeared to him in the plains of Mamre,
and he was sitting at the entrance of the tent when
the day was hot. (Bereishis 18:1)

וירא אליו ה'. ס"ת אוה. מלמד שאוה לשכון באהלו של אברהם.

Hashem appeared to him — The last letters (of these first three words of the
pasuk) form the word ivah, "desired." This teaches that Hashem desired to
dwell in the tent of Avraham. (Baal HaTurim)

Rashi in *Parashas Lech Lecha*, quoting the Gemara in *Pesachim* 117b,
explains what Hashem's promise to Avraham of והיה ברכה, you shall be a
blessing, involved:

והיה ברכה: הברכות נתונות בידך, עד עכשיו היו בידי, ברכתי את אדם ואת נח ואותך,
ומעכשיו אתה תברך את אשר תחפוץ. דבר אחר, ואעשך לגוי גדול זהו שאומרים אלקי
אברהם, ואברכך זהו שאומרים אלקי יצחק, ואגדלה שמך זהו שאומרים אלקי יעקב. יכול
יהיו חותמין בכולן, תלמוד לומר והיה ברכה, בך חותמין ולא בהם.

And you shall be a blessing — The blessings are entrusted into your hand.
Until now, they were in My hand; I blessed Adam, Noach, and you, and
from now on, you may bless whomever you wish. Another explanation:

*"And I will make you into a great nation" — this is [the basis] for saying
"Elokei Avraham" [in the first berachah of Shemoneh Esrei]; "And I will
bless you" — this is [the basis] for saying "Elokei Yitzchak;" "And I will
aggrandize your name" — this is [the basis] for saying "Elokei Yaacov." You
might think that this berachah should be concluded by mentioning them
all, therefore, the pasuk states, "and [you shall] be a blessing" — with
you [Avraham] they will conclude, and not with them. [That is to say,
we conclude the berachah with the words Magen Avraham, "the shield of
Avraham," and not with "the shield of Avraham, Yitzchak, and Yaacov."]
(Rashi, Bereishis 12:2)*

A beautiful idea is presented in the *Mayanah Shel Torah* in the name
of the *Ohel Torah* to further explain Rashi's words:

נאמר במשנה: "על שלשה דברים העולם עומד, על התורה, על העבודה ועל גמילות חס־
דים" (אבות פ"א מ"ב).שלושת עמודי עולם אלה הם כנגד שלושת האבות. אברהם היה
גמילות חסד. יצחק – עבודה, שהקריב עצמו קרבן לה'. יעקב – התורה, שהרי היה "איש
תם יושב אהלים", באהלי תורה. בדורות האחרונים שלפני ביאת המשיח תתמעטנה התו־
רה והעבודה, ולא יגאלו ישראל אלא בזכות צדקה וגמילות חסדים, כמו שאמר הכתוב:
ציון במשפט תפדה ושביה בצדקה (ישעיה א-כז). וזהו הרמז בדברי רש"י: "בך חותמין"
חתימת הגלות, כלומר סיומה תהיה רק "בך" – בגלל מידת גמילות חסד שבך שכן לדאבון
הלב תהיינה התורה והעבודה במידה מועטת ביותר.

*The Mishnah states (Avos 1:2): "Upon three things the world stands: On the
Torah, on the Holy Temple service, and on acts of kindness." These three central pillars holding up the world correspond to the three Patriarchs. Avraham
stands for doing kindness; Yitzchak for the Divine service, for he himself
offered a sacrifice; and Yaacov is Torah, for he was a "dweller of tents" — in
the tents of Torah.*

*In the final generations prior to the coming of the Mashiach, Torah and
Divine service will diminish, and it will be only in the merit of charity and
acts of kindness that Israel will be redeemed. As is written, "Tzion will be redeemed with judgment, and its returnees — with charity" (Yeshayahu 1:27).*

*This is what Rashi alludes to when he says about Avraham, "With you, Israel
will conclude [the first blessing in Shemoneh Esrei]." He means that the Exile
will conclude specifically with "you, Avraham," i.e., with that which Avraham
stands for: acts of kindness — for unfortunately, as we said, in the final
generations, Torah and service of Hashem will be on a very low level. (Ohel
Torah, cited in Mayanah shel Torah)*

The *Ohel Torah* provides an alternative idea to that which the Gemara teaches, regarding the conclusion of the first *berachah* of *Shemoneh Esrei* with the mention of Avraham. He explains that the "conclusion" here refers to the end of the *galus*. It is specifically with Avraham's special attribute of *chessed*, kindness, that we will be rendered worthy of being redeemed.

Avraham Alone

Yet there is another attribute that Avraham personified as he courageously stood alone against the polytheistic worship that surrounded him. Avraham didn't simply "go with the flow," but rather thought for himself and arrived at his own conclusions, irrespective of what the majority believed. We can assume he was not very popular for this approach. Surely, at first, he must have been mocked for expressing his revolutionary ideas to the masses. Avraham was one person opposing the whole world, but he remained unyielding and stood firm regardless of the repercussions of being ridiculed.

The *Mesilas Yesharim* offers advice and guidance relating to this very issue:

ואם יארע לו שימצא בחברת מי שילעג עליו, לא ישית לבו אל הלעג ההוא, אדרבא, ילעג על מלעיגיו ויבזם, ויחשוב בדעתו כי לולי היה לו להרויח ממון הרבה, ההיה מניח מה שהיה צריך לזה מפני חבריו שלא ילעגו?! כל שכן שלא ירצה לאבד נשמתו מפני לעג.[14]

If he happens to find himself in the company of those who mock him, he should not give heart to this mockery. On the contrary, let him mock them and shame them. Let him consider what he would do if he had an opportunity to profit a great amount of money: Would he abandon what he needed to do to this end so that they would not mock him?! How much more so, would he not act this way not to destroy his soul for the sake of sparing himself some mockery. (Mesilas Yesharim chapter 5:3)

This particular trait is especially important today, when Western culture dictates so much of the way we live our lives. We are surrounded by immoral behavior, which has become the norm of our society. Over

---

14 . וכן כתב השולחן ערוך (אורח חיים סימן א סעיף א): ולא יתבייש מפני בני אדם המלעיגים עליו בעבודת השם יתברך.

time, we risk losing our sensitivity toward negative trends that have become commonplace and a part of our everyday lives. Expressing opposition to that which has become accepted but is morally and ethically wrong requires courage and tenacity. It demands a clear and unbendable reaction via which we withstand the influence of the masses. We need to be prepared to stand alone despite the contemptuous response we may experience from others. Avraham was alone and likely knew that the ideas he was voicing were not going to

We need to be prepared to stand alone despite the contemptuous response we may experience from others.

be palatable for most. For him, it was living for Hashem and spreading the truth that motivated him, regardless of what it might cost him in his social standing.

The *Navi* Yechezkel describes Avraham as "One":

בן אדם יושבי החורבות האלה על אדמת ישראל אומרים לאמור אחד היה אברהם ויירש את הארץ ואנחנו רבים, לנו ניתנה הארץ למורשה:

Son of man, the dwellers of these ruins on the soil of Israel speak, saying: Avraham was one, and he inherited the land; we are many, [and so] the land has [surely] been given to us for an inheritance. (Yechezkel 33:24)

Perhaps this, too, is the attribute with which Avraham began his journey of discovering Hashem and with which our *galus* will conclude. It is the feeling and awareness of being distinct and "one," while simultaneously remaining strong in our beliefs and practices, that remains with us at the End of Days and connects us to the distinctive characteristic of Avraham.

End of Days

To conclude, we can suggest that it is this idea of the *Ohel Torah* and the insight of the *Baal HaTurim* that is expressed in this *pasuk*:

כי בחר ה' בציון אוה למושב לו:

For Hashem chose Tzion, He desired it as His dwelling. (Tehillim 132:13)

At the End of Days, with the "conclusion of the *Galus*," when B'nei Yisrael have shown to persevere with that unique character trait of

Avraham Avinu, standing alone and remaining committed to the standards mandated by the Torah; we too will be visited by Hashem, as Avraham Avinu was, because of Hashem's desire (אוה), to make Eretz Yisrael — with the B'nei Yisrael living in it — His dwelling place.

Chayei Sarah

וַיְהִי כַּאֲשֶׁר כִּלּוּ הַגְּמַלִּים לִשְׁתּוֹת וַיִּקַּח הָאִישׁ נֶזֶם זָהָב בֶּקַע מִשְׁקָלוֹ
וּשְׁנֵי צְמִידִים עַל יָדֶיהָ עֲשָׂרָה זָהָב מִשְׁקָלָם:

And it was, when the camels had finished drinking,
that the man took a golden nose ring, weighing half [a shekel],
and two bracelets for her hands, weighing ten gold [shekels].

(Bereishis 24:22)

Rashi derives important messages from the gifts that Eliezer gave Rivkah:

בקע: רמז לשקלי ישראל בקע לגלגלת.

Half [a shekel] — *This alludes to the shekels of Israel, half a shekel per head.*

ושני צמידים: רמז לשני לוחות מצומדות.

And two bracelets — *An allusion to the two Luchos paired together.*

עשרה זהב משקלם: רמז לעשרת הדברות שבהן.

Weighing ten gold [shekels] — *An allusion to the Aseres HaDibros [inscribed] on them.*

Immediately after Eliezer and his camels finish drinking the water given to them by Rivkah, the *pasuk* details the gifts given to her by Eliezer. Rashi sees their weight in gold as symbolizing, respectively,

31

the *machatzis hashekel* (half-*shekel*) and the *Luchos*, the paired Tablets
of the Law.

Three Pillars

The *Maharal*, Rav Yehudah Lowe in his *Gur Aryeh*, questions the significance of Eliezer's gifts as symbolizing the future *machatzis hashekel*
and *Luchos*:

- Were there no other *mitzvos* that could have been chosen to be
  signified during this gift-giving ceremony?
- What deeper messages were the gold nose ring and the two
  bracelets communicating to Rivkah?

ואם תאמר למה רמז לה זאת המצוה יותר משאר מצות? אלא נראה שראה אותה גומלת
חסד ורמז לה עוד העבודה והתורה בשני צמידים על ידיה כמו שמסיק, והשתא תהא
לה שלשה דברים שעל שלשתן העולם עומד התורה והעבודה וגמילות חסדים ורמז לה
מאחר שיש לה עמוד אחד שיהיה לה כל שלשתן.[15]

*If you will, ask why did he allude this mitzvah to her more than others? It
appears that Eliezer recognized her to be one who embodied kindness, and
therefore he hinted to her the additional attributes of Divine Service and
Torah, via the two bracelets for her hands. And now she would have the three
items upon which the world exists — Torah, avodah, and kindness — and he
alluded to these (additional two) since she already had one pillar (kindness),
so that she would (in the future) have all three.*

The *Maharal* explains that Eliezer observed in Rivkah the trait of
being a *gomeles chessed*, quick to perform kindness, in the manner in
which she offered water to him and his camels. Eliezer wanted to introduce Rivkah to the two remaining spiritual traits that are important for
one who would join the family of Avraham and which she would merit
through her child. With these gifts, he showed her Torah and *avodah*.
The nose ring weighing a half-*shekel* represented the *korbanos* purchased
with the annual communal half-*shekel* collection; this is also an allusion

---

15   עיין בתורת משה להחתם סופר שכתב כעין זה.

to Yitzchak, the man she would soon marry.[16] The two bracelets represented the two *luchos*, the Torah,[17] alluding to her future son Yaacov.[18]

Interdependence

The *Shem MiShmuel*, Rav Shmuel Bornstein, *zt"l*, the second Sochatchover Rebbe, offers another approach based on Rashi above.

ונראה עוד לומר עפ"י מה שאמרנו במק"א בטעם בקע לגלגולת כי קרבן ציבור אינו קרבן שותפין רק שכולם כאיש אחד והדרך להיות כאיש אחד שכל אחד ירגיש בעצמו חסרונו ואין לו השלמה אלא מזולתו עי"ז נדבק אחד בחבירו כמו אבר האדם עצמו באבר אחד מאבריו ולזה בא הרמז מחצית השקל שיהי' רואה את עצמו כאילו הוא רק חצי הגוף. וזה שנתן לה נזם בקע משקלו לרמוז לה שבשביל לה מדת גמילות חסדים שבה תזכה לעבודה כנ"ל.

*We can also explain according to that which we said elsewhere regarding the "beka (half-shekel) for each person" (Shemos 38:26): A "communal sacrifice" is not a sacrifice in which all are partners; it rather belongs to the entire community as one entity, one person. And the way we can come to feel "as one person" is when each person realizes his own shortcomings and that these can be compensated for only via someone else, that is, via his ties with others. This is just like a body's organs: they are incomplete without each other. This is what is alluded to by the fact that each person pays a **half**-shekel: he should view himself as if he is only half, incomplete. And the fact that Eliezer gave Rivkah a ring worth a half-shekel symbolized that in the merit of her kindness, she would merit "Divine service," as above.*

Rashi explains that Eliezer's gift of a *beka* alludes to the half-*shekel* that B'nei Yisrael would in the future give toward the communal offerings, a half-*shekel* per person. The *Shem MiShmuel* explains that the reason Hashem commanded each person to donate a half-*shekel*, as opposed to a whole *shekel*, was to impress upon the nation that no individual person is ever complete without the other; each and every person is important, possessing a unique role in Klal Yisrael's destiny. Every individual contribution is significant, as we all make up a "half," i.e., a part, of the whole.

---

16 Yitzchak's *middah* was *avodah*; ויצא יצחק לשוח בשדה.
17 See the *Gur Aryeh* where he explains in detail the symbolism of the two bracelets relating to the *Luchos*.
18 Yaacov's *middah* was Torah: ויעקב איש תם ישב אהלים.

This sense of connection to the greater *klal* (community) and availability for others in time of need was Avraham's strength, as he proved when beseeching Hashem on behalf of even the wicked city of Sedom. Similarly, he was known for his outreach, making himself available for the less fortunate.

This was Avraham's demand of Eliezer: to ensure that the future wife of Yitzchak recognized her role as both an individual and part of the greater *klal*. When Rivkah assisted Eliezer at the well and he realized that she personified this *middah*, he gave her a gift valued at a half-*shekel*, representing her understanding of the need to assist others and view herself as an important part/half of the broader *klal*.

Mikdash Me'at

Perhaps this idea can be further extended to a marriage relationship. When a man and woman marry, their new situation allows for constant opportunities and circumstances in which they will make choices that can either result in self-growth and character refinement, or reveal their incomplete and raw soul with all its failings and shortcomings. Marriage allows for particular *middos* to be exercised and developed, simply because living with another individual requires interactions that are considerate, attentive, understanding, sympathetic, concerned, helpful, unselfish, kind, compassionate, and caring. The building of a marriage in effect represents the half-*shekel*, the individual spouse who recognizes that he or she is part of a whole and that together their successful relationship completes the whole *shekel*.

> The building of a marriage in effect represents the half-shekel, the individual spouse who recognized that he or she is part of a whole.

The awareness that we as individuals are incomplete on our own, and that marriage is a tool by which we may refine ourselves and work toward spiritual growth, is that which the Torah teaches us with the description of Eliezer's unique gift to Rivkah.

This may also lend itself to the idea that each new home built through marriage is termed a *mikdash me'at*, a miniature/micro Beis HaMikdash. It is no coincidence, then, that the half-*shekel* was specifically given for the building of the *Mishkan*, and it is the individual symbolized by the half-*shekel* that builds their own form of *Mikdash* with their spouse.

The Gemara in *Maseches Pesachim* teaches:

תנו רבנן, לעולם ימכור אדם כל מה שיש לו וישא בת תלמיד חכם וישיא בתו לתלמיד חכם. משל לענבי הגפן בענבי הגפן דבר נאה ומתקבל.

The Sages taught: One should sell all he has [if he must] in order to marry the daughter of a Torah scholar and in order to marry off his daughter to a Torah scholar. This type of marriage can be compared to grapes of a vine that become intertwined with grapes of a vine, something which is beautiful and acceptable. (Pesachim 49a)

The obvious question is: Why are grapes, of all things, used as a metaphor to describe the beauty of a marriage? The *halachah* is that the *berachah* recited on grapes is *borei pri ha'etz*. However, when the grapes are squeezed, their juice is considered a higher-level food item and the *berachah* of *borei pri hagefen* is instead recited. This *halachah* is unique to grapes and their juice, whereas all other liquids squeezed from fruits fall to the lower-level *berachah* of *shehakol*. This teaches us a lesson about marriage: Each spouse has the opportunity to transform and improve the other by "squeezing out" all his selfishness and other faulty *middos* he or she has gathered during the years prior to marriage. This is done by putting the other's needs first which in turn allows for character refinement and improves the individual as well as the marriage, raising the union between husband and wife to a whole new and lofty level. What was once merely a "grape" of a relationship, is now the actual and more exalted juice thereof.

Toldos

וַיֹּאמֶר הִנֵּה נָא זָקַנְתִּי לֹא יָדַעְתִּי יוֹם מוֹתִי:

And he said, "Behold now, I have grown old; I did not know
the day of my death. (Bereishis 27:2)

It is fascinating to note that prior to the giving of the *berachos*,
Yitzchak asks Eisav to prepare delicacies in order to facilitate the
blessing:

וַעֲשֵׂה לִי מַטְעַמִּים כַּאֲשֶׁר אָהַבְתִּי וְהָבִיאָה לִי וְאֹכֵלָה בַּעֲבוּר תְּבָרֶכְךָ נַפְשִׁי בְּטֶרֶם
אָמוּת:

And make for me tasty foods as I like, and bring them to me, and I will eat,
so that my soul will bless you before I die. (Bereishis 27:4)

The question is obvious: Why was it necessary for Yitzchak to satisfy
himself with a meal in order to bless Eisav?

In addition, the wording Yitzchak uses is *"lo yadati yom mosi — I did
not know the day of my death,"* in the past tense. Would it not have been
more logical for him to say that he "does not know" the day of his death,
in the present tense? What message is the *pasuk* teaching us with this
choice of words?

Rabbi Tzvi Elimelech of Dinov, the *B'nei Yissaschar*, explains in his

Igra DeKalah the connection between Yitzchak's request for delicacies and the giving of the *berachos*:

הנה נא זקנתי לא ידעתי וכו': יש לדקדק "לא ידעתי" לשון עבר, היה לו לומר "לא אדע"
לשון הווה. אך הוא דהנה רצה לברכו, וציוה להביא לעצמו מאכל לאכול ולשתות מעדנים
ומטעמים, ומה ענין זה לברכות. אך הוא דזה ענין הצדיקים הגדולים שכל עבודתם להבורא
ית' בשמחה ובטוב לבב, ובפרט כשרוצים שתשרה עליהם רוח הקודש, אזי מטיבים את
לבם בשמחה ובטוב לבב, כי העצבות דבר מגונה בעיניהם ומונע העבודה ורוח הקודש, וזה
עניני סעודת מצוה וסעודות שתלמידי חכמים מסובין בה, שעל ידי התענוג הגשמיי מטיבין
את לבם לרוח הקודש.

וזה מ"ש בדברי חז"ל (ברכות ה' ע"א) לעולם ירגיז אדם יצר טוב על יצר הרע, נצחו מוטב
ואם לא וכו' ואם לאו יזכיר לו יום המיתה, הוא רפואה בדוקה יותר מקריאת שמע ותורה,
מה היא המניעה שלא יזכיר לו תיכף וינצל מכל רע. אך הוא בוודאי שאינו מהראוי לעורר
יראה פחותה הלזו המביאה לידי עצבות, אם לא על צד ההכרח שיראה שאין עוזר לו נגד
היצר הרע, על כן מוטב לו לבא לידי עצבות, ולא יעבור על התורה לשמוע לעצת היצר
הרע, אבל כל זמן שיש באפשרי לעמוד נגד יצר הרע באיזה תחבולה אחרת, ירחיק את
עצמו מיראת העונש ומזכרון יום המיתה, בכדי שלא יבא לידי עצבות, כי על ידי זה ירע
לבבו ולא יעבוד את הש"י בשמחה ויסתלק ממנו הרוח הקודש, הגם שהיראה הפחותה
הלזו נצרכת מאוד לשפלי מצב אשר אין להם יד שם יד בגדולות ונפלאות עבודתו ית"ש,
לגדולי הערך היא יראה פחותה מאוד, כמבואר העניין בזהר בראשית (ח"א י"א ע"ב) אית
יראה ואית יראה וכו', עיין שם.

והנה יצחק אבינו מדתו מדת היראה, אך היה מתנהג תמיד ביראת הרוממות שהוא
מתוך שמחה, ומעולם לא עלתה על דעתו יראת העונש, וזה היה הענין בכאן שהיה
רוצה שתשרה עליו השכינה ורוח הקודש לברך ברוך קדשו את אשר גזר הבורא
שראויין אליו הברכות, אזי צוה לעשות לעצמו מטעמים לשמח את לבבו, ואז תשרה
עליו רוח הקודש.

ובזה נבא אל הכוונה שהיה רוצה לומר לבנו הענין הנרצה שרוצה לברכו, על כן
בהכרח שיהיה זה מתוך שמחה, על כן יעשה לו מטעמים. ובכדי שלא יקשה לו הדבר לבנו
הלא מדתו מדת היראה ושמחה מה זו עושה, על כן הקדים מאמרו והודיעו לבנו שמעולם
שמר את עצמו מיראה הפחותה, ואמר הלא תראה הנה נא זקנתי, ואף על פי כן עדיין לא
ידעתי יום מותי, מעולם לא עלתה על דעתי ומחשבתי הזכרת יום המיתה שהוא יראה
הפחותה, רק אני מתנהג ביראת הרוממות הבאה מתוך שמחה של מצוה ורוחב לב, על כן
ועתה שא נא וכו', והבן.

This wording must be understood: Why did Yitzchak say, "I have not known," in the past tense, when it would seem that he should have said, "I do not know the day of my death"?

In addition, Yitzchak wanted to bless Eisav — so why did he ask him to bring him tasty food? What do condiments have to do with a blessing?

The explanation is that the way of great tzaddikim, whose entire service to the blessed Creator is founded upon joy and good cheer — and particularly when they desire to have ruach hakodesh (Divine Spirit) upon them — is to gladden their hearts with happiness. Sadness is repulsive to them, preventing Divine service and obstructing ruach hakodesh. This is the point of a seudas mitzvah, a "mitzvah meal," and other meals in which Torah scholars participate: via physical pleasure, they prepare their hearts to accept ruach hakodesh.

This is precisely what our Sages have taught (Berachos 5a): "One must always incite his yetzer hatov to fight against the yetzer hara — and if it defeats it, well and good...but if not, he should remind himself of the day of death."

The Gemara says that this reminder is actually a stronger "cure" for his sins than even saying Shema or learning Torah. We must understand: Why should he not begin, then, with remembering the day of death, guaranteeing that he not sin?

The answer is clearly that it is not advisable to arouse the base emotion of fear, which brings sadness, unless he truly has no other recourse to help him withstand the yetzer hara. If this is the case, he must choose the path of fear of death and the resulting sadness, and not violate the Torah. But if he has other methods by which he can stand up to the yetzer hara, he should distance himself from the fear of punishment and the memory of his future death — for this will lead to sadness, preventing him from serving G-d with joy and receiving ruach hakodesh.

It is true, nonetheless, that this debased level of "fear" is necessary for those of a low stature, those who have no connection with the greatness and wonders of the true service of Hashem. But for those of a high stature, this level is most lowly, as explained in the Zohar,[19] which states that there are two different types of fear; see there.

Returning to Yitzchak Avinu: His special trait was that of "fear" — but it was a high-level type of fear: an awe of Hashem's greatness, yiras haromemus. It never occurred to him to concern himself with the fear of Divine punishment. This explains why he asked Eisav for tasty food: he wanted the Shechinah and ruach hakodesh to dwell upon him so that he could deliver the blessing to the son upon whom the Creator deemed worthy for the blessings. He therefore instructed Eisav to prepare good food for him to gladden his heart, thus enabling ruach hakodesh to dwell upon him.

19   *Bereishis I 11b.*

Yitzchak wished to express this to Eisav and have him understand that he wanted to bless him — which must necessarily stem from joy, brought about by Eisav's good food. But in order that Eisav not be puzzled as to why physical joy was important or necessary, Yitzchak introduced his words by saying, in the past tense, "I never considered the day of my death; that is, I always distanced myself from sad thoughts of that nature. 'Behold, I have grown old,' and yet you see that 'I never knew my day of death,' I never stooped to the low level of fear of my own death; I rather always had only yiras haromemus, the awe of G-d's greatness, amid the joy and broad-heartedness of mitzvah — 'and therefore take your bow and arrow,' etc." Strive to understand this. (Igra DeKalah)

Yitzchak wanted to ensure that the *Shechinah* and *ruach hakodesh* would rest upon him so that the *berachos* he gave would be presented in a manner that they would be fulfilled.

The *B'nei Yissaschar* explains that the *Shechinah* rests upon the *tzaddikim* specifically when they are in a state of happiness. Being in a state of depression and sadness restrains them from reaching greater heights in their *avodas Hashem* and experiencing *ruach hakodesh*.[20]

Two Kinds of Fear

The Gemara in *Berachos* 5a tells us that a person should always attempt to agitate his *yetzer hara* with his *yetzer tov*. The Gemara details a list of tactics to use in the event that one particular method isn't able to conquer the *yetzer hara*. The Gemara concludes that if one is not successful, then as a last resort, he should remind himself of the day of death as a remedy to protect himself from his *yetzer hara*.[21]

The *B'nei Yissaschar* explains that reminding oneself of the day of death is clearly a last-ditch effort, only to be used when all other options have been exhausted. Why? Because this is likely to leave one with sadness and fear, leading down a path where one will be unable to

---

20 The *Talmud Yerushalmi* (*Succah* 5:1) says אין רוח הקודש שורה אלא על לב שמח.

21 א"ר לוי בר חמא אמר ר"ש בן לקיש לעולם ירגיז אדם יצר טוב על יצר הרע שנאמר רגזו ואל תחטאו. אם נצחו מוטב ואם לאו יעסוק בתורה שנאמר אמרו בלבבכם אם נצחו מוטב ואם לאו יקרא קריאת שמע על משכבכם אם נצחו מוטב ואם לאו יזכור לו יום המיתה שנאמר ודומו סלה.

serve Hashem with happiness. Serving Hashem through *yiras ha'onesh*, fear of retribution or punishment, is not the ideal. The optimal way to serve Hashem is with *yiras haromemus*, awe of Hashem's greatness, the ultimate level of veneration of the Divine majesty. This is not fear per se, but rather a sense of reverence and humility before the greatness of Hashem, which in itself serves as a deterrent from sin.

Yitzchak served Hashem with *yirah*, but never with *yiras ha'onesh*, fear of punishment. His recognition of Hashem's greatness allowed him to serve with *yiras haromemus*. This, says the *B'nei Yissaschar*, was actually his request to Eisav; "Please gladden my heart with delicacies so that I could bless my children amid a state of happiness and with the *Shechinah* and *ruach hakodesh* resting upon me." When Yitzchak says to Eisav in the past tense, *I did not know the day of my death*, the deeper message was, "I have never served Hashem through fear of punishment or death, so please, Eisav, go and prepare for me delicacies so that my *berachos* will be given in a state of happiness, and with continued *yiras haromemus*."

This may also explain why earlier in this *perek*, the Torah tells us that Yitzchak loved Eisav "*ki tzayid b'fiv* — game was in his mouth," while "Rivkah loved Yaacov."[22] The Torah gives a reason for Yitzchak's love for Eisav, but not for Rivkah's love for Yaacov. The question really is why the Torah explained Yitzchak's love for Eisav; Rivkah's love for Yaacov needs no explanation, as this is the natural state of affairs; Yitzchak clearly loved him as well. In addition, Yaacov was the ideal child, the "*ish tam yosheiv ohalim* — a wholesome person, abiding in tents."[23]

But the Torah explains Yitzchak's love for Eisav, because he had a particular reason for loving him: his ability to be *tzayid b'fiv* and keep him in a state of joy, which in turn kept the *Shechinah* and *ruach hakodesh* resting upon himself. This idea is also alluded to in the very words, "for game was in his mouth"; it was with Yitzchak's "mouth" that ate from Eisav's trappings which enabled Yitzchak to bless with his "mouth," since the *Shechinah* was with him.

---

22 ויאהב יצחק את עשו כי ציד בפיו, ורבקה אוהבת את יעקב. (בראשית כה:כח)
23 *Bereishis* 25:27.

David HaMelech asked of Hashem:

הורני ה' דרכך אהלך באמתך, יחד לבבי לירא השמך.

Teach me Your ways, that I will go in Your truth; give me an undivided heart
(or, unite my heart) so I may fear Your Name. (Tehillim 86:11)

The emphasized word יחד can also come from the root meaning "joy," as in "*vayichad Yisro — and Yisro rejoiced.*"[24] In this vein, perhaps David was asking Hashem, "make my heart joyful so that I may fear Your Name with *yiras haromemus*, and not fall to *yiras ha'onesh.*"

Parents desire their child to relate to them not out of fear or because of punitive consequences, but out of respect and appreciation for all the time they dedicate for the child's welfare. Hashem, too, wishes that we respect Him and follow in His ways not out of distress and fear of His ability to punish, but with recognition of His greatness and awesomeness.

Imagine being in the home of someone that has just freed you from an overwhelming debt. The level of gratitude and graciousness felt is

Hashem wishes that we respect Him and follow in His ways not out of fear, but with recognition of His greatness and awseomeness.

inconceivable, and while in his presence, your feelings of joy and appreciation are simply indescribable. You would be ready to comply with any of his possible needs or requests, with great respect and admiration for his act of kindness. This is the feeling with which we must relate to Hashem. Recognizing His greatness and magnitude, and that He alone is responsible for all we have, should help negate feelings of fear and dread when we think of Hashem; they should motivate us to serve Him with great love and joy, seeking to fulfill His every wish and demand.

24 *Shemos* 18:9. See Rashi.

Vayeitzei

וַיְהִי בַבֹּקֶר וְהִנֵּה הִוא לֵאָה וַיֹּאמֶר אֶל לָבָן מַה זֹּאת עָשִׂיתָ לִּי
הֲלֹא בְרָחֵל עָבַדְתִּי עִמָּךְ וְלָמָּה רִמִּיתָנִי:

It came to pass in the morning, and behold, she was Leah.
Yaacov said to Lavan, "What is this that you have done to me?
Did I not work with you for Rachel? Why did you trick me?"

(Bereishis 29:25)

Rashi quotes the Gemara in *Megillah* 13b which describes the events that unfolded as Lavan deceived Yaacov by switching Leah in place of Rachel as he had previously promised. Rashi states:

ויהי בבקר והנה היא לאה: אבל בלילה לא היתה לאה? לפי שמסר יעקב לרחל סימנים,
וכשראתה רחל שמכניסין לו לאה אמרה עכשיו תכלם אחותי, עמדה ומסרה לה אותן
סימנים.

And it came to pass in the morning, and behold she was Leah — But at night, she was not Leah?! Rather, Yaacov had given signs to Rachel, but when she saw that they were bringing in Leah (instead), Rachel said, "My sister will now be put to shame" [for she will not know the signs], and so she transmitted those signs to Leah.

Yaacov and Rachel had already anticipated Lavan's deceptive scheme to give him Leah instead of Rachel. Yaacov therefore preempted this possibility by giving Rachel signs by which she could identify herself to him. When Rachel realized that Leah would be humiliated by this plan, she decided to forego her original plan with Yaacov and reveal the signs, sparing her sister the shame.

If we study the sequence of events, we find that Rachel was overcome with emotion and concern for her sister's impending shame. Why, then, did she plan with Yaacov from the start to use the signs to identify herself? If they both suspected Lavan would give Leah instead of Rachel, was it not clear that Leah stood to be embarrassed by not having the signs? What was Rachel's original plan, and what happened in the interim to make her change her mind?

Seeing Is Believing

Perhaps the answer lies in a deeper insight into human emotions, particularly that of empathy. As the popular saying goes, "seeing is believing." Hearing about someone else's difficult situation makes an impression, but not always a powerful one. Actually seeing the pain of others brings it to life and makes it tangible. Rashi uses the word וכשראתה, when Rachel *saw* Leah being brought in, the devastating pain and embarrassment that Leah was about to experience became very real to her. Disregarding her previous plans with Yaacov, she thereupon gave Leah the signs, so that she wouldn't suffer pain and humiliation.

This is an important lesson regarding sharing in someone else's pain and suffering. Many of us find it difficult to *daven* or empathize for someone ill, a Jew in prison, or even for a family in the midst of a crisis; we struggle to connect to the abstract and intangible. Perhaps it would help to close our eyes and use our imagination to visualize the actual hospital room with a heart monitor and IV drip connected to the patient and the worried family awaiting news from the doctor on the patient's test results, or a prison cell with three bare concrete walls and a rusty steel gate, bed, and urinal, while the prisoner sits alone.

Maybe picture the image of a child crying under his blanket knowing that his parents don't get along and are on the brink of divorce, or of a girl whose father lost his job and her parents worry about paying their monthly bills. Actually imagining an individual with a disability crying and hoping to walk again, or a mother in Israel afraid of her child not coming home from school because of a terror attack, could do the trick. Visualize the scene of a couple so distraught because efforts to have a child they wish for so badly have failed them again, or of a lonely young man or woman hoping to find their *shidduch* and build a family. Perhaps these mental exercises can trigger our hearts to truly feel for another and make our *tefillos* more meaningful and significant. We may even shed a tear as we imagine ourselves experiencing their pain.

Allowing Another's Pain to Penetrate Your Heart

This episode of Rachel giving the signs to Leah teaches us that in order to really feel and share in another's pain, it is required of us to connect to their experience in a manner that allows their pain to penetrate our hearts. This is perhaps what led Rachel to abandon her original plan with Yaacov after *witnessing* her sister Leah being chosen and the dramatic consequence that was about to follow.

> *To really feel and share in another's pain, it is required of us to connect to their experience.*

The *pasuk* tells of Moshe Rabbeinu's initial encounter with B'nei Yisrael and observing their suffering.

וַיְהִי בַּיָּמִים הָהֵם וַיִּגְדַּל מֹשֶׁה וַיֵּצֵא אֶל אֶחָיו וַיַּרְא בְּסִבְלֹתָם וַיַּרְא אִישׁ מִצְרִי מַכֶּה אִישׁ עִבְרִי מֵאֶחָיו:

It happened in those days, Moshe grew and went out to his brothers and saw their suffering; he saw an Egyptian man striking a Hebrew man of his brethren. (Shemos 12:1)

Rashi explains:

וירא בסבלתם: נתן עיניו ולבו להיות מיצר עליהם.

And looked at their burdens *— He directed his eyes and his heart to be distressed over them.*

Surely, Moshe had *heard* about the burden of B'nei Yisrael. However, what actually resulted in him taking action was *seeing* the distress his brothers were suffering and his wish to experience first-hand what they were living through. Seeing is a powerful tool and allows us to connect and feel another person's struggle in a real and almost tangible way.

The *pasuk* in *Koheles* says:

טוֹב לָלֶכֶת אֶל בֵּית אֵבֶל מִלֶּכֶת אֶל בֵּית מִשְׁתֶּה בַּאֲשֶׁר הוּא סוֹף כָּל הָאָדָם וְהַחַי יִתֵּן אֶל לִבּוֹ:

It is better to go to a house of mourning than to go to a house of feasting, for that is the end of all men, and the living will take it to his heart. (Koheles 7:2)

Going to the home of a mourner brings to mind the day of death and has the ability to make a lasting impression on us. Unfortunately, just hearing of someone's passing is something to which we have become largely immune, and may not be sufficient to truly affect us. However, visiting the actual mourner and interacting with him or her will provide us the visual cue that leads to thinking about death and ultimately pierces the heart.

Rachel Experiences the Pain of Her Children

This may also explain Rashi in *Parashas Vayechi*. Yaacov had excused himself to Yosef for not burying Rachel as honorably as he himself had requested to be buried. Rashi says:

ואקברה שם: ולא הולכתיה אפילו לבית לחם להכניסה לארץ, וידעתי שיש בלבך עלי [תרעומת], אבל דע לך שעל פי הדבור קברתיה שם שתהא לעזרה לבניה כשיגלה אותם נבוזראדן, והיו עוברים דרך שם, יצאת רחל על קברה ובוכה ומבקשת עליהם רחמים, שנאמר (ירמיה לא יד) קול ברמה נשמע נהי רחל מבכה על בניה וגו', והקב"ה משיבה (ירמיה לא טו) יש שכר לפעולתך נאם ה' ושבו בנים לגבולם (מח:ז):

And I buried her there — *And I did not take her even to Beis Lechem to bring her into a populated area[25] and I know that you hold it against me; but you should know that I buried her there by Divine command, so that she would be of assistance to her children. [How so?] When Nevuzaradan will exile them [B'nei Yisrael], and they pass by there, Rachel will emerge from her grave and weep and beg mercy for them, as it is said: "A voice is heard on high,*

---

25 See *Sifsei Chachamim* who explains Rashi in this manner.

[lamentation, bitter weeping, Rachel is weeping for her children]...'There will be a reward for your work,' says Hashem,...'and the children shall return to their own border.'" (Yirmiyahu 31:14–15)

Is it necessary for Rachel to wait until B'nei Yisrael pass her burial place before she stands and *davens* for them? Using the same thought as above, we can understand that Rachel *davens* when she *sees* and experiences the pain of her children. When she sees them exiled into *Galus* this prompts her to cry and ask Hashem to have mercy on them.

Levi Selects Names for His Children

A beautiful idea from Rav Yeshaya HaLevi Horowitz, the *Shelah HaKadosh*, accentuates this idea of what it means to relate to another person's suffering.

אלה ראשי בית אבותם בני ראובן וגו' ובני שמעון וגו' ואלה שמות בני לוי (שמות ו: יד) ק'
למה אמר תיבת שמות אצל לוי יותר ממה שאמר בראובן ושמעון. הענין הוא כי שבט לוי
לא היו בגלות ולוי ידע דבר זה ורצה להשתתף בצרת הצבור מה עשה קרא שמות לבניו
ע"ש הגלות דהיינו שם גרשון ע"ש כי גרים הם בארץ לא להם ושם קהת על שם שיניהם
קהות ושם מררי ע"ש שמררו את חייהם זה שאמר ואלה שמות בני לוי ומכאן ילמוד האדם
להשתתף בצער הציבור אע"פ שאין הצרה מגעת לו וכו'.

"These were the heads of their fathers' houses: The sons of Reuven, etc., the sons of Shimon, etc., these are the names of the sons of Levi." — The pasuk is difficult to understand. Why did the Torah choose to use the word "names" with Levi and not with Reuven, Shimon, and the other families? [The Shelah answers] that the children of all of the Twelve Tribes were enslaved except for the children of Levi. Levi felt that he and his family should participate in the communal suffering of their brethren. What did Levi do? He named his children in a way that would remind them of the galus. Gershon originated from the word "ger," meaning "stranger," for the Jews were strangers in a land not their own. Kehas originated from the word "dull," for B'nei Yisrael's teeth were dulled by their suffering. And the name Merari originated from "mar" which means "bitter," for their lives were made bitter by the galus. And from this we should learn to participate in the communal suffering even though the actual suffering may not reach us.

Levi understood that to truly empathize with his brothers, it was going to take more than simply knowing about their suffering. A constant reminder and a way to connect was implemented so as not to become immune to B'nei Yisrael's grief and misery.

The famous nineteenth century poet Walt Whitman wrote:

"I do not ask the wounded person how he feels; I myself become the wounded person."

Vayishlach

קָטֹנְתִּי מִכֹּל הַחֲסָדִים וּמִכָּל הָאֱמֶת אֲשֶׁר עָשִׂיתָ אֶת עַבְדֶּךָ כִּי בְמַקְלִי עָבַרְתִּי אֶת הַיַּרְדֵּן הַזֶּה וְעַתָּה הָיִיתִי לִשְׁנֵי מַחֲנוֹת:

I have become small from all the kindnesses and from all the truth that You have rendered Your servant, for with my staff I crossed this Jordan, and now I have become two camps.

(Bereishis 32:11)

קטנתי מכל החסדים: נתמעטו זכיותי על ידי החסדים והאמת שעשית עמי לכך אני ירא שמא משהבטחתני נתלכלכתי בחטא ויגרום לי להמסר ביד עשו.

I have become small — My merits have diminished because of the kindnesses and the truth that You have rendered me. Therefore, I fear lest I have become sullied with sin ever since You promised me, causing me to be delivered into Eisav's hands. (Rashi)

After splitting his family into two camps, Yaacov is afraid for his life and says to Hashem, "Even though You promised to return me to my home and birthplace and do good with me, perhaps I will not be deserving of Your previous promise." Rashi explains that Yaacov is in essence saying, "My merits have been reduced through the kindness you have shown me in the past."

48

Taking Life for Granted

Perhaps we can add an additional idea. Yaacov was teaching us that when one is showered with an abundance of Hashem's goodness day after day, he can become immune to recogniz-
ing Hashem's kindness and actually not notice the good provided to him. The *pasuk* then is communicating this idea that a person can become *katan* (קָטֹנְתִּי), diminished and lacking in his appreciation to Hashem. What might be the cause of this? The answer is, מִכֹּל הַחֲסָדִים, "all the kindness" that Hashem has provided can

When one is showered with an abundance of Hashem's goodness day after day, he can become immune to recognizing Hashem's kindness.

create a rote behavior of living and expectations that the good will persist and continue on.

This thought is further seen in the *pasuk* as it continues with, *ki b'makli avarti*, I've gone through life with my staff and all my needs were met and satisfied which caused me to take them for granted and forget my Benefactor.

Rabbeinu Bachya ibn Pakuda, the *Chovos Halevavos*, in his introduction to *Shaar HaBechinah*, the Gate of Examination, lends an insight to this idea. He provides several reasons why people tend to become apathetic to Hashem's kindness and don't reflect on the good He bestows upon them. The second one is this:

והשני: צאתם אל העולם הזה והם נמשלים כבהמות סכלות וכעייר כמו שאמר הכתוב
איוב יא ועיר פרא אדם יולד והתגדלם בטובות האלוקים העודפות והתגלגלם בהם, עד
ששבו אצלם רגילות וידועות, כאילו הם עצמיות להם, בלתי סרות מאתם ולא נפרדות
מהם כל ימיהם. וכאשר ישכילו, ותתחזק הכרתם, יסכלו טובות הבורא עליהם, ואינם
משימים על לבם חיוב ההודאה עליה, מפני שאינם יודעים מעלת הטובה והמטיב בה
אליהם ומשלם בזה לתינוק שמצאו איש אחד מאנשי החסד במדבר, וחמל עליו, ויאספהו
אל ביתו ויגדלהו ויאכילהו וילבישהו, ויתנדב עליו בכל הטוב לו, עד שהשכיל והבין אופני
דרכי טובתו ואחר כן שמע האיש ההוא על אסיר שנפל ביד שונאו, והגיעו אל תכלית הצער
והרעב והעירום ימים רבים, ונכמרו רחמיו על צערו, ופיים לשונאו, עד שהתירו ומחל לו
את דמיו. ויאספהו האיש אל ביתו והיטיב לו במקצת הטוב אשר היטיב בו לתינוק והיה
האסיר מכיר בטובת האיש עליו ומודה עליה, יותר מן התינוק שגדל בה, מפני שיצא מעניין
העוני והצער אל עניין הטובה והשלווה בעת שהכרתו בה גמורה. על כן הכיר טובת האיש
החסיד וחסדו מאוד והתינוק לא הבין מעלת הטובה עליו, אף על פי שהתתחזקה הכרתו

והתיישב בדעתו, מפני שהיה רגיל בה מימי נערותו ואין איש מאנשי השכל מסתפק שח־
סדו וטובו על התינוק כוללים ונראים יותר, ושהוא חייב בהתמדת הודאה והשבח עליהם
יותר וזה דומה למה שאמר הכתוב (הושע יא) ואנכי תרגלתי לאפרים קחם על זרועותיו,
ולא ידעו כי רפאתים.

The second reason is that human beings, when they come into this world, are like ignorant beasts and donkeys, as it says: "A man is born a wild donkey" (Iyov 11:12). They grow up so accustomed to G-d's abounding favors that [these favors] seem routine and ordinary to them, as if they were innate, interminable, and inseparable from them for the rest of their lives. When their intelligence develops and their perception sharpens, they remain ignorant of G-d's favors. It does not occur to them that they have an obligation to express gratitude for them, because they realize neither the magnitude of the favor nor [the magnitude] of the One Who bestows it.

In this respect they may be compared to an infant found in the desert by a man who was a devotee of lovingkindness. The man had pity for the child, took him into his home, raised him, fed him, clothed him, and provided him generously with all that was good for him, until the child [matured and] was able to comprehend the man's kind favors.

Later, the man heard of someone whose enemy had taken him captive and had subjected him to extremes of suffering, starvation, and exposure over a lengthy period of time. The man's compassion was aroused by the suffering of this prisoner. He appeased the enemy, who then freed the prisoner and forgave him his debt. [The man] then took him into his home, and treated him kindly, but this came to only a fraction of all the kindness which he had shown the infant. Yet this [freed] prisoner had more appreciation and expressed more gratitude for the man's favors then did the child who had been raised on them. This was because he had passed from a state of poverty and suffering to a state of well-being and tranquility at a point in his life when he could fully appreciate this. As a result, he was exceedingly grateful for the devout man's favors and kindnesses.

The infant [now a young man], however, could not appreciate the magnitude of the favor that had been done for him — even though his perception had sharpened and his mind had matured — for he had been used to these favors from earliest childhood. Still, no rational person will doubt that the love and kindness showered upon the infant were wider in scope and more striking, and that he is under greater obligation to express constantly his thanks and appreciation. This is like what the pasuk says: "It was I who accustomed

Efrayim to being taken up in his arms, and they did not know that I had healed them" (Hoshea 11:3).[26]

The Need for a Kidney

Hardly a week goes by without an email or other media plea for someone in dire need of a kidney donation. This has become so routine that it may not even cause us to actually contemplate the individual in need. We may not be prepared to take the bold step and donate a kidney or perhaps we aren't the appropriate candidate from a medical perspective. However, these requests for people less fortunate than us, in need of vital medical care, should at the minimum cause us to reflect on the kindness that Hashem so graciously provides us day in and day out. We should at the very least think to ourselves how blessed we are that our kidneys and other organs are functioning properly. We should use these events as reminders from Hashem for us to appreciate that which we have, and not to fall into a habitual, prosaic mode of life in which we feel "entitled" to health and wellbeing, taking these gifts for granted.

A beautiful idea is presented in the name of Reb Simcha Bunim of Peshischa relating to the risk of falling into rote living. He comments on the following *pasuk*:

וְהוֹצֵאתִי אֶתְכֶם מִתַּחַת סִבְלֹת מִצְרָיִם:

I shall take you out from under the burdens of Mitzrayim. (Shemos 6:6)

הקשה על זה רשכבה"ג מרן הרבי ר' בונם זצלל"ה זי"ע מפשיסחא: מדוע לא נכתב "עב־
דות" או לשון אחר, רק לשון "סבלות". והשיב כי בתחילת השיעבוד היה אצלם קשה
הדבר, אבל אחר כך גם הם התרגלו והיה אצלם רגילות, כי הרגל נעשה טבע, וכאשר ראה
השי"ת שהם כבר רגילים לעבודת פרעה ומשוקעים בחומר ובלבנים ואינם מרגישים כלל,
אמר "והוצאתי אתכם מתחת סבלות מצרים" — "אז עטס קאנט שוין סובל זיין די מצרים,
טויג נישט, וועל איך ענק אויסלייזן" [אם אתם כבר יכולים לסבול את מצרים, זה לא טוב,
וצריך לגאול אתכם], ע"כ לשון קדשו, ודפח"ח. (שיח שרפי קודש ח"ג אות תפ"א)

The Rashkebehag (Head of the Diaspora), Reb Bunim, zt"l, of Peshischa, asked: "Why did it not say 'from under the bondage of Mitzrayim,' or

---

*some other similar language, but rather used the word 'sivlos' [which
has the connotation of a burden that can be borne, even if with great
difficulty]?"*

*He answered that the beginning of the subjugation was very hard for
B'nei Yisrael, but after a while, they became accustomed to it; it became part of their routine, and the "routine becomes natural." When
Hashem saw that they had grown accustomed to the work that Pharaoh
placed upon them, and that they were totally engrossed in bricks and
mortar without even realizing or feeling [the pain] — at that point,
Hashem said, "I will extricate you from the sivlos of Mitzrayim." It is as
expressed in Yiddish: "If you can bear the suffering of Egypt, then it's
really bad; you have to be redeemed already." (Siach Sarfei Kodesh, part
III, section 481)*

Hashem, in His endless kindness, desires us to simply recognize the
good He provides. According to Reb Simcha Bunim, as he homiletically
interprets the *pasuk*, Hashem "needed" to redeem us because the burdens of Mitzrayim were having less of an effect on us.

Let us not put ourselves in a situation where Hashem "needs" to create new tests for us so that we come to appreciate His kindness. If we
live life with our eyes wide open and resist falling into the walking slum-
ber of taking all for granted, we can continue experiencing Hashem's
goodness without a lapse.

David HaMelech's Request of Hashem

David HaMelech says in *Tehillim*:

אַחַת שָׁאַלְתִּי מֵאֵת ה' אוֹתָהּ אֲבַקֵּשׁ שִׁבְתִּי בְּבֵית ה' כָּל יְמֵי חַיַּי לַחֲזוֹת בְּנֹעַם יְהֹוָה וּלְבַקֵּר
בְּהֵיכָלוֹ:

*One thing I asked of Hashem that I shall seek, that I dwell in the House of
Hashem all the days of my life to behold the delight of Hashem and to visit in
His Sanctuary. (Tehillim 27:4)*

David seems to be making two contradictory requests:

- First, he asks to sit in the House of Hashem all of his life.
- Then, he follows with the request to *visit* Hashem in the *Heichal*.

Which one is it? Eternal life with Hashem, or just an occasional visit? Many commentators answer that David was asking to dwell all the days of his life in the House of Hashem, but that his time there should remain as if it were only a visit, with the same freshness, excitement, and novelty of the first day's experience. He was requesting that he not fall into the trap of becoming apathetic to Hashem's generosity to a point where he would no longer appreciate it.

Vayeishev

וַיִּשְׁמַע רְאוּבֵן וַיַּצִּלֵהוּ מִיָּדָם וַיֹּאמֶר לֹא נַכֶּנּוּ נָפֶשׁ:

Reuven heard and he saved him from their hand[s] and said,
"Let us not deal him a deadly blow." (Bereishis 37:21)

As the brothers planned to rid themselves of their brother Yosef, Reuven developed his own plan to save Yosef's life. He suggested that they put him into a pit, and Rashi explains[27] that his intention was to return later and rescue Yosef.

The Midrash on *Megillas Rus* teaches:

אמר רבי יצחק בר מריון: בא הכתוב ללמדך, שאם אדם עושה מצוה יעשנה בלב בשלם. שאלו היה ראובן יודע שהקדוש ברוך הוא מכתיב עליו (בראשית לז:כא) וישמע ראובן ויצילהו מידם — בכתפו היה מוליכו אצל אביו. ואילו היה יודע אהרן שהקב"ה מכתיב עליו (שמות ד:יד) הנה הוא יוצא לקראתך — בתופים ובמחולות היה יוצא לקראתו. ואלו היה יודע בעז שהקדוש ברוך הוא מכתיב עליו ויצבט לה קליות אכל ותשבע ותותר — עגלות מפוטמות היה מאכילה. ר' כהן ור' יהושע דסכנין בשם ר' לוי: לשעבר היה אדם עושה מצוה והנביא כותבה ועכשיו כשאדם עושה מצוה מי כותבה אליהו כותבה ומלך המשיח והקדוש ב"ה החותם על ידיהם הדא הוא דכתיב אז נדברו יראי ה' איש אל רעהו וגו' (משלי ג:טז).

Rabbi Yitzchak Bar Maryon said: The pasuk comes to teach you that if a person does a good deed, he should do it with his whole heart. For if Reuven

---

27   To *pasuk* 22.

had known that Hashem would write about him in the Torah, "Reuven heard, and saved him from their hand" (Bereishis 37:21), he would have actually carried Yosef on his shoulders back to his father. And if Aharon had known that Hashem would write about him, "Behold he [Aharon] is going out to meet you [Moshe]" (Shemos 4:14), he would have greeted Moshe with tambourines and dancing. And if Boaz had known that Hashem would write about him, "And he gave her parched corn and she ate and was satisfied and left over thereof" (Rus 2:14), he would have fed her with fattened calves.

Rav Cohen and Rav Yehoshua of Sachnin said in the name of Rav Levi: In the past, when a man performed a good deed, the prophet placed it on record; but nowadays when a man performs a good deed, who records it? Eliyahu records it and Mashiach and Hashem will, so to speak, sign His Name next to their's. This is the meaning of the pasuk, "They that feared Hashem then spoke with one another and Hashem hearkened, and heard, and a book of remembrance was written before Him" (Malachi 3:16). (Midrash Rus Rabbah 5:6)

Rav Aharon Kotler, *zt"l*, in his *Mishnas Rabbi Aharon* offers insight to this Midrash and the perpetual value of even a seemingly small good deed:

והנה עוד יותר יש בזה, שהרי כשהציל יוסף את ראובן היה בזה מעשה הצלה עד אין
ערוך, הצלה כללית לכל העולם שהרי על ידי יוסף ניצלו כל הארצות ממיתת רעב, גם
זן וכלכל את כל בית יעקב, גם לעתיד לבא כתוב: והיה בית יעקב אש, ובית יוסף להבה,
ובית עשיו לקש, ודלקו בהם ואכלום (עובדיה א', יח), ואמרו חז"ל: אין זרעו של עשיו
נמסר אלא ביד זרעו של יוסף (ב"ב קכג) [ויהושע החליש כחו של עמלק], ונמצא
שבמעשיו היו מונחים תוצאות גדולות מאד. וכן אצל בועז הרי יצא ממעשיו ומצוותיו
מלכות בית דוד ומלך המשיח. ויש לפרש עפי"ז מה שאמרו חז"ל אילו היו יודע, דקאי
על כל אלו התוצאות, דהרי כתיבתו בתורה זהו הנצחיות של המעשים וזה שאמרו אילו
היה יודע שהקב"ה מכתיב עליו, דווקא.

There is even more to this. For when Reuven saved Yosef, this was an inestimable act of rescue — a salvation for the entire world, which was saved by Yosef from the famine, and especially for the family of Yaacov, which he fed and supported then, and [a salvation for Israel] in the future as well, as the Prophet says, "The House of Yaacov will be fire, and that of Yosef will be flames, and that of Eisav will be straw, and [Yaacov and Yosef] will blaze and consume Eisav" (Ovadiah 1:18); our Sages taught (Bava Basra 123b): "The descendants of Eisav will be delivered only into the hands of the descendants of Yosef." [And in fact it was Yehoshua who weakened the strength of Eisav's descendant Amalek, as written in Shemos (17:13), and thus Reuven's actions led to very great results indeed.

Similarly, regarding Boaz: His deeds resulted in the Kingdom of the House of David [Boaz's descendant via Rus] and the King Mashiach.

Accordingly, we can explain that which the Sages said, "If [Reuven or Boaz] had known…" as referring [not merely to the very writing down of their deeds in the Torah, but] to the great consequences of what they did — because being written in the Torah is actually the "eternity" of these deeds. Thus, the Sages say specifically, "If Reuven/Boaz had known that the Torah would write about him," meaning, if they had known that their deeds would have such eternal consequences. (Mishnas Rabbi Aharon)

Even a small good deed, explains Rav Aharon, goes further than we can imagine. It is very precious to Hashem, a thought to keep in mind when we engage in a seemingly small mitzvah.

Hashem's Business

We are well aware that Hashem knows the deepest thoughts of man and that our actions cannot be hidden. What message, then, is the Midrash teaching by saying that Hashem places His seal on each recorded mitzvah?

Perhaps this can be understood and compared to the CEO of a large business. While he busies himself with running a successful company, an accounting staff is hired to manage the day-to-day finances of the company. Unlike the CEO who doesn't involve himself in the trivial dealings of his business, Hashem's seal is placed on each mitzvah. The Midrash emphasizes that we should not think that a small deed goes unnoticed or holds little value. Hashem takes great pleasure in our small deeds which, without our knowledge, go a long way and have lasting effects.

Yet this Midrash remains difficult to understand:

- Normally, we are never encouraged to perform a mitzvah based on the fanfare and reward that may result from our actions, and surely not for that which will be written publicly. Why, then, is this aspect so aggrandized here?
- Additionally, we are speaking of Reuven, Aharon, and Boaz, all great personalities; surely their mitzvah performance was

not motivated by what would be written about them later, but rather with pure untainted intentions. For what value or significance would the knowledge that the Torah would praise them for their good deeds have to them in any event?

A Fire in the Rav's Home

Rav Yosef Shalom Elyashiv, *zt"l*, presents[28] a beautiful metaphor of a devastating fire that broke out one evening in a small town. The rabbi's house went up in flames, resulting in total destruction of all its furnishings and contents. After the clean-up effort began, with the congregants pitching in to restore their rabbi's home, they found among the ruins a thick envelope labeled "Eulogies." Unable to contain their curiosity, they opened the envelope to see its contents. What they discovered left them all horror-stricken and shocked. Apparently, in an effort to save time and be prepared for the untimely passing of one of his congregants, the rabbi had prepared eulogies in advance for all of the members of the shul. Each person found a neatly written eulogy describing his life's work and accomplishments. This left them with feelings of anger toward the rabbi. After all, they were alive and well. How morbid could their rabbi be to write a eulogy for living people?

However, after these feelings subsided, they were left with a deep sense of amazement. They reasoned to themselves that this was perhaps the catalyst for some much-needed introspection for the manner in which they lived their lives. Each one was astounded with the limited accomplishments and inadequate good deeds he had performed throughout his lifetime. They immediately accepted upon themselves to accomplish more and attain a greater commitment in serving Hashem, so that they could be remembered after their passing in a more positive light.

Perhaps the Midrash is teaching us that thinking about how we will be remembered or what will be written about us after our passing is not a reason in itself to do good — but it can act to motivate and direct us

---

28   *Divrei Aggadah, Parashas Chayei Sarah.*

in performing mitzvos with a whole heart and help keep us focused on achieving more in our *avodas Hashem*. The message for us is that the day will come where something will be written about us — and the question is: What will it be?

A simple walk through a cemetery will show that never is the amount of money a person amassed written on his or her tombstone. Nor is the extent of their lavish lifestyle written on stone. It is rather the good deeds and *chessed* to which we committed ourselves that is displayed and serve as an example for others.

The message of the Midrash is not that if only Reuven knew what would be written about him he would have acted differently. Such a reading of the Midrash is too simplistic and unbefitting of great people such as Reuven, Aharon, and Boaz. Rather, since our actions are eventually recorded and remembered, we stand to benefit if we would question ourselves about how genuinely we would greet people, make time for those less fortunate, and dedicate ourselves to Hashem if we had the vision of the future written in front of us at all times.

We stand to benefit if we would question ourselves about how genuinely we would greet people, make time for those less fortunate, and dedicate ourselves to Hashem if we had the vision of the future written in front of us at all times.

Reuven may have acted differently — but not for the fame and prominence it would have left him. Rather, had he known that what he did was of such great value and importance, worthy of being written in the Torah as a lesson for others, he would have planned to rescue Yosef even more dedicatedly than he did.

Mikeitz

וַיִּקְרָא יוֹסֵף אֶת שֵׁם הַבְּכוֹר מְנַשֶּׁה כִּי נַשַּׁנִי אֱלֹקִים אֶת כָּל עֲמָלִי וְאֵת
כָּל בֵּית אָבִי: וְאֵת שֵׁם הַשֵּׁנִי קָרָא אֶפְרָיִם כִּי הִפְרַנִי אֱלֹקִים בְּאֶרֶץ עָנְיִי:

*And Yosef named the firstborn Menashe, for "Hashem has
caused me to forget all my toil and all my father's house." And
the second one he named Ephraim, for "Hashem has made me
fruitful in the land of my affliction."*

(Bereishis 41:51)

The *pasuk* tells of Yosef choosing to name his firstborn Menashe
because his birth enabled him to forget all his troubles and his father's house.

Rav Moshe Shternbuch, in his work *Taam Vodaas*, asks this question
(as do others): Was Yosef proud of forgetting his grieving father? Was
this something to commemorate in his firstborn's name? In addition,
it is perhaps true that Yosef was finally feeling that times were getting
better for him, after his kidnapping and incarceration. However, the
pasuk seems to communicate that he was comforted specifically by
the birth of his son and that it was this that now enabled him to put
memories of his father's home behind him. What was special about
Menashe's birth?

Rav Moshe answers that Yosef realized that his fate was to be away from his father and that he was prohibited by a *cherem*[29] declared by his brothers from revealing to his father that he was alive and well in Mitzrayim. Yosef was trapped with a longing and yearning for his father's household. He suffered from the constant thoughts and memories of what life once was. Yosef was unable to free himself of the thought that his father was so close, yet so far away. Now, with the birth of a child, it allowed him to focus his emotions and strong feelings on his child, diverting his thoughts and his passionate feelings away from the memories of his father's house. Yosef was finally able to live again without emotional pain continuously gnawing at him.

The Fruits of Our Labor

As we go through life, we are met with many challenges while working toward our specific goals. We keep trying and trying, often without much success, until finally our hard work pays off and we succeed. The pain and hardship of the past can then be forgotten and minimized, because the fruits of our labor have appeared. After much hard work, we can be sure that what will ultimately be remembered and enjoyed is that which we produced and worked toward; the immense pleasure that awaits us afterwards will help us forget all the hardships along the way.

What Is Galus?

It happened that a local water utility notified an entire town that because of a major break in the main water pipeline, there would be no water for one week. The residents ran to stock up on as much bottled water as possible, bracing

---

29 Yosef's brothers proclaimed a *cherem*, solemn ban, forbidding anyone from divulging to Yaacov what had occurred. According to *Sefer Chassidim* the oath applied even to Yosef, and prohibited him from attempting to return to Yaacov, or even to notify him by word of mouth or letter of his whereabouts, without the consent of his brothers. This explains why Yosef did not contact Yaacov throughout his twenty-two years in Mitzrayim. He was bound by the oath, for when a qualified quorum of ten invokes a solemn ban, it is binding on all. Yitzchak, who was still alive, knew prophetically what had happened, but he was forced to endure Yaacov's anguish in silence because of this oath. (See Artscroll Chumash, Stone ed., 37:27.)

themselves for a week of no running water to cook with or shower. Finally, the week passed, and the water utility reported that the issue was more severe than originally thought and that it would take another five to seven days to repair. The bottled water supply was scarce, and people began to make plans to move into their relatives' homes in areas not affected by the water outage. Two weeks went by and little progress was made. Residents were now notified that it would take another two weeks, and they urged people to be patient as they worked around the clock to resolve the issue. At this point, people started actually moving much of their belongings into their friends' and relatives' homes, while some even rented temporary apartments or moved into hotels miles away from their homes so that they could live decently. They were distraught over the upheaval, and longed for normalcy to return. They remembered a time when daily life was easy and routine, when they lived in happiness and comfort with all of their conveniences in their small town. Their communities and neighborhoods had been wonderful, with feelings of warmth and closeness among friends and neighbors. All this had now changed. Two additional weeks passed and the water company announced that it would most likely take another five months before complete restoration of the water supply. The company apologized profusely and offered a free month of water supply for all those customers affected. Realizing that they were now in for the long haul, people were seen moving out of their homes in tears, trying to take with them as much as possible as they transplanted their once normal lives into their new dwellings.

A long eight months later, the call finally came that they could all return to their homes, as water had been restored. Most people, however, had already established themselves in their new communities and were at peace with their new living arrangements. They had already forgotten about their old lifestyles and lost their interest in returning. People had found new friends and became accustomed to the new shopping and school routines. In fact, they all decided to just stay put, not interested in the tensions and planning involved with moving again. Life had finally become normal again, comfortable for most, and they weren't interested in remembering what their lives were once like and how much they had once wished and yearned for their old town.

This is *galus*.

We've been away from our true home for so long. We've become so complacent and comfortable with the *galus* and fascinated by the surroundings of our new home that we have forgotten our original feelings of sadness and grief when we were driven out of our home in Yerushalayim. We have also forgotten the purpose of the *galus:* to rebuild within us the desire to be close with Hashem. The opposite has occurred. We've found a new life which has caused us to become more distant.

Initially, the change must have been most difficult and we hoped it would only be a short while — perhaps two months, six months, or maybe ten months. But as time went on, we lost our desire and hope of returning, because we had found new life in a foreign place and had surrounded ourselves with all its conveniences. We simply forgot that things used to be so much better. Hashem now calls on us to come home. He seeks to remind us how much better life is with the Beis HaMikdash, in His Land, and with each other. Unfortunately, we have accustomed ourselves to the status quo. We feel so satisfied, with so little lacking, that we are at times incapable of hearing Hashem's calling for us to return. This *galus* has then created a struggle within us to direct our hearts to Hashem's promise of redeeming us.

Of course, Hashem knew that the *galus* was to be difficult and demanding, with many struggles of personal and communal pain. He, therefore, surrounded us with many remedies to help distract us and sweeten the exile so that life would be manageable and even palatable. But Hashem does not want us to use these gifts to help us forget Him, nor allow our success to result in our forgetting the Beis HaMikdash. We must continue to yearn for the days that once were and for our return to the homes we were once forced to leave.

Perhaps there is an allusion to this idea in the *pasuk* above. Yosef said *ki nashani Elokim es kol amali ve'es kol beis avi*, for "Hashem has caused me to forget all my toil and all my father's house." This can be read and understood homiletically that throughout this long and painful *galus* we forgot Hashem and all our suffering[30] as well as Hashem's House, the Beis HaMikdash. This occurred because of *ki hifrani Elokim b'eretz anyi*, because Hashem has made us prosper and succeed in our land of suffering, in *galus*. Since we have been surrounded by so much good which was intended to alleviate the hardship of the *galus*, we have forgotten Hashem and our interest in returning to our true home.

Yosef's Lesson While in the Land of His Affliction

Yosef says, *ki hifrani Elokim b'eretz anyi*, Hashem has made me fruitful in the land of my affliction. He realizes that Hashem made him successful and prosperous, but nevertheless he is still in the land of his affliction. He did not completely forget that even with all the power and success he had achieved in Mitzrayim, it was still not the ideal. He had not lost sight of his goal, despite all the blessings he had received.[31]

Remove the Knife

The *Mishnah Berurah*, in the name of Rabbeinu Simcha, provides an incredible reason for the custom to cover or remove the knife from the table at the time of *Bircas HaMazon*:

נוהגים לכסות הסכין בשעת ברכת המזון ונהגו שלא לכסותו בשבת ויום טוב (שו"ע סימן קפ סעיף ה).

---

30   Intended to help us yearn for the Redemption.

31   See *Abarbenel* for a similar idea.

לכסות הסכין: בב"י ב' טעמים האחד דברזל מקצר ימי האדם ואינו דין שיהיה מונח על
השלחן שדומה למזבח שמאריך ימי האדם דע"כ כתיב לא תניף עליהם ברזל וע"כ אחר
שגמר אכילתו ורוצה לברך בהמ"ז מכסה הסכין וטעם שני בשם רבינו שמחה לפי שפעם
אחד הגיע אחד לברכת בונה ירושלים ונזכר חורבן הבית ותקע סכין בבטנו וע"כ נהגו
לסלקו בשעת ברכה.

It is customary to cover the knife during Bircas HaMazon…[32]

To cover the knife — The Beis Yosef offers two reasons [for this custom]: The first is that iron curtails life [as weapons are made from this material], and it is therefore inappropriate to have it rest on the table which is similar to the Altar which represents that which lengthens one's life…The second reason is given in the name of Rabbeinu Simcha: It once happened that one was reciting the blessing about the rebuilding of Jerusalem during Bircas HaMazon, and he was reminded of the destruction of the Beis HaMikdash [which caused much emotional pain] and as a result he stabbed himself in the stomach. Therefore our custom is to remove the knife while reciting the berachah.[33]

There existed those who yearned for the Beis HaMikdash in unimaginable ways; they truly recognized the value of what they were missing.

While it is unlikely that we will ever experience the intense emotions that Rabbeinu Simcha describes, we should at the minimum be aware that there existed those who yearned for the Beis HaMikdash in unimaginable ways; they truly recognized the value of what they were missing.

Let us strive to stay focused and yearn for the coming of *Mashiach* and our return to Yerushalayim in all its glory, as we say three times daily in our *Shemoneh Esrei*: *u'mitzapim tamid leyeshuah*, "always awaiting [Hashem's] salvation."

---

32   *Shulchan Aruch, Orach Chaim* 180:5.
33   *Mishnah Berurah*, ibid, note 11.

Vayigash

In one of the most emotionally charged dramas in the Torah, Yosef finally reveals himself to his brothers:

וַיֹּאמֶר יוֹסֵף אֶל אֶחָיו גְּשׁוּ נָא אֵלַי וַיִּגָּשׁוּ וַיֹּאמֶר אֲנִי יוֹסֵף אֲחִיכֶם אֲשֶׁר מְכַרְתֶּם אֹתִי מִצְרָיְמָה:

Yosef said to his brothers, "Approach me, please," and they approached. He said, "I am Yosef your brother whom you sold to Egypt." (Bereishis 45:4)

Rashi explains why Yosef asked his brothers to come closer and the reason he used that exact wording to address them:

גשו נא אלי: ראה אותם נסוגים לאחוריהם, אמר עכשיו אחי נכלמים, קרא להם בלשון רכה ותחנונים, והראה להם שהוא מהול.

Please approach me — He saw them drawing backwards and said, "Now my brothers are embarrassed" (based on Tanchuma, Vayigash 5). He called them tenderly and pleadingly, and showed them that he was circumcised. (Rashi)

According to Rashi, Yosef sought to comfort his brothers. Observing their discomfort and embarrassment, he spoke to them kindly and revealed to them that he was circumcised.

This Rashi needs some explanation. What is he teaching us? After all, if the brothers were suffering from embarrassment, how would showing that he was circumcised ease their humiliation and shame?[34]

Perhaps Yosef had already envisioned his brothers' reaction and shame to the revelation long before this day and planned to counter these events by his policy enacted of having the Egyptians circumcise themselves prior to receiving grain during the famine years. But how would making them circumcise themselves comfort his brothers?

Rashi in *Parashas Mikeitz* explains that Yosef commanded all those who came to receive food to first have themselves circumcised:

אשר יאמר לכם תעשו: לפי שהיה יוסף אומר להם שימולו, וכשבאו אצל פרעה ואומרים כך הוא אומר לנו, אמר להם למה לא צברתם בר, והלא הכריז לכם ששני הרעב באים, אמרו לו אספנו הרבה והרקיבה, אמר להם אם כן כל אשר יאמר לכם תעשו, הרי גזר על התבואה והרקיבה, מה אם יגזור עלינו ונמות.

Whatever he tells you, do — [Pharaoh said this] because after Yosef had ordered them to circumcise themselves, they came to Pharaoh and told him as much. The king then said, "Why didn't you gather grain [instead]? Didn't he announce to you that years of famine were coming?" They replied, "We gathered much, but it rotted." Pharaoh replied, "If so, do whatever he tells you. He issued a decree upon the grain, and it rotted. What if he issues a decree upon us and we die?" (Rashi to Bereishis 41:55)

Yosef knew that the Egyptians would mock the brothers for being circumcised, and he therefore devised a plan to preclude this, by setting circumcision as the prerequisite for receiving food.

One might think that Yosef would have been pleased to see his brothers' humiliation, retribution for what they had done to him. Does not a measure of embarrassment pale in comparison to the twenty-two years of Yosef's suffering and separation from his father and his brother Binyamin? But Yosef reacts differently, and in effect tells his brothers, "Look at my *bris*. I am circumcised, and I even made all the Egyptians

---

34   Most commentators understand that Yosef wished to show his brothers that he was "one of them." However, this is difficult, because we know that Yosef required all the Egyptians to be circumcised as a prerequisite for receiving grain; what then is proven by showing them his own circumcision? See *Chizkuni, Tzeidah Laderech,* and *Kli Yakar.*

circumcise themselves, so that you wouldn't feel different or uncomfortable among them. I've made a serious effort in sparing you from feeling shamed." Yosef truly wished to spare them from pain and embarrassment, and went the extra mile to put them at ease.

This showed the brothers Yosef's true feelings toward them. They saw that he was sincere when he said to them:

> *Yosef truly wished to spare them from pain and embarassment, and went the extra mile to put them at ease.*

וְעַתָּה אַל תֵּעָצְבוּ וְאַל יִחַר בְּעֵינֵיכֶם כִּי מְכַרְתֶּם אֹתִי הֵנָּה כִּי לְמִחְיָה שְׁלָחַנִי אֱלֹקִים לִפְנֵיכֶם:

But now do not be sad and let it not trouble you that you sold me here, for it was to preserve life that Hashem sent me before you. (Bereishis 45:5)

Yosef meant what he said — and he proved it with his actions.

The Mitzvah of Milah

The *Sefas Emes*, Rav Yehudah Aryeh Leib Alter, zt"l, in *Parashas Lech Lecha* shares a deep and fundamental insight relating to the mitzvah of *milah* which illuminates Yosef's actions toward his brothers.

הסוד. כי ע"י המילה מתגלה קדושה פנימיות שגנז הקב"ה באדם והמילה עליה נאמר (תהילים קי״ח, כ) זה השער לה' צדיקים יבואו בו. והוא כמו השבת דכתיב (יחזקאל מו, א) ביום השבת יפתח והוא מגלה הקדושה שנסתרת בימי המעשה כמו כן בגוף המילה מגלה מה שמכסה הגוף וגולה סוד ה' ולכן לא נברא האדם מהול ולא ניתן פתיחת השער רק לבנ"י שהם שומרים הברית כמו שכתוב (בראשית יז, ט) ואתה את בריתי תשמור שידע הקב"ה שבני ישראל הם בני שמירה.(שפת אמת, לך לך, תרנ"ב)[35]

The secret: For via the milah (circumcision), the inner sanctity that Hashem hid inside man is revealed. And the milah, about which is written, "This is the gate to Hashem, the righteous will enter through it" (Tehillim 118:20) — is like the Shabbos, as is written, "On the Shabbos day [the Beis HaMikdash gate] will be opened" (Yechezkel 46:1), revealing the holiness that is hidden on weekdays. Similarly, in the body: the milah reveals what the body hides, and Hashem's secret is revealed. This is why a person is not born circumcised. In addition, the gate is opened only for B'nei Yisrael, because they preserve the covenant of milah, as is written, "And you

---

35 See the full text of the *Sefas Emes* for a more elaborate and in-depth understanding of this idea.

[Avraham] shall keep My covenant" (Bereishis 17:9) — for Hashem knew
that B'nei Yisrael were to be capable of keeping it.

In other words, the *Sefas Emes* draws a beautiful parallel between *milah* and Shabbos: Both have the ability to reveal that which is hidden. Shabbos reveals holiness which during the weekday cannot easily be found. *Milah*, too, reveals what the body hides. Shabbos and *Milah* offer much but only revealed to those that keep Shabbos properly and are careful with *kedushas habris*. The more one is careful with *shemiras Shabbos* and *kedushas habris;* the more which is hidden and can be achieved both through Shabbos and *Milah* are revealed.

Perhaps, by Yosef showing his brothers he was circumcised, he was alluding to the nature of *bris* which reveals that which is hidden (in the body). This represented the hidden nature of Hashem's master plan to have Yosef sold by the brothers so that food would be available for them during the years of famine. Attempting to convince his brothers not to blame themselves and feel ashamed of their actions, he reveals to them his circumcision — alluding to the chain of events which were meant to occur as part of a hidden plan only now making sense and fitting — in to the larger picture.

Yosef tells his brothers *geshu na eilai, please come closer.* The *pasuk* uses the word *geshu* with Yosef telling them to come closer as if to tell them the following; don't simply look at things on the surface and superficially. Come close and see the hidden message in all that transpired, as it all turned out for the best.

We too are capable of understanding the ways of Hashem on a deeper and more complex level. While it is not always revealed to us why certain events in our life occur contrary to the way in which we would like; let us comfort ourselves in knowing that just like the episode of Yosef and his brothers was a source of much grief and pain but ultimately led to them having a food supply during the famine; the same is true for us as Hashem always acts in a kind and just manner.

Vayechi

Yaacov, on his deathbed, blesses his sons, beginning with his *bechor*, Reuven:

פַּחַז כַּמַּיִם אַל תּוֹתַר כִּי עָלִיתָ מִשְׁכְּבֵי אָבִיךָ אָז חִלַּלְתָּ יְצוּעִי עָלָה:

[You have] the restlessness of water; [therefore] you shall not have superiority, for you ascended upon your father's couch; then you profaned [Him Who] ascended upon my bed. (Bereishis 49:4)

Rashi explains this blessing as follows:

אל תותר: אל תרבה ליטול כל היתרות הללו שהיו ראויות לך.

You shall not have superiority — *You shall no longer receive all these superior positions that were fit for you.*

Bechorah, Kehunah, and Malchus

The *Midrash Tanchuma* expounds on what positions Reuven was worthy of and what had been intended for him:

יתר שאת ויתר עז שלשה כתרים היו בידך כהונה מלכות ובכורה, שאת זו כהונה שנאמר (ויקרא ט) וישא אהרן את ידיו, עוז זו מלכות שנאמר (שמואל א ב) ויתן עוז למלכו, יתר בכורה שהיא שני חלקים שנאמר (דברים כא) לתת לו פי שנים.

"Superior in rank (yeser se'es) and superior in power (yeser oz)" (Bereishis 49:3) —
Yaacov tells Reuven that he had been given three crowns: priesthood, royalty,
and birthright:

Se'es stands for priesthood, as is written, "Aharon lifted (vayisa, from the
same root as se'es) his arms" (Vayikra 9:22). Oz is royalty, as is written, "He
shall give strength (oz) to his king" (Shmuel I 2:10).

Yeser, meaning "more," stands for the double portion that the firstborn receives,
as is written, "to give him two-fold" (Devarim 21:17). (Midrash Tanchuma 9)

From the Midrash, we understand that Reuven was worthy of receiving the *bechorah* (birthright), *kehunah* (priesthood), and *malchus*
(royalty) — but forfeited them all by acting in haste and moving his
father's bed following his mother's passing. The commentators describe
Reuven's misdeed in a variety of ways; regardless, however, how did this
punishment match the crime? Furthermore, Yaacov was giving his last
and final *berachos* to his children before his imminent death. Why, then,
do his words to Reuven seem like more of a curse[36] than a blessing?

Reb Chaim Volozhiner, in his *Nefesh HaChaim*,[37] describes the relationship between *yiras Hashem* (fear of G-d) and the acquisition of
Torah and *deveykus* (lit., cleaving; spiritual ecstasy):

ולפי ערך גודל אוצר אוצר היראה אשר הכין לו האדם, כן ע"ז הערך יוכל ליכנס ולהשתמר ולהת־
קיים בתוכו תבואות התורה כפי אשר יחזיק אוצרו. כי האב המחלק תבואה לבניו, הוא מחלק
ונותן לכל א' מדת התבוא' כפי אשר יחזיק אוצרו של הבן אשר הכין ע"ז מקודם. שאף אם
ירצה האב וידו פתוחה ליתן לו הרבה, אמנם כיון שהבן אינו יכול לקבל יותר מחמת שאין
אוצרו גדול כ"כ שיוכל להחזיק יותר, גם האב א"א לו ליתן לו עתה יותר. ואם לא הכין לו הבן
אף אוצר קטן, גם האב לא יתן לו כלל, כיון שאין לו מקום משומר שתתקיים אצלו.

כן הוא ית"ש ידו פתוחה כביכול להשפיע תמיד לכל איש מעם סגולתו רב חכמה ובינה
יתירה, ושתתקיים אצלם צלם ויקשרם על לוח לבם, להשתעשע אתם בבואם לעולם המנוחה
ותלמודם בידם. אמנם הדבר תלוי לפי אוצר היראה שתקדם אל האדם. שאם הכין לו
האדם אוצר גדול של יראת ה' טהורה, כן ה' יתן לו חכמה ותבונה ברוב שפע כפי שתחזיק
אוצרו, הכל לפי גודל אוצרו. ואם לא הכין האדם אף אוצר קטן שאין בו יראתו יתב' כלל
ח"ו, גם הוא ית' לא ישפיע לו שום חכמה כלל, אחר שלא תתקיים אצלו. כי תורתו נמאסת
ח"ו כמשרז"ל. וע"ז אמר הכתוב (תהלים קי"א) ראשית חכמה יראת ה'.

36   See Rashi to 49:28, s.v. *"vezos"* and s.v. *"berach osam."*
37   4:5.

The size of one's treasure-house of yiras shamayim (fear or awe of Hashem) is that which determines the amount of fruits of Torah that one can accept and retain. It is like a father who distributes grain to his sons, giving to each the amount that his particular storeroom can hold. Even if the father is generous and wishes to give more, he cannot give more than can fit in his son's stockroom. And of course, if the son did not prepare a stockroom at all, the father won't be able to give him any grain at all.

The same is true for Hashem, may His Name be blessed. Always is His hand outstretched to give wisdom and understanding to every member of His treasured nation. He desires that they retain it and bind it to their hearts,[38] so that He can take great pleasure in them when they come to the World of Rest with their knowledge in hand. However, this is dependent upon the storeroom of yiras shamayim that each individual comes with. One who prepared a large supply of pure yiras shamayim, Hashem will shower upon him wisdom and understanding in great abundance, in accordance with what he can hold. But if he did not prepare even a small storeroom and does not have even a small amount of fear of Hashem, Heaven forbid, Hashem will not give him any wisdom at all, for it will have no place to be stored; his Torah is reviled, Heaven forbid, as the Sages taught. This is what we read in Tehillim (111:10): "The beginning of wisdom is fear (awe) of G-d."[39]

The *Nefesh HaChaim* teaches that in order to receive Torah and for it to have permanence, we need a mechanism by which to safeguard it, namely, Fear of Hashem. Just as a father can give his sons only what they can hold, the same is true with the Torah. Hashem wants to benefit his children with the Torah, but wants to be sure that they can preserve it faithfully. The more fear and awe of Hashem we have, the more He can provide us with the blessings of Torah.

This, perhaps, is how we can understand Yaacov's *berachos* to his children. Yaacov saw Reuven as lacking the tools necessary to lead with *malchus*, serve Hashem with the *kehunah*, and maintain the *bechorah*. This was precisely the correct time to tell him, and all his children: "Now as I bless each and every one of you, it is your past actions and personalities that will assist and guide me in deciding specifically what each child

38   See *Mishlei* 6:21.
39   *Nefesh HaChaim* 4:5.

should be blessed with and what is his ability to retain the blessing."[40] As the *Nefesh HaChaim* explained, the receptacle in which to preserve the grain must precede the distribution. Yaacov thus tells Reuven *al tosar*, "do not take more," and as Rashi elaborated: "You shall no longer receive all these superior positions that were fit for you — not because I don't want to give them to you, but because you have proven that they will not be properly cared for; you lack the requisite receptacle for these superior privileges."

We must demonstrate that our homes are spiritually healthy, that we are honest with our wallets, so that there exists a place for Hashem's berachah to be stored safely.

This idea is so very relevant in our relationships with Hashem and regarding our requests for His gifts. We ask Hashem for physical health, financial security, fine children, healthy relationships, and the ability to connect with Him and His Torah — but we must first ascertain that there exists a place for the *berachah* to be stored safely. We must demonstrate that our homes are spiritually healthy, that we are honest with our wallets, and that we can be relied upon to distribute His blessing to the less fortunate. We need to show evidence that we are engaged in refining our character traits, enabling us to keep His Torah safe with us. Our actions must show that we have what it takes to manage the blessings for which we beseech Hashem, and we can then merit His ultimate *berachos*.

When one seeks to make an investment with his money, he will naturally vet the investment by looking at its past performance and returns, the integrity of the person running the investment, and the stability it will guarantee. The same is true for one who looks to be a worthy repository for Hashem's blessings.

---

40   See Rashi to 49:28, s.v. *"berach osam."*

Shemos

Shemos

וְכַאֲשֶׁר יְעַנּוּ אֹתוֹ כֵּן יִרְבֶּה וְכֵן יִפְרֹץ וַיָּקֻצוּ מִפְּנֵי בְּנֵי יִשְׂרָאֵל:

As much as they would afflict them, so did they multiply and so did they gain strength, and they were disgusted [vayakutzu] because of the People of Israel. (Shemos 1:12)

Rashi explains the contextual meaning of the word *vayakutzu:*

ויקצו: קצו בחייהם. ורבותינו דרשו כקוצים היו בעיניהם.

And they were disgusted — *They were disgusted with their lives [i.e., the Mitzrim (Egyptians) were disgusted with themselves]. Our Rabbis, however, interpreted it to mean that the B'nei Yisrael were like thorns (kotzim) in the eyes of the Egyptians.*

The Ramban in his commentary on this *pasuk* says the following:

והשרים האלה צוו אותם שיבנו ערים לפרעה. ויבן העם ערי מסכנות לפרעה במס הזה, וכאשר ראו שלא יזיק זה לעם קצו בחייהם מפניהם, וגזרו שיעבידו כל מצרים את העם, וכל איש מצרי שיצטרך בעבודה ימשול לקחת מהם אנשים שיעשו עבודתו.

The officers commanded them to build cities for Pharaoh. The people built storage cities for Pharaoh under this program of conscripted labor. When the Egyptians saw that this did no harm to the Israelites, they became "disgusted with their lives," and decreed that all Egyptians may put the nation to work:

Any Egyptian man who needed work done had the authority to take men
from among B'nei Yisrael to do his work for him.

These two interpretations in Rashi, together with the Ramban's comment, can be understood as one, offering much insight into the unique
character traits embedded in every Jew: tenacity and resilience.

The *pesukim* describe the way in which the Mitzrim devised all sorts
of methods and did their utmost to break the morale and spirit of the
B'nei Yisrael. Whether it was harsh taskmasters supervising the forced
labor, the requirement that the B'nei Yisrael produce their own stones
and bricks, or the cruel beatings they endured, the system in Mitzrayim
was designed to physically destroy and emotionally devastate the Jews.
But the more the Egyptians oppressed them, and the harder their re-
strictions upon them, the more B'nei Yisrael increased and multiplied.

We can suggest that the Mitzrim's failure to destroy B'nei Yisrael led
them to become envious of Israel's tenacity, resilience, and ability to
remain resolute in face of their suffering. As the Ramban commented:
"When the Mitzrim saw that this did no harm to the Israelites, they
became 'disgusted with their lives.'" What specifically prompted them
to be disgusted with their lives?

Perhaps we can understand that they were dissatisfied with themselves and their own failings, while simultaneously witnessing the
intensity of a nation so strong-spirited and unwavering that it did
not abandon its core values even under physical and emotional pain.
The Egyptians were disgusted with themselves because their failure
to break the B'nei Yisrael, despite their harsh treatment of them,
caused them to recognize their deficient moral fiber. Suddenly, the
contrast between the two nations was blinding. This invoked among
the Egyptians feelings of guilt and shame, to a point where they were
repulsed with themselves. As Rashi said, they were disgusted with
themselves in front of the B'nei Yisrael; compared to the B'nei Yisrael,
their wickedness was glaring.

It is characteristic of a person trapped with feelings of guilt and infe-
riority to then find fault in one who triggers this feeling in him. Doing

so discredits the other's good deeds, and no longer must he always be reminded of his inadequacies when in the company of the other.

The Mitzrim, in an effort to discount the great strength of the Jews, needed to find something negative about them, something to be disgusted with. This would help the Egyptians once again feel comfortable with themselves, and be released from the feelings of shame brought to the surface whenever they were around the B'nei Yisrael. This is what is meant by Rashi's comment: "they [Israel] were like thorns in their eyes." Each time they attempted to destroy the spirits of B'nei Yisrael and were unsuccessful, their own shortcomings were highlighted, as thorns in their eyes.

What Is a Jew?

The Egyptians saw our greatness and reacted with negativity. If only they had seen in Israel that which the well-known author Leo Tolstoy saw. He described our uniqueness in his essay entitled, "What is a Jew?" as follows:

> What is a Jew? This question is not as strange as it may seem at first glance. Let's examine this free creature that was insulated and oppressed, trampled on and pursued, burned and drowned by all the rulers and the nations, but is nevertheless living and thriving in spite of the whole world.
>
> What is a Jew that did not succumb to any worldly temptations offered by his oppressors and persecutors so that he would renounce his religion and abandon the faith of his fathers?
>
> A Jew is a sacred being who procured an eternal fire from the heavens and with it illuminated the earth and those who live on it. He is the spring and the source from which the rest of the nations drew their religions and beliefs.
>
> A Jew is a pioneer of culture. From time immemorial, ignorance was impossible in the Holy Land, even more so than nowadays in civilized Europe. Moreover, at the time when the life and death of a human being was worth nothing, Rabbi Akiva spoke against the death penalty which is now considered to be an acceptable punishment in the most civilized countries.
>
> A Jew is a pioneer of freedom. Back in primitive times, when the nation was divided into two classes, masters and slaves, Moses' teaching forbid holding a person as a slave for more than six years.

A Jew is a symbol of civil and religious tolerance, "So show your love for the alien, for you were aliens in the land of Egypt." These words were uttered during distant, barbarian times when it was commonly acceptable among the nations to enslave each other.

In terms of tolerance, the Jewish religion is far from recruiting adherents. Quite the opposite, the Talmud prescribes that if a non-Jew wants to convert to the Jewish faith, then it has to be explained to him how difficult it is to be a Jew and that the righteous of other religions also inherit the heavenly kingdom. A Jew is a symbol of eternity.

The nation which neither slaughter nor torture could exterminate, which neither fire nor sword of civilizations were able to erase from the face of earth, the nation which first proclaimed the word of Lord, the nation which preserved the prophecy for so long and passed it on to the rest of humanity, such a nation cannot vanish.

A Jew is eternal; he is an embodiment of eternity.

Leo Tolstoy, 1891

Jewish Resilience

A beautiful story told by Rabbi Paysach Krohn[41] illustrates the resilience embedded and displayed within Jews throughout the millennia despite the great pain and suffering they experienced.

At an Agudath Yisrael dinner in 1995 commemorating the fiftieth year since the liberation of Jews from the Nazi death camps, Mr. Yosef Friedenson, editor of the noted magazine "Dos Yiddishe Vort," told a moving personal story. It lent a historical perspective to the trials and tribulations that Jews have undergone throughout their nearly two thousand years in the Diaspora. The story is this:

> After being a prisoner and slave laborer in numerous camps, R' Yosef was transported to a steel factory labor camp in Starachowitz, Poland, in 1943, where armaments were manufactured for the German war effort. The

---

41   *Along the Maggid's Journey,* by Rabbi Paysach Krohn, pg. 168, Artscroll/Mesorah.

brutality of the German officers was unspeakable. Adults and children alike suffered torturous pain and death at the hands of barbarians who roared, "No Jew will escape us, not even a child!"

At this particular camp, however, there was one German factory chief, Herr Bruno Papeh, who was kind to Jews whenever he could be. He would provide them with extra rations of food and was a bit more tolerant when the prisoners failed to complete their labor assignments on time.

While R' Yosef was at Starachowitz, a Gerrer chassid from Cracow was brought to the camp. Akiva Goldstoff, a wine merchant, was close to forty when he arrived, frightened and disoriented. But before his first Friday night in the camp arrived, he had already organized a minyan for Kabbalas Shabbos. Akiva and Yosef, who was twenty at the time, became close friends. Despite the difficult circumstances, they exchanged Torah thoughts and encouraged each other in faith and belief.

A few weeks before Pesach, Akiva called Yosef to the side and said, "I think we should ask Herr Papeh if he would allow us to bake matzos for *Yom Tov.*"

"You must be mad," replied Yosef. "Herr Papeh has been kind to us in certain circumstances, but he will never allow us such a luxury!"

"I am older than you," said Akiva. "Listen to me; I believe he will be receptive."

After some intense debate, Yosef agreed to go with Akiva to ask the factory chief for permission to bake matzos. When Herr Papeh heard their request, he was incredulous. "Don't you have any other worries? Is this all that is on your minds?" he asked in disbelief. "Yes," replied Yosef. "This is what we are concerned about, and it would mean a great deal to us if you granted permission."

Herr Papeh thought about it for a moment and then said, "All right. If you have the flour, go ahead. Just talk to the Polish workers who are in charge of the smiths' ovens and tell them I gave the consent." "But we don't have any flour," Yosef said quietly, embarrassed at being granted his wish and not having the means to fulfill it.

At that same time, a Polish factory worker was seeking a furlough from Herr Papeh, who controlled the work schedule. Papeh knew that the Polish workers could get the prize commodities of meat and butter from the local villagers and then bring them into the labor camp. Papeh was no saint. He would allow himself to be bribed. "I'll tell you what," Papeh said, turning to the Polish worker. "You get me a kilo of butter and a kilo of flour, and you can have the time off that you want."

The Polish worker agreed, and within a day Yosef and Akiva were called into Herr Papeh's office, where he clandestinely gave them the flour for the matzos. The two thanked him profusely, but secretly they worried that he could — and with his Nazi temper, would — rescind his permission at any moment. They set off to bake the matzos.

Several women, including R' Yosef's wife, Gittel, kneaded the dough and baked the unleavened dough in the large melting ovens, heated to a temperature of two thousand degrees. There was an air of controlled ecstasy in the barrack as the matzos emerged from the ovens, ready for those who wanted them.

On the first morning of Pesach, Herr Papeh walked into the factory and suddenly became furious. As always, at 10 a.m., baskets containing slices of bread were passed around the factory and every worker would take a meager slice. Each slice was accounted for, and no one would dare take more than his share. But this day, instead of taking their slice, many prisoners left the bread in the doorway. Herr Papeh looked around at the people eating matzah and realized they had purposely declined the bread. In a violent, bloodcurdling, voice he suddenly yelled, "Your G-d has forsaken you, and you are still loyal to Him?!"

Papeh scanned the room and then roared, "Friedenson! Eat your bread or you will die!" Everyone froze. The fury they had feared had suddenly exploded, and at the worst time. None of the men moved as they waited to see what he would do.

Herr Papeh walked directly over to Akiva and yelled, "Has your G-d not forsaken you here?" Akiva, standing tall and ready to accept the worst, replied softly but with certainty, "Not totally and not forever."

Papeh was taken aback by the answer. He could not comprehend such conviction. He knew well the suffering and torment of the Jews. "Not totally!?" he demanded, raising his voice.

"You let us bake matzos, didn't you?" Akiva replied.

This *middah* (trait) of unwavering strength in the face of hardships and difficulties is implanted in us. We are characterized in the Torah as an *am keshei oref*, a stiff-necked nation, and this *middah* can assist us in our *avodas Hashem*.

A Miracle Nation

The term "miracle baby" is commonly used when a child is born healthy after all medical odds were stacked against him, or when a young infant recovers despite a serious and grave illness. Perhaps we, the B'nei Yisrael, are to be termed the "miracle nation." While the odds have not been in our favor, and according to the norms we should have been long forgotten and done with, we know that we survive and exist with a different set of rules and statistics. We rely, instead, on Hashem's promise that He will never forsake us.

Va'Eira

וְהֵבֵאתִי אֶתְכֶם אֶל הָאָרֶץ אֲשֶׁר נָשָׂאתִי אֶת יָדִי לָתֵת אֹתָהּ לְאַבְרָהָם
לְיִצְחָק וּלְיַעֲקֹב וְנָתַתִּי אֹתָהּ לָכֶם מוֹרָשָׁה אֲנִי ה': וַיְדַבֵּר מֹשֶׁה כֵּן אֶל
בְּנֵי יִשְׂרָאֵל וְלֹא שָׁמְעוּ אֶל מֹשֶׁה מִקֹּצֶר רוּחַ וּמֵעֲבֹדָה קָשָׁה:

I will bring you to the Land, concerning which I raised My hand
to give to Avraham, to Yitzchak, and to Yaacov, and I will give
it to you as a heritage; I am Hashem. Moshe spoke thus to B'nei
Yisrael, but they did not listen to Moshe because of [their]
shortness of breath and because of [their] hard labor. (Shemos 6:8–9)

וַיְדַבֵּר ה' אֶל מֹשֶׁה וְאֶל אַהֲרֹן וַיְצַוֵּם אֶל בְּנֵי יִשְׂרָאֵל וְאֶל פַּרְעֹה מֶלֶךְ
מִצְרָיִם לְהוֹצִיא אֶת בְּנֵי יִשְׂרָאֵל מֵאֶרֶץ מִצְרָיִם:

Hashem spoke to Moshe and to Aharon, and He commanded
them concerning B'nei Yisrael and concerning Pharaoh,
the king of Mitzrayim, to let the B'nei Yisrael out of the land
of Mitzrayim. (pasuk 13)

Moshe informs the B'nei Yisrael that Hashem will fulfill the promise
He made to the *Avos* and bring them to Eretz Yisrael. The Torah then
tells us that the B'nei Yisrael were unable to hear these words because of
[their]... hard labor." The Ramban explains the nature of this "hard labor":

82

ועבודה קשה: הוא הדוחק שהיו הנוגשים אצים בהם ולא יתנום לשמוע דבר ולחשוב בו.

The hard work was the pressure with which the taskmasters pressed them, not allowing them to hear any idea or to reflect upon it. (Ramban, Shemos 2:9)

The Ramban explains that the B'nei Yisrael could not arouse within themselves optimism or hope with which to hear Moshe's words of encouragement. This was because their hard work and the emotional burden they bore were so great that they simply could not focus on or even consider his message. Their minds were so overburdened that Moshe's message was just words without any actual meaning for them. They could not contemplate the prospect of entering Eretz Yisrael while being so overwhelmed.

Rav Moshe Chaim Luzzatto, the *Ramchal*, in his *Mesillas Yesharim*, relates this idea to our constant battle with the *yetzer hara*:

ואולם הנה זאת באמת אחת מתחבולות היצר הרע וערמתו להכביד עבודתו בת־
מידות על לבות בני האדם עד שלא ישאר להם ריוח להתבונן ולהסתכל באיזה
דרך הם הולכים, כי יודע הוא שאלולי היו שמים לבם כמעט קט על דרכיהם, ודאי
שמיד היו מתחילים להנחם ממעשיהם, והיתה החרטה הולכת ומתגברת בהם עד
שהיו עוזבים החטא לגמרי. והרי זו מעין עצת פרעה הרשע שאמר (שמות ה, ט)
תכבד העבודה על האנשים וגו', שהיה מתכוין שלא להניח להם ריוח כלל לבלתי
יתנו לב או ישימו עצה נגדו, אלא היה משתדל להפריע לבם מכל התבוננות בכח
התמדת העבודה הבלתי מפסקת כן היא עצת היצר הרע ממש על בני האדם, כי
איש מלחמה הוא ומלמד בערמימות, ואי אפשר למלט ממנו אלא בחכמה רבה
והשקפה גדולה.

In reality, this is one of the clever devices of the yetzer hara — to mount pressure unrelentingly against the hearts of men so as to leave them no leisure to consider and observe the type of life they are leading. For it realizes that if they were to devote even a slight degree of attention to their ways, there is no question but that they would immediately begin to repent of their deeds and that regret would wax in them until they would leave sinning altogether. It is this consideration which underlay the counsel of the wicked Pharaoh in his statement (Shemos 5:9), "Intensify the men's labors..." His intention was not merely to deprive them of all leisure so that they would not come to oppose him or plot against him, but he also strove to strip their hearts of all thought by means of the enduring, interminable nature of their labor. (Mesillas Yesharim chap. 2)

No Time to Think

The *Ramchal* here references the *pasuk* where Pharaoh commands the Mitzrim to intensify the workload emplaced upon the B'nei Yisrael. He explains that this command was designed so that the B'nei Yisrael should have neither the time nor the state of mind to plan a revolt or even think about a way to defy his orders. By enslaving them with back-breaking labor, they would be so embittered and overwhelmed with their predicament that they would not be able to contemplate their situation or devise a plan to free themselves.

The *Mesillas Yesharim* draws a parallel to the nature of the *yetzer hara*. In order for us not to think about our spiritual needs and contemplate strategies to prevail over the temptations of the *yetzer hara's* trappings, he creates situations with which we must constantly busy ourselves. He creates circumstances that demand so much of our attention that no time remains for introspection or reflection on our *ruchniyus* (spirituality). The *Ramchal* therefore advises us to designate a time to take an accounting of our spiritual standing, so that we can strategize to protect ourselves from the frivolous pursuits and idle pleasures of this world that the *yetzer hara* masterfully presents to us as necessities.

> *He creates circumstances that demand so much of our attention that no time remains for introspection or reflection on our ruchniyus (spirituality).*

The *Meshech Chochmah*, Rav Meir Simcha of Dvinsk, presents a beautiful insight on this *pasuk* explaining B'nei Yisrael's failure to listen to the words of Moshe Rabbeinu.

וידבר משה כו' ולא שמעו אל משה, פירוש ענין הבאה לא"י מקוצר רוח ומעבודה קשה כי
דרך קשי יום אשר יחפוצו לשמוע רק כדי לצאת מצרתם ולא לשמוע בהבטחות עתידות
ובהצלחות נפלאות כו' ולכן וידבר ה' וכו' ויצוום אל ב"י ואל פרעה וכו' להוציא בנ"י מארץ
מצרים כלומר לדבר רק אודות זה וכמו שנזכר לקמן (דו"ק ותשכח) והבן ע"ד צחות.

"They could not hear him because of their anguish of spirit and hard work." What they could not hear was the idea of being taken to Eretz Yisrael. For the way of day-laborers is that they wish to hear only that which will help extricate them from their [immediate] troubles, but not future promises and great wonders, etc. Therefore we read (Shemos 6:13) that Hashem

_told Moshe and Aharon to speak to B'nei Yisrael and Pharaoh "to bring the
People of Israel out of Mitzrayim," that is, to speak only about that…Study
it carefully and you will understand it clearly._

Moshe was telling them that the day will come when we will enter
Eretz Yisrael and Hashem will fulfill His promise to the _Avos_. This, however, provided no encouragement to the embittered and enslaved Jews
pining for even the slightest easing of their suffering.

An Immediate Solution

Why is this? When someone is in pain, explains the _Meshech Chochmah_,
he needs an immediate and accessible solution to his problem. Telling
B'nei Yisrael that they will enter Eretz Yisrael did nothing to release
them from their current misery. It is analogous to someone suffering
outdoors in freezing cold temperatures; the last thing he wants to hear
is that the weather will get warmer two months from now. What he
needs immediately is warm clothing to shield himself from the frigid
cold. In the midst of their suffering the Jews could not listen to promises of entering Eretz Yisrael, as these could not help them now. It is for
this reason that Hashem speaks to Moshe again with a new command:
"…to take B'nei Yisrael out of Egypt." This time, there is no mention
of entering Eretz Yisrael. The message is simple and straightforward,
one which they needed to hear for immediate consolation, and for relief
from their sufferings in Mitzrayim.

When a person is suffering, we must be careful with the advice and
guidance that we offer. We must address their immediate needs and not
just the end result, even if it is a positive one in itself.

Perhaps the ideas of the _Ramchal_ and the _Meshech Chochmah_ can be
interwoven. When we finally dedicate time for introspection and ana-
lyze our ways in order to develop a plan with which to battle the _yetzer
hara_, we need to carefully and in a measured manner select a strategy
which can succeed. People tend to accept upon themselves big changes
when committing to a path of _teshuvah_ and intense resolutions, but
they are liable to fail, given their inability to maintain the demanding
change. Instead, these resolutions need to take place gradually, with

attainable immediate gains, so as to inspire perpetual growth. From the *Meshech Chochmah* and the *Ramchal* we can learn that even when looking to inspire ourselves to be better and return to Hashem, let us be careful not to take on something too distant and extreme. If we attempt to climb the ladder too fast, we may fall and, this may cause us to lose hope in trying again. Alternatively, small steps and more immediate and achievable goals will help us succeed in our battle with the *yetzer hara*, and this success will inspire even more success in the future.

Bo

דַּבֶּר נָא בְּאָזְנֵי הָעָם וְיִשְׁאֲלוּ אִישׁ מֵאֵת רֵעֵהוּ וְאִשָּׁה מֵאֵת רְעוּתָהּ
כְּלֵי כֶסֶף וּכְלֵי זָהָב:

Please speak into the ears of the people, and let them borrow,
each man from his friend and each woman from her friend,
silver vessels and golden vessels. (Shemos 11:2)

Rashi explains why Moshe was told to "please" speak to the nation:

דבר נא: אין נא אלא לשון בקשה, בבקשה ממך הזהירם על כך שלא יאמר אותו צדיק
אברהם (בראשית טו יג) ועבדום וענו אותם קיים בהם, (שם יד) ואחרי כן יצאו ברכוש
גדול לא קיים בהם.

Please speak — The word na, please, is an expression of request. [Hashem is
saying:] "I ask you to warn them [about asking their neighbors for vessels]
so that the righteous man, Avraham, will not say that [G-d] fulfilled [His
promise] of 'and they will enslave them and oppress them' (Bereishis 15:13),
but did not fulfill His promise that 'afterwards they will go forth with great
possessions' (ibid. 15:14)." (Berachos 9a)

The *pasuk*, as interpreted by the Gemara in *Berachos*, begins with
Hashem telling Moshe to warn[42] the B'nei Yisrael to ask the Mitzrim for

---

42   See *Sifsei Chachamim* who offers a reason as to why they needed to be warned and not just told.

their gold and silver vessels. Rashi, quoting the Gemara, explains the choice of the word *na*, meaning "please," in that Hashem truly needs Moshe to collect the gold and silver vessels from the Mitzrim so that Avraham Avinu would not argue that Hashem didn't fulfill His promise that B'nei Yisrael would leave with great possessions.

This Gemara quoted by Rashi is puzzling and needs explanation. Rav Avraham Shmuel Binyamin Sofer, zt"l, the *Ksav Sofer*, asks the following questions: Is Hashem's reason for keeping His promise only that Avraham shouldn't complain? Why wasn't Hashem's command to ask the Mitzrim for their possessions necessary simply because Hashem made the promise, regardless of Avraham Avinu's reaction? So writes the *Ksav Sofer*:

דבר נא באזני העם: בש"ס ברכות [ט.] אין נא אלא לשון בקשה שלא יאמר אותו צדיק ועבדום ועינו אותם קיים בהם ואח"כ יצאו ברכוש גדול לא קיים בהם. צריך להבין איך בלא תלונת אברהם לא הי' מקיים ה' הבטחתו ברוך שומר הבטחתו לישראל תמיד ואיך לא היה מקיים עתה. ונ"ל הנה מי שמעודו הי' בעוני ודוחק גדול, לא ראה טובה כל ימיו מבית אבותיו, כשיהיה לו מעט מזעיר, לעושר והון יחשב בעיניו. אבל מי שהי' תמיד בהצלחה לא יחשב לו רק כשיגיע לו הון רב אז יחשב בעיניו וישמח בו. והנה מאחר שהיו ישראל משועבדים ומעונים, כשיביאו עמם ממצרים מעט, יהי' להון ורכוש בעיניהם ולא היו צריכים לשאול כלי כסף וזהב. ולא אמר ה' לאברהם מה שיביאו עמהם רק יצאו ברכוש גדול מה שבעיניהם רכוש גדול אבל מאחר שבעיני אברהם לא יהיה נחשב לכלום, שהיה מעולם משופע בעושר ונכסים צאן ובקר, לכן אמר ה' שלא יאמר אברהם קיים בהם ואח"כ יצאו ברכוש גדול, כנ"ל וק"ל.

Hashem asked Moshe to "please" ask the nation to borrow silver and gold utensils from the Egyptians before the Exodus. The Gemara (Berachos 9a) explains [as cited by Rashi above]. This Gemara must be understood: Would Hashem not have fulfilled His promise without Avraham's complaint?! We say that Hashem is blessed for always keeping His promises to Yisrael! How could He not have kept it in this case?

It appears to me to explain as follows: One who was always poor and downtrodden, and who grew up without seeing material blessing — when he receives a small amount, it seems like a great treasure to him. However, for one who grew up with abundance, only a tremendous amount will gladden him. Therefore, if B'nei Yisrael, who were enslaved and tortured in Mitzrayim, take out a small amount of wealth with them, it will seem like a great treasure for them — and they would see no need to ask for silver and gold utensils in addition. But Hashem told Avraham that they would leave with "great wealth" — referring to what Avraham, who had come from a world of riches, would consider great wealth. This is why Hashem "feared" that if they would not leave with gold and silver, Avraham would think that the promise of "great wealth" was not fulfilled. (Ksav Sofer)

While this insight by the *Ksav Sofer* explains the wording of the *pasuk* well, one could ask why it was so important for B'nei Yisrael to ask the Mitzrim for their gold and silver at this point altogether. Could they not have waited until they crossed the Red Sea *(Krias Yam Suf)*? After all, the spoils they collected there could certainly have been considered a fulfillment of Hashem's promise to Avraham to enrich them when they left Mitzrayim!

Avraham: A Master of Chessed

Perhaps there is something deeper here. Avraham was known as the master of *chessed*. His whole life was dedicated to caring for others and bringing them into his tent to share with them knowledge of Hashem and, of course, providing their material needs as well. Avraham wasn't satisfied with just being available for those in need; he actually searched to do good, taking a proactive approach to his acts of *chessed*. Whether it was the four entrances he built for his tent to ensure he wouldn't miss a guest, or sitting outside looking for visitors on a scorching hot day while recovering from major surgery *(bris milah)*, or attempting to save the people of Sedom even if their lives were antithetical to everything he believed, Avraham's acts of kindness were surely a step above the plain meaning of *chessed*. In terms of B'nei Yisrael's forefather Avraham, it would have gone against the grain of all the *chessed* that Avraham stood for if B'nei Yisrael were to leave Mitzrayim without great possessions, wondering what happened to the Divine promise that they were to leave with great wealth. Even if Hashem were to provide for them later at the Red Sea, they would have been left for seven days without the fulfillment of that promise, perplexed with the apparent nullification of the pledge Hashem made to Avraham Avinu.

Going Above and Beyond the Call of Duty

This, then, is what Hashem meant when he told Moshe that he was concerned with what the righteous Avraham would say. Avraham's complaint would have been this: "Since I have devoted my life to doing the *middah* of *chessed* in an above-and-beyond manner, it is inappropriate to have my descendants B'nei Yisrael leave Mitzrayim in a state of emptiness and doubt — even if in the end they will soon collect the spoils at the *Yam Suf*." For this reason, it was important specifically for B'nei Yisrael to leave Mitzrayim with these great possessions already in hand, being treated to the trait of Avraham in the way he himself practiced it.

When performing acts of kindness with others, we should make sure to treat them so that it is evident that we are willing to go the extra mile.

An important lesson can be learned from this incident. When performing acts of kindness with others, we should make sure to follow in the way of Avraham Avinu. We must treat them so that it is evident that we are willing to go the extra mile, or even inconvenience ourselves, in order to benefit them.

Following the Middah of Hashem's Kindness

We may also think of the kindness we are provided with by Hashem daily which is delivered to us with all the trimmings. The simplicity of drinking a cup of water can cause us to forget that there was a time, and still is in some parts of the world, where one needed to visit the well to get water. Food preparation and producing clothing was not as automated as today and required great effort and work. The world we live in today is overflowing with Hashem's kindness, and, when reciprocating to Hashem, let us commit to inconveniencing ourselves if the need arises to serve Hashem, just as He maintains His world, with an abundant of kindness in an above-and-beyond manner.

Beshalach

As the B'nei Yisrael prepared to experience a miracle that would forever be remembered as a symbol of Hashem's glorious might, the Torah
tells us:

וַיָּבֹאוּ בְנֵי יִשְׂרָאֵל בְּתוֹךְ הַיָּם בַּיַּבָּשָׁה וְהַמַּיִם לָהֶם חוֹמָה מִימִינָם וּמִשְּׂמֹאלָם:

*Then the B'nei Yisrael came into the midst of the sea on dry land,
and the waters were to them as a wall from their right and from their left.
(Shemos 14:22)*

Just a few *pesukim* later, we read almost the same words again:

וּבְנֵי יִשְׂרָאֵל הָלְכוּ בַיַּבָּשָׁה בְּתוֹךְ הַיָּם וְהַמַּיִם לָהֶם חֹמָה מִימִינָם וּמִשְּׂמֹאלָם:

*But the B'nei Yisrael went on dry land in the midst of the sea, and the water
was to them like a wall from their right and from their left.(Shemos 14:29)*

The *Vilna Gaon* (the *Gra*), Rav Eliyahu ben Shlomo Zalman, in his work
Kol Eliyahu, asks several questions on these seemingly identical *pesukim*.
Two of them are particularly notable: In *pasuk* 22, the Torah writes first
that the Jews went into the sea, then afterwards onto the dry land. Yet
in *pasuk* 29, we read first "on the dry land" and then afterwards, "into the
sea." Why the difference? Secondly, why is the word *chomah*, wall, written
in *pasuk* 22 with the letter *vuv*, while in *pasuk* 29 it is written without a *vuv*?

בפסוק ויבואו בני ישראל בתוך הים ביבשה והמים להם חומה מימנם ומשמאלם. והנה בפסוק כ"ט כתיב ובני ישראל הלכו ביבשה בתוך הים והמים להם חמה מימינם ומשמאלם.

ויש לבאר אמאי שינו בהלשון, דמקודם כתיב דהלכו בני ישראל בתוך הים ביבשה, ואחרי זה כתיב דהלכו ביבשה בתוך הים — מקודם יבשה ואחר כך בתוך הים. ועוד יש לדקדק למה כתיב שני פעמים על בני ישראל דהלכו בים? וגם כפל לשון דהמים להם חומה מימנם ומשמאלם. גם יש לדקדק מדוע כתיב בפסוק כ"ט חמה חסר וי"ו — ודרשו חז"ל חמה כתיב דנתמלא עליהם חמה.

אבל הכל יבוא על נכון: דהנה בבני ישראל היו שתי כתות, אנשים צדיקים המאמינים בה' ובעלי בטחון, והם הלכו תיכף לים עד כי בא מים עד נפש, וכדאיתא במדרש דקפץ נחשון בן עמינדב ואחריו כל שבט יהודה. והנה איתא במדרש דהיה קטרוג מה נשתנו אלו מאלו? הללו עובדי ע"ז והללו עובדי ע"ז. והשיב השי"ת זכות האמונה והבטחון כדאי להם. א"כ לפי זה גבי בני ישראל דהלכו בתוך הים מקודם בהאמונה והבטחון, כתיב אצלם "ויבואו בני ישראל בתוך הים," ואחרי זה היה היבשה ושפיר היה להם המים חומה כחומה. אבל כת השניה דלא היו מאמינים כל כך עד שראו בעיניהם היבשה, לכן כתיב עליהם דהלכו "ביבשה בתוך הים" — מקודם יבשה, לכן היו להם המים ר"ל הקטרוג מה נשתנו אלו מאלו כנז"ל.

"B'nei Yisrael entered into the water on the dry land, and the water was a wall for them on their right and on their left." (Shemos 14:22) In pasuk 29, the Torah says something similar: "B'nei Yisrael walked on the dry area in the sea, and the water was a wall for them on their right and on their left." This needs to be explained: Why does it first say that they walked in the water on the dry land, and afterwards it says the opposite, that they went on the dry area in the water?

In addition, why does it say twice that B'nei Yisrael walked in the sea? And why does it say twice that the water was a wall for them on their right and left? And why in pasuk 29 is the word "wall" spelled ches-mem-hei, without a vuv? On the last point, the Sages derived that the sea became "angered" at them — for anger is spelled ches-mem-hei.

But everything can be explained as follows: There were two groups within B'nei Yisrael. One group was the righteous people, those who believed and trusted in Hashem. They went immediately into the sea, up to the point that the water endangered them; the Midrash teaches that Nachshon ben Aminadav went in first, followed by the entire Tribe of Yehudah.

Another Midrash says that there was criticism of the B'nei Yisrael: "How are these [Israelites] different than these [the Mitzrim]? Both worship idols, so why is one punished and the other is saved?" And Hashem answered that the B'nei Yisrael have the merit of faith and trust in Hashem.

Accordingly, those of B'nei Yisrael who walked with faith and trust went into the water first and only afterwards on the dry part — that is, where the water split and left dry land. For them, the wall was truly a wall.

The other group of B'nei Yisrael were not such believers, and did not trust Hashem until their eyes actually saw the dry part of the sea — and therefore about them it was written that they walked first on the dry part and then in the water. And for them the wall was "anger," that is, denunciation and criticism that they were no different than the Mitzrim. (Kol Eliyahu)

The Malachim's Argument

The Vilna Gaon cites the Midrash that teaches that when the Jews were standing trapped between the Mitzrim and the sea, the angels complained to Hashem, saying, "Why are these Jews worthy of being saved? Both the Jews and the Mitzrim worshipped idols. Why should the Jews be saved and merit having the sea split open for them? They are just standing passively, waiting for a miracle to happen!"[43] Hashem answered, "Look, there are Jews who have such great *emunah* (faith) that they are jumping into the sea even before it is split." This was referring to Nachshon ben Aminadav and the rest of the Tribe of Yehudah who followed him.

Therefore, explains the *Gra*, *pasuk* 22 is referring to Nachshon and his fellow tribesman who went with tremendous *bitachon*, trust in G-d, into the sea before it split, and only then did it become dry land. In that *pasuk*, "wall" is written with a *vuv*; the water was truly a wall for them because of their *bitachon*, and the word is understood according to its plain meaning. However, *pasuk* 29 tells us about those who walked on dry land in the midst of the sea, referring to the Jews who waited until it was already dry before entering what had been the sea. Concerning those people who lacked the *emunah*, the *pasuk* continues that the water was a wall — but without a *vuv*, spelling "anger." The waters were upset at these Jews because they were no better than the Mitzrim as the Midrash says: "Both are idol-worshipers; why should one be saved over the other?"

---

43 מלאכי השרת אמרו (מדרש תהלים א, כ; טו, ה, זהר תרומה קע:, ילקוט ראובני בשלח סי' פב, פט):הללו עובדי עבודה זרה והללו עובדי עבודה זרה. מדוע אתה מציל את ישראל ומטביע את המצרים בים, הרי אין הבדל ביניהם: אלו ואלו עובדי עבודה זרה.

Acheinu, Our Brothers

Perhaps a connection can be made with the *tefillah* we say on Monday and Thursday and also commonly recited after saying *Tehillim* when beseeching Hashem for mercy. Known as *Acheinu*, the *tefillah* reads:

אחינו כל בית ישראל, הנתונים בצרה ובשביה, העומדים בין בים ובין ביבשה, המקום ירחם עליהם,
ויוציאם מצרה לרווחה, ומאפלה לאורה, ומשעבוד לגאלה, השתא בעגלא ובזמן קריב, ונאמר אמן

*Regarding our brothers [amid] the whole House of Yisrael, who are given over
to trouble or captivity, whether they abide on the sea or on the dry land: May
Hashem have mercy upon them, and bring them forth from narrow straits to
expansiveness, from darkness to light, and from subjugation to redemption —
now, speedily and very soon, and let us say Amen.*

According to the Vilna Gaon's interpretation, the words "whether they abide on the sea or on the dry land" can take on a deeper meaning. There are Jews today who find themselves with much faith in Hashem, like those on the Red Sea who had great faith — and then there are those who unfortunately aren't there yet; like those who remained on the land when the sea split, they struggle with their faith and are perhaps not committed to a Torah lifestyle, yet we still ask Hashem: "Even those on the *yabashah*, the dry land — please have mercy on them, too."

We ask Hashem to remove them from the narrow vision in which they have yet to recognize Your great and mighty Hand.

Furthermore, we plead "and bring them forth from narrow straits to expansiveness." We ask Hashem to remove them from the *narrow* vision in which they have yet to recognize Your great and mighty hand and grant them *expansiveness*, the ability to see Your ways so that they put their faith in You.

Regarding both groups of Jews, we beseech Hashem to have mercy on them and bring them forth from their troubles. This idea is especially relevant nowadays when we ask Hashem to protect Jews in Eretz Yisrael and around the world. Let us keep in mind our brothers, regardless of their spiritual state, and relate to them in their struggle.

Yisro

וַיִּשְׁמַע יִתְרוֹ כֹהֵן מִדְיָן חֹתֵן מֹשֶׁה אֵת כָּל אֲשֶׁר עָשָׂה אֱלֹקִים לְמֹשֶׁה
וּלְיִשְׂרָאֵל עַמּוֹ כִּי הוֹצִיא ה' אֶת יִשְׂרָאֵל מִמִּצְרָיִם:

*And Moshe's father-in-law Yisro, the priest of Midian, heard
all that Hashem had done for Moshe and for Yisrael His
people, in bringing Israel out of Egypt.* (Shemos 18:1)

Rashi elaborates on what specifically Yisro heard.

וישמע יתרו: מה שמועה שמע ובא, קריעת ים סוף ומלחמת עמלק.

And Yisro heard — *What news did he hear that [made such an impression that] he came? He heard of the splitting of the Yam Suf and the war
with Amalek.*[44]

After reading the *pasuk* with Rashi, two questions emerge:

- First, why wasn't *Krias Yam Suf* alone sufficient to prompt
  Yisro to convert and join the B'nei Yisrael? Was it only after
  the war with Amalek that finally caused the turning point for
  him? After all, as the *pasuk* says in *Shiras HaYam* in *Parashas*

---

44   Based on the views of Rabbi Yehoshua and Rabbi Eliezer, *Maseches Zevachim* 116a.

Beshalach, "the nations heard [about *Krias Yam Suf*] and were agitated and afraid" — they were stunned and frightened of Hashem's great power. Surely this miracle alone should have been sufficient for Yisro to make a fair assessment and result in his decision to join B'nei Yisrael?

• If the surrounding nations actually heard of *Krias Yam Suf* and were frightened, why then was Yisro the only one to come forth and join Klal Yisrael?

Yisro's Turning Point

Perhaps Rashi is teaching us something more about Yisro's character and what truly was the ultimate driving force behind his decision. In *Sefer Devarim*, the Torah recounts the episode of Amalek's battle with B'nei Yisrael, and describes Amalek's manner of attack:

אֲשֶׁר קָרְךָ בַּדֶּרֶךְ וַיְזַנֵּב בְּךָ כָּל הַנֶּחֱשָׁלִים אַחֲרֶיךָ וְאַתָּה עָיֵף וְיָגֵעַ וְלֹא יָרֵא אֱלֹקִים:

How he (Amalek) happened upon you on the way and cut off all the stragglers at your rear, when you were faint and weary, and he did not fear Hashem. (Devarim 25:18)

What is meant by *karcha*, "happened upon you"? What specific trait of Amalek is the *pasuk* teaching us? Rashi elaborates with a beautiful insight into the root of the word:

אשר קרך בדרך: לשון מקרה. דבר אחר, לשון קרי וטומאה, שהיה מטמאן במשכב זכור. דבר אחר, לשון קור וחום, צננך והפשירך מרתיחתך, שהיו כל האומות יראים להלחם בכם ובא זה והתחיל והראה מקום לאחרים. משל לאמבטי רותחת שאין כל בריה יכולה לירד בתוכה, בא בן בליעל אחד קפץ וירד לתוכה. אף על פי שנכוה, הקרה אותה בפני אחרים.

How he happened upon you on the way — [The word קָרְךָ is] an expression denoting a chance occurrence (מִקְרֶה). Alternatively, it is an expression denoting seminal emission (קֶרִי) and defilement; Amalek defiled the Jews [with] homosexual acts. Yet another explanation: it is an expression denoting heat and cold (קוֹר); Amalek cooled you off and made you [appear] tepid, after you were boiling hot, for the nations were afraid to fight with you, [just as people are afraid to touch something boiling hot]. But then Amalek came forward and showed the way [of fighting Israel] to others. This can be compared to

a bathtub of boiling water into which no one could descend. Along came a
good-for-nothing and jumped headlong into it! Although he scalded himself,
he cooled it off for the others.

Rashi presents three ideas relating to the word *"karcha."* We can suggest that the first and third share a common theme. Amalek interpreted
Hashem's miracles as *"mikreh"* a chance occurrence; not impressed by
Hashem's glorious might, he instead saw them as a normal act of nature, nothing to get excited about. Related to this is Rashi's third idea
that *karcha* means "cold," as in the word *"kor."* Just imagine the talk
among the nations of the world: B'nei Yisrael were untouchable, with
the fear of G-d's wrath upon all following the destruction of Mitzrayim.
Then comes along Amalek to "cool off" the passions with which everyone related to Hashem's miracles. He calmed everyone down, making
light of G-d's greatness to the point that the fear of His strength waned
and diminished in the view of the nation's, concluding that what had
occurred was a simple coincidence.

With this understanding in mind, we can now answer the original
questions about Yisro and the need for two miracles to prompt his conversion. Perhaps Rashi is telling us that Yisro actually came to convert
after hearing about *Krias Yam Suf* alone.

Yisro was not the only one that considered conversion. All the nations trembled and were in awe of Hashem's power but then Amalek
came along and began making light of all that happened and eventually
cooled off the reactions to the great miracles witnessed by all. In other
words, it was *Krias Yam Suf* alone that prompted Yisro to come, but
what guided him to be impervious to Amalek's mocking was hearing
about the actual war with Amalek. After seeing Amalek construing the
miracles as a simple chance occurrence, cooling off the passions of the
nations, Yisro decided not to allow himself to be influenced like the
others but instead kept his inspiration and passion alive and came to
join the B'nei Yisrael. This is what Rashi means when he says that he
came after *Krias Yam Suf* and *Milchemes Amalek*. It was the great miracle
of *Krias Yam Suf* that opened up Yisro's eyes to the truth, followed with

the war of Amalek, which reinforced his awe of Hashem and did not allow him to be "cooled off" and lose the initial inspiration.

Open versus Hidden Miracles

Actually, everything in our lives should really be viewed as a miracle, but at times Hashem brings about a supernatural event that breaks with the rules of "nature."

There are always those who attempt to downplay an open miracle and find a reason to explain it as nothing more than nature at work. Actually, everything in our lives should really be viewed as a miracle, but at times Hashem brings about a supernatural event that breaks with the rules of "nature" to inspire and renew our recognition of His control over all that occurs. A miraculous event is no greater than a natural one; but miracles serve their purpose by preventing us from forgetting that even the *teva*, nature, which surrounds us is actually an awesome sign of Hashem's complete control.

Mishpatim

אִם כֶּסֶף תַּלְוֶה אֶת עַמִּי אֶת הֶעָנִי עִמָּךְ לֹא תִהְיֶה לוֹ כְּנֹשֶׁה לֹא תְשִׂימוּן
עָלָיו נֶשֶׁךְ: אִם חָבֹל תַּחְבֹּל שַׂלְמַת רֵעֶךָ עַד בֹּא הַשֶּׁמֶשׁ תְּשִׁיבֶנּוּ לוֹ: כִּי
הִוא כְסוּתֹה לְבַדָּהּ הִוא שִׂמְלָתוֹ לְעֹרוֹ בַּמֶּה יִשְׁכָּב וְהָיָה כִּי יִצְעַק אֵלַי
וְשָׁמַעְתִּי כִּי חַנּוּן אָנִי:

*When you lend money to My people, to the poor person
[who is] with you, you shall not behave toward him as a
lender; you shall not impose interest upon him. If you take
your neighbor's garment as security, by sunset you shall
return it to him, for it is his only covering; it is his garment
for his skin. With what shall he lie? And it shall be [that] if
he cries out to Me, I will hear because I am gracious.*

(Shemos 22:24–26)

The Torah tells us about the lender that takes the poor person's garment as a security (*mashkon*) for payment. At sunset, the lender must
return it to him, "for it is his only covering."

In *Parashas Pekudei* we read:

אֵלֶּה פְקוּדֵי הַמִּשְׁכָּן מִשְׁכַּן הָעֵדֻת אֲשֶׁר פֻּקַּד עַל פִּי מֹשֶׁה עֲבֹדַת הַלְוִיִּם בְּיַד אִיתָמָר בֶּן
אַהֲרֹן הַכֹּהֵן:

99

These are the accounts of the Mishkan, the Mishkan of the Testimony, which were counted at Moshe's command; [this was] the work of the Levi'im under the direction of Isamar, the son of Aharon the Kohen. (Shemos 38:21)

Rashi explains the double use of the word *Mishkan* based on the *Midrash Tanchuma*:

המשכן משכן: שני פעמים, רמז למקדש שנתמשכן בשני חורבנין בשני עונותיהן של ישראל.

The Mishkan, the Mishkan — [The word Mishkan is written] twice. This alludes to the Beis HaMikdash, which was taken as security by the two destructions, for B'nei Yisrael's sins. [Midrash Tanchuma 2, Shemos Rabbah 51:3](Rashi)

From Rashi, we learn that the two *Batei Mikdash* were taken as a *mashkon*, collateral, and will be returned in the form of the Third and final Beis HaMikdash when we return to Hashem by committing ourselves to *teshuvah*.

Rav Chaim Palagi[45] has a beautiful idea which relates to this Rashi. He asks if the *Batei Mikdash* were taken as collateral *(mashkon)*, as Rashi explained based on the Midrash, then it is proper that it be returned to us before sunset — as is required by the Torah in the normal case of collateral taken by a lender?

A Place to Sleep

He answers that the Torah uses the words *"bameh yishkav* — with what shall he lie?"* to describe the borrower's state when sunset arrives, and his collateral has not yet been returned. The Torah shows *rachmanus*, mercy, to the borrower since, after all, with what will he sleep at night if not for his garment.

Hashem is ready to return the collateral, the Third Beis HaMikdash, but we need to have the perception of *bameh yishkav*, with what shall he lie? We must feel that we have nowhere to go; we must sense the absence of a place to call our home, no place to rest and find comfort from this dreadful and painful *Galus*. This is the condition for returning the *mash-kon* and until then Hashem keeps it as a security waiting for us to return to Him and signaling that we feel a void with no place to call home.

Let us take this idea a step further:

Hashem is waiting for us to return, and will then bless us with the Third Beis HaMikdash and His presence in our midst. Simply showing a genuine desire and an intense yearning, feeling that we are in dire need of the *Geulah*, redemption, can facilitate Hashem's mercy. Perhaps the *pasuk* alludes to this when it says:

וְהָיָה כִּי יִצְעַק אֵלַי וְשָׁמַעְתִּי כִּי חַנּוּן אָנִי:

When he cries out to Me, I will hear him, for I am merciful. (Shemos 22:26)

The Language of Crying

Hashem is so gracious and He will listen to us, but we must first "cry out" and show we are in distress, with no other plan other than relying on His mercy to bring us the final *Geulah*. We must demonstrate a display of discomfort and not being satisfied with our current state. Communicating with Hashem in this manner will prove our true desire for Him to redeem us.

We must first "cry out" and show we are in distress, with no other plan other than relying on His mercy.

Another allusion to this idea may be found in the *tefillah* of *Shemoneh Esrei*, when we ask Hashem,

ותשכון בתוכה כאשר דברת.

And may You dwell in Jerusalem as You spoke.

It can be suggested that we are requesting that Hashem return the *mashkon, vesishkon besochah*, just as He said, *ka'asher dibartah*, in the above-cited *pasuk* of *vehayah ki yitzak eilai*. We need to shed a tear in this *berachah* and realize our need to be released from this *Galus* with the recognition of how much we are lacking without the Beis HaMikdash to call our home.

Another idea to keep in mind is that all the difficulties which we encounter today are sourced globally in the destruction of the Beis HaMikdash. Without it we lack the Divine closeness which provides us with Hashem's constant blessing. When we pray for Hashem to redeem us, included in this request is for Him to remove all the distress and grief we experience originating from the distance we created between us and Him.

Terumah

וְזֹאת הַתְּרוּמָה אֲשֶׁר תִּקְחוּ מֵאִתָּם זָהָב וָכֶסֶף וּנְחֹשֶׁת:

And this is the offering that you shall take from them:
gold, silver, and copper. *(Shemos 25:3)*

Rabbeinu Ephraim, in his commentary on the Torah, quotes the
following idea:

זהב וכסף ונחושת שנדרש על נותני צדקה. זהב נוטריקון זה הנותן בריא, ר"ל קודם
שיפול בסכנה או בחולי נותן צדקה לעני תמיד והוא עומד בבריאותו, ולכן נמשל לזהב
שהוא משובח מן הכל, אבל מי שלא יתן עד שיפול בסכנה הוא נמשל לכסף שהוא קל
מזהב, וזהו נוטריקון של כסף כשרואה סכנה פותח. והנמשל לנחשת זה אינו נותן עד
שיחלה אח"כ הוא נותן הנדר שעשה, וזהו נוטריקון של נחשת נדר חולה שיאמר תנו.
ע"כ תם תם.

*The pasuk categorizes three different levels of giving tzedakah, beginning
with gold and ending with copper. Rabbeinu Ephraim explains that the most
noble manner of giving is when one gives when all is fine and good with him.
A remez (allusion) to this is* ז"ה ה"נותן ב"ריא *— one who gives when he is healthy
and fit; the roshei teivos (initial letters) of these words spell* זהב, *gold. The
second category is* כ"שרואה ס"כנה פ"ותח; *when tragedy strikes he opens his wallet,
with the hope of remedying his situation; the roshei teivos are* כסף, *silver. The
third and lowermost level of giving is* נ"דר ח"ולה ש"יאמר ת"נו *— the promise of a
sick person who says "Give!," ready to do anything to heal himself and better
his situation. The initials of these words spell* נחשת, *copper.*

Relationships Made of Gold

Rabbi Baruch Simon, in his *sefer Imrei Baruch*, teaches an important lesson relating to our relationships with others that can be learned from the words of Rabbeinu Ephraim. He explains that we shouldn't wait until a difficult situation arises to improve our relationships with others. Instead, we should work to get along and be at the level of "gold," one who has a good relationship with others when all is good and does not wait for a tragedy or some other event to cause togetherness and friendship. This is especially true on the community level. There are times when the differences in a community are allowed to become very deep and cause divisiveness among friends — yet when tragedy strikes, all come together to support each other. Such support is nice, but it is only on the level of *tzedakah* given like "copper;" it would be better had there been peace and friendship all along.

Another approach can be suggested as well. Many of us may relate to Hashem as a figure to Whom we turn when in need of help, whether it be difficult times with earning a living, raising children, or when someone is sick. We then turn to Hashem in *tefillah*, beseeching Him for a favorable outcome.

Toward a Meaningful Connection with Hashem

The problem with a relationship of this nature is that Hashem wants more connection with us. We are His joy and pride, and He wants to be close with us. He loves us and wants us to make Him a part of our lives, during both the good and the challenging times. This is analogous to a child who only speaks to his father when he needs money or the like, yet at other times will not let him know how he is doing or call him to thank him for his past favors. The same is true with Hashem. Our relationship must be one with depth, where we live with Hashem daily and speak with Him about the good in our lives in the same manner as we plead with Him when things don't go our way. We need to bring Hashem into our lives and speak with Him constantly, so that the relationship is not merely needs-based.

We need to bring Hashem into our lives and speak with Him constantly, so that the relationship is not merely needs-based.

The Torah tells us after the sin of Adam and Chava that the Snake that enticed them to sin was cursed to crawl in the dust and eat the dirt of the ground. Rav Yitzchak Meir Alter, *zt"l,* known as the *Chidushei HaRim,* asks: Since dirt is always available and easy to come by, why was this curse considered a punishment for the Snake? It would seem that the Snake was rewarded in having an endless amount of food easily obtainable!

אמרו חכמינו, כי על ידי זה שנתקלל הנחש לאכול רק עפר, הרי תמיד מזונותיו מזומנים לפניו. עולה לגג, מזונותיו עמו. וכן אמרו חכמינו הרואה נחש בחלום פרנסתו מזומנת לו (ברכות נ"ז). קשה איפוא, מה קללה היא זו.

ברם, הקללה היתה בכך שהורחק כל כך מן הקדושה, עד כדי למנוע ממנו שיצטרך אי פעם לשאת עיניו אל השמים, כדרך ברואים אחרים המחפשים להם מזונותיהם ונושאים לפעמים עיניהם השמימה, לבקש מזון מאת ד' יתברך, כגון הכפירים שואגים לטרף ולבקש מאל אכלם (תהילים ק"ד כ"א).

את קולו של הנחש אין רוצים בכלל לשמוע, בבחינת קח לך את שלך והסתלק מנגד עיני, לבל אראך ולבל אשמעך עוד.

Our Sages said that in being cursed with having to eat only dirt, the Snake's food supply is always in abundance; even if it goes up on a roof, it has what to eat. And our Sages similarly taught: "He who sees a snake in his dream, it means his living (sustenance) is assured" (Berachos 57a). The question is therefore clear: What kind of punishment is this?

The answer is that the Snake was cursed in being distanced from anything having to do with sanctity — to the extent that even the need to ever look heavenward is taken from it. It is not like other creatures that seek their food and sometimes lift their eyes to the heavens to ask Hashem to provide them. For instance, "The young lions roar for their prey, and seek their food from G-d" (Tehillim 104:21). The sound of the Snake's call is not at all desired in the Heavens, as if it were being told, "Take your food and get out of my sight! I don't want to see you or hear you." (Chidushei HaRim, Bereishis)

Explains the *Chidushei HaRim* as follows: Hashem cursed the Snake by making his food so easily accessible, in effect severing His relationship from the Snake, that it now had no need to ask Hashem for its sustenance. This was the Snake's punishment; being distanced from having a relationship with Hashem. In essence, the Snake was now on its own, with no connection to Hashem — and with no reason for one.

Don't Be Like the Snake

Perhaps we can now have a deeper understanding of Rabbeinu Ephraim's *remez* to the word נחשת, copper. As discussed above, "copper" alludes to the lowest level of giving *tzedakah*, one in which the action is taken only after a difficult situation arises. This idea is similar to the individual who seeks no relationship with Hashem until the need occurs, and he then searches for Hashem out of desperation. The root of the word נחשת is נחש — the Snake that was cursed and lost the opportunity to be close to Hashem. The message is: Do not be like the נחש, the Snake, that was cursed and banned from the privilege of having a relationship with Hashem. We should look to make Hashem a part of our lives and speak to Him daily, because Hashem loves us and wants our closeness as a true father-son relationship. We dare not wait for misfortune to prompt this bond. Instead, let us join the category of זה ה' נותן ב"ריא, one who seeks to forge a relationship with Hashem even when he is healthy and all is well.

Tetzaveh

וְעָשִׂיתָ מִזְבֵּחַ מִקְטַר קְטֹרֶת עֲצֵי שִׁטִּים תַּעֲשֶׂה אֹתוֹ:

You shall make an Altar for bringing incense up in smoke; you shall make it out of shittim wood. (Shemos 30:1)

The Torah commands the building of the *Mizbei'ach HaKetores*, the Altar of Incense. Aside from having the actual *ketores* (incense) offered upon it once in the morning and then again in the evening, it was used once a year on Yom Kippur during the service (*avodah*) of the Kohen Gadol when he sprinkled on its corners the blood of the *chatas Yom HaKippurim*, the Yom Kippur sin-offering.

The Need for Two Altars

The *Kli Yakar* has a fascinating idea which explains the need for two altars: the *Mizbei'ach Ha'Olah*,[46] which was situated in the *Azarah* (Courtyard), and the *Mizbei'ach HaKetores*,[47] positioned in the *Kodesh HaKodashim*, the Holy of Holies. Why was one altar not sufficient for both the *korbanos* as well as for the *ketores* offerings?

---

46   Also called the *Mizbei'ach HaNechoshes*, the Bronze Altar, and the *Mizbei'ach HaChitzoni*, the Outer Altar.
47   Also called the *Mizbei'ach HaZahav*, the Golden Altar, and the *Mizbei'ach HaPnimi*, the Inner Altar.

כפי הנראה שב' מזבחות אלו נערכו שניהם לכפר על הנפש החוטאת כי מזבח הנחושת, בא
לכפר על חלקי החומר והגוף הנגוף באבן החטא, ועליו מקריבים הבעלי חיים הבאים תמורתו כי
יש להם דמיון אל חומר האדם ותמונת המזבח יוכיח כי זאת קומתו דמתה לקומת אדם בינוני ג'
אמות, וכן הבהמות הנקרבים דומים אל נפש הבהמית שבאדם נפש תמורת נפש כי מטעם זה
נאמר במנחת עני ונפש כי תקריב (ויקרא ב,א) כי אין בידו להקריב נפש הבהמה תמורת נפשו
והוא מביא מנחת סולת על כן אמר הכתוב ונפש מעלה אני עליו כאילו הקריב נפש אבל מ"מ גם
הנשמה צריכה כפרה אחרי אשר הוטמאה בגוף הנגוף הזה ואינה מתכפרת בנפש הבהמה כי אין
דמיון זה לזה, כי רוח בני אדם עולה למעלה ורוח הבהמה יורדת למטה ואיך תהיה נפש הבהמה
הכלה ונפסד תמורה לנשמת אדם הקיימת לנצח, ע"כ צוה אל חי לעשות מזבח הקטרת,
המעלה עשן וריח ניחוח לה' לכפר על רוח בני האדם העולה היא למעלה כעשן הקטורת והיא
גם היא מקוטרת מור ולבונה (שיר ג,ו) של מעשים טובים. ולהורות נתן בלבבנו מ"ש (שמות
ל,לו) ושחקת ממנה הדק רמז לנשמה דקה מן הדקה שצריכה גם היא כפרה כדי להעלותה אל
מקום חוצבה, ומספר אמות מזבח זה יוכיח כי בו נאמר אמה ארכו ואמה רחבו. אמות יחידות
לכפר בו על הנשמה שנקראת יחידה כמו שהקב"ה אחד כך היא יחידה, ואמתיים קומתו. כי
רוח בני האדם היא העולה למעלה למקומה בזולת מקום שיש לה תוך הגוף וזמן הקטרתו בבקר
ובערב, כי הנשמה בבקר היא באה בילדותו זמן זריחת שמשו ובערב היא שבה אל אביה כימי
נעוריה והלואי שתהא יציאה כביאה בלא חטא, ובא הקטורת בהטיבו את הנרות בבוקר, ובערב
בהעלות את הנרות, ומראה הערב והבוקר אמת, כי הוא מתייחס לנר אלקים נשמת אדם כי
הבוקר זמן הטבת נר אלקים נשמת אדם להטיב מעשיה ולנקות עצמה מכל חלודת אפר ובערב
זמן שקיעת שמשו הוא זמן העלאת הנשמה אל מקום חוצבה ובא הקטרה זו לכפר על הנשמה
כדי שתהא היציאה מן העולם בלא חטא כביאה.

It appears that the two altars were designed to atone for the sinner (lit., the
"soul that sins"). The Bronze Altar [for the incense] comes to atone for the
tangible, i.e., for the body afflicted with the millstone of sins, and upon it are
offered the animals that come in place of the person, for they are physically
similar to man. And the shape of the Altar proves this, for its height is that
of an average man: three amos, and the animals offered upon it are likened
to the "animalistic nature" of man — a soul for a soul. This is why the Torah
states regarding the minchah offering of a poor man (Vayikra 2:1), "And
if a soul offers..." (and not "if a man offers") — for the poor man does not
have the wherewithal to offer an animal soul for his own soul, and instead
he brings a meal offering. This is why the Torah says "soul," for Hashem says,
"I regard him as if he had sacrificed his soul before Me" (Menachos 104b).

At the same time, however, his spiritual side (neshamah) also requires
atonement, after having been defiled in its afflicted body. It is not atoned
for together with the animalistic soul, because they are not the same: Man's
spirit ascends, while the animal spirit descends; how can an animal soul that
is transitory and feeble come in place of the human soul that is eternal?

For this reason, the Living G-d commanded to make an Incense Altar, from which smoke and the pleasant fragrance ascend to Hashem — to atone for man's spirit which ascends like the smoke of the incense, and which is also "perfumed [from the same Hebrew root as incense] with myrrh and frankincense" (Shir HaShirim 3:6) of good deeds.

And the Torah enlightened us by stating "You shall beat some of it [the incense] very fine" (Shemos 30:36) — an allusion to the soul, the finest of the fine, which too needs atonement to raise it to its source.

The amount of the Incense Altar's amos [in length] — "its length is an amah, and its width is an amah" (Shemos 30:2) — is an indication: Individual amos to atone for the soul which is called Yechidah, unique and individual; just as Hashem is One, so too the soul is individual.

"And its height was two amos" (ibid.) — for the spirit of people ascends upward to its place, in addition to its place within the body.

And the time of the offering of the incense is in the morning and evening — just as the soul comes to the world as a baby in the "morning" when its sun rises, and it returns to its Father like in its youthful days in the evening; would it be that its return would be like its first coming, without sin. Similarly, the incense is offered when the Kohen arranges the Menorah's candles in the morning, and in the evening when he kindles them. This comparison-image of morning and evening is true, because it relates to the pasuk (Mishlei 20:27) "The candle of G-d is the soul of man" — for the morning is the time of arranging the candle of Hashem that is the soul of man, to arrange (improve) its deeds and to cleanse it of all dirt and ash; and the evening, the time of its setting sun, is the time of raising the soul to its source. And this offering of the incense comes to atone for the soul so that its departure from the world should be without sin, as it was when it came into the world. (Kli Yakar)

For Body and Soul

The *Kli Yakar* teaches that the outer *Mizbei'ach*, which was used for the actual *korbanos*, served to offer forgiveness for the *guf* (body), or the person's physical act of the sin committed. However, the *neshamah* (soul) also needed forgiveness. The *Mizbei'ach HaKetores* served this purpose since it represented the soul of the person. He explains that the dimensions of the *mizbei'ach* used for the *ketores* were one *amah* by one *amah*. This singular measure represents the *neshamah* (of which one of its names is *Yechidah*) which is similar to Hashem, Who is referred to as *Echad*, One. Furthermore, the height of this Altar measured two *amos*, symbolizing the *neshamah* returning — ascending — to the One Hashem. With regard to the process of preparing the *ketores*, the Torah (*Shemos* 30:36) says "You shall beat of [the incense] very fine." The *ketores* was finely ground, similar to the *neshamah* which is refined and pure but still needs to purify itself to achieve forgiveness and return to its original place. Finally, the *ketores* was offered twice daily, morning and evening, similar to the *neshamah* which goes up in the evening and is returned in the morning.[48]

A Pleasant Aroma

The *Rambam* in his *Moreh Nevuchim* (*Guide to the Perplexed*) offers a practical reason for the *ketores* as follows:

וכיון שהמקום המקודש נשחטין בו זבחים רבים בכל יום, ומחתכיו בו בשר, ונקטר ונרחצין
בו הקרבים אין ספק שאלו הניחוהו כפי המצב הזה בלבד היה ריחו כריח בתי המטבחים
ולפיכך צווה בו בהקטרת: הקטורת פעמים בכל יום בבקר ובין הערבים, כדי לבשם ריחו
וריח בגדי כל העובדים שם, כבר ידעת אמרם מיריחו היו מריחין ריח הקטורת גם זה ממה
שמקיים יראת המקדש אבל אילו לא היה לו ריח טוב, כל שכן אילו לו היה ההפך, הייתה
ההרגשה הפך הרוממות, כי הנפשות ניוחות מאוד לריחות הבשמים ונמשכות אליהן,
וקצות מן הריחות הרעים ומתרחקות מהם.

Since many korbanos were slaughtered daily in the Beis HaMikdash, the flesh cut in pieces, and the entrails and legs burnt and washed, the smell of the place would undoubtedly have been like the smell of slaughterhouses, if nothing had been done to counteract it. They were therefore commanded to burn incense there twice every day, in the morning and in the evening, in order to give the place and the garments of those who worked there a pleasant odor. There is a well-known saying of our Sages, "In Yericho they could smell the ketores." This provision likewise supported the dignity and awe of the Beis HaMikdash. If there had not been a good smell, let alone if there had been a stench, it would have produced in the minds of the people the reverse of respect, for our heart generally feels elevated in the presence of a good odor and is attracted by it, but it abhors and avoids a bad smell. (Moreh Nevuchim 3:45)

---

48   See the *Kli Yakar* for additional similarities between the *ketores* and the *neshamah*.

From the Rambam, we understand that the purpose of the *ketores* was so that people would leave the Mishkan or Beis HaMikdash with a positive feeling and with respect for this holy place, counteracting the negative smell that could mar the experience.

Humility and Optimism

Perhaps with the understandings of the *Kli Yakar* and the Rambam together, we can suggest the following as the purpose of the *Mizbei'ach Haketores*. It was to offer the *neshamah* forgiveness, and then allow one to leave after bringing his *korban* with a feeling of positivity and recognition of still being valued in Hashem's eyes *keviyachol*, despite the sin that was committed. The act of bringing a *korban* was to humble oneself and view the animal in place of oneself while receiving forgiveness but then remain with an encouraging spirit, realize that the whole experience was meant to bring the person closer to Hashem, leaving with a pleasant odor and his *neshamah* feeling elevated and renewed. The purpose of coming to the Mishkan or Beis HaMikdash was for the person to be revitalized, spiritually strengthened, and not feeling dejected because of his sin. The pleasant aroma of the *ketores* was intended to achieve this goal.

> The purpose of coming to the Mishkan or Beis HaMikdash was for the person to be revitalized, spiritually strengthened, and not feeling dejected because of his sin.

Inside and Outside

Perhaps the locations of the Altars also make this point. The *Mizbei'ach HaKetores*, the Inner Altar, was placed in the Inner Sanctuary, the *Kodesh*, symbolizing the *neshamah* which is hidden inside the *guf*, the body. The *Mizbei'ach Ha'Olah*, on the other hand, is the Outer Altar, symbolizing the body, and therefore its place was most appropriate in the Outer Courtyard.

The fire on the *Mizbei'ach HaKetores* was ignited with the burning coals of the *Mizbei'ach HaNechoshes*; this again binds the two together, alluding to the *guf-neshamah* relationship.

The Family of Beis Avtinas

The Mishnah in *Yoma*[49] tells of those families that are remembered in a disgraceful manner for not sharing their special talents used in the Beis HaMikdash. One family, Beis Avtinas, knew the recipe for the production of the *ketores*, and the Gemara[50] teaches that they attempted to excuse themselves by arguing that they did not want the *ketores* to be abused and utilized for idol worship. Nevertheless, the *Chachamim* (Sages) did not accept their argument. The *Talmud Yerushalmi*, on the other hand, teaches that their argument was accepted by the *Chachamim*. This leads some commentators[51] to explain that the curse against these families — *veshem reshaim yirkav*, "may the name of the wicked rot" — refers to other families, but not Beis Avtinas, the family that held the secret to the *ketores*.

Perhaps this further alludes to the nature of the *guf*-and-*neshamah* bond. The *ketores* and its Altar symbolized the *neshamah* and the vital importance that it be kept secret and hidden from any possible threat.

While it is easy for us to care for our bodies which give us constant reminders in the form of feeling hungry, tired, and pain; our *neshamos* can be neglected as they remain hidden and protected out of sight. However, the same way in which we would not let a physical wound go untreated, we need to think about our soul in a similar manner. The soul waits patiently but also cries and awaits the *guf* to care of it and its needs.

49   3:11.
50   *Yoma* 38a.
51   *Meiri, Tosafos Yom Tov.*

Ki Sisa

וְעָשִׂיתָ כִּיּוֹר נְחֹשֶׁת וְכַנּוֹ נְחֹשֶׁת לְרָחְצָה וְנָתַתָּ אֹתוֹ בֵּין אֹהֶל מוֹעֵד וּבֵין הַמִּזְבֵּחַ וְנָתַתָּ שָׁמָּה מָיִם:

You shall make a Kiyor (wash basin) of copper and its base of copper for washing, and you shall place it between the Tent of Meeting and the Altar, and you shall put water therein.

The Sochatchover Rebbe, Rav Shmuel Bornstein, *zt"l*, asks in his *Shem MiShmuel*:

- Why is the commandment of building the *Kiyor* (wash basin) not mentioned together with the other Mishkan vessels earlier on, in *Parashas Terumah*?
- Why did Hashem command Moshe to place the *Kiyor* between the *Ohel Moed* (Tent of Meeting) and the *Mizbei'ach* (Altar)? This would mean that when the Kohanim enter the *Azarah* (Courtyard), they would need to pass the *Mizbei'ach* to reach the *Kiyor,* and then return to the *Mizbei'ach*. Would it not have made more sense to position the *Kiyor* first so that the Kohanim would encounter that vessel first, and then the *Mizbei'ach*?

113

יש להתבונן בפרשיות הכיור שלא נכתבה בין הכלים אלא אחר פרשת שקלים, וגם מקומו הקבוע של הכיור בין אוהל מועד ובין המזבח אף שמשוך כלפי דרום, מ"מ לפי דרך הפשוט יותר יצדק אם הי' לפני המזבח במזרח.

ונראה דהנה בתרגום יונתן (פ' פקודי) דהכיור רומז לתשובה, וכן הוא בפשיטות דרחיצת ידים ורגלים רומז להכתוב (ישעי' א') רחצו הזכו הסירו רוע מעלליכם מנגד עיני וגו'. והנה תשובה מעומקא דלבא לאיש המטונף בעבירות קשה מאוד, כי (יומא ל"ט.) עבירה מטמטמת לבו של אדם ואינה מניחתו לעשות תשובה, וצריך סיוע מזכות הרבים, וע"כ (שם פ"ו:) יחיד שעשה תשובה מוחלין לכל העולם כולו, כי יש לכולם חלק בתשובתו, אבל מאחר שחטא ממילא נעשה נבדל מכלל ישראל. וכמו שארץ ישראל מקיאה את עוברי עבירה כדכתיב (ויקרא י"ח) כאשר קאה את הגוי אשר לפניכם, כן היא כנסת ישראל למעלה. אבל העצה היעוצה שלא להשגיח על שום דבר רק לאגד עצמו עם הציבור כמ"ש ויעשו כולם אגודה אחת לעשות רצונך בלבב שלם, ואף שעדיין מצואתו לא רחץ, מ"מ מאחר שהוא נותן את לבו להיות בכלל האגודה של ציבור שוב אין כלל ישראל מקיא אותו, וכמו החלבנה בסממני הקטורת. וזהו הענין בשקלים שכל ישראל עושין אגודה אחת להתחיל מחדש בעבודה, ואז זכות הרבים מסייעת לו שיהי' ביכלתו לעשות תשובה ולהתרחץ בטנופת של מעשיו כדכתיב רחצו הזכו וגו' כנ"ל.

אך כ"ז הוא אם האדם יודע בעצמו שהוא עומד מבחוץ, וכמו גר שבא להתגייר, אם אומר יודע אני ואיני כדאי אין מקבלין אותו כבש"ס יבמות (מ"ז.). וזה עצמו מרומז בחלבנה, דהנה יש להבין בסממני קטורת שהם אחד עשר, וידוע שכל עשרה הוא בקדושה ומספר י"א הוא בחיצוניות כמספר י"א ארורים, ולמה בקטורת שהיא מהיותר נכבדים שבקרבנות כדכתיב (משלי כ"ז) שמן וקטורת ישמח לב יהי' המספר י"א סממנים. אך יש לומר דבטל כמאן דליתא, וחלבנה בפני עצמה ריחה רע אלא שבטלה לעשרה סממנים שריחן טוב, ע"כ שוב אין כאן אלא עשרה דהחלבנה בטלה לגביהו וכטל כמאן דליתא, וכ"ז אם אינו נחשב ליש בפני עצמו אלא שבטל לאינך, אבל אם נחשב ליש בפני עצמו שוב אינו מתקבל.

והנה זה עצמו מרומז במקום הכיור, שמקומו בין מזבח לאוהל מועד רומז שבלתי אפשר לבא אל הכיור הרומז לתשובה אלא באמצעות המזבח שהוא רומז לכנסת ישראל כנודע. ויש בזה רמז במשנה דש"ס תמיד (פ"א מ"ד) אין אדם נכנס עמו ולא נר בידו אלא מהלך לאור המערכה [בכהן שתורם את המזבח שחרית שהולך לקדש את ידיו ורגליו מן הכיור], היינו שאין דרך לבא לקידוש הרומז לתשובה בנר בידו או בסיוע חברו רק לאור המערכה שהוא רומז לאור של כל כנסת ישראל, ואם הוא חושב את עצמו שיש לו אור שלא מן הכלל כולו רק מצד עצמו שהוא נר בידו, או חברו הפרטי, אין לו כלום כמו חלבנה הבלתי מתבטלת לעשרה הסממנים האחרים.

Let us consider: Why are the passages of the Kiyor (the washing basin in the Mishkan) not written among the other holy vessels, but rather after Parashas Shekalim? In addition, why is the Kiyor located between the Tent of Meeting and the Altar? True, it is somewhat to the south, but it would still seem more straightforward and correct to locate it before the Altar in the east?

The explanation appears to be as follows. The Targum Yonasan (in Parashas Pikudei) says that the Kiyor alludes to repentance, and this in fact is straightforward — for washing the hands and feet alludes to the pasuk "wash and become clean, remove the evil of your wrongdoings" (Yeshayahu 1:16). Real heartfelt teshuvah for one who is steeped in sin is very difficult, for "sin muddles one's heart" (Yoma 39a) and does not allow him to repent; he needs assistance from the "communal merit." This is why "in the merit of one individual who repents, the sins of the entire world are forgiven" (Yoma 86b), because everyone has a share in his teshuvah — but because he sinned, he is separated from Klal Yisrael. And just like Eretz Yisrael vomits out sinners, as is written, "as it vomited out the nation that preceded you" (Vayikra 18:28), so too is Knesses Yisrael loftier.[52] Rather, the best counsel is not to pay attention to anything other than binding to the community, as we say in our prayers, "They shall form one union to do Your Will wholeheartedly" — and even though he has not yet rinsed off his filth, still, since he intends to be part of the community of Klal Yisrael, it will no longer vomit him out, just like the chelbenah,[53] a foul-smelling ingredient of the incense. And this is the idea of the shekalim, that all of Israel forms one community to begin the service anew, and then the "communal merit" aids him to be able to do teshuvah and to wash off the filth of his misdeeds, as is written, "wash and become clean," as above.

But all this applies only if the person himself knows that he is "standing outside," just like a convert before his conversion: If he says, "I know [that Israel is abused by the Gentiles] and I am not worthy [of joining]," then we accept him, as the Gemara states (Yevamos 47a). And this itself alludes to the chelbenah — for we must understand: It is known that every "ten" is holy, while "eleven" is chitzoniyus, external — such as the eleven curses in Ki Savo. Why then regarding the incense, which is among the more honorable offerings, as written, "Oil and incense will gladden the heart" (Mishlei 27:9), are there eleven ingredients? We can answer that chelbenah, whose odor is bad, is canceled out among the ten others whose odor is pleasant, and therefore, there are essentially only ten ingredients, for the chelbenah is voided. But this is only if it is not considered an entity in and of itself, but is rather voided among the others; but if it is an entity in itself, it is not accepted.

---

52   And like Eretz Yisrael cannot tolerate the sinner.
53   Even with its foul-smelling quality, it was still included and was an integral part of the *Ketores*.

This precisely is indicated by the location of the Kiyor, between the altar and the Tent of Meeting — showing that one can approach the basin, representing teshuvah as stated above, only via the Altar, which alludes to Klal Yisrael, as is known.

And this is alluded to in the Mishnah (Tamid 1:4) which states that when the Kohen who removes the ashes from the Altar [the act of terumas hadeshen] comes in the morning to wash his hands and feet, "No one enters with him, nor does he come in with a candle; he rather walks by the light of the fire on the Altar." This tells us that there is no way to approach sanctification [washing], alluding to teshuvah, with a candle or with help from a friend — other than by the light of the burnt-offerings on the Altar, which alludes to the light of Knesses Yisrael. And if he thinks that he has light that does not originate with the Klal, but rather has his own candle, or light from his individual friend — then he has nothing; he is like the chelbenah that is not canceled out by the other ingredients. (Shem MiShmuel, Parashas Ki Sisa/Parah, 5672)

This *Shem MiShmuel* requires explanation. He begins with an introduction to that which the *Kiyor* symbolized, in accordance with the following *Targum Yonason* (to *Shemos* 40:7):

וְתִתֵּן יַת כִּיּוֹרָא בֵּינֵי מַשְׁכַּן זִמְנָא וּבֵינֵי מַדְבְּחָא וְתִתֵּן תַּמָּן מוֹי מְטוּל חוֹבַיָּא דְהַדְרִין בִּתְיוּבְתָּא וְשָׁדְיָין עֲקַמּוּמִיתְהוֹן הֵי כְמַיָּא.

And you should place the Kiyor between the Ohel Moed and the Mizbei'ach and you should put water in it for the sinners that repent and throw their crookedness (wickedness) away like water. (Targum Yonason)

Another reference to water symbolizing *teshuvah* is from the *pasuk* in *Yeshayahu.*

רַחֲצוּ הִזַּכּוּ הָסִירוּ רֹעַ מַעַלְלֵיכֶם מִנֶּגֶד עֵינָי חִדְלוּ הָרֵעַ.

Wash yourselves, make yourselves clean; Remove the evil of your deeds from My sight. Cease to do evil. (Yeshayahu 1:16)

Again, we see that water signifies cleansing oneself from evil and sinful ways.

Joining the Klal as a Path to Teshuvah

The *Shem MiShmuel* explains that *aveiros* can burden the individual to a point that true *teshuvah* can be a struggle when going at it alone. However, with the *zechus* of the *tzibbur*, i.e., the merit of being connected with a community, the individual can merit *teshuvah* that leads to forgiveness. Once a person connects himself to the *tzibbur*, the *teshuvah* process becomes easier and more accessible. It is for this reason that a *taanis tzibbur* (communal fast day) needed to include even the *poshei Yisrael*, the sinners of Klal Yisrael. Similarly, the ingredients used in the production of the *ketores* must include even the foul-smelling *chelbenah* spice.[54] The same is true with the *machatzis hashekel* which required including both the poor and the rich in an equal manner so that there would be no division amongst Klal Yisrael and they would embody *achdus* which could act as a *zechus* for even those not worthy on their own merit. The *Mizbei'ach*, too, signified the *tzibbur* coming together as one, for it was there that the *korbanos* of the *tzibbur* were offered. Therefore, the *Mizbei'ach* and *Kiyor* were placed such that one first reached the *Mizbei'ach*, unifying the sinner with the entire nation and facilitating the merit of the entire nation, and only afterwards would he reach the *Kiyor*, where he would cleanse himself from the sin.

The *Mishnah* in *Yoma* says:

בן קטין עשה עשר שנים עשר דד לכיור, שלא היו בו אלא שניים; אף הוא עשה מוכני לכיור,
שלא יהו מימיו נפסלין בלינה.

Ben Katin made twelve spouts for the kiyor, for it formerly only had two; he also made a machine (muchni) for the kiyor so that its water should not become unfit by remaining overnight. (Yoma 3:10)[55]

The Twelve Spouts of the Kiyor

Does it not seem strange that a vessel commanded by Hashem to be built would be constructed in a manner that would later require improvement and enhancements? Why wasn't the *Kiyor* originally built

---

54   See *Maseches Kerisus* 6a.
55   See the *Bartenura* commentary to this Mishnah, explaining in greater detail the reason for the twelve-spout enhancement and the need for the pulley system.

with twelve spouts so that all the *Kohanim* on shift would be able to wash and sanctify themselves simultaneously? Additionally, if the water in the *Kiyor* was susceptible to *linah*,[56] would it not have been more sensible to build the special mechanism as part of the original design and thus avoid disgracing one of the *Klei HaMikdash* by emptying the water from the *Kiyor* each morning when the water was unfit to use because of its overnight status?

> *The Kiyor was purposely made with imperfections and flaws — but so was the sinner who came to the Beis HaMikdash with imperfections and missing parts, in need of a "redesign" to function better and lead a more spiritually positive life.*

Perhaps we can understand this *Mishnah* with greater insight according to the *Targum Yonason* above. The *Kiyor*, as explained, symbolized *teshuvah* and the act of repairing one's ways. It was to clean away the sin and allow for a new start. It is for this very reason that the *Kiyor* was built so that it needed to be improved and enhanced. It was purposely made with imperfections and flaws — but so was the sinner who came to the Beis HaMikdash with imperfections and missing parts, in need of a "redesign" to function better and lead a more spiritually positive life.

This is the message of the *Kiyor* to those steeped in sin. The *Kiyor* was a holy vessel used daily in the *Mishkan*, yet it too was not perfect — and still and all, it was privileged to be in a holy environment, and was eventually rebuilt to serve in perfection.

---

56   Once sacrificial objects are placed in a *kli shareis* (sanctified vessel) they must be offered or used before the next morning. If they are left overnight they become disqualified due to remaining overnight. Since the *Kiyor* (washbasin for the Kohanim) was a *kli shareis*, any water remaining in the *Kiyor* overnight was subject to this disqualification of *linah* and could no longer be used. Ben Katin made a wheel with which to lower the *Kiyor*. Rashi explains that with this pulley they would lower the *Kiyor* each night underground and this prevented the water from becoming *pasul*, as something which is attached to the ground is not susceptible to the laws of *linah* (*Yoma* 37a).

Vayakhel

וַיֹּאמֶר מֹשֶׁה אֶל בְּנֵי יִשְׂרָאֵל רְאוּ קָרָא ה' בְּשֵׁם בְּצַלְאֵל בֶּן אוּרִי בֶן חוּר לְמַטֵּה יְהוּדָה: וַיְמַלֵּא אֹתוֹ רוּחַ אֱלֹקִים בְּחָכְמָה בִּתְבוּנָה וּבְדַעַת וּבְכָל מְלָאכָה:

Moshe said to the B'nei Yisrael, "See, Hashem has called by
name Betzalel, the son of Uri, the son of Chur, of the tribe
of Yehudah. He has imbued him with the spirit of G-d, with
wisdom, with insight, and with knowledge, and with [talent
for] all manner of craftsmanship." (Shemos 35:30–31)

Moshe commands B'nei Yisrael to "see" that Hashem has appointed Betzalel to construct the Mishkan, and that He has imbued him with great talent to carry out this monumental task.

Rav Moshe Feinstein, *zt"l*, in his *Darash Moshe*, asks what message does the Torah wish to convey to us with the word "see"? What in particular were B'nei Yisrael supposed to see? When the Torah describes Aharon's appointment as *Kohen Gadol*, no such wording was used. What, then, is the specific lesson to be learned from this *pasuk*? Rav Moshe writes:

לכאורה לא מובן איך רואים בנ"א זה, מ"ש מבחירת אהרן שלא נאמר זה? ונראה משום שהי"ת שנתן להאדם איזה כח צריך לידע שניתן לו רק כדי שיעשה בכח זה רצון הי"ת לצורך ישראל ולצורך כבוד שמים, ואף שלא נגזר עליו שיהיה מוכרח לעשות, משום שזה

תלוי בבחירה, אבל בכל אופן נברא לזה ויתבעו ממנו חשבון על מה שלא עשה כפי כוחו
שניתן לו. וממילא הוא כפשוטו שהרי אתם רואים בעיניכם כי ה' קרא בשם את בצלאל
שיעשה המשכן, דהרי מלא אותו ה' כל הדברים שצריך לזה, ומזה ידעינן שכל אדם בין
שניתן לו חכמה בין שניתן לו גבורה בין שפע ברכה בכסף ובנכסים הוא רק כדי לעשות
רצון ה', וכשרואים הרבה בנ"א שניתן להם חכמה וגבורה וכספים ואין עושים רצון הי"ת,
הוא משום שהבחירה בידם ובחרו ברע, ויתבעו מהם חשבון על הכספים שניתן לו מה
עשה בהם וכן החכם מה עשה בחכמתו אם למד ולימד.

It is not clear how people are supposed to see that Betzalel was appointed, and how is this different than when Aharon was appointed and the Torah did not say that B'nei Yisrael should see that?

The explanation appears to be that when Hashem gives a person a talent or strength, he must know that it was given to him only so that he use it to fulfill Hashem's Will on behalf of the B'nei Yisrael and Hashem's Honor. True, it was not decreed that he must necessarily do so, because ultimately, it is up to his Free Choice — but in any event, the person was born for this purpose, and he will have to make an accounting for what he did not do in accordance with the abilities he was given. As such, the pasuk is to be understood straightforwardly: "You (B'nei Yisrael), look and see clearly with your own eyes that Hashem has chosen Betzalel to fashion the Mishkan — for Hashem filled him with all the abilities and talents needed for this mission."

And from this we know that any person with wisdom, or great might, or great wealth — the purpose is always so that he use it to fulfill Hashem's will. And when we see many people who were given wisdom, might or wealth, and yet do not fulfill Hashem's will, it is because the choice was left up to them — and they chose evil. They will be called to task for the wealth that they were given, and will be challenged to show what they did with it; similarly, those who were given wisdom will have to show whether they studied and taught others. (Darash Moshe)

Using Our G-d-Given Talents

Rav Moshe answers by explaining an important concept about our G-d-given talents and unique personalities. Moshe Rabbeinu was telling B'nei Yisrael, "Look at the talent and wisdom which Betzalel was given." Betzalel was selected with the task of constructing the Mishkan and with it he was handed the tools or talents to carry out his mission. Rav Moshe continues that the *pasuk* is a directive to us all about the various aptitudes and talents with which we are born. We have a choice: Will we use these gifts to their fullest and direct our energies toward spiritual endeavors? Or will we waste them on foolishness and squander the privileges and opportunities we have been given? Some of us are granted great wealth, a brilliant mind, or the ability to influence people positively. Hashem leaves us with the free will to choose how we will utilize these talents and gifts throughout our lives — and He will eventually hold us accountable if we failed to use them appropriately.

Rashi, on the above *pasuk* adds the following:

חור: בנה של מרים היה.

Chur — He was Miriam's son.

Why is this piece of family lineage important at this point?

Rav Shabsi ben Yosef, author of the *Sifsei Chachamim* commentary on Rashi, says that Rashi was answering this question: Why is Betzalel mentioned here as having descended both from Uri and Uri's father Chur? Would it not have been sufficient to mention only that he is the son of Uri? He explains that Chur was the son of Miriam who was a *neviah*, prophetess, and therefore the Torah emphasizes that she merited a great and holy grandchild like Betzalel.

דקשה לרש"י למה לא יחסו אלא עד חור או לא היה לו לומר אלא בצלאל בן אורי למטה
יהודה. ומתרץ ואמר חור בנה של מרים היה שהיתה נביאה לכך זכה לכל זה.

Rashi was bothered with why the pasuk didn't provide the lineage [of Betzalel] up until Chur, or just say Betzalel ben Uri of the tribe of Yehudah. And he [Rashi] answers that Chur was the son of Miriam who was a prophetess and therefore merited all this [that her grandchild Betzalel was entrusted with building the Mishkan]. (Sifsei Chachamim, Shemos 35:30)

Lineage versus G-dly Spirit

Perhaps, however, we can provide an alternative answer to Rashi's question. Moshe intended to teach the B'nei Yisrael to "רְאוּ — look" at Betzalel and appreciate that although his lineage is impressive and notable — his grandfather was Chur and his great-grandmother was

Miriam HaNeviah — this alone did not make him eligible to build the Mishkan. Regardless of his lineage, he was chosen only because וַיְמַלֵּא אֹתוֹ רוּחַ אֱלֹקִים בְּחָכְמָה בִּתְבוּנָה וּבְדַעַת וּבְכָל מְלָאכָה, Hashem instilled within him a G-dly spirit, with wisdom and understanding[57] — and for this reason alone he was successful and effective in his task of erecting a *Mishkan*.

Putting aside each person's origins and their family pedigree, we must recognize that our *neshamos* are G-dly and holy, made by Hashem, with the ability to accomplish and attain great heights of holiness and purity. Whether or not we originate from famous ancestry, our chances of being successful are available to the degree that Hashem intends for us to be, as He has infused each of us with the requisite faculties needed to achieve our goals. Our pureness and G-dliness are hidden away and protected in the depth of our *neshamos*, and we need to dig deep to reveal these hidden tools and utilize them to our advantage as we navigate *Olam HaZeh*. The *pasuk* tells us "*re'u*," look deeply into yourselves and perceive the hidden treasures you were given.

Look deeply into yourselves and perceive the hidden treasures you were given.

The great Italian sculptor and painter Michelangelo is quoted as saying, "Every block of stone has a statue inside it, and it is the task of the sculptor to discover it." Let us put our past and family roots aside and discover the richness and splendor of our *neshamos* by chiseling away at the thick grime of the *guf* and negativity with which our surroundings have influenced us. Let us not place excessive value on externals; let us remember that we were plucked from beneath the *Kisei HaKavod*, the Heavenly Throne, before arriving in this world.

---

57   *Shemos* 35:30.

Pekudei

וַיָּבִיאוּ אֶת הַמִּשְׁכָּן אֶל מֹשֶׁה אֶת הָאֹהֶל וְאֶת כָּל כֵּלָיו קְרָסָיו קְרָשָׁיו
בְּרִיחָיו וְעַמֻּדָיו וַאֲדָנָיו:

*And they brought the Mishkan to Moshe: the tent
and all its furnishings, its clasps, its planks, its bars,
its pillars, and its sockets. (Shemos 39:33)*

Rashi explains why they brought the *Mishkan* to Moshe and what his
role was in erecting it.

ויביאו את המשכן וגו': שלא היו יכולין להקימו, ולפי שלא עשה משה שום מלאכה במ־
שכן, הניח לו הקדוש ברוך הוא הקמתו, שלא היה יכול להקימו שום אדם מחמת כובד
הקרשים, שאין כח באדם לזקפן, ומשה העמידו. אמר משה לפני הקדוש ברוך הוא איך
אפשר הקמתו על ידי אדם, אמר לו עסוק אתה בידך נראה כמקימו, והוא נזקף וקם מאליו,
וזהו שנאמר (שמות מ יז) הוקם המשכן, הוקם מאליו.

*Now they brought the Mishkan to Moshe, etc. — Because they could not erect
it. Since Moshe had done no work in the Mishkan, Hashem left for him the task
of erecting it, since no human being could erect it [by himself] because of the
heaviness of the planks; and no human was strong enough to put them up, but
Moshe [was able to] put it up. Moshe said before Hashem, "How is it possible
for a human being to build it?" Hashem replied, "Work with your hands." Moshe
appeared to be erecting it, and it arose by itself. This is [the meaning of] what it
says: "the Mishkan was set up" (Shemos 40:17) — it was set up by itself.*

123

Who's Running the Show?

Rashi cites the *Midrash Tanchuma* that teaches us that Hashem told Moshe to make it appear as if he was putting the planks into the sockets and the Mishkan then arose by itself and fell into place. This, says Rashi, is what the *pasuk* means later when it says, "the Mishkan was set up,"[58] in the passive form — for no human could have actually done it himself.

This Rashi serves as a reminder that, in truth, even the situations that don't require great strength, it is only because of Hashem's intervention that we are able to succeed at anything. As the Gemara in *Maseches Chullin* teaches:

ואמר ר' חנינא אין אדם נוקף אצבעו מלמטה, אלא אם כן מכריזין עליו מלמעלה.

A person does not lift a finger down here (in this world) unless it is announced up above first. (Masesches Chullin 7b)

Rashi teaches us that Moshe was told to make it seem *as if* he was building the *Mishkan*, and then it would be set up on its own. This is true in general: Our actions are merely at the level of "going through the motions," but in truth, we aren't really capable of doing much on our own without Hashem's constant assistance and support.

Work...It Will Be Done

The *pasuk* in *Parashas Vayakhel* says:

שֵׁשֶׁת יָמִים תֵּעָשֶׂה מְלָאכָה וּבַיּוֹם הַשְּׁבִיעִי יִהְיֶה לָכֶם קֹדֶשׁ שַׁבַּת שַׁבָּתוֹן לַה' כָּל הָעֹשֶׂה בוֹ מְלָאכָה יוּמָת.

Six days work shall be done, but on the seventh day you shall have sanctity, a day of complete rest to Hashem; whoever performs work [on this day] shall be put to death. (Shemos 35:2)

Many of the *meforshim* comment on the Torah's use of the passive form of תֵּעָשֶׂה,[59] as opposed to תַּעֲשֶׂה,[60] which is the active form and would

---

58   40:17.
59   Will be done.
60   You will do.

be translated as *should be done*. Perhaps here too the Torah describes working to earn a livelihood in the passive form instead of the active form — תֵּעָשֶׂה — similar to the idea above with regard to the *Mishkan*: The Torah is telling us to go through the motions of working — but ultimately Hashem is providing for us. We too need to recognize our work and toil as a simple token performance, but not to think that we are actually capable of anything on our own.[61]

This poignant and beautiful parable of the *Dubno Maggid*[62] highlights the importance of recognizing Hashem's role in every area of our lives:

A poor man was walking on his way with a satchel over his shoulder. The route was long and the load was heavy and the poor man trudged along, barely making any progress. Suddenly, a wealthy merchant passed by in a carriage hitched to powerful horses. When the wealthy man noticed the poor man trudging along the road, he ordered his driver to stop the carriage and invited the poor peddler to board the carriage so that they could travel together to their destination. The poor man, thrilled by the invitation, climbed into the carriage and took a seat. The carriage took off again at a fast clip.

Sometime later, the wealthy man noticed that the poor man was still carrying his satchel over his shoulder. "Why don't you put your bag down?" the rich man asked. "Why are you still holding it like that?"

"Oh, it's enough that you're taking me," said the poor man. "How can I impose upon you to take my heavy bundle as well?"

"Fool!" the wealthy man chuckled. "It is the wagon that is carrying both you and your bundle!"

---

61 Perhaps this is also another reason the commandment of working six days (and resting on the seventh, *Shabbos*) and building the *Mishkan* are written in proximity to each other; because of their shared common theme.

62 *Diamonds from the Dubno Maggid*, Rabbi Yisrael Yosef Bronstein, Israel Bookshop Publications.

Worrying in Vain

It is perplexing to think that many of us go to sleep each night and don't think twice about how we will awake the next morning, whether we'll make it home alive while traveling, or if we will choke while eating dinner. Yet, we worry to no end about earning a livelihood, whether we'll have enough money to pay our bills, and whether our savings will carry us through retirement. We agonize and torment ourselves, constantly devising new ideas and strategies to earn more, looking for the highest return on investment, and planning our financial future to a point where we seek to mitigate any potential risk. In truth, just as we subconsciously rely on Hashem to help us arrive at our destination, swallow our food safely, and miraculously wake up each morning, we must also rely on Him to provide for us monetarily, now and in the future. After all, do we really think that by making sure to carry our sack of *parnasah* it will lighten Hashem's load? Hashem is already taking care of every minute detail of our lives, most of which we give no thought to or are not even aware of, such that providing for our *parnasah* is certainly no extra burden upon Him!

Just as we subconsciously rely on Hashem to help us arrive at our destination, swallow our food safely, and miraculously wake up each morning, we must also rely on Him to provide for us monetarily.

Let us remind ourselves of David HaMelech's promising words:

וְיִבְטְחוּ בְךָ יוֹדְעֵי שְׁמֶךָ כִּי לֹא עָזַבְתָּ דֹרְשֶׁיךָ ה'.

And they will trust in You, those who know Your Name, for You have not forsaken those who seek You, Hashem. (Tehillim 9:11)

Vayikra

Vayikra

דַּבֵּר אֶל בְּנֵי יִשְׂרָאֵל וְאָמַרְתָּ אֲלֵהֶם אָדָם כִּי יַקְרִיב מִכֶּם קָרְבָּן לַה' מִן הַבְּהֵמָה מִן הַבָּקָר וּמִן הַצֹּאן תַּקְרִיבוּ אֶת קָרְבַּנְכֶם:

Speak to B'nei Yisrael and say to them: When a man from [among] you brings a sacrifice to Hashem, from animals, from cattle or from the flock shall they bring their sacrifices. (Vayikra 1:2)

אדם כי יקריב מכם: כשיקריב, בקרבנות נדבה דבר הענין.

When a man from [among] you brings a sacrifice — *When he brings; [the Torah is not dealing here with an obligatory sacrifice, in which case it would have said, "a man shall bring;" rather,] the Torah is speaking here of voluntary sacrifices. (Rashi)*

The *pasuk* begins in the singular form: When *a man* from among you brings a korban, and concludes in the plural form, shall *they* bring their korban. Why did the Torah phrase the *pasuk* in this manner and not maintain grammatical consistency? The *Kli Yakar*, Rav Shlomo Ephraim Luntschitz, asks this question and makes the following observation:

אדם כי יקריב מכם קרבן לה'. התחיל בלשון יחיד וסיים בלשון רבים תקריבו קרבנכם, ומה שפירש"י מלמד שב' מתנדבים עולה בשותפות אינו מספיק ליישב המקרא לחברו מראשו לסופו כי לא ידענו היכן הפסיק הענין. ונ"ל שרצה להזהיר כל מקריבי קרבן לה'

שלא יכשלו בב' דברים אשר בהם נכשלו קין והבל שהיו ראשונים בהקרבת קרבן, כי קין
נכשל במה שהביא מן הפחות והגרוע והוא זרע פשתן והחטאים בנפשותם צריכין להביא
נפש הבהמה תמורת נפשם ובדוחק התיר הקב"ה לעני להביא מנחה שאין בה נפש ומעלה
עליו כאילו הקריב נפשו כמו שפירש"י על פסוק ונפש כי תקריב מנחה (ב:א) והבל אע"פ
שהביא מבכורות צאנו מ"מ לא טוב עשה שלא נתעורר אל הקרבן מעצמו ולא נזדרז למ־
צוה זו מעצמו, רק אחר שראה שהקריב קין קרבן אז נתקנא בו והבל הביא גם הוא להשוות
עצמו אליו כמבואר למעלה פר' בראשית.

ע"כ אמר אדם כי יקריב מכם לשון יחיד, לומר לך שהמקריב יהיה כאדה"ר בקרבנו שהיה
יחידי בעולם, וכשם שמזה הצד היה ניצול מן הגזל שהיה יחידי והיה הכל שלו, כך מזה הצד
היה ניצול מן הדבר שנכשל בו הבל כי מצד שהיה יחידי בעולם ודאי נתעורר אל הקרבן
מעצמו ולא מצד שראה אחרים עושין, ועל זה אמר אדם כשיהיה כאדה"ר כי יקריב מכם
שתהיה ההקרבה מכם ולא מזולתכם כי מכם ובכם יבא ההתעוררות אל המקריב, זהו קרבן
לה' כי ודאי אין כוונתו כ"א לשם ה' לאפוקי מי שאינו נתעורר מעצמו זהו אינו מכם ואינו
קרבן לה'. אינו מכם, שהרי ההתעוררות בא לו מאחרים ולא מכם ממקריב הקרבן עצמו,
ואינו קרבן לה', כי כל מה שהוא קנאת איש מרעהו אינו עושה כי אם להתהדר עצמו בפני
הבריות ונמצא שאינו קרבן לשם ה' כ"א לשם הבריות. וזה"ש (שבת כח:) שור שהקריב
אדה"ר קרן אחת היה לו במצחו לכך נזדמן לו שור אחת כי היה דומה כי היה דומה אל האדם
שהיה קרן א' ר"ל שהיה יחידי בעולם ולא גזל משום אדם, ולא נתעורר משום אדם, כ"א
מעצמו דהיינו מכם ע"כ עלה קרבנו לרצון נמצא שקרבן לה' הפסיק העניין. ואח"כ אמר
מן הבהמה וגו' להוציא זרע פשתן אלא שהביא כהבל יעשה פשתן שהביא מבכורות צאנו. ומה שאמר
תקריבו קרבנכם היינו מחלביהן החלק המובחר שאדם בוחר לעצמו הנקרא קרבנכם הקריב
הקריב לגבוה ונקט קרבנכם לשון רבים כפירש"י לומר שב' מקריבין בהמה.

Why does the pasuk start out in singular and end in plural? Rashi's explanation — that two people may bring an olah offering in partnership — does not suffice to explain the entire pasuk from beginning to end and how it must be punctuated. It appears to me that the Torah wishes to warn all those who bring sacrifices to Hashem not to make the two grave errors made by Kayin and Hevel — the first to ever bring sacrifices.[63] *Kayin's failure was in bringing from the lowest quality, namely, flaxseed, whereas those who sin with their souls must bring a live animal — a soul in exchange for their own. In fact, Hashem barely permitted a poor person to bring a minchah sacrifice without an animal component, considering it as if he had sacrificed his soul, as Rashi explains on the pasuk, "A soul who brings a minchah offering..." (Vayikra 2:1)*

And Hevel, though he brought a sacrifice from the first-borns of his sheep, nonetheless did not act correctly in not realizing on his own that he should do

---

63   The *Kli Yakar* notes below that Adam also brought sacrifices; perhaps he did so after Kayin and Hevel.

this mitzvah. Instead, he offered the sacrifice only after he saw Kayin bring his; this aroused his jealousy of Kayin, and so he brought a sacrifice in order to match Kayin, as explained above in Parashas Bereishis.

This is why the Torah said here "A man who offers" in singular, teaching that one who brings a sacrifice must be like Adam in this regard: Just as Adam was alone in the world and was thus saved from the sin of stealing — for he was alone, and everything was his — similarly he was also saved from the sin of jealousy of which Hevel was guilty. For since Adam was alone in the world, his desire to bring a sacrifice certainly came from within himself, and not because he saw others doing so. For this the Torah says, "A man — using the Hebrew word, 'Adam' — who offers" — that is, when a man is like Adam in bringing a sacrifice "from amongst you" — and the sacrifice is from "you" and not because of someone else; the arousal to do so should be "from amongst you" — it will then truly be "a sacrifice to Hashem," for then his intention is certainly exclusively for G-d. This is in contrast with one who is aroused to do so from without: such a sacrifice is not "from amongst you" and is not "a sacrifice to Hashem," as the source is not from you but from others. Everything done from jealousy is done only to aggrandize the doer before other people; such a sacrifice is not for Hashem, but rather for others...

And the Torah then continues with "you [plural] shall bring your sacrifice" — you shall bring the fats, the choicest parts of the animals. That is, that which you would choose for yourself is called "your sacrifice" — and it is that which you should offer to Hashem as a sacrifice. And why is the word "sacrifices" in plural? — As Rashi explained, it teaches that two people can bring one sacrifice in partnership.

With Pure Intentions

The *Kli Yakar* begins by explaining that the Torah is warning the one bringing the *korban* not to falter in two areas which were prevalent with Kayin and Hevel, pioneers in bringing sacrifices to Hashem. Kayin brought a *korban* of flax, a poor choice, being from the lowest grade; but since a sacrifice serves in place of the sinner — the animal is being killed in his stead — it should have been from an animal with a life force, a soul. Hevel too, although he selected a *korban* from his cattle, brought his sacrifice only after Kayin brought one. His motivation was one of jealousy.

The *pasuk* in *Bereishis* (4:4) tells us: *V'Hevel heivee gam hu mibechoros tzono*, And Hevel brought, he as well, from the first-born of his flock...The words *he as well* teach that his act was in reaction to that which Kayin had done. Therefore, explains the *Kli Yakar*, our *pasuk* begins in the singular form to teach us that just like Adam surely didn't bring a *korban* from a stolen source — as there was no one to steal from — so too, he did not bring a sacrifice out of envy, as Hevel did, for there was no one else around to be envious of. Adam brought his *korban* on his own and sincerely, without duplicating someone else's actions. The *pasuk* is teaching us to be like Adam and bring the *korban* "from you," from your own desire and interest, and not with ulterior motives. Then, continues the *pasuk*, it will be a true sacrifice unto G-d, because your true intentions are to get closer to Hashem and not just to exceed or outdo others.

The *pasuk* continues with *min habeheimah*, from the animals, making it clear that the choice sacrifice is an animal — like that which Hevel brought — and not items such as flax and plants, which do not serve as a parallel for the sinner's soul. The *pasuk* then concludes with *korbanchem*, your sacrifice, in the plural form — as this is symbolic of the choicest and finest grade of cattle, worthy of and appropriate for a sacrifice to Hashem.

Torah, Honey, and Chametz

Later on in the *parashah*, we find that the Torah prohibits the bringing of *chametz* and honey when offering a *korban minchah* (meal offering):

כָּל הַמִּנְחָה אֲשֶׁר תַּקְרִיבוּ לַה' לֹא תֵעָשֶׂה חָמֵץ כִּי כָל שְׂאֹר וְכָל דְּבַשׁ לֹא תַקְטִירוּ מִמֶּנּוּ אִשֶּׁה לַה': קָרְבַּן רֵאשִׁית תַּקְרִיבוּ אֹתָם לַה' וְאֶל הַמִּזְבֵּחַ לֹא יַעֲלוּ לְרֵיחַ נִיחֹחַ.

No meal offering that you sacrifice to Hashem shall be made [out of anything] leavened. For you shall not cause to [go up in] smoke any leavening or any honey, [as] a fire offering to Hashem; [however,] you shall bring them as a first [fruit] offering to Hashem; nevertheless, they shall not go up on the mizbei'ach as a pleasing fragrance to Hashem. (Vayikra 2:11–12)

קרבן ראשית תקריבו: מה יש לך להביא מן השאור ומן הדבש קרבן ראשית שתי הלחם של עצרת הבאים מן השאור שנאמר (ויק' כג יז) חמץ תאפינה, ובכורים מן הדבש, כמו בכורי תאנים ותמרים.

You shall bring them as a first [fruit] offering — What can you bring from
leaven and honey? A first [fruit] offering, namely: a) the Two Loaves [of
bread] brought on Shavuos, which come from leaven, as it is said: "they shall
be baked leavened" (Vayikra 23:17), and b) the First Fruits which [contain]
honey, such as the first fruits of figs and dates. (Rashi)

Again, the *Kli Yakar* enlightens us with a deeper understanding of
the *pasuk*:

כי כל שאור וכל דבש לא תקטירו וגו', קרבן ראשית תקריבו אותם לה' ואל המזבח לא
יעלו לריח ניחוח. פירש"י שתי הלחם של עצרת באים מן השאור וביכורים מן הדבש.
ביאור הדברים כי כל אדם יש לו תאוה לכל חמדות העה"ז המכונים בדבש כי כמו
שהדבש מתוק לחיך ורבויו מזיק כך כל חמדות העה"ז הם הכרחיים ורבויים מזיק, וזאת
העצה היעוצה שישתמש האדם במוכרחות והמותר יחרים. והשאור הוא דוגמא אל
היצר הרע כמ"ש ר' אלכסנדרי בתפלתו (ברכות יז.) רצוננו לעשות רצונך אלא ששאור
שבעיסה מעכב, וב' אלו הכרחיים למציאות האדם כ"א לא ישתמש בצרכיו ההכרחיים
המכונים בדבש ימות ולא יחיה ולא יהיו אבריו חזקים אף בריאים להטריח במצות ה',
ואלמלא היצר הרע לא היה האדם נושא אשה ולא בונה בית ונמצא העולם חרב. וב' אלו
קודמים בזמן אל עסק התורה והמצות כי אם לא יאכל תחילה קמח אין תורה, אבל עסק
התורה ראשית במחשבה ובמעלה לפי שהשאור והדבש שהזכרנו אין בהם שלימות
מצד עצמם לעלות לריח ניחוח לה' אך שהם ראשית והתחלה אל האדם שעל ידם הוא
יכול לבא לידי שלימות הנפש.
על כן נאמר כל שאור וכל דבש לא תקטירו ממנו אשה לה'. כי מצד עצמם אין בהם שום
צד שלימות אשר יעלה לריח ניחוח לה' אך קרבן ראשית תקריבו אותם, כדי להורות שהם
ראשית והתחלה אל האדם להביאו לידי השלימות האמיתי אשר א"א להשיגו בלעדם,
ומזה הטעם אין מקריבין מהם כ"א השאור לקרבן ראשית ביום מ"ת כי התורה כמו תבלין
אל היצר הרע והיו ב' הלחם של עצרת מן החמץ כי התורה שנתנה בו רפאות תהא לשריך,
והביכורים באים מן הדבש כי בזמן שיתן אל ה' ראשית פרי אדמתו מכל מאכל מאכל אשר
יאכל, אז יאכל כל ימיו חולין שנעשו על טהרת הקודש כי זה הוראה שאכילתו על כוונה זו
שהשלימות האמיתי הוא ראשון אצלו במחשבה. וכן טעם הביכורים הוא לשבר תאותו
כמו שיתבאר בע"ה בפר' כי תבא.

*Rashi explains that the offering of Two Loaves on Shavuos is brought from
leaven, and first-fruits are brought from honey. The explanation is this:*

*Every person feels a passion for the pleasures of the world. These are
referred to as "honey," for honey is sweet to the palate, yet too much
of it is harmful — as is true for all pleasures, which on the one hand
are necessary, but their over-abundance brings harm. We are therefore
advised to use them only to the necessary degree, and no more. Leaven,*

on the other hand, stands for the Evil Inclination, as Rav Alexandri wrote in his prayer (Berachos 17a): "We desire to do Your will, but the 'leaven in the dough' is blocking us." Both honey and leaven are required for our existence, because one who does not fill his minimal needs with "honey," will die and not live, that is, his limbs will not be strong enough to perform G-d's commands; and if he did not have an Evil Inclination, he would not get married or build a home, leading to the destruction of the world. These two (honey and leaven) must precede, chronologically, even the study of Torah and the performance of mitzvos, for if one does not eat, he will not have Torah. But in terms of the Divine Plan and importance, the study of Torah precedes them — because the leaven and honey have no completeness in and of themselves; they cannot be offered on the Altar "for a pleasing fragrance to Hashem" — even though they are first in terms of man's physical needs and help him reach spiritual completion.

This is why the Torah tells us not to include leaven or honey in our incense offering to Hashem: They have no inherent complete value that can rise up as a pleasing fragrance to Him. However, as the pasuk states, "you may bring them as a first offering to Hashem," showing that they are first for man's physical needs; without them, he cannot reach true completion.

This is why leaven is brought as a first offering specifically on Shavuos, the day of the Giving of the Torah — because the Torah is like a "sweetener" for the Evil Inclination (Bava Basra 16a), and the "First" offering on Shavuos is from leaven, because the Torah has the ability to cure ("It shall be healing for your navel," Mishlei 3:8). And the first-fruits are offered from the honey, because when one brings to Hashem the first of every food that grows from his land, it means that he lives his life eating "non-sacred food that was prepared in sanctity" — for this teaches that he should eat knowing that "true completion" is first in his thoughts.

> *The prerequisite for an individual to develop his relationship with Hashem may be by utilizing the honey and chametz.*

Similarly, the reason for the first-fruits is to break his lust, as we will explain, please G-d, in Parashas Ki Savo.

The *Kli Yakar* explains that all people have materialistic desires as well as materialistic needs. Too much of either one can be harmful. Even that which is needed serves us well, but if taken in excess, it harms our spiritual development. *Chametz* is symbolic of the *yetzer hara*,[64] which is also a necessity for the world's existence; without it, no one would marry and build a family. It is for this reason, then, that the Torah refers to these two offerings, the *bikkurim* (first-fruits) and *Shtei Halechem* (Two Loaves), with the word *reishis*, "the first"; to teach us that the prerequisite for an individual to develop his relationship with Hashem may be by utilizing the honey and *chametz*. It is also these offerings in particular that honey and *chametz* were included because the *Shtei HaLechem* were brought on Shavuos — the *Yom Tov* on which we celebrate the Giving of the Torah — and the message was that material goods may precede the Torah, allowing the Torah itself to be more accessible and palatable to man. The *bikkurim* incorporated dates (honey), since it represented that first in his thoughts while taking part in materialistic pursuits was its purpose — to be able to acquire spiritual greatness. With regards to other offerings these two items were excluded as they had no inherent relevance after the *reishis*, "the first," and can possibly cause harm and hinder future spiritual development.

When first beginning our journey in our *avodas Hashem*, service of G-d, surely these additional ingredients are needed to sweeten the deal and help motivate us. Afterwards, however, we need to separate and detach ourselves from them, and they are no longer necessary in our efforts to build a closer relationship with Hashem. This is represented by the fact that the other *korbanos* are forbidden to be brought with honey and *chametz*.

Commonality of Bikkurim and Shtei HaLechem Offerings

Perhaps another reason can be offered as to why *bikkurim* and *Shtei HaLechem* are the exceptions to the rule and may be brought with honey and leaven. The *Kli Yakar* that we quoted above explained that the Torah's choice of words was designed to teach us the importance of bringing a *korban* with pure intentions and self-motivation. Why then should there be an exception for the *bikkurim* and *Shtei HaLechem*, which

---

64   See *Maseches Berachos* 17a.

are brought with ingredients symbolic of anything but pure intention and true willingness to obtain a closer relationship with Hashem?

Perhaps the common denominator between these two offerings is that the whole *tzibbur* was equal in bringing them:

- The *Bikkurim* were each individual's first fruits, and
- The *Shtei HaLechem* were brought on Shavuos, witnessed by all those being *oleh regel*, that is, the pilgrims who came to Yerushalayim.

All of B'nei Yisrael were equal and there wasn't any room for individual tainted intentions in their offerings. As such, special dispensations could be made to allow for honey and *chametz*. In contrast, the *pasuk* of *adam ki yakriv mikem*, a man among you who brings, deals with a *korban nedavah*, a private and voluntary sacrifice, and there the temptation to stand out and bring a *korban* for reasons other than for its true purpose may be motivated. Therefore, honey and *chametz* representing character flaws and the *yetzer hara* were forbidden ingredients.

Let us appreciate our self-worth and recognize our own strengths, without the need to be motivated by those around us and driven to act falsely in a *shelo lishmah* manner, for impure motives.

Tzav

וּכְלִי חֶרֶשׂ אֲשֶׁר תְּבֻשַּׁל בּוֹ יִשָּׁבֵר וְאִם בִּכְלִי נְחֹשֶׁת בֻּשָּׁלָה
וּמֹרַק וְשֻׁטַּף בַּמָּיִם:

An earthenware vessel in which it [the sin-offering]
is cooked shall be broken, but if it is cooked in a copper vessel,
it shall be purged and rinsed with water.

(Vayikra 6:21)

Rashi explains:

ישבר: לפי שהבליעה שנבלעת בו נעשה נותר, והוא הדין לכל הקדשים:

Shall be broken — [Why? Because] that which was absorbed in the vessel
becomes nosar.[65] The same is true for all holy sacrifices.[66]

What Rashi means is that if the time for eating the sacrifice has
passed, even the flavor that was absorbed in the vessel is forbidden.
Since the absorbed flavor in an earthenware vessel cannot be removed
or made kosher, the vessel must be destroyed.

---

65   Sacrificial offerings which were not consumed within the designated time and thereby
      became invalid for consumption.
66   And not exclusive to the *chatas* sin-offering.

Rashi further states:

ומרק ושטף: לפלוט את בליעתו, אבל כלי חרס למדך הכתוב כאן שאינו יוצא מידי
דפיו לעולם.

Purged and rinsed — *To expel its absorption. [This is in the case of a metal vessel,] but regarding an earthenware vessel, we are taught here [by the requirement that it be broken] that it can never rid its walls [of the flavor].*

The Torah teaches us how to *kasher* (purge) the vessel that is used in the preparation for the *korban chatas*, sin-offering:

- If it was made of a metal material, the vessel can be *kashered*.
- But if made of earthenware, the vessel cannot be *kashered*, since it is impossible to purge the taste particles from a porous utensil. There is no way to make its use permissible again.

The Torah explains that after a day and a night, anything remaining of the *chatas* becomes *nosar*, forbidden leftover. Therefore, taste particles of the *chatas* absorbed in a metal vessel are *kashered* and this process will purge the leftover taste; but for the earthenware vessel, destroying it. This is the only solution; no method of *kashering* will succeed in expelling the taste absorbed in the walls of the utensil.

Purging Vessels and Sins

The *Kli Yakar*, Rav Shlomo Ephraim Luntschitz, asks why the Torah chose to teach the *halachah* requiring one to destroy an earthenware vessel specifically with regard to a sin-offering and not with other *korbanos*? After all, the law of *nosar* applies equally to other *korbanos*, as does the process of purging vessels of their absorbed taste.

וכלי חרס אשר תבושל בו ישבר וגו'. פירש"י והוא הדין לכל הקדשים, ומ"מ הדבר צריך
ביאור למה כתבה התורה דין זה דווקא גבי חטאת הבא לכפרה.

ועל צד הרמז קרוב לשמוע, שטהרת הכלים יש להם דמיון לטהרת החוטא המקריב
חטאת, כי כמו שהכלים יש מהם שבולעים הרבה מן האיסור ולא יוכל לצאת ע"י שטיפה
ואין להם תקנה כ"א בשבירה, ויש מהם שאינם בולעים הרבה מן האיסור ויש להם תקנה
בשטיפה, כך יש לך אדם חוטא שבולע הרבה מן האיסור וקשה לו לעזוב ההרגל ואין לו
תקנה כ"א בשבירת לבו כי הוא הכלי שנתבשל בו האיסור, ויש לך אדם שאינו בולע הרבה

ויש לו תקנה בכל דהו כדרך שארז"ל (ערכין טו:) מאי תקנתיה של מספר לה"ר אם ת"ח
הוא יעסוק בתורה שנאמר (משלי טו:ד) מרפא לשון עץ חיים. ואם עם הארץ הוא ישפיל
עצמו שנאמר (שם) וסלף בה שבר ברוח. ומן חטא לה"ר יוקח לכל חטאת ולכל עון שבזמן
שאין ב"ה קיים אין תקנה לעם הארץ כ"א בשבירת לבו שנתבשל בו החטא, ולת"ח
יש תקנה בכל חטא ע"י ת"ת, וחטא בני עלי יוכיח שאינו מתכפר בזבח ומנחה אבל מתכפר
הוא בת"ת (ר"ה יח)

ע"כ כתבה התורה דין הכלים אצל החטאת, לומר לך שבזמן שאין זבח ומנחה אז טהרת
החוטא כטהרת הכלים, כי כל עם הארץ נמשל לכלי חרס ואינו יוצא מידי דופיו כ"א בשבי-
רת לבו, וכל ת"ח יש לו דין כלי נחושת שיש לו תקנה ע"י מריקה ושטיפה מבית ומחוץ, כך
כל ת"ח יש לו תקנה ע"י התורה שנמשלה למים המטהרו מבית ומחוץ כי ע"י התורה יהיה
תוכו כברו כמ"ש מבית ומחוץ תצפנו (שמות כה.יא) כדרך שנתבאר שם בפר' תרומה, וזה
הדבר שאמרנו שכל אדם דומה לכלי מה.

"An earthenware vessel in which it is cooked shall be broken, etc." — Rashi explains that this refers [not only to sin-offerings, but] to all sacred meat. Why, then, did the Torah teach this law specifically regarding the sin-offering that comes to atone?

Using derech haremez, the method of allusion, we might say that the purification of utensils is similar to the purification of the sinner bringing a sin-offering: There are some utensils that absorb large amounts of the forbidden substance, in which case they cannot be purified by washing; they must be broken. However, others do not absorb much of the forbidden substance, and they can be purified by washing.

Similarly, there are people who sin and who take in much of the sin, in that it is hard for them to abandon their sinful ways to which they have grown accustomed. For such a person, there is no remedy other than breaking his heart — for that is the utensil in which the forbidden substance was "cooked."

There are also people who do not absorb so much of the forbidden behavior and can be easily remedied, as our Sages taught (Arachin 15b): "What is the remedy for one who speaks lashon hara? If he is a Torah scholar, he should engage in Torah, as is written, "A healing tongue is a tree of life" (Mishlei 15:4), and if he is an ignoramus, he should humble himself, as the same pasuk continues, "but if there is perverseness in it, it causes destruction by wind."

And from the sin of lashon hara we can derive a lesson for all sins, for when there is no Beis HaMikdash, we see that there is no remedy for the ignoramus other than humbling himself, that is, "breaking his heart" in which the sin was "cooked." For a Torah scholar, studying Torah will help him for every sin — and the sin of the sons of Eli the Kohen is proof, for it was not atoned for via sacrifices, but only via the study of Torah (Rosh Hashanah 18a).

This, then, is why the Torah taught this law of the utensils regarding the sin-of-fering, to tell you: When there is no opportunity for sacrifices, then the purification of the sinner is similar to that of utensils — as every ignoramus is likened to earthenware vessels and cannot be purged of his impurity other than by breaking his heart. Torah scholars, on the other hand, have the status of metal vessels, which can be purged via heating and rinsing, inside and out — for via the Torah, his inside will be like his outside [i.e., he will be sincere and not hypocritical], as is written, "Plate [the Ark] with gold inside and outside" (Shemos 25:11), as was explained there in Parashas Terumah. And this is what we said, that every person is likened to a certain utensil.

Our neshamos become so soiled and accustomed to sin that removing the stain can only be effected when we "break" our hearts that "cooked" the sin.

The *Kli Yakar* offers a beautiful and vital insight. He explains that when a sinner seeks forgiveness, the sin-offering arouses within him feelings of remorse, for he realizes that an animal is being put to death in place of himself. However, when *korbanos* cannot be offered,[67] the same concept still applies: The Torah tells us that the purification and repentance process is similar to the way in which we purge vessels of their impurities. Just as with vessels that absorb forbidden flavors, some are purged through *kashering*, while others need to be broken because of their impurities:

- The *tzaddik* or *talmid chacham* may sin, but he is similar to a metal vessel which can be *kashered* — for the sin isn't so heavily absorbed, nor does the sin stain his *neshamah* to a large degree. The *tzaddik* hasn't habituated himself to the sin and it can easily be cleansed.
- Other individuals however, fall into the category of the earthenware vessel which, when it absorbs, receives the taste deep in its walls; removing the sin becomes impossible. Our *neshamos* become so soiled[68] and accustomed to sin that removing the

---

67   Such as when the Beis HaMikdash hasn't yet been rebuilt.
68   See *Nefesh HaChaim, shaar* 1 *perek* 18, in which he discusses the *neshamah* element of the soul never being affected by sin because it is rooted in a higher world. The *neshamah* here is not meant in literal terms, but refers rather to the *ruach* element of the soul which can be affected and restored through *teshuvah*.

stain can only be effected when we "break" our hearts that "cooked" the sin and made it so much the norm to which our bodies became so accustomed.

This is why the Torah chose to teach us how to purge an impure vessel of its forbidden taste specifically regarding the sin-offering.

Kashering Our Souls

Perhaps we can interpret life's challenges and difficulties as a method by which Hashem seeks to *kasher* our souls[69] by breaking our hearts, thus helping us recognize and take an accounting of our sinful ways. It is easy to get caught up in sin while all is fine and well. When people suffer, however, it prompts a reckoning of their ways, and they are likely to look to improve and eliminate their unhealthy habits. The *kashering* process can be painful, because for some of us, our sinful behaviors are so deeply embedded. Purging the *neshamah* of these behaviors and sinful traits may require additional suffering as a means of rectifying an original sin. We may take comfort, however, knowing that we will then merit returning our souls to Hashem in the pristine condition it was given to us. Let us remind ourselves when the *yetzer hara* tempts us to sin that if we succumb to his temptation we will need to follow-up with the *kashering* process as the principle of *k'bolo kach polto*[70] dictates, the way in which it absorbed, is the way in which it must be purged.

To take this idea a step further, we can suggest a thought about *nosar*, the forbidden leftover.

Nobody Wants Leftovers

The definition of *nosar* is that which is left over past the time the sacrifice should have been eaten. It must then be burned. Hashem has placed us in this world so that we can use our bodies to serve Him — but many times, the *guf* (body) takes an alternate route and attaches itself to behaviors incompatible with our holy *neshamos*, souls. The *neshamos*

---

69   See *Mishnah Berurah* 222:4.
70   A basic principle with regards to *hagolas keilim*.

must be returned to Hashem in the pure state in which we received them. These behaviors are represented by *nosar* — the leftovers or foreign materials that don't belong with the *neshamah*; before leaving this world, they need to be burned and detached because of their incompatibility. This, then, is the lesson of the *pasuk*: We must break the harmful *middos* (traits) that attach to our *neshamos* during our lifetime, so that there are no leftovers to deal with when it is time to return our souls.

Shemini

וַיֹּאמֶר מֹשֶׁה אֶל אַהֲרֹן הוּא אֲשֶׁר דִּבֶּר ה' לֵאמֹר בִּקְרֹבַי אֶקָּדֵשׁ וְעַל פְּנֵי
כָל הָעָם אֶכָּבֵד וַיִּדֹּם אַהֲרֹן:

Moshe said to Aharon, "This is what Hashem spoke [when He said], 'I will be sanctified through those near to Me, and before all the people I will be glorified.'" And Aharon was silent. (Vayikra 10:3)

Rashi tells us:

הוא אשר דבר וגו': היכן דבר ונועדתי שמה לבני ישראל ונקדש בכבודי (שמות כט
מג). אל תקרי בכבודי אלא במכובדי. אמר לו משה לאהרן אהרן אחי יודע הייתי
שיתקדש הבית במיודעיו של מקום והייתי סבור או בי או בך, עכשיו רואה אני שהם
גדולים ממני וממך.

This is what Hashem spoke — *When did He speak this? [It was when He said,] "And I will meet with B'nei Yisrael, and [the Mishkan] will be sanctified through My glory (בִּכְבֹדִי)" (Shemos 29:43) — Do not read בִּכְבֹדִי, "through My glory," but rather, בִּמְכֻבָּדַי, "through My honorable ones." Moshe said to Aharon, "Aharon, my brother! I knew that this House was to be sanctified through the beloved ones of the Omnipresent, and I thought it would be either through me or through you. Now I see that they [Nadav and Avihu] were greater than me and you!"*

143

Rashi continues:

בקרבי: בבחירי.

With those near to Me — My chosen ones.

The Ramban adds:

וטעם וידום אהרן שהיה בוכה בקול ואז שתק.

And the reason Aharon was silent is because he was crying loudly, but then was quiet.

In the midst of one of the most joyous moments for B'nei Yisrael, while they were celebrating the inauguration of the Mishkan, tragedy struck and two sons of Aharon were taken away. The *meforshim* offer various reasons explaining Nadav and Avihu's misdeed in offering a strange fire to Hashem. The *pasuk* tells us of Moshe's words of comfort to his brother Aharon, that Hashem was referring to them when he said He will be sanctified through those nearest to Him and glorified before all the people. Moshe was communicating, as Rashi explains, that Nadav and Avihu were of a greater caliber than even Aharon and himself, since they were chosen as the vehicle for Hashem's sanctification and glory, for it was their act that led to Hashem demonstrating His greatness. Aharon is then comforted and remains silent.

Let's try and understand this on a deeper level.

Our Children's Secret Identity

If one were asked to describe their child, he would likely begin by describing the child's physical features, such as, "average height, skinny, brown hair, blue eyes." This would usually be followed by describing his personality as "fun, loving, always smiling, a great kid and a good heart." Surely, these characteristics are all correct, as they illustrate the child in terminology we humans use to describe people. The question is, however, is that where it ends? Does this really describe the true

Beneath their physical appearance and behavior is a neshamah, a soul, that has a deep history and a unique mission.

essence of our children? To think of them only in these terms may be leaving out their true essence and core identity.

In truth, beneath their physical appearance and behavior is a *neshamah*, a soul, that has a deep history and a unique mission — but one that can be very foreign to parents who have only viewed the child as the sum of his physical needs. This *neshamah* may have been that of a holy person in a previous life and has returned to rectify a specific *middah*. Perhaps the child was born into this family to help them accomplish their mission in life.

Let us contemplate parents surrounded by four, five, or six children. This means that much more holiness, purity, and unknown are found in their home, with each child holding an impenetrable secret about him or herself. In some ways, they are like strangers. We see only their physical aspects, and can only imagine the true nature of their holy *neshamos*. This thought can be overwhelming and humbling, as we may actually be in the company of people much greater than we are.

Now we must ask ourselves: If we would know the true nature of the *neshamos* underfoot in our home, would we expose them to certain environments which may offend the *neshamah*? Would we not be more cautious with the foods, both spiritual and physical, that we feed them? Would we not attempt to surround them with greater purity and holiness?

Children lying in bed at night and admired by their parents, have within them a holy *neshamah* entrusted to parents to care for its maintenance while it visits this world. Do we really know what their *neshamah* requires? After all, we provide for their physical needs, keeping them well nourished, giving them necessary medical care, and even providing a loving environment. Do we also put sufficient effort and thought into caring for their *neshamos*, ensuring that their spiritual needs are met? We would never allow a child to go hungry — it is instinctual to feed and nurture them — but our children's *neshamos* may be starving and neglected. Can we really consider ourselves good parents if we fail to care and provide an integral need where the *neshamah* is crying on deaf ears to be cared for? We must constantly check and double-check that we are investing our parenting efforts in both the physical and spiritual needs of the children Hashem has placed in our care.

I Can't Imagine

The following article entitled "I Can't Imagine"[71] depicts this point in a most poignant and moving way.

> I can't imagine the feelings of a father as he tries to shield his little boys. I can't imagine the terror of a child as he tries to crawl to save himself. I can't imagine a little girl in the grips of evil, facing a gun. I can't imagine the horror of a father as his little girl died in his arms. I can't imagine the pain of a father as he died along with his sons. And I can't imagine the grief of the parents who lost their children and grandchildren or the shattering wails of the mother and widow who lost so much.
>
> But I Can Imagine...
>
> A discussion in Heaven the Holy One had with a group of some very holy souls. "There is coming a time for My People that will be fraught with danger. They are beset by their enemies, yet they have not the merits to be redeemed and they have not yet repented. Are there any holy *neshamos* that are prepared to rescue their brethren?"
>
> "Yes," many answered at once, "but how will we save them?"
>
> "Your *neshamos* will return to the world below. Your life and death will be an atonement and will serve to inspire my People to repent. Some of you will die as infants, others with sickness. For some it will be shootings, and yet others will perish by enemies with bombs. Bombs that kill babies and parents, little boys and girls, school children and teachers, soldiers, and *chassanim* and *kallahs* too."

---

71   Written by L. Isaacs, appears on www.matzav.com.

"Do you still agree to save your brethren?" the Holy One asked.

"Yes," they answered.

Then the Holy One went to an even higher level, so very close to His Throne, and He asked, "Are there any *neshamos* here that are prepared to save their brethren in the world below?"

"Yes," some *neshamos* answered. "What do we need to do?"

"You are needed to be the parents and grandparents, brothers and sisters, husbands and wives and children of those who will die to sanctify My Name. You will need to bear the unspeakable pain of losing loved ones. Do you accept?"

"Yes, we do for the sake of Your People, Hashem," they answered. And then one *neshamah* asked the Holy One, "What would Your People need to do to stop the terrible suffering?"

The Holy One answered, "If they pray to me with a broken heart, I will redeem them in an instant."

I can't imagine being silent any longer.

Contemplating these words, no longer are our children defined as mere simple physical beings. While their outer appearance can be deceiving, their inner existence has more to tell us then what actually meets the eye.

The *pasuk* tells us that Aharon was comforted and, according to the Ramban, refrained from crying after Moshe said the words, "I will be sanctified through those near to Me," or, according to Rashi, "through My chosen ones." Perhaps Aharon was inspired by Moshe's words and learned something striking about his children that immediately comforted him. These two sons, it turned out, were Hashem's honorable and chosen ones, privileged to be the *neshamos* that served as Hashem's medium to demonstrate His glory.

This should serve as a profound lesson to us in changing our perspectives and the way we relate to our children. There's a part of them that will forever remain hidden. We may recognize a specific *middah* that they embody, or a holiness that permeates their *avodas Hashem*, but their true inner spirit is forever concealed — a reminder for us to "handle with spiritual care."

Plant It... Water It... Grow It...

Planting grass is not a simple task. To succeed requires several steps of nurture and care which eventually produces a green lawn. Some fresh soil and grass seed are of course the basics. Birds will likely follow and feast off of the grass seeds making one wonder why the grass won't grow. To prevent this from happening it will be wise to spread hay atop the seeds so it is safe from the lurking birds. Now ample sun and water are needed to allow the seed to germinate and grow into grass.

Our children are no different. Their *neshamos* are similar to the seedling which has enormous potential but the *yetzer hara* — like the hungry birds — looks to eat away at this holy seed. It is the parent's responsibility to protect and secure the *neshamah* so it is safe from the *yetzer hara's* predatory behavior, creating a holy environment in which the child is spiritually safe. Hashem then provides the sun which is the component of raising children out of our human control. It is the parents that then must water them and instill the proper values for the young and fragile *neshamos*. Our children's success is very much dependent on our dedication, willingness, and commitment to their success.

Tazria

וְהַבֶּגֶד כִּי יִהְיֶה בּוֹ נֶגַע צָרָעַת בְּבֶגֶד צֶמֶר אוֹ בְּבֶגֶד פִּשְׁתִּים:

And the garment that has the lesion of tzaraas upon it,

on a woolen garment, or on a linen garment. (Vayikra 13:47)

The Ramban on this *pasuk* offers a fundamental idea relating to what types of items could receive the impurity of *tzaraas*. He discusses the phenomenon of *tzaraas* on inanimate objects such as houses and clothing:

והבגד כי יהיה בו נגע צרעת: זה איננו בטבע כלל ולא הווה בעולם וכן נגעי הבתים אבל בהיות ישראל שלמים לה' יהיה רוח השם עליהם תמיד להעמיד גופם ובגדיהם ובתיהם במראה טוב וכאשר יקרה באחד מהם חטא ועון יתהוה כיעור בבשרו או בבגדו או בביתו להראות כי השם סר מעליו ולכך אמר הכתוב (להלן יד לד) ונתתי נגע צרעת בבית ארץ אחוזתכם כי היא מכת השם בבית ההוא.

והנה איננו נוהג אלא בארץ שהיא נחלת ה' כמו שאמר (שם) כי תבאו אל ארץ כנען אשר אני נותן לכם לאחוזה ואין הדבר מפני היותו חובת קרקע אבל מפני שלא יבא הענין ההוא אלא בארץ הנבחרת אשר השם הנכבד שוכן בתוכה ובתורת כהנים (מצורע פרשה ה ג) דרשו עוד שאין הבית מטמא אלא אחר כבוש וחלוק ושיהא כל אחד ואחד מכיר את שלו והטעם כי אז נתישבה דעתם עליהם לדעת את ה' ותשרה שכינה בתוכם וכן אני חושב בנגעי הבגדים שלא ינהגו אלא בארץ ולא הוצרך למעט מהן חוצה לארץ כי לא יארעו שם לעולם.

An article of clothing that has tzaraas — This situation is not found in nature at all, nor does it generally occur in the world altogether. The same is

149

true for the tzaraas afflictions of houses. However [the explanation is this],
When the People of Israel are completely faithful to Hashem, His Spirit will
rest upon them constantly, so as to maintain their bodies and their garments
and their houses with a good appearance; and when an incident of sin or
iniquity occurs with one of them, there will appear a discoloration on his flesh
or his garment or his home, to indicate to him that the spirit of Hashem has
departed from him. As such, the pasuk states, "I will place a tzaraas affliction
upon a house in the land of your possession," for it is a strike by Hashem
against that house.

Now, tzaraas of houses is applicable only in the Land of Israel, which is the
heritage of Hashem, as the pasuk states, "When you arrive in the land of
Canaan…and I will place a tzaraas affliction upon a house in the land of your
possession." And this fact is not due to its being a land-related obligation;
rather, it is because this supernatural situation can occur only in the Chosen
Land, in the midst of which dwells the Glorious Name (Hashem). And in
Toras Kohanim,[72] [the Sages] expounded further that a house becomes subject to contamination through tzaraas only after the conquest of the Land
and its apportionment among the tribes, and at the time that each and every
individual knows his portion and his possession. And the reason for this is
that only at that point would they have peace of mind for them to be able to
truly serve and know Hashem, and only then would His Divine Presence re-
side among them. And I think that the same is true concerning the afflictions
of garments: they would not be applicable except in the Land of Israel, but it
was not necessary for the pasuk to explicitly exclude garments outside of the
Land from being susceptible to afflictions, because it will never occur there.
(Ramban al HaTorah)

Tzaraas as a Privilege

The Ramban teaches that tzaraas appearing on clothing or a home
was not a natural phenomenon, but rather a sign that Hashem's
Presence had left because of the sin committed by the individual.
Hashem's Spirit was present amid B'nei Yisrael as long as they main-
tained their holiness — but when it could no longer remain because of
the impurity of the sin, tzaraas would take its place, serving as a catalyst

72   The halachic Midrash known as Sifra.

for the person to repent. The Ramban continues that the emergence of *tzaraas* on clothing and on the walls inside homes was not something that occurred outside of Eretz Yisrael; this was an affliction appropriate only for the chosen place, the Land of Eretz Yisrael, which Hashem favored and in which He preferred to rest his *Shechinah*.

Tzaraas was a sign that Hashem cared deeply for him and his spiritual state, but sought to assist him in correcting his ways.

We can infer from the Ramban that *tzaraas* was a privilege for one who was close to Hashem but regrettably sinned and caused His Presence to leave him. This was a sign that Hashem cared deeply for him and his spiritual state, but sought to assist him in correcting his ways by sending this affliction his way. The afflicted person, called a *metzora*, was provided with a process of purifying himself by becoming aware of the effect speaking ill of others had on his soul, in the form of a spiritual illness.

Becoming a *metzora*, it could be suggested, was, in a sense, a badge of honor, attesting to Hashem's Desire and longing for the person to rectify his ways and allow Hashem's *Shechinah* to rest on him once again, despite his sin.

Let us apply this to the people who committed the first sins in history. The Torah tells us that after the sin of Adam and Chava, the Snake that enticed them to eat from the Tree of Knowledge was cursed by having to crawl in the dust and eat the dirt of the ground. Rav Yitzchak Meir Alter, *zt"l*, the *Chidushei HaRim*, asks as follows: Since dirt is always available for the Snake and easy to come by, why was this curse considered a punishment? Was this not actually a reward for the Snake, who now has an endless supply of food easily obtainable and always at his disposal?

אמרו חכמינו, כי על ידי זה שנתקלל הנחש לאכול רק עפר, הרי תמיד מזונותיו מזומנים לפניו. עולה לגג, מזונותיו עמו. וכן אמרו חכמינו הרואה נחש נאה בחלום פרנסתו מזומנת לו (ברכות נ"ז). קשה איפוא, מה קללה היא זו.

ברם, הקללה היתה בכך, שהורחק כל כך מן הקדושה, עד כדי למנוע ממנו שיצטרך אי פעם לשאת עיניו אל השמים, כדרך ברואים אחרים המחפשים להם מזונותיהם ונושאים לפעמים עיניהם השמימה, לבקש מזונם מאת ד' יתברך, כגון הכפירים שואגים לטרף

ולבקש מאל אכלם (תהילים ק"ד כ"א). את קולו של הנחש אין רוצים בכלל לשמוע,
בבחינת קח לך את שלך והסתלק מנגד עיני, לבל אראך ולבל אשמעך עוד.

Our Sages said that in being cursed with having to eat only dirt, the Snake's
food supply is always in abundance; even if it goes up on a roof, it has what
to eat. And our Sages similarly taught: "He who sees a snake in his dream,
it means his living (sustenance) is assured" (Berachos 57a). The question is
therefore clear: What kind of punishment is this?

The answer is that the Snake was cursed in being distanced from anything
having to do with sanctity — to the extent that even the need to ever look
heavenward is taken from it. It is not like other creatures that seek their food
and sometimes lift their eyes to the heavens to ask Hashem to provide them.
For instance, "The young lions roar for their prey, and seek their food from
G-d" (Tehillim 104:21). The sound of the Snake's call is not at all desired in
the Heavens, as if it were being told, "Take your food and get out of my sight!
I don't want to see you or hear you." (Chidushei HaRim, Bereishis)

Banished Forever

Explains the *Chidushei HaRim* as follows: Hashem cursed the Snake
by making his food so easily accessible, in effect severing His relationship from the Snake, that it now had no need to ask Hashem for its
sustenance. This was the Snake's punishment; being distanced from
having a relationship with Hashem. In essence, the Snake was now on
its own, with no connection to Hashem — and with no reason for one.

On the other hand, one who needs to turn to Hashem for his sustenance and constantly remain "in line" to be deserving of Hashem's
kindness will naturally have a close and deep relationship with Him.
This is in contrast to the Snake; whose food is readily available at all
times but has no opportunity for a relationship with Hashem. Hashem
sends us difficulties so we may turn to Him and ask for His assistance,
as a son turns to his father. Naturally then, a relationship is built and
developed as a result. As long as we perceive ourselves invulnerable and
with no need for Hashem in our lives, even if only passively, Hashem
will send us opportunities to get closer to Him. While we work to grow
the relationship, it may be difficult sometimes grim, but ultimately, we
will benefit as we look back in introspection.

Perhaps with the understanding of the Ramban above we can view *tzaraas* as Hashem's message that He still wants to be close with us and desires the relationship. It is our sins, namely *lashon hara* which result in His *Shechinah* departing and the affliction of *tzaraas* introduced in its stead. This is to offer us the opportunity to undergo a process of *teshuvah* so that we may reunite with His spirit and revive our relationship.

In Honor of Miriam

The Gemara tells how Miriam, the sister of Moshe and Aharon, was confined[73] when she became a *metzora*:

> מרים מי הסגירה א"ת משה הסגירה משה זר הוא ואין זר רואה את הנגעים וא"ת אהרן הסגירה אהרן קרוב הוא ואין קרוב רואה את הנגעים, אלא כבוד גדול חלק לה הקב"ה למרים אותה שעה אני כהן ואני מסגירה אני חולטה ואני פוטרה.

> *Who was the Kohen who declared Miriam leprous and thus caused her to be confined? If you say that it was Moshe, that is problematic, because Moshe was not a Kohen and could not inspect negaim. And if you say Aharon confined her, Aharon was a relative of Miriam and a relative cannot inspect negaim. Rather, Hashem Himself accorded great honor to Miriam at that time by taking charge of her case. He said, "I am a Kohen and I confine her; I declare her a leper, and I exempt her." (Zevachim 102a)*

The question can be asked: Would not Hashem's confirmation of Miriam as a *metzora* and then His confinement of her attract undue attention to her misdeed of speaking negatively about her brother? Would not Miriam have been better off had the entire process been done in a quieter and more hushed manner, with less publicity, without Hashem honoring her by acting as the Kohen?[74]

---

73 The Torah prescribes the process and treatment of one afflicted with *tzaraas*. After the *Kohen* inspects the *nega* and declares it as *tamei*, the individual is confined and sent outside of the camp in which B'nei Yisrael dwelled.

74 At the end of *Parashas Beha'aloscha*, Rashi explains that the B'nei Yisrael delayed their journeying in honor of Miriam to wait until she was able to re-enter the camp and could travel with them. This too, seems like anything but honor. Now all of B'nei Yisrael knew that because of Miriam's sin they were unable to continue with their travels.

In fact, however, the exact opposite is true, and Miriam's episode teaches us a critical lesson about a *metzora*. The Gemara's words are carefully selected: *kavod gadol chalak lah HaKadosh Baruch Hu l'Miriam osah sha'ah*, Hashem accorded Miriam great honor at that time. What great honor does the Gemara refer to if after all she was guilty of speaking ill of her brother? The answer is since Miriam HaNeviah was a holy woman and shared a special closeness with Hashem she was *worthy* of being afflicted with *tzaraas* and having Hashem Himself confirm her status, a sign from Hashem to her of His so called own pain relating to what had occurred and took charge of the process to initiate her repentance. Hashem wanted to be close with Miriam again and be involved in her healing process.[75]

This idea can be further supported by the following. In *Parashas Metzora* the Torah says regarding *tzaraas* found in a home:

> כִּי תָבֹאוּ אֶל אֶרֶץ כְּנַעַן אֲשֶׁר אֲנִי נֹתֵן לָכֶם לַאֲחֻזָּה וְנָתַתִּי נֶגַע צָרַעַת בְּבֵית אֶרֶץ אֲחֻזַּתְכֶם.
>
> When you come to the Land of Canaan, which I am giving you as a possession, and I place a lesion of tzaraas upon a house in the land of your possession. (Vayikra 14:34)

Rashi adds this explanation:

> ונתתי נגע צרעת: בשורה היא להם שהנגעים באים עליהם, לפי שהטמינו אמוריים מט־
> מוניות של זהב בקירות בתיהם כל ארבעים שנה שהיו ישראל במדבר, ועל ידי הנגע נותץ
> הבית ומוצאן.
>
> And I will place a lesion of tzaraas — This is [good] news for them that lesions of tzaraas will come upon them, because the Emorites had hidden away treasures of gold inside the walls of their houses during the forty years that B'nei Yisrael were in the desert, and because of the lesion in his home, he will [have to] demolish the house and find the treasures.

---

75   This idea is futher highlighted in the Six Rememberances which some have the custom to recite daily after *Shacharis*. One of them is a *pasuk* which recalls Miriam's sin. זכור את אשר עשה ה' אלוקיך למרים בדרך בצאתכם ממצרים, *Remember that which Hashem, your G-d did to Miriam on the way of leaving Mitzrayim* (Devarim 24:9). Again, if this was a negative episode to remember what honor would it be to Miriam if we would recall this event daily? Rather, we recall the great love Hashem showed Miriam and for that reason it is important to remember daily the supernatural closeness and care Hashem has for all His people.

A True Treasure

If *tzaraas* were sent to afflict one's home as a sign from Hashem to change his sinful behavior, why was he rewarded with a treasure hidden behind the wall? Perhaps we can explain that the Midrash quoted by Rashi is hinting to the idea that *tzaraas* was a *besurah*, good news, in the literal sense. That is, not only would he find a treasure, but he would also undergo a process of becoming aware of his wrongdoings and thus heal his soul. He would thus find the "treasure" to the correct path, leading to a more spiritual existence.

One who invites Hashem into his life can expect to be reprimanded at times and face hardship or suffering. However, it is important to recognize that this may be the result of his deep relationship with Hashem that makes him worthy of Hashem taking a special interest in him to help correct and mend his ways. This is unlike the Snake that was prevented from having a relationship with Hashem and never experienced the need to appeal to Him for assistance.

Metzora

כִּי תָבֹאוּ אֶל אֶרֶץ כְּנַעַן אֲשֶׁר אֲנִי נֹתֵן לָכֶם לַאֲחֻזָּה וְנָתַתִּי נֶגַע צָרַעַת בְּבֵית אֶרֶץ אֲחֻזַּתְכֶם:

When you come to the Land of Canaan, which I am giving you as a possession, and I place a lesion of tzaraas upon a house in the land of your possession. (Vayikra 14:34)

The *Midrash Tanchuma* on this *pasuk* teaches as follows:

לפיכך הקדוש ברוך הוא מתרה בהם ומלקה בתיהן כדי שיעשו תשובה, שנאמר: ונתתי נגע צרעת בבית ארץ אחזתכם. חזר בו מוטב (ואם לאו לוקה בגופו) שכן בפרשה אחרת אומר איש איש כי יהיה זב בבשרו לפיכך האבנים לוקות תחלה. חזר בו, מוטב. ואם לאו, בגדיו לוקין, שנאמר: והבגד כי יהיה בו נגע וגו' חזר בו, מוטב. ואם לאו, מלקה בגופו.

Hashem warns them and plagues their houses so that they should do teshuvah, as is written: "I will place a plague of tzaraas on the home of the land of your inheritance" (Vayikra 14:34). If the home-owner repents, good, (but if not, he will be plagued bodily), as is written in another passage, "If any man has a discharge from his flesh" (ibid. 15:2) — therefore, the stones [of the house] are stricken first: If he repents, good, but if not, his clothing will be stricken, as is written, "And the cloak that has a plague..." (ibid. 13:47) — and if he repents, good, but if not, he is stricken bodily. (Tanchuma, Metzora 4)

Asking a similar question as the *Tanchuma*, the *Ohr HaChaim*, Rav Chaim ben Moshe Attar, establishes a fundamental of the laws of *tzaraas*:

והוא לצד שהקדים לומר נגעי בני אדם, והוא הפך האמור בבעל הרחמים, לזה אמר מה שהקדמתי נגעי בני אדם הוא לצד שעדיין לא באתם אל הארץ ואין בתים לנגוע בהם, אבל כי תבואו אל הארץ אז לא אתן הנגע באדם תחלה אלא ונתתי נגע בבית ארץ וגו' תחלה. וטעם שלא סדר הכתוב נגע הבית קודם, לצד שנגעי אדם ישנם תיכף ומיד מהדיבור ואילך נוהגים ונגעי הבית הוא כי יבואו, לזה הקדים הצריך תיכף ומיד.

Why did the Torah speak first of leprosy on one's body [in Parashas Tazria] and only afterwards about leprosy in the home? This contradicts that the All-Merciful would not strike people first! To this Hashem answers: "I spoke first of body leprosy because you have not yet come to the Land, and there are no houses yet. But 'when you come to the Land,' I will not allow the leprosy to strike you there first, but rather 'I will place leprosy in your houses' first."

And why did the Torah not discuss house-leprosy first? It is because bodily plagues can happen immediately after Hashem spoke to them, whereas house-leprosy can happen only "when you come to the Land," and therefore the Torah spoke first of that which is immediately necessary. (Ohr HaChaim)

Levels of Lesions

The *Ohr HaChaim* explains the interesting order in which the Torah chose to present the laws of *tzaraas*. The *Midrash Tanchuma* teaches that there were essentially three different levels of *tzaraas*, each with a very different level of significance:

- When a *nega* (lesion) was found in one's home, it was a warning sign for the individual to reflect on his behavior and eliminate the bad *middah* which caused the *nega* to appear, ensuring that the punishment not become more severe.
- If that wasn't successful, Hashem sent the lesion one step closer — affecting the clothing of the person as a more personal sign that it was imperative for the individual to change his ways.
- Finally, if these two spiritual signs had no awakening effect on the person, the *nega* was sent in its most severe form, afflicting the individual physically in a manner that could no longer be disregarded.

In other words, Hashem, in His merciful nature, does not immediate-ly punish physically, but rather seeks first to spiritually rouse us in a less harsh and punitive manner.

Parenthetically, this *Midrash* serves as an important lesson in our modern lives as well: We must recognize the signs Hashem sends us through the loss of material items, and improve our ways before the need arises for stricter measures such as those that affect us physically. We must interpret the small and minor annoyances in life as the *tzaraas* that would have in the past befallen one's home or garment, so that we may spare ourselves the dreadful physical afflictions that may be sent the next time around.

Based on this *Midrash*, asks the *Ohr HaChaim*, it would follow that the laws relating to *negaim* afflicting a home should be taught first, fol-lowed by *negaim* found on a garment, and finally on the person's flesh. After all, this is the order that these afflictions would actually occur. Instead, the Torah taught us in *Parashas Tazria* the laws of *tzaraas* found on one's skin and on garments, and afterwards, in *Parashas Metzora*, we are taught the laws relating to a house stricken with *tzaraas*. Why?

Tzaraas Outside of Eretz Yisrael

The *Ohr HaChaim* offers a few approaches to answer this question. He explains that the Torah emphasizes that the laws of leprosy only apply once we enter Eretz Yisrael. Since at the time B'nei Yisrael had not yet entered the Land, meaning that *tzaraas* in homes was not yet something that could occur, the Torah chose not to begin with the laws of house-lesions.

Rav Shalom Schwadron, zt"l, in a talk given about *teshuvah*,[76] explains that one of the reasons it is so difficult for us to inspire ourselves to te-shuvah is because of the habituation process that takes place even when there are significant reasons to repent. Rav Shalom questions how it was possible that the generation of Noach was not inspired to repent even after hearing Noach's warnings and even though they were well

---

76   *Sefer Kol Dodi Dofek.*

aware of his greatness. Later, too: They all witnessed the great miracles in the way the animals came peacefully in pairs to Noach, without the stronger ones devouring the weaker. Instead, all came in a calm and organized manner, a phenomenon completely against the laws of nature. They saw Noach's warnings begin to materialize when people tried to destroy the *teivah*, Hashem miraculously surrounded it with bears and lions to protect it. Even when the rain began to fall the people remained reluctant to repent. How was this possible? As stubborn as they may have been, shouldn't their perspectives have changed once they saw that what was promised began to take effect?

Waiting 120 Years for the Mabul

The answer is they had become immune to the warnings relating to the Flood, because they had already been hearing them for 120 years until it actually happened. If Noach would have warned them that Hashem was to bring a flood "next week" if the people didn't repent, surely they would have taken his words more seriously and with greater concern. However, when hearing about a cataclysmic event set to take place 120 years later, it becomes hard for anyone to heed the warning. The people likely rationalized, "We have so much time…why inconvenience ourselves now? When the flood gets closer, we'll deal with it then." However, when it truly came closer, it was too late, for they had become immune to hearing about it — and so there was nothing to motivate a change within themselves.

We must act when an experience is fresh in our minds and has made an impression on us.

The Gemara teaches:

כל הרואה סוטה בקלקולה יזיר עצמו מן היין.

If one witnesses a sotah being disgraced, he should separate himself from wine. (Sotah 2a)

Why should he do so? The answer is that it is important to act when being inspired, so as not to lose the intensity of what was experienced. This is a message for life: We must act when an experience is fresh in our minds and has made an impression on us. One who listens to the appeal of an unfortunate father sharing his heart-breaking story — pain and suffering in his family, wife and children suffering from illnesses, enormous medical costs and deep financial debt — is likely to make a mental vow to offer a significant donation to ease the father's agony. Yet, after just a few hours, the initial feelings dwindle and the emotional intensity that originally inspired the vow becomes lost. This was because he allowed the thought to linger, instead of acting on it immediately.

Don't Take Advantage of Hashem's Mercy

This perhaps was the intention of the Torah in its carefully crafted, out-of-order sequence and presentation with regard to the laws of *negaim*. It's true that *negaim* will first befall the individual in his home and garments, as the *Midrash* taught — but let this not fool us into overlooking these spiritual wake-up calls. If we read the *pesukim* in the Torah in the order that the *Midrash* presents the events of *negaim* we may view the occurrence of these afflictions as not being so severe, leading to a laxity in our own response to the appearance of a *nega*. We may rationalize that we have time to repent before it gets to our physical bodies, and that *negaim* in our homes and garments are tolerable. To counter this approach, the Torah makes it clear immediately at the outset of its presentation of the laws of *negaim* in *Tazria* that these afflictions are liable to befall you on your flesh. The most severe option is taught first, so that we do not allow the message to linger and our inspiration to evaporate.

Acharei-Mos

וַיְדַבֵּר ה' אֶל מֹשֶׁה אַחֲרֵי מוֹת שְׁנֵי בְּנֵי אַהֲרֹן בְּקָרְבָתָם לִפְנֵי ה' וַיָּמֻתוּ:

And Hashem spoke to Moshe after the death of Aharon's two sons, when they drew near before Hashem, and they died.

(Vayikra 16:1)

Rashi comments on this *pasuk*:

ודבר ה' אל משה אחרי מות שני בני אהרן וגו': מה תלמוד לומר, היה רבי אלעזר בן עזריה מושלו משל לחולה שנכנס אצלו רופא. אמר לו אל תאכל צונן ואל תשכב בטחב. בא אחר ואמר לו אל תאכל צונן ואל תשכב בטחב שלא תמות כדרך שמת פלוני. זה זרזו יותר מן הראשון, לכך נאמר אחרי מות שני בני אהרן.

And Hashem spoke to Moshe after the death of Aharon's two sons —
What does this teach us [when it specifies "after the death of Aharon's two sons"]? Rabbi Elazar ben Azariah illustrated [the answer] with a parable of a patient, whom a physician came to visit. [The physician] said to him, "Do not eat cold foods, and do not lie down in a cold, damp place." Another [physician] then visited him and advised him, "Do not eat cold foods or lie down in a cold, damp place, so that you will not die the way so-and-so died." This one warned the patient more effectively than the former. This is why the Torah says, "after the death of Aharon's two sons" [i.e., Hashem said to Aharon, "Do not enter the Kodesh HaKodashim in a prohibited manner, so that you will not die as your sons died"].

161

Preparing for Prophecy

Let us consider the following quote from *Chazal* which can shed light and offer us a better understanding of this *pasuk* with Rashi's explanation to it. Hashem performed unbelievable miracles at the parting of the *Yam Suf* (Red Sea), and the *Mechilta* describes the enormity of what took place:

ראתה שפחה על הים מה שלא ראה יחזקאל בן בוזי.

A maidservant saw at the Sea [i.e., reached a most spiritual lofty level] that which Yechezkel ben Buzi did not [see or experience]. (Mechilta, Shemos 3)

The Prophet Yechezkel merited to be shown an incredible prophetic vision — the *Maaseh Merkavah*, the Works of the Holy Chariot — but the *Mechilta* tells us that B'nei Yisrael were so privileged during *Krias Yam Suf* that even a simple maidservant saw more than that when Hashem split the sea.

Rav Chaim Shmulevitz, *zt"l*, in his *Sichos Mussar* asks:

- Why, then, is the maidservant a maidservant and not a prophet, just as Yechezkel was known for his great prophecy? From the words of *Chazal*, we understand that her prophecy was even greater; why, then, is she still referred to as a lowly maidservant?

- Furthermore, how was it possible after witnessing an event so grand, the people could falter later on by serving the *Eigel HaZahav* (Golden Calf) and directing multiple complaints toward Moshe? Could they actually have lost all faith?

Rav Chaim explains:

והנה, במה שאמרו חז"ל ראתה שפחה על הים מה שלא ראו הנביאים, יש להתבונן, כי
לכאורה כיון שראתה השפחה יותר מן הנביאים, היה לה להיות במדרגה נעלה מהם,
ועם כל זאת, הנביאים הם נביאי ה', ואילו השפחה נשארה בדרגתה השפלה והפחותה
-שפחה, הגם שזכתה לראות בהתגלות ה' יותר מן הנביאים. מבואר מזה, כי על ידי גודל
ההשגה וההכרה כשלעצמה, לא תתהפך מהותו של האדם ולא ישתנה במאומה, כי הגם
שרואה וזוכה להכרה נעלה ועמוקה, הרי הוא עצמו נשאר כמו שהיה במדרגתו הקודמת.
ולכן אע"פ שראתה השפחה על הים יותר מישראל משראו הנביאים, עם זאת נשארה שפחה
כשהיתה. וכל זה זה אמור במי שזכה להשגה גבוהה והכרה נעלה בלא הכנה ועבודה, וזוכה
מן ההפקר. לא כן הנביאים, שמעלתם נקנתה להם בגודל יגיעתם ועבודתם, שעלו מדרגה

לדרגה עד שהגיעו בהכנתם לדרגת נביא, להם הנבואה היא עליה גדולה בעצם מהותם, כי
נבואה זו באה להם ע"י שינוי עצמיותם וגודל הכנתם ויגיעתם.

*Chazal taught: "That which a maidservant saw at the Red Sea crossing,
the Nevi'im (Prophets) did not see." Let us consider: It would seem that
after the maidservant saw more than the Nevi'im, she would be on a
greater level than them — yet we see that the Nevi'im are the "Prophets
of Hashem," while the maidservant remained on her lowly level and is still
called "maidservant," even though she merited to see Hashem's revelation
more sublimely than the Nevi'im.*

*This tells us that merely "seeing" or "experiencing" does not change the
essence of a person at all. For even if he merits a great vision and deep understanding, he himself remains the same as he was, on the same level. This is
what happened with the maidservant, who remained as she was even after
seeing the great revelation at the Red Sea.*

*However, this is true regarding one who merited great vision and understand-
ing without prior preparation and effort on his part, as if he had simply found
it on the street. But the Nevi'im are different: They acquired their high level by
virtue of their hard work, climbing up from level to level until, by their efforts,
they reached the level of "Navi." For them, prophecy is a major ascent in their
very essence, for it comes to them by virtue of an inner change within them as
a result of their great preparations and hard work. (Sichos Mussar, Ki Sisa)*

Rav Chaim explains that seeing and experiencing an event, even one
as great as *Krias Yam Suf*, will alone not suffice to change the person
indefinitely. Only if the experience and inspiration is prepared for and
then cultivated as a springboard for change, will it have a lasting effect:

- The maidservant saw a great vision and experienced a once-
  in-a-lifetime moment — but the next morning she was still a
  maidservant because she didn't equip herself prior to the event
  so that she could use the experience and take it to the next level.
- Yechezkel, on the other hand, acquired the lofty level of a
  prophet by preparing himself with holiness. Thus, when he
  received a vision, even one of a lower level than that which
  the maidservant experienced, it took him much further. This
  was because he was pre-programmed to absorb the message
  of the vision.

As cited above, Rashi explains that the Torah emphasized the death of Aharon's sons in order to reinforce the prohibition of entering the *Kodesh HaKodashim*. If the *Kohanim* were given the opportunity to contemplate what had occurred to the sons of Aharon who attempted to enter when they weren't commanded to, surely the warning would have a greater impact than a simple and skeletal warning. Warnings alone can at times fade away and lose their intensity, but when coupled with an iteration of the consequence, a strong association is then formed which leaves a much more lasting impression.

Interpreting Life Events Seriously

Perhaps the *mashal* of Rabbi Elazar ben Azarya quoted by Rashi was chosen specifically here because of its hidden message. The physician told the man, "Do not eat cold foods or lie down in a cold, damp place, so that you will not die the way so-and-so died." Perhaps the message is, "Do not live a cold existence, where every experience or inspirational event in your life is interpreted in a reticent manner, ignoring its point and the warmth and meaning it is destined to deliver. Don't follow the ways of those who dampen and seek to remove all seriousness that a holy experience has to offer — typical of some who seek to put their guilty conscience to rest."

Don't follow the ways of those who dampen and seek to remove all seriousness that a holy experience has to offer.

We all have moments of inspiration when we are convinced that our lives have now been changed forever. Hopefully, we've enabled ourselves through the proper preparation to feel the power of the message, and make commitments to change. Unfortunately, even the most powerful message fades and loses its intensity the morning after. The goal is to act immediately; to take the message to heart and contemplate it so that the commitment is cemented at the moment of inspiration. Hashem sends us inspiring messages at times to give us a boost and make it easier for us to heed His warning. We can either let them pass — or seize the opportunity and grow from them.

Kedoshim

מֹאזְנֵי צֶדֶק אַבְנֵי צֶדֶק אֵיפַת צֶדֶק וְהִין צֶדֶק יִהְיֶה לָכֶם אֲנִי ה' אֱלֹקֵיכֶם
אֲשֶׁר הוֹצֵאתִי אֶתְכֶם מֵאֶרֶץ מִצְרָיִם:

You should have true scales, true weights, a true ephah, and a true hin. I am Hashem, your G-d, Who brought you out of the land of Mitzrayim. (Vayikra 19:34)

Rashi offers us two explanations on these last words:

אשר הוצאתי אתכם: על מנת כן. דבר אחר, אני הבחנתי במצרים בין טפה של בכור לטפה
שאינה של בכור, ואני הנאמן להיפרע ממי שטומן משקלותיו במלח להונות את הבריות
שאין מכירים בהם.

Who brought you out etc. — *on this condition [i.e., that you observe these commandments]. Another explanation: Hashem says, "In Mitzrayim, I discerned between the drop [of sperm that led to the conception] of a firstborn and the drop [of sperm that did] not [lead to the conception] of a firstborn. [Likewise,] I am the One faithful to exact punishment upon someone who secretly stores his weights in salt [thus altering their weight] in order to defraud people who do not recognize them [as weights that have been tampered with]."*

This *pasuk* teaches and warns about the importance of being truthful in setting accurate weights and scales for measurement purposes when selling goods. The Torah connects this commandment with Hashem taking us out of Mitzrayim. As Rashi explains, the parallel is made with Hashem's ability to differentiate at the time of *Makas Bechoros* between those that were first-born and those that weren't and so too He can discern those that secretly tamper with weights and scales to cheat and defraud the public.

It is interesting that of all *mitzvos* that are listed in *Parashas Kedoshim*, it is this particular one that is connected with leaving Mitzrayim. In addition, as Rashi added, the Torah is warning us that Hashem knows all that is hidden just as He was able to discern a *bechor* from a non-*bechor*. Clearly, we need to better understand the connection between leaving Mitzrayim, *Makas Bechoros*, and using accurate weights and scales.

He Knows Your Thoughts

Furthermore, an additional two prohibitions are taught in this week's *parashah* which are paired with a very specific warning. The first one is this:

לֹא תְקַלֵּל חֵרֵשׁ וְלִפְנֵי עִוֵּר לֹא תִתֵּן מִכְשֹׁל וְיָרֵאתָ מֵאֱלֹקֶיךָ אֲנִי ה':

You should not curse a deaf person. You shall not place a stumbling block before a blind person, and you shall fear Hashem. I am Hashem. (Vayikra 19:14)

Again we consult Rashi:

ויראת מאלקיך: לפי שהדבר הזה אינו מסור לבריות לידע אם דעתו של זה לטובה או לרעה, ויכול להשמט ולומר לטובה נתכוונתי, לפיכך נאמר בו ויראת מאלקיך המכיר מחשבותיך. וכן כל דבר המסור ללבו של אדם העושהו ואין שאר הבריות מכירות בו, נאמר בו ויראת מאלקיך.

And you shall fear Hashem —[Why is this mentioned here?] Because this matter [of misadvising someone] is not discernible by people, whether this person had good or evil intentions, and he can avoid [being recriminated by his victim afterwards] by saying, "I meant well!" Therefore, it says concerning this, "and you shall fear Hashem" Who knows your thoughts! Likewise, concerning anything known to the one who does it, but no one else has knowledge of, the Torah says, "and you shall fear Hashem."

Later in this *perek*, the Torah commands as follows:

מִפְּנֵי שֵׂיבָה תָּקוּם וְהָדַרְתָּ פְּנֵי זָקֵן וְיָרֵאתָ מֵאֱלֹקֶיךָ אֲנִי ה'.

*You shall rise before a venerable person and you shall respect the elderly, and
you shall fear Hashem. I am Hashem. (Vayikra 19:32)*

Rashi teaches:

והדרת פני זקן: איזהו הדור, לא ישב במקומו ולא ידבר במקומו ולא יסתור את דבריו.
יכול יעצים עיניו כמי שלא ראהו, לכך נאמר ויראת מאלקיך, שהרי דבר זה מסור ללבו של
עושהו, שאין מכיר בו אלא הוא, וכל דבר המסור ללב נאמר בו ויראת מאלקיך.

And you shall respect the elderly — *What is meant by "respecting" [the
elderly]? One may not sit in his place, speak in his stead [when it is the
elder's turn to speak], or contradict him. One might think that he may close
his eyes [when the elder approaches], as if he did not see him [and evade the
obligation to rise before him]. This is why the Torah adds here, "and you shall
fear Hashem," for this matter is privately known to the one who commits it,
and no one else knows about it, and, concerning any matter known only in
the heart [of one person], the Torah says, "and you shall fear Hashem" [for
Hashem knows man's thoughts].*

Regarding both of these prohibitions the Torah says, "Fear your G-d; I
am Hashem." Rashi explains that whenever a matter is privately known
only to the one that commits it, there the Torah gives this warning, for
Hashem knows each person's true intentions and motives.

One could ask why the act of tampering with scales and weights,
which, as Rashi noted, is intended to "defraud people who do not recognize them," is not also included in this category? After all, it is a matter
that is only known to the one who tampers with the weights and scales!
Why does the Torah not tell us here as well to "fear your G-d"?

To achieve clarity, perhaps we need to gain a deeper insight into the
plague of *Makas Bechoros* and understand its connection, according to
Rashi, with the Torah's prohibition of manipulating weights and scales.

The Social Structure of Mitzrayim

What was it about the firstborns in the Egyptian homes that caused
them to be singled out to be killed by this last plague? Weren't all the

Mitzrim equally at fault and liable for the enslavement and affliction of B'nei Yisrael?

Rav Yosef Dov Soloveitchik, *zt"l*,[77] paints the backdrop for *Makas Bechoros*, shedding light on an important aspect of Egyptian culture at the time of the enslavement in *Mitzrayim*. In order to fully understand this plague, we must appreciate the hierarchy within Egyptian civilization. The firstborn in Egypt occupied an elite position of social aristocracy in that society. They represented authority and might, and used their power abusively and politically to influence their authority over the Jews. As we know, even the households of Egyptian slaves and prisoners were affected by the plague, because they, too, played a role in persecuting the Jews or rejoicing at the Jewish suffering. The eldest member of every household, even if not the halachic *bechor*,[78] was killed because these individuals were of that upper echelon of Egyptian society and culture. Attacking the firstborns wasn't about attacking specific individuals or groups, but rather attacking the philosophy and culture of Egyptian power — represented by the firstborns, who so offensively wielded their higher social class power. With *Makas Bechoros*, Hashem designed an assault over this abuse of power that existed in Mitzrayim in which people were exploiting those less fortunate or of a lower political class.

Hashem used this as a teaching moment, instructing that a *bechor* has a responsibility greater than other members of his family. The lesson was that firstborn status was not to be used to impose physical might over others, but rather to fulfill the added responsibility that comes with the position. This was the significance of *Makas Bechoros*: teaching B'nei Yisrael how to view power and how it is to be utilized in a responsible manner. It was about restoring social justice and creating a new model of what it means to be a *bechor*. Power means more responsibility, and using it to take advantage of those less fortunate and vulnerable is an abuse of the power given to a firstborn.

....

77   *Festival of Freedom*, Rav Yosef Dov Soloveitchik, *zt"l*, pg. 140, Ktav Publishing House.
78   I.e., the *bechor* was living out of his home at that time or even a *bechor* from the mother.

Rav Naftali Tzvi Yehudah Berlin, the *Netziv*, in his *Ha'amek Davar*[79] describes this idea as well with a lesson from the *Shiras HaYam*, the Song of the Sea:

> סוס ורכבו רמה בים. זהו תמצית השירה כמובן משירת הנשים. והענין דבמשמעות סוס ורוכבו נכלל הכל. דכמו הסוס המוכן למלחמה נשמע לרוכבו, כך האיש חיל הוא כסוס לאדוניו להתהלך באש ובמים. והגדול ממנו הוא כסוס לשר האלף. ושר האלף לראש שרי צבאות עד פרעה עצמו. וגם נכלל בזה השר העליון הרוכב על המערכה העליונה של פרעה. ולאותו השר העליון הרי כל המערכה נחשבת כסוס. וכל אלה רמה בים.

"Horse and its rider He threw into the sea." — This is, as we see from the song the women sang, the upshot of the entire Song of the Sea. This is because the words "horse and its rider" include everything: Just like the horse that is ready for war obeys its rider, similarly, the soldier listens to his commander, willing to go [even] through fire and water. On a higher level is one who is like a horse to the battalion commander, and even greater is one who is subservient to the division commander, all the way up to Pharaoh himself. This also includes the highest-ranking commander who rides on Pharaoh's highest chariot; for him, the entire army is considered like a horse. All of these — Hashem threw into the sea.

What does it mean that the rider and horse were hurled into the sea? The *Netziv* explains that Hashem destroyed the Egyptian concept of a power hierarchy by killing the horse and rider model. This *pasuk* sums up the defeat of *Mitzrayim* and its admiration of the horse-and-rider mentality.

Just as the rider directs the horse, so must the rider listen to the officer and be prepared to enter any situation in which he is commanded to enter. That officer takes orders from his general, and that general listens to his commander all the way up to Pharaoh. According to the *Netziv*, this was Egyptian society, a series of horses-and-riders, and the Jewish slaves became the lowest entity supporting the entire chain

Using weights and scales in a dishonest manner and exploiting those who don't know any better is, in essence, returning to the days of Egyptian culture.

---

79   *Shemos* 14:1.

of command. This system collapsed with *Makas Bechoros* and *Krias Yam Suf*, in which Mitzrayim and its political structure was destroyed and brought to its knees.

The Responsibility of Power

With this thought in mind, we can perhaps understand why keeping honest weights and scales is paired with the plague of *Makas Bechoros*. The Torah is teaching us that Hashem brought the plague to destroy the hierarchy of power which existed in Mitzrayim and which took advantage of those vulnerable and less fortunate. Using weights and scales in a dishonest manner and exploiting those who don't know any better is, in essence, returning to the days of Egyptian culture in which those who had more power than others used it to abuse those underneath them. To this, the Torah lays out a strong warning — even stronger than that of "Fear Hashem your G-d" — namely, the mention of *Yetzias Mitzrayim* and *Makas Bechoros,* a punishment designed to completely eradicate those who abused their power and to remind us of their bitter end.

Let us recognize that being in a position of power is a serious responsibility, one which is granted to bestow good upon others and assist the less fortunate. If not treated carefully and with the sensitivity demanded of it, it can be taken away.

Emor

וְכִי תִזְבְּחוּ זֶבַח תּוֹדָה לָה׳ לִרְצֹנְכֶם תִּזְבָּחוּ:

And when you slaughter a thanksgiving offering to Hashem,
you shall slaughter it so that it should be offered willingly.

(Vayikra 22:29)

The *pasuk* teaches about a *korban todah*, an offering brought by those obligated to thank Hashem after recovering from an illness, being freed from prison, and crossing the sea or desert safely.

The *Ksav Sofer*, Rav Avraham Shmuel Binyamin Sofer, makes the following observation:

וכי תזבחו זבח תודה לה׳ לרצונכם תזבחוהו, עיין הפלאה [פנים יפות] בפ׳ אחרי בפסוק וכי תזבחו זבח שלמים עיי״ש, ונ״ל דהנה מי שנעשה לו נס ונוצל מליסטים וכדומה יביא תודה על הטוב שגמלוהו, והנה אם גם כי שמח מי הצילו ה׳ מרעה שבאה עליו מ״מ אינו לרצון לאדם, כי הי׳ טוב לו יותר אם לא בא מעיקרא לידי סכנה ולא וא״כ צריך לנס וא״כ אין קרבן תודה לרצון לפני האדם. אבל באמת ישמח האדם ביסורים שעברו עליו כי לא על חנם באו עליו אם לא שחטא לפני ה׳, ורק ע״י רחמי וחסדי ה׳ ניצל, וא״כ גם ביסורים ישמח ויודה לה׳ כי הענישו בעולם הזה ונתכפרו עוונתיו וכדמצינו בחז״ל ששמחו ביסורים, וכמו שאמר דוד המלך ע״ה (תהלים צד,יב) אשרי הגבר אשר תיסרנו י-ה, וז״ש וכי תזבחו זבח תודה לרצונכם תזבחוהו שלא יהי׳ שלא לרצון כל עיקר הדבר שעי״ז תתחייבו תודה אלא לרצון יהי׳ לפניכם וכהנ״ל:

When you offer a thanksgiving sacrifice, do so that it should be to your
desire — See the Haflaah (Panim Yafos) to Parashas Acharei-Mos on the

171

pasuk "when you offer a shelamim sacrifice."[80] It appears that one for whom a miracle was wrought — he was saved from thieves, for instance — must bring a thanksgiving offering for the goodness that was done to him. Now, granted that he is happy that Hashem has saved him from evil; but still, the situation is not fully to his satisfaction — for he would rather the danger not have come upon him in the first place, and then he would not have needed the miracle! Thus, the thanksgiving offering is never truly totally to one's desire and liking. However, by saying that it should be desirable to us, the Torah is teaching that one should in fact be gladdened by the suffering that has come upon him, because it was not in vain; it means he has sinned before Hashem, and only by Hashem's mercies was he saved. He should therefore be happy even for his suffering and should thank Hashem for punishing him in This World and atoning for his sins.

In this vein, we know that our Sages were happy with the suffering that came upon them, and as David HaMelech wrote (Tehillim 94:12), "Fortunate is the man whom You torment." And this is what this pasuk means when it says that the thanksgiving sacrifice must be "to your satisfaction" — that your obligation to bring the sacrifice should not be undesirable to you in any way, but should rather be totally desirable.

I Never Asked for It in the First Place!

When a person offers thanks to Hashem for a miracle that he experienced, or after being rescued from a dangerous situation, in the back of his mind he may be thinking, "While I'm thankful for what Hashem has done for me, why did I have to be placed in this situation in the first place?" With that thought process, the person is essentially bringing the korban without the true ratzon, will, which the Torah requires of him; as the pasuk says, "It should be offered willingly." The Ksav Sofer continues to explain that Hashem may have brought the hardship upon the person as a way to offer him atonement in this world; through His mercy and kindness, He thus spared him from an even more challenging situation. Therefore, a person should rejoice in the suffering that has come his way and recognize its silver lining — namely, that it is to

---

80 This pasuk does not appear in Acharei-Mos, but rather elsewhere; in Acharei-Mos 17:5, it says
וְזָבְחוּ זִבְחֵי שְׁלָמִים לה'.

his ultimate advantage and benefit. Hashem has a master plan, and at times, we merit seeing only afterwards why things needed to work out the way they did. This is what the *pasuk* means when it commands to bring a *korban* of thanksgiving *lirtzonchem*, willingly; the *korban* should be brought with the understanding that encountering the dangerous situation in the first place was for our own benefit.

Rashi on this *pasuk* explains that the Torah warns of having improper thoughts when offering the *Korban Todah*:

לרצנכם תזבחו: תחלת זביחתכם הזהרו שתהא לרצון לכם.

> **You shall slaughter it willingly** — *From the very beginning of your slaughtering, take care that it should be acceptable (to Hashem) for you (with proper intentions so it does not become pigul[81]).*

Perhaps we can interpret Rashi's words in a homiletic manner alluding to the *Ksav Sofer's* idea. The word *techilas*, "from the very beginning," can be understood as one should not think to himself that he would have been better off without needing the miracle in first place but instead, recognize that "from the very beginning" of what took place it was necessary and for your own benefit. With that recognition, *zvichaschem*, one should bring "the slaughtering" so that it is a pure offering without any improper thought such as wishing that Hashem would have spared you the illness or prison sentence in the first place.

The Berachos Will Find You

This idea recalls the words of the *Degel Machaneh Ephraim*, Rav Moshe Chaim Ephraim of Sudilkov. In *Parashas Ki Savo*, he discusses Hashem's promise that if we follow the Torah, He will provide us with blessing:

וּבָאוּ עָלֶיךָ כָּל הַבְּרָכוֹת הָאֵלֶּה וְהִשִּׂיגֻךָ

And all these blessings will come upon you and overtake you. (Devarim 28:2)

---

81 *Pigul* occurs when one who brings the *korban* had in mind that it will be eaten after the proper time, or that the parts designated for burning will be burned after the proper time. In such a case, the *korban* may not be eaten.

The *Degel Machaneh Ephraim* explains:

ובאו עליך כל הברכות האלה והשיגוך. צריך להבין זה שאין לו ביאור לכאורה היה ראוי
לומר להיפך שהוא ישיג את הברכות ולא שהברכות ישיגו אותו אך דהענין הוא כמ"ש
דהמע"ה אך טוב וחסד ירדפוני וכו'. והיינו כי לפעמים אדם בורח מן הטוב מחמת קוצר
דעתו שאינו יודע אם הוא טוב ולכך התפלל דהמע"ה אך טוב וחסד ירדפוני שהם ירדפו
אחרי וישיגו אותי אף שאיני יודע לרדוף אחריהם והוא שמרמז ובאו עליך כל הברכות
האלה והשיגוך והבן.

*"And all these blessings will come upon you and overtake you" — This pasuk
appears to lack explanation, for it would have been more appropriate to state
the opposite: "you will reach the blessings" and not "the blessings will reach
you." However, the point is similar to that which David HaMelech wrote
(Tehillim 23:6), "Only good and kindness shall pursue me." Since at times one
runs away from the intended good because of his inability to recognize it, and
therefore David HaMelech prayed that "good and kindness should pursue me
and reach me even though I don't know to run after
them." And this is what the pasuk here alludes to
when it says, "And all these blessings will come upon
you and overtake you."*

*We need to habituate
ourselves to relinquish
all control and believe
that Hashem seeks to
deliver only that which
is in our best interest.*

The *Degel Machaneh Ephraim* asks: The phras-
ing of the *pasuk* seems to be odd as it would have
been more proper to phrase the words "you will
reach the blessings" instead of "the blessings
will reach you"? We can also ask that if Hashem will give you blessings,
why the need for the words "and overtake you"? Surely, someone who is
on the receiving end will gladly accept blessings and there's no need for
it to overtake[82] the person?

He answers that in truth, at times we run away from the good that
Hashem grants us, not recognizing the hidden blessing awaiting us
even when at first the opposite is perceived. We need to habituate
ourselves to relinquish all control and believe that Hashem seeks to
deliver only that which is in our best interest. The *pasuk* is teaching
that the blessings will reach you even if you are refusing to accept

82   Implying unwillingly.

them, thinking that they aren't for your benefit. This is what David HaMelech alluded to when he said, אַךְ טוֹב וָחֶסֶד יִרְדְּפוּנִי כָּל יְמֵי חַיָּי (*Tehillim* 23:6). David asked Hashem for good and kindness to run after him, so that even when he runs away from what he thinks is to his detriment, Hashem should allow the good and kindness to reach him — as He knows what's truly best.

A Personal Thank You

Rabbi David Abudraham, in his commentary on the *siddur*, notes that we appoint a *shaliach tzibbur* for all of *chazaras hashatz*, from whom we listen to all the *berachos* and may thereby fulfill our obligation of *Shemoneh Esrei*. But one *berachah* — that of *Modim* — requires those listening to respond with *Modim D'Rabanan*; listening to the *Shaliach Tzibbur* alone will not suffice. Why is that? And in what way is *Modim*, or giving thanks to Hashem different than all other parts of *Shemoneh Esrei* of which we rely on the one reciting out loud?

וכשיגיע ש"ץ למודים וכורע כל העם שוחין ואומרין הודאה קטנה המתחלת כמו כן במו־
דים שאין דרך העבד להודות לרבו ולומר לו אדוני אתה על ידי שליח אלא כל אדם צריך
לקבל בפיו עול מלכות שמים ואם יקבל על ידי שליח אינה קבלה גמורה שיוכל להכחיש
ולומר לא שלחתיו. אבל בשאר התפלה שהיא בקשה יכול לתבוע צרכיו על ידי שליח שכל
אדם חפץ בטובתו ולא יכחיש ויאמר לא שלחתיו וזהו שאמר דוד אמרתי לה' ה' אתה אני
בעצמי אמרתי לו ולא על ידי שליח.

And when the leader of the congregation reaches Modim and bows, the listeners bow and prostrate and respond with a small praise which also begins with the words Modim [Modim D'Rabanan]. This is because it is not proper for a servant to praise his master and say "you are my master" through a messenger; rather, each person needs to accept upon himself the yoke of heaven with his mouth. And if he accepts this upon himself through a messenger, it is not considered a complete acceptance since he can deny and argue that he never sent the messenger [with that message]. However, regarding other areas of tefillah that are requests, one may use an intermediary to ask for his needs, since everyone wants the best for himself and there is no fear that he will deny [having sent the messenger]. This is what David HaMelech said, "I said to Hashem, Hashem you are" (Tehillim 16:2) — I myself said this to Him and not by messenger. (Abudraham)

The *Abudraham* explains that when it comes to giving thanks, appointing a *shaliach* does not satisfy our obligation. One needs to show appreciation on his own with sincerity, lest he come to deny Hashem's superiority.

Perhaps we can offer another reason for the need for an individual to say *Modim* without the *shaliach tzibbur* acting as an intermediary. According to the *Ksav Sofer* quoted above, we need to welcome the difficult situation Hashem brings our way, recognizing that it is for our good even if it may seem at first to our detriment. Consequently, it is important that when giving thanks to Hashem, we do it on our own to ensure that it is completely "our will," as the *pasuk* said: *lirtzonchem*. But if we use an intermediary, this would allow for the possibility that we continue to hope in our heart that Hashem would have never tested us in the first place. Offering thanks on our own, will require one to remove those negative feelings and give thanks willingly, with complete gratitude and recognition that Hashem has our best interests in mind.

Behar

דַּבֵּר אֶל בְּנֵי יִשְׂרָאֵל וְאָמַרְתָּ אֲלֵהֶם כִּי תָבֹאוּ אֶל הָאָרֶץ
אֲשֶׁר אֲנִי נֹתֵן לָכֶם וְשָׁבְתָה הָאָרֶץ שַׁבָּת לַה':

Speak to B'nei Yisrael and say to them: When you come
to the land that I am giving you, the land shall rest,
a Shabbos to Hashem. (Vayikra 25:2)

וְקִדַּשְׁתֶּם אֵת שְׁנַת הַחֲמִשִּׁים שָׁנָה וּקְרָאתֶם דְּרוֹר בָּאָרֶץ לְכָל
יֹשְׁבֶיהָ יוֹבֵל הִוא תִּהְיֶה לָכֶם וְשַׁבְתֶּם אִישׁ אֶל אֲחֻזָּתוֹ וְאִישׁ
אֶל מִשְׁפַּחְתּוֹ תָּשֻׁבוּ:

And you shall sanctify the fiftieth year, and proclaim freedom
[for slaves] throughout the land for all its inhabitants. It
shall be a Jubilee for you, and each of you shall return to his
property, and each of you shall return to his family. (25:10)

Parashas Behar begins with two essential *mitzvos* relating to the land of Eretz Yisrael, namely, *Shemittah* and *Yovel*. The Torah commands that every seven years the owner of a field must cease all farming activity and allow the field complete rest. The second mitzvah requires sanctifying the fiftieth year, and all land must be returned to its original owners.

Eretz Yisrael: A Delicate Land

Rav Yosef Dov Soloveitchik, zt"l,[83] explains a fundamental concept behind these *mitzvos*, delving into Eretz Yisrael's role relating to *Shemittah* and *Yovel*. At the end of *Parashas Acharei-Mos*, the Torah warns us to be careful regarding our behavior and the way we conduct ourselves in Eretz Yisrael:

וַתִּטְמָא הָאָרֶץ וָאֶפְקֹד עֲוֹנָהּ עָלֶיהָ וַתָּקִא הָאָרֶץ אֶת יֹשְׁבֶיהָ... וְלֹא תָקִיא הָאָרֶץ אֶתְכֶם בְּטַמַּאֲכֶם אֹתָהּ כַּאֲשֶׁר קָאָה אֶת הַגּוֹי אֲשֶׁר לִפְנֵיכֶם:

And the land became defiled, and I visited its sin upon it, and the land spit out its inhabitants...And let the land not spit you out for having defiled it, as it spit out the nation that preceded you. (Vayikra 18:25–28)

Rashi likens the Land to the son of a king:

ולא תקיא הארץ אתכם: משל לבן מלך שהאכילוהו דבר מאוס, שאין עומד במעיו אלא מקיאו, כך ארץ ישראל אינה מקיימת עוברי עבירה. ותרגומו ולא תרוקין, לשון ריקון, מריקה עצמה מהם.

And let the Land not spit you out — *This can be compared to a prince who was fed spoiled food, which could not remain in his intestines, and so he vomited it out. Likewise, Eretz Yisrael cannot retain transgressors in its midst [and thus, it vomits them out]. The Targum renders וְלֹא תָקִיא as:* וְלֹא תְרוֹקֵן, *meaning "emptying out"* (רִקּוּן), *i.e., the Land empties itself of transgressors.*

Rashi compares the land of Eretz Yisrael to a prince who is sensitive and requires a special diet. Rav Soloveitchik explains that we see from the Torah's narrative that Eretz Yisrael takes on an almost human dimension. It has a special, unique sensitivity to sin, and cannot tolerate sinful behavior within its borders. The Torah tells us that every seven years the land should rest and be sanctified. Similar to human beings who rest on Shabbos, the land is also given rest. The promise for those who keep *Shemittah* is that their land will yield crops in the sixth year that are sufficient for three years. Eretz Yisrael is not simply a land

---

83   See *Dorosh Dorash Yosef*, by Rabbi Avishai David, where he references this thought from his *rebbi* and many other examples portraying Eretz Yisrael's human-like features.

designated for the B'nei Yisrael's physical dwelling. Rather, it is infused with holiness demanding special care and sensitivity, and if not treated properly, it will cause its inhabitants to be removed and ejected.

Yaacov Is the Guf and Yisrael the Neshamah

This brings to mind the role of the *neshamah*, the soul, that is housed inside the *guf*, our physical body. This, too, can be compared to Eretz Yisrael's relationship with its inhabitants. The *guf* and *neshamah* are designed to work in tandem, but if the *guf* involves itself with sins which are the antithesis of what the *neshamah* seeks, then the latter will separate itself from the *guf*, as its *kedushah* and sensitive needs don't allow for a sustainable relationship with it.

The *Shem MiShmuel* in *Parashas Yisro* explains this idea in the following manner.

לכלל ישראל ישנם ב' שמות, יעקב וישראל. כללות ישראל בגופם נקראים יעקב, ונשמתם נקראת ישראל. ושם ישראל אף פעם לא נתבטל מהם, כי אף על פי שחטא, ישראל הוא, אלא כשנכשל וחוטא הנשמה מתרחקת ממנו ומחכה עד שישוב, ועצם עיקר החטא הוא בגוף והגוף גורם שהנשמה תכשל ותסתלק, וזהו מה שאמר כי כשלת בעונך על ידי הגוף.

Klal Yisrael has two names, Yaacov and Yisrael. Their physical entities are represented by Yaacov, and their neshamos by Yisrael. The name Yisrael never departs from them[84] even when they commit sins. However, if they stumble in sin, this will result in the neshamah distancing itself and waiting for repentance (and will then connect again with the physical body). The actual sin is with the physical body, and the body causes the neshamah to depart. And this is what the pasuk means when it says, "for you have stumbled in your iniquity" (Hoshea 14:2) — through the physical body. (Shem MiShmuel, Yisro)

> *The neshamah cannot tolerate the guf when it engages in ways antithetical to its holiness.*

Perhaps Rashi's analogy which compares Eretz Yisrael to a prince with a special diet can be applied to the *guf/neshamah* relationship as well. Rashi commented: כך ארץ ישראל אינה מקיימת עוברי עבירה, Eretz Yisrael cannot retain sinners. Just as a prince cannot tolerate food which is repulsive,

---

84   See *Maseches Sanhedrin* 44a.

similarly, Eretz Yisrael cannot bear transgression and wrongdoing in its presence and will rid itself of such impurities in order to maintain the innate *kedushah* it encompasses. According to the *Shem MiShmuel*, the words of Rashi may also be read *kach Eretz Yisrael*, so too Yisrael, which represents the *neshamah*, cannot tolerate the *guf* when it engages in ways antithetical to its holiness. Just as Eretz Yisrael was infused with a human-like entity and needs to be treated with holiness lest it spit out its inhabitants, our *neshamos* too are spiritually alive and full of spiritual energy, sensitive to ideas not in sync with its holiness. Our task is to keep our *neshamah* and *guf* in a spiritual and peaceful partnership so that together they can achieve their intended purpose.

We tend to think that our *neshamos* are "just another part of us" and forget that they are in reality a G-dly gift, a *Chelek Elokah Mimaal*, a part of Hashem's Essence, created from the highest source of holiness. It is an incredible privilege to be walking around with a *neshamah*! Imagine being awarded twenty-five thousand dollars and then placing it in your pocket. Aside from guarding it carefully and checking your pocket every minute to ensure it is still safely there, you also walk with a sense of pride knowing what's hidden away in your pocket.

The gift of being the carrier of a *neshamah*, too, should instill within us a sense of pride. We must remember that there is a G-dly component inside of us, and this will help us recognize the importance of protecting this most prized possession, treating it with its deserved *kedushah* and respect.

Bechukosai

אִם בְּחֻקֹּתַי תֵּלֵכוּ וְאֶת מִצְוֹתַי תִּשְׁמְרוּ וַעֲשִׂיתֶם אֹתָם:

If you follow My statutes and observe
My commandments and perform them…

(Vayikra 26:3)

Rashi tells us that this highlights the study of Torah:

אם בחקתי תלכו: יכול זה קיום המצות, כשהוא אומר ואת מצותי תשמרו, הרי קיום
המצות אמור, הא מה אני מקיים אם בחקתי תלכו, שתהיו עמלים בתורה.

*If you follow My statutes — One might think that this refers to the fulfill-
ment of the commandments. However, when the Torah says, "and observe
My commandments," the fulfillment of the commandments is thus already
stated. So what is the meaning of, "If you follow My statutes"? It means that
you must toil in the study of Torah.*

Rashi teaches us that the words *im bechukosai teileichu* are specifically teaching us about a form of Torah learning described as being
amel, "toiling" in the study of Torah. What is it about toiling and
laboring over the Torah that Hashem promises such great reward
for it?

181

The Beneficial Rays of Torah

Rav Shimshon Pincus[85] shares a beautiful idea on the topic of modest dress which can perhaps shed some light on our discussion related to toiling in Torah.

We all know that a pregnant woman should not enter an x-ray room; a large sign hangs on the door announcing this. Why? What's the problem? The problem is that there is radiation in the x-ray room that can be damaging to the fetus. When a child is born with a defect, the doctors will try to figure out the prenatal cause. If a pregnant woman enters such a room and then gives birth to a child with certain defects or health problems, the doctors will attribute it to those x-rays that affected the fetus while it was in its mother's womb. The mother will claim, "But I didn't feel anything!" She did not taste these damaging rays with her tongue, nor did she see them with her eyes, nor did she hear them with her ears. And she surely did not touch them with her fingers. But it is a fact: x-rays are damaging to a fetus.

Rav Pincus explains that the same is true with one's *ruchniyus* in which at times can be negatively affected without feeling or experiencing a physical act. The mere negative environment impacts us in a harmful manner.

Perhaps we can apply this idea to toiling in the study of Torah. Torah is not simply another topic of study, nor is Torah learning an intellectual exercise designed to provide knowledge. The knowledge one acquires while studying Torah is a byproduct of the toiling, but is not its sole — or even main — purpose. Toiling in Torah is an opportunity for us and our souls to connect with Hashem in a way that's beyond anything the physical world can offer. It is a supernatural experience which allows for one to elevate his *neshamah* and gain access to a greater level of closeness with Hashem. We experience this not by hearing, seeing, or touching something; nevertheless, it happens through the rays of holiness emanating from working hard to understand Torah and has a direct impact on our *neshamos*. Just like an x-ray machine, whose effects can-

85   Based on *Nefesh Chaya*, Rav Shimshon Pincus, Feldheim.

not be seen or heard, yet can still affect our bodies, the same is true for Torah and its effect on our souls.

Those who study with passion to acquire Torah are positively affected in unimaginable ways, and they allow themselves a relationship with Hashem in which the *neshamah* can ascend to the greatest of spiritual heights.[86]

Toiling in Torah is an opportunity for us and our souls to connect with Hashem in a way that's beyond anything the physical world can offer.

The benefits of *ameilus b'Torah* do not end there. An additional advantage is that when we learn Torah sincerely, our *neshamos* themselves go through a spiritual transformation wherein they can be repaired and restored with holiness. Aside from feeling physically invigorated and spiritually uplifted after intense Torah learning, having ingested food for the soul, our *neshamos*, too, are altered for the better and given a new and different status.

The Transformative Nature of Honey and Torah

Let us elaborate upon this idea with the following thought from the *Chofetz Chaim*, Rav Yisrael Meir HaKohen Kagan, *zt"l*:

ומה שכתב ומתוקים מדבש וגו' כי ידוע שיש בטבע הדבש כת המתיקות גדול עד שאם יפול בה איזה דבר לחם או בשר וכדומה וישתהא בה שיהוי רב במשך הזמן יתהפך הלחם והבשר לדבש גמור. והנה לרוב הפוסקים אפילו אם נפל בה דבר איסור חוזר להיות היתר גמור וזהו שאמר הכתוב שכח מתיקות התורה הוא גדול הרבה יותר מדבש ונופת צופים דהיינו אם אדם שוקד על התורה ומתדבק בה כראוי אפילו אם טבע נפשו היה מתחלה רע מאוד כח התורה מטהרתו ומקדשתו ונהפך להיות איש אחר ממש.

Regarding that which is written [that Hashem's laws are] "sweeter than honey" (Tehillim 19:11), it is known that the sweetness of honey is so strong that if something falls into it, such as bread or meat or the like, and remains in the honey for a long while, it becomes honey itself. According to most halachic decisors, even if that which fell in was forbidden, it becomes totally permitted. This is what is written here: The power of the sweetness of Torah is much stronger even than honey and the honeycomb, meaning that if a man studies Torah diligently and clings to it strongly, then even if the nature of his

---

86   See chap. 9 in the *Sefer Chovas HaTalmidim* of the Piacezner Rebbe *Hy"d* who elaborates incredibly on this idea.

soul was originally very bad, the power of Torah purifies and sanctifies him, and he becomes literally a new man.

Rabbeinu Yonah in *Maseches Berachos*[87] rules that if a piece of forbidden food falls into honey and remains there for a period of time until it dissolves within the honey, the entire food is deemed permissible. This is because the nature of honey is to completely transform anything that falls within it into honey itself. The *Chofetz Chaim*, quoted above from his introduction to his *Likutei Halachos* on *Zevachim*, explains that the Torah, too, has this ability to change a person whose soul is evil into a righteous individual. The reason is because the nature of the Torah is to transform the soul of those who toil in it. Again, we encounter a lofty concept related to our *neshamos* in which Torah learning can influence us and change our being, as our *neshamos* are rooted in the spiritual realm and not bound by the limits of the physical world that they are visiting.

An All-in-One Spiritual Tool

Perhaps this is the meaning of the *pasuk* in *Tehillim* which states, *Toras Hashem temimah meshivas nafesh,* "the Torah of Hashem is perfect, restoring the soul."[88] The Torah was built with the ability to repair and restore the damaged *neshamah*. It is essentially the all-in-one spiritual tool for repairing the broken soul.

What Does Hashem Say?

Rav Chaim Volozhiner, the *Nefesh HaChaim*, teaches us a most fundamental idea about toiling in Torah and Hashem's actual role in our learning:

כי גם באותו העת שהאדם עוסק בתורה למטה כל תיבה שמוציא מפיו הן הן הדברים
יוצאים כביכול גם מפיו ית' באותו העת ממש. כדאשכחן בפ"ק דגיטין גבי פלגא בגבע'
ותזנה עליו פלגשו ר' אביתר אמר זבוב מצא לה רי"א נימא כו'. ואשכחי' ר"א לאלי' א"ל
מאי קעביד קב"ה א"ל עסיק בפלגיש בגבעה ומאי קאמר אביתר בני כך הוא אומר יונתן בני
כך הוא אומר. והיינו מפני שר"א ור"י עסקו ביניהם בענין פלגיש בגבע' אז באותו עת גם הוא
ית' שנה דבריהם ממש. והוא ית"ש ודבורו חד. וכמפורש בתוה"ק במשנה תורה לאהבה

---

87   36b.
88   *Tehillim* 19:8.

את ה' אלהיך כו' ופירשוהו רז"ל בנדרים (ס"ב א) דקאי על עסק התורה ע"ש וסיפי' דקרא
ולדבקה בו. ולכן אמר דוד המע"ה טוב לי תורת פיך כו'. אמר כי לבי שמח בעמלי בתורה
הקדושה ברוב עוז ובהעלותי על לבי שהיא תורת פיך שכל תיבה ממש מהתורה שאני
עוסק בה כעת הכל יצא יצא וגם עתה היא יוצאת מפיך יתב'.

*While engrossed in Torah study down on earth, every word one utters em-
anates at the same time, keviyachol, from Hashem's Mouth. This is evident
from the Gemara in Maseches Gittin[89] where Rav Aviyasar and Rav Yonason
argue on the subject of the Pilegesh BeGivah. Soon afterwards, Rav Aviyasar
met Eliyahu and said to him, "What is Hashem doing up in the heavens?"
Eliyahu replied, "He is discussing the question of the Pilegesh BeGivah."*

*"What does He say?" asked Rav Aviyasar. Eliyahu said, "He says: my son
Aviyasar says such-and-such, and my son Yonason says such-and-such."
This was because, at that very moment, Rav Aviyasar and Rav Yonason
were debating that issue, and so Hashem was also repeating their words.
And when David said, "The Torah of Your mouth is better for me than
thousands of gold and silver," he meant to say, "I rejoice in my arduous
study of the holy Torah, realizing that it is the Torah of Your Mouth;
every word that I learn came from and comes from Your Mouth." (Nefesh
HaChaim 4:6)*

What a remarkable insight from the *Nefesh HaChaim*: While we study
the Torah, Hashem involves Himself in our learning to the point where
He repeats our words! This gives us a new perspective on the loftiness of
being *amel* in Torah, which we can use as a means to attain an intimate
relationship with Hashem, raising the bar of our existence to a whole
new spiritual level.

Rav Moshe Chaim Luzzatto in his *Derech Hashem* has an entire chapter dedicated to describing the tremendous influence Torah study has
on the one studying it and its illuminating effect on this world. One
passage discusses the inherent power of Torah and its ability to remedy
even one so distant from Hashem.

אעפ"כ רז גדול גילו לנו החכמים ז"ל, שאילו לא היו הרשעים עוזבים את תלמוד התורה,
סוף שהיו חוזרים למוטב. כי אף על פי שאין בכוחם להמשיך שום המשך מלפניו יתברך
כמו שכתבתי, כבר דברי התורה בעצמם מקודשים ועומדים מצד עצמם, עד שבהתמיד

העסק בהם יגיע מהם פעם אחר פעם קצת התעוררות, וכמו דמות הארה קטנה שבקטנות,
אל העוסק בם, שסוף סוף תגבר עליו ותחזירהו למוטב. והוא מה שכתבו ז"ל: "הלואי אותי
עזבו ותורתי שמרו, שהמאור שבה מחזירן למוטב".

*Our Sages have revealed a very great mystery, however, namely, that if the
wicked would only not abandon the study of the Torah, they would ultimately
return to G-d. Even though they do not have the power to transmit anything
from G-d, as discussed above, the words of the Torah themselves are intrinsi-
cally holy. One who consistently involves himself with the Torah therefore constantly receives a small measure of spiritual motivation from it. Even though
this is the barest possible shadow of the true Illumination, the fact that it is
constantly reinforced gives it the power to ultimately overcome a person and
make him good again. Our Sages thus teach us that G-d said, "If they would
only have kept my Torah, the Light in it would bring them back to the good."[90]*

The *Ramchal* teaches us about the Torah as almost having a therapeutic
component to it. While the resulting influence of Torah study on this
world will vary according to the degree of one's reverence and other
pre-conditions[91] needed to be eligible for the Torah's great benefits; simply studying its words has the power to transform the person. At times
the broken and worn-out soul searches high and low in an attempt to heal
and restore his relationship with Hashem. While being so distanced from
anything spiritual or G-dly and feeling unwelcomed to enter the broad
waters of the Torah, Hashem tells him "stop searching; it is the Torah
itself that has the ability to heal." While we are accustomed to seeking
the guidance of medical professionals when overwhelmed with physical
ailments we must accustom ourselves to using the Torah to heal the spectrum of spiritual ailments that visit us throughout our lives.

---

90   *The Way of God*, Feldheim.
91   See the *Ramchal's* words earlier in this chapter where he elaborates on this idea in great detail.

Bamidbar

Bamidbar

וַיְדַבֵּר ה' אֶל מֹשֶׁה בְּמִדְבַּר סִינַי לָמָּה בְּמִדְבַּר סִינַי, מִכָּאן שָׁנוּ חֲכָמִים בִּשְׁלֹשָׁה דְבָרִים נִתְּנָה הַתּוֹרָה, בָּאֵשׁ, וּבַמַּיִם, וּבַמִּדְבָּר. בָּאֵשׁ וכו', וְלָמָּה נִתְּנָה בִּשְׁלֹשָׁה דְבָרִים הַלָּלוּ, אֶלָּא מָה אֵלּוּ חִנָּם לְכָל בָּאֵי הָעוֹלָם כָּךְ דִּבְרֵי תוֹרָה חִנָּם הֵם, שֶׁנֶּאֱמַר, הוֹי כָּל צָמֵא לְכוּ לַמַּיִם.

"And Hashem spoke to Moshe in the Desert of Sinai."
(Bamidbar 1:1) — Why in the Desert of Sinai? From here our
Sages taught [that] the Torah was given in three ways: through
fire, through water, and in the desert. And why was it given in
these three ways? [To point out that] just as these are free for
all the inhabitants of the world, so too the words of Torah are
free, as is written "Ho, whoever is thirsty, go to the water."

(Yeshayahu 55:1) (Midrash Rabbah 1:6)

Free for All

The Midrash teaches us a fundamental principle in acquiring Torah and growing in *avodas Hashem*. The Torah isn't reserved for an elite or privileged group of people. It doesn't belong to a certain sect of Jews over another. It is available for all who seek the word of Hashem, free for the taking. It was

> The Torah isn't reserved for an elite or privileged group of people.

given in the desert to demonstrate the point that no individual or group should argue at a future time that they are the proprietors of the Torah or that they have a closer relationship with the Giver of the Torah.

A fascinating Gemara in *Maseches Taanis* teaches us the importance of recognizing each individual's right to attain his own share in the Torah and develop his spirituality.

תנו רבנן לעולם יהא אדם רך כקנה ואל יהא קשה כארז. מעשה שבא רבי אלעזר (בן ר')
שמעון ממגדל גדור מבית רבו והיה רכוב על החמור ומטייל על שפת נהר ושמח שמחה
גדולה והיתה דעתו גסה עליו מפני שלמד תורה הרבה. נזדמן לו אדם אחד שהיה מכוער
ביותר אמר לו שלום עליך רבי ולא החזיר לו אמר לו ריקה כמה מכוער אותו האיש שמא
כל בני עירך מכוערין כמותך אמר לו איני יודע אלא לך ואמור לאומן שעשאני כמה מכוער
כלי זה שעשית. כיון שידע בעצמו שחטא ירד מן החמור ונשתטח לפניו ואמר לו נעניתי
לך מחול לי אמר לו איני מוחל לך עד שתלך לאומן שעשאני ואמור לו כמה מכוער כלי זה
שעשית. היה מטייל אחריו עד שהגיע לעירו יצאו בני עירו לקראתו והיו אומרים לו שלום
עליך רבי רבי מורי מורי אמר להם למי אתם קורין רבי רבי אמרו לו לזה שמטייל אחריך
אמר להם אם זה רבי אל ירבו כמותו בישראל אמרו לו מפני מה אמר להם כך וכך עשה
לי אמרו לו אעפ"כ מחול לו שאדם גדול בתורה הוא אמר להם בשבילכם הריני מוחל לו
ובלבד שלא יהא רגיל לעשות כן. מיד נכנס רבי אלעזר בן רבי שמעון ודרש לעולם יהא
אדם רך כקנה ואל יהא קשה כארז.

The Rabbis taught: "A person should always be soft like a reed and not hard like a cedar."

Once, Rabbi Elazar the son of Rabbi Shimon was coming from his teacher's house in Migdal Gedor, riding on a donkey. He was traveling along the bank of the river with a feeling of great joy and a sense of arrogance, because he had learned a great deal of Torah. A very ugly person happened upon him. The ugly person said, "How are you, Rebbe?" Rabbi Elazar did not respond, but rather said, "Empty one — how ugly this fellow is! Are all the people of your town as ugly as you?" The ugly person responded, "I don't know, but you should go to the Craftsman who made me and tell Him how ugly is the vessel He made." Rabbi Elazar knew that he had sinned. He got off the donkey, prostrated himself before the other fellow and said, "I have misspoken before you. Forgive me." The man said, "I will not forgive you until you go to the Craftsman who made me and tell Him how ugly is the vessel He made." Rabbi Elazar followed him until they came to his town. All the townspeople came out to greet Rabbi Elazar and they said, "Welcome, our Rabbi, our Rabbi, our teacher, our teacher." The ugly fellow said, "To whom are you referring as

> *Torah is available for all who seek the word of Hashem, free for the taking.*

*your rabbi?" They said, "The one who is walking behind you." He said to them,
"If this is a rabbi, let there not be more like him in Israel." They said, "Why?" He
said to them, "He did such-and-such to me." They said to him, "Nevertheless,
forgive him because he is a great Torah scholar." He said to them, "For your sake
I forgive him, but on condition that he not become accustomed to act this way."
Rabbi Elazar immediately entered [the Beis Midrash] and taught, "A person
should always be soft like a reed and not hard like a cedar." (Taanis 20a–20b)*

The *Keren Orah*, Rav Yitzchak of Karlin explains this complex Gemara
with the following idea:

מזה נראה שעסק התורה העיקר בזה להזריח מאורה לזולתו גם כן ולהביאן אל השלימות,
ולא ח"ו להתגדר בה לאמר לי לבדי ניתנה הארץ, כי בזה הוא נותן מחסור בברואיו ח"ו,
ועיקר שלימות התורה הוא להשלים הבריאה ולא יהיה בה שום חסרון, וזה שאמרו ז"ל
(נדרים א לח) אין השכינה שורה אלא על חכם גבור עשיר ועניו, כי אחרי כל המעלות אם
ח"ו מחמת זאת יתן מחסור לזולתו כל מעלותיו לחסר תבואנו, על כן צריכה מדת ענוה
להיות עמהם, ובלעדה כולם כאין, ולזה בשביל שהיתה דעתו של ר"א גסה עליו נזדמן לו
אדם שהיה מכוער ביותר לנסותו אם יתן בו חסרון, או תורתו יעמוד לו שלא ליתן חסרון
בשום בריה, ואדרבה להשלים את הכל לתכלית, ולא עמד בנסיון והתחיל לבזותו ולספר
בחסרונו, והשיב לו האיש לך לאומן שעשאני, לרמוז לו כי כל החכמה שלמד הוא ח"ו בלא
יועיל אם על ידי זה הוא נותן חסרון בבריות.

*In telling over this story, the Gemara emphasizes that it occurred just after
Rabbi Elazar returned from studying Torah. This teaches us that the main
point of Torah learning is to shine its light on others, and have them thus
reach perfection. One must not study Torah so that, Heaven forbid, he may
take pride in it and say, "This is all for me" — for by doing so, he relates to the
other creations of Hashem as if they are lacking, Heaven forbid, whereas the
primary aspect of Torah perfection is to raise up and perfect all of Creation,
leaving no deficiency.*

*This, too, is the lesson of the Sages in Nedarim 38a: "The Divine Presence
dwells only on one who is wise, mighty, wealthy, and humble." Why is "humility" included among these other striking traits? The explanation is that if
one is wise, mighty and wealthy, but this leads him to look askance, Heaven
forbid, at others — then all of his great traits will lead him to be lacking!
This is why he must have humility together with the other traits; without it,
everything else is worthless.*

*Thus, it was precisely because Rabbi Elazar was feeling too proud of himself
that he chanced upon this homely man — to test him and to see if he would*

*look down upon him and see only his shortcomings, or, preferably, if his
Torah would help him not see a lack in anyone else, but on the contrary:
would rather help him perfect all, as is the ultimate purpose.*

*Rabbi Elazar did not pass the test, and instead denigrated the man, em-
phasizing his negative side. The man responded, "Go and complain to the
Craftsman Who made me" — hinting to him that all the Torah wisdom he
had amassed was, Heaven forbid, of no worth if it leads him to see the shortcomings of others. (Keren Orah, Maseches Taanis)*

Each of Us Unique

The *Keren Orah* understands Rabbi Elazar's error as rooted in his arrogance, developed from his extensive Torah learning and his inability to
see the value of others not involved in the pursuit of the highest degree
of Torah learning. Of course, the ugliness to which Rabbi Elazar refers
is the spiritual ugliness of observing a man void of Torah. This may be
further understood regarding those people that look down at others for
not practicing their *avodas Hashem* in the identical manner as they do.
The Torah, as the Midrash stated, was given in the *midbar* to illustrate
the point that it is available for all to engage in, and that no one group
has the capacity to intimidate others with their way being the better or
only way to serve Hashem. We are all created with a unique purpose and
with a targeted spiritual growth to achieve during our sojourn in *Olam
HaZeh*, but we may not try to measure the growth of another *Yid*.

Perhaps the "ugly" person was telling Rabbi Elazar to "go to the
Craftsman that made me and ask Him why I was created with the simple purpose of reaching the level of saying a *berachah*, or just giving
tzedakah, and why reaching great levels in Torah is not my intended
purpose. Go to the Craftsman and ask Him how He runs His world."

Looking Down from Way Up

The *Maharal*, Rav Yehudah Lowe of Prague, in his *Nesivos Olam*, develops a beautiful idea based on the location in which this story takes place:

ומעשה שבא ר' אלעזר בן ר"ש ממגדל גדר... והשם הזה ממגדל גדר לא מצינו בשום
מקום ומה בא לאשמועינן בזה שבא ממגדל גדר, בודאי אם היה המקום הזהמיוחד בתורה

יותר מן שאר מקום יש לומר דבשביל כך זכר המקום אבל לא מצאנו זה במקום אחר. לכך
נראה שבא לומר כי לא היה ח"ו חטא בצדיק הזה שילבש ח"ו גאוה, רק שהתורה היא
למעלה למעלה על הכל כמו המגדל לכך ישבת"ח קצת גאוה, ולפיכך אמרו בפ"ק דסוטה
שצריך שיהיה בת"ח אחד משמונה בשמינית ... מכל מקום שמעינן מזה כי הגאוה הוא על
בעל תורה בטבע וכל זה מצד הגדולה והמעלה שיש לתורה, ולכך אמר שבא ממגדל גדר,
שנקראת התורה בשם זה כי יש בתורה המעלה העליונה שנרמז בשם מגדל שהוא גבוה
למעלה, והתורה היא נבדלת מכל העולם כמו הגדר הזה שהוא נבדל מן רשות הרבים,
ומפני כך בעל התורה יש בו קצת גאוה שרואה עצמו ג"כ גבוה ונבדל משאר הבריות. ור"א
בשביל שלא היה נזהר ונשמר מאד מן הגאוה בא אל דבר הזה שאמר כמה מכוער אדם זה,
והיה מבזה הבריאה שהיא מן הש"י ודבר זה אין ראוי לגדול בתורה כמו שהיה ר"א בעל
תורה, כי אם היה נולד חסרעין ממעי אמו כיון שאין זה כדרך עולם ובריאות הש"י היא
בשלימות אין לומר על זה לך לאותו שעשאני ואמור אליו למה עשה אותי כך כי אין זה
מעשה אומן, אבל זה שלא היה בו מום, זה, בודאי מעשה אומן כי כך היא הבריאה בעצמה,
ופירש"י כי זה האדם שנזדמן לו היה אליהו ז"ל וכדי להציל אותו מן החטא עשה לו אליהו
ז"ל דבר זה אליו שידע שחטא, וכמו שאמר אח"כ אליו ובלבד שלא ירגיל לעשות כך.

The Gemara begins the story by stating that Rabbi Elazar came from Migdal Gader. We have not seen this name Migdal Gader anywhere else in the sources; what does the Gemara wish to tell us by emphasizing that he came from there? Certainly, if this location was somehow special in the Torah more than any other, we could assume that this is the reason why the Gemara here mentions it — but in fact it is mentioned nowhere else.

It therefore appears that the Gemara wishes to explain the source of the righteous Rabbi Elazar's feeling of superiority. It did not come, Heaven forbid, from a source of sin. Rather, the Torah is very high above all, like a migdal (tower) — and this is why a Torah scholar has a measure of pride. In fact, the Gemara in the first perek (chapter) of Maseches Sotah teaches that a Torah scholar must have 1/64th of the attribute of pride.

... In any event, we learn from this that pride is found in the very nature of a Torah man — precisely because of the greatness of Torah. This is why we are told that Rabbi Elazar came from Migdal Gader — for this name refers to the Torah: The Torah has the great virtue alluded to in the word migdal in that it towers above all else. The Torah is also distinct from the world, just like a gader (fence) which by its nature is distinct from the public domain — and this is why a man of Torah has a measure of pride, as he sees himself, like the Torah, towering over and separate from everyone else.

And because Rabbi Elazar did not sufficiently guard himself from arrogance, he reached the point where he was able to say, "How ugly is this man," thus abusing a creation of Hashem. Such a thing is not worthy of a great Torah scholar such as

Rabbi Elazar — unless the man would have been missing an eye from birth, [in which case Rabbi Elazar would have been justified in saying what he said,] for this is not the way of the world, as the Creation of Hashem is perfect. In such a case, it would not have been right [for the man] to respond, "Go to He Who made me and ask Him why He made me this way" — for the handiwork was not of high quality. But one who was born with no abnormal imperfection — this is certainly high-caliber handiwork, for Creation itself is perfect [and therefore the man was right in responding to Rabbi Elazar as he did].

And Rashi explains that the man whom Rabbi Elazar encountered was Eliyahu HaNavi, and that Eliyahu's purpose in causing this to befall Rabbi Elazar was to have him realize his sin and thus repent of it — as the man said afterwards, "I will forgive him on condition that he not do it again." (Maharal, Nesivos Olam II, Nesiv Ha'Anavah 7)

The Maharal observes that the story takes place in Migdal Gedor, and focuses on the words "tower" and "fence" in the name of this unfamiliar location. A tower is a tall structure from which one can look down upon others, and a fence symbolizes a boundary that separates one from the public. These two items symbolize how Rabbi Elazar's Torah learning influenced the way he interacted with the ugly person. Rabbi Elazar developed an arrogance which, if measured and tempered, is acceptable for those who toil in Torah, since the Torah itself is paramount. However, Rabbi Elazar wasn't cautious with this trait and it led him to shame a person he met while traveling home. Living in the proverbial tower can be dangerous, causing us to look down at others and focus on their negatives. Similarly, when we build borders to highlight our prominence in society, we are in effect communicating that Hashem was deficient in His work and fashioned a human that is lacking — when clearly the opposite is true: We were all created with specific objectives, and one person's failure in *avodas Hashem* may be another's success.

Eventually, Rabbi Elazar's apology was accepted — provided that he gave his word to limit this behavior. For us, the lesson is clear. While at times it is important to set clear dividing lines in situations where the truth can become blurred, it is important for us to see those who are less religious than we not as ugly people but rather as those with a different role and purpose, and we must do all that we can to inspire them.

Transporting the Vessels of the Mishkan

The *pasuk* in our *parashah* that discusses the manner in which the *Mishkan's* vessels were transported while B'nei Yisrael journeyed alludes to the above idea.

וְלָקְחוּ בֶּגֶד תְּכֵלֶת וְכִסּוּ אֶת מְנֹרַת הַמָּאוֹר וְאֶת נֵרֹתֶיהָ וְאֶת מַלְקָחֶיהָ וְאֶת מַחְתֹּתֶיהָ וְאֵת כָּל כְּלֵי שַׁמְנָהּ אֲשֶׁר יְשָׁרְתוּ לָהּ בָּהֶם: וְנָתְנוּ אֹתָהּ וְאֶת כָּל כֵּלֶיהָ אֶל מִכְסֵה עוֹר תַּחַשׁ וְנָתְנוּ עַל הַמּוֹט:

They shall take a blue cloth and cover the Menorah for lighting and its lamps, its tongs, and its scoops, and all its oil vessels used in performing its service. They shall put it and its vessels into a covering of tachash skin and place it on a pole. (Bamidbar 4:9–10)

When the major vessels in the *Mishkan* were transported, they were covered and carried via poles inserted on their sides. The Menorah, however, was not fashioned with carrying poles on its side. Instead, it was covered and then placed on a pole which was then moved to transport when traveling in the *Midbar*. Perhaps the Menorah, which represented the Torah,[92] was specifically designed in this manner without carrying poles on its side in order to symbolize that no person or group can ever argue that they alone "carry" the Torah or that they have a more privileged right to it. The Torah was given to us all and is free for the taking for all of Klal Yisrael. The Menorah's lights represent the Torah which should not be contained with rigid borders and fences, but must rather shine and share its rays for all to experience and gain benefit.

A Bouquet of Flowers

The Viener Rav, Rav Asher Anshel Katz, explains in his *sefer Shemen Rosh*[93] that each *shevet* had its own banner waving above its place of encampment, colored with the same color that represented the *shevet* on the *Choshen* worn by the *Kohen Gadol*. In addition to the unique insignia on each banner, every individual *shevet* had a different color on

---

92   The Gemara *Bava Basra* 25b says אמר רבי יצחק, הרוצה שיחכים ידרים, ושיעשיר יצפין. וסימניך שולחן בצפון ומנורה בדרום.

93   *Bamidbar, chelek chamishi.*

its banner — signifying its uniqueness and importance even as it chose its own individual path in serving Hashem. Rav Katz adds that this may be the reason for our custom to beautify our shuls and homes with flowers on Shavuos. Flowers look their best when the bouquet is mixed with an array of colors, and the Twelve Tribes, too, were a combination of colors represented by their distinctive paths in *avodas Hashem*, each an integral part of B'nei Yisrael's overall structure.

Naso

דַּבֵּר אֶל בְּנֵי יִשְׂרָאֵל וְאָמַרְתָּ אֲלֵהֶם אִישׁ אוֹ אִשָּׁה כִּי יַפְלִא לִנְדֹּר נֶדֶר נָזִיר לְהַזִּיר לַה':

Speak to the People of Israel and say to them:
A man or woman who sets himself apart by making a Nazirite
vow to abstain for the sake of Hashem…(Bamidbar 6:2)

כי יפלא: יפריש. למה נסמכה פרשת נזיר לפרשת סוטה, לומר לך שכל הרואה סוטה בקלקולה יזיר עצמו מן היין, שהוא מביא לידי ניאוף.

Who sets himself apart — *Why is the section dealing with the Nazir juxtaposed with the section of the wayward wife? To tell us that whoever sees a Sotah in her disgrace should vow to abstain from wine, for it leads to adultery. (Rashi)*

Rav Zalman Sorotzkin, *zt"l*, in his *Oznaim LaTorah*, asks why it was necessary to become a *Nazir* after witnessing the *Sotah* in her disgrace. If, as Rashi quotes the Gemara as teaching, wine can lead to adulterous behavior, then it would be wise and prudent to stay away from wine alone! Why is there a need to become a *Nazir* and forbid oneself from all grape products, from cutting one's hair, and from becoming contaminated by a human corpse?[94]

---

94 See the *Oznaim LaTorah* for his remarkable explanation.

Interestingly, we find many parallels between a marital relationship and the laws to which a *Nazir* must adhere. The unraveling of a marriage typically does not occur overnight. Rather, it develops in a progression after months or years of neglect. The relationship between husband and wife must never reach the auto-pilot mode where the relationship remains in a slumbered state of no movement or renewal. Marriage requires constant maintenance, with small and frequent gestures of kindness and thoughtfulness to counteract the decay that can root itself over time. It is not a battery-operated machine which, once the batteries are replaced, can go unchecked until the next time the low-battery alert beeps. Marriage rather requires daily care so that it may operate properly, as does any meaningful relationship.

Marriage requires constant maintenance, with small and frequent gestures of kindness and thoughtfulness.

The *Nazir* accepts upon himself to become holy and separate himself for the sake of Hashem. Simply separating from wine alone without the necessary preventive measures and boundaries to ensure success will likely result in failure. Therefore, the Torah prohibits all grape products, and enacts other boundaries as well, to ensure holiness. This will keep the *Nazir* holy and prevent him from falling off course.

Safety Measures

A nuclear energy site is equipped with extensive security measures and backup safety systems which provide layer upon layer of safety in the event of an emergency. Similarly, marriage needs to have a plan to guarantee that the relationship does not turn stale. Preventive measures in a relationship are the boundaries which need to be established so that the relationship is kept fresh and exciting. One who witnesses the degradation of the *Sotah* should separate himself from wine, reminding him of the boundaries that the Torah established for the *Nazir*. This will inspire him to set his own boundaries and allow his marriage to flourish and thrive.

But what role do these boundaries play in a marriage? How do they work to cultivate the relationship between husband and wife?

Wine and Marriage

Perhaps the wine prohibited to the *Nazir* is symbolic of the building, or dismantling, of a relationship. It is the nature of wine to slowly intoxicate, with every additional sip adding to the alcohol's influence. A marriage, too, can be destroyed by a slow process of disregard for a spouse, sip after sip, leading eventually to "inebriation" and the resulting inability to repair months of neglect.

The same is true in a successful marriage. It also develops progressively, sip after sip. Great marriages require diligence and nurturing, with careful planning and effort. A small thank you, a pleasant word, and a spontaneous sign of affection will breed a healthy relationship and respect between the two partners. Thinking of one's spouse in the midst of a hectic day with a short phone call or an unexpected gift of appreciation contributes to an entire life of happiness together.

Witnessing the plight of the *Sotah* brings to mind the dangers of wine: the "sip after sip" of neglect, as well as the missed opportunities of not taking the small sips or steps to enrich and enhance the closest human relationship possible between two people.

Of course, all human relationships correspond to the epitome of the holiest and deepest relationship that an individual can develop: Our connection with Hashem. This too does not take effect instantaneously, but rather needs to be nurtured and cared for with a genuine will, which can then over time reach the highest levels of closeness with Hashem.

Small Steps toward Peace

Rav Avraham Yitzchak HaKohen Kook[95] offers a beautiful insight into peaceful relationships and the mechanism through which they can be achieved. We ask Hashem each night in our *Maariv*: *U'fros aleinu succas shlomecha*, "Spread over us the *succah* shelter of Your peace." What exactly is the connection between peace and the shelter of a *succah*? Rav Kook explains that a *succah* that lacks the necessary three walls, or appears to be otherwise invalid, can still be validated if certain well-known

---

95   *Moadei HaRei'ah, Succos.*

halachic principles can be applied. These principles include *gud achis*,[96] *gud asik*,[97] *lavud*,[98] *dofen akumah*,[99] and two-plus-a-*tefach*.[100] The same is true with peace: It can be difficult to attain, but is so precious that even if it cannot be achieved completely, one should still strive for as much as possible. Even if the peace that is realized is only at the level of a *succah* that is *halachically* valid only via special *halachic* mechanisms that are put into place, such peace is still admirable and worthwhile.

It is the small gestures that will help us build and nurture harmonious relationships.

---

96   A wall that starts from the top of the *succah* and reaches within approximately thirty-nine inches of the ground is viewed as though it reaches the ground.

97   As long as the wall is ten *tefachim* tall, the principle of *gud asik* teaches that the wall is considered to reach *ad lashamayim*, connecting with the *sechach* at whatever height it happens to be.

98   Two parts of a wall are viewed as if they are connected, despite a space of less than three handbreadths between them.

99   Invalid *sechach* is viewed as if it is part of the wall leading up to it.

100   Two walls and part of a third.

Beha'aloscha

דַּבֵּר אֶל אַהֲרֹן וְאָמַרְתָּ אֵלָיו בְּהַעֲלֹתְךָ אֶת הַנֵּרֹת אֶל מוּל פְּנֵי הַמְּנוֹרָה
יָאִירוּ שִׁבְעַת הַנֵּרוֹת:

Speak to Aharon and say to him, "When you light the lamps,
the seven lamps shall cast their light toward the face
of the Menorah." (Bamidbar 8:2)

בהעלתך: למה נסמכה פרשת המנורה לפרשת הנשיאים, לפי שכשראה אהרן חנוכת
הנשיאים חלשה דעתו, שלא היה עמהם בחנוכה, לא הוא ולא שבטו, אמר לו הקב"ה חייך,
שלך גדולה משלהם, שאתה מדליק ומטיב את הנרות.

When you light — *Why is the portion dealing with the Menorah juxtaposed*
with the portion dealing with the Nesi'im (tribal princes)? For when Aharon saw
the dedication [offerings] of the Nesi'im, he felt distressed that neither he nor his
tribe joined them in this dedication. So Hashem said to him, "By your life, yours is
greater than theirs, for you will light and prepare the lamps." (Rashi)

וְזֶה מַעֲשֵׂה הַמְּנֹרָה מִקְשָׁה זָהָב עַד יְרֵכָהּ עַד פִּרְחָהּ מִקְשָׁה הִוא
כַּמַּרְאֶה אֲשֶׁר הֶרְאָה ה' אֶת מֹשֶׁה כֵּן עָשָׂה אֶת הַמְּנֹרָה:

This was the work of the Menorah: hammered gold,
from its base to its flower it was a hammered work;
according to the form that Hashem had shown Moshe,
so did he construct the Menorah. (Bamidbar 8:4)

201

וזה מעשה המנורה: שהראהו הקב"ה באצבע לפי שנתקשה בה, לכך נאמר וזה.

This was the work of the Menorah — *Hashem showed it to him with His Finger, for Moshe had difficulty with [constructing] it. That is why it says, "And this is [the work]."* (Rashi)

וַיֹּאמְרוּ הָאֲנָשִׁים הָהֵמָּה אֵלָיו אֲנַחְנוּ טְמֵאִים לְנֶפֶשׁ אָדָם לָמָּה נִגָּרַע
לְבִלְתִּי הַקְרִיב אֶת קָרְבַּן ה' בְּמֹעֲדוֹ בְּתוֹךְ בְּנֵי יִשְׂרָאֵל:

Those men said to him (Moshe), "We are ritually unclean [because of contact] with a dead person; [but] why should we be excluded so as not to bring the offering of Hashem in its appointed time, with all of B'nei Yisrael? (Bamidbar 9:7)

Parashas Beha'aloscha is filled with several different events that took place while B'nei Yisrael were journeying in the *Midbar*. There is, however, one central consistent theme that is interwoven into the above *pesukim*, which communicates an important lesson as to how we must relate to *mitzvos* in general.

The *pasuk* begins with Aharon HaKohen being awarded the mitzvah of lighting the Menorah. Rashi, quoting the *Midrash Tanchuma*, explains that Aharon felt distressed and left out of the inauguration of the *Mishkan* since he and his *shevet* were not included in the dedication offerings. Hashem appeased him with the honor of lighting the Menorah.

How do we define this *chalishus hadaas*, distress, that Aharon experienced? He certainly knew his role as *Kohen Gadol (High Priest)*, and if he wasn't given a part in the *Mishkan's* inaugural ceremonies, why was he not satisfied with the knowledge that he would be serving Hashem regularly in the *Mishkan*?

Later on, the *pasuk* describes how the Menorah was constructed, as Moshe was taught in *Parashas Terumah*. Moshe was instructed that the Menorah must be hammered out from one chunk of gold. That is, instead of connecting each branch separately to the Menorah's base, the builders were to fashion the entire Menorah from one solid piece of gold. For Moshe, this was difficult to understand — until Hashem showed him an image of what it was to look like. Rashi, in *Parashas*

Terumah, further describes this episode and says that after Hashem saw Moshe's difficulty, He instructed him to throw the gold into the fire, from which it was then created by Hashem alone.

The question may be asked: If it was humanly possible to manufacture a Menorah out of a single chunk of gold, what was Moshe's difficulty? Why did Hashem ultimately not allow for it to be constructed in that manner? Moshe was first given a description of its complex components and later shown an image to make it more understandable to him — yet this still wasn't sufficient and Hashem had him throw the chunk of gold into the fire. Why?

A few *pesukim* further, the Torah introduces us to the group of people that came to Moshe with a complaint: "Why should we be left out of the *korban Pesach* offering? Just because we are impure, as a result of performing the mitzvah of being involved with the casket of Yosef, should we be excluded from this mitzvah?"

What was it specifically that bothered this group of people? The Torah forbids one who is *tamei* to bring a *korban Pesach* and they were therefore excluded. They were not being penalized, but rather exempted.[101] Why did they not realize that their obligation no longer applied because of their impure state? Why did they complain?

The Common Denominator

Perhaps we can suggest that the common denominator connecting these three events — Aharon's distress, Moshe's difficulty in constructing the Menorah, and the complaints of those whose impurity exempted them from bringing the *korban Pesach* — is a strong will and desire to fulfill the *ratzon Hashem*, G-d's desire. They were all not satisfied with taking the easy way out. There are those who are overjoyed when *tachanun* is not said, or when the rabbi is away and no *derashah* will be said that Shabbos. For Aharon, Moshe, and the group of men who were *tamei* this was not the case. They

They were not satisfied with the easy way out.

---

101   This is the principle of *onehs derachmana patrei*; see *Avodah Zarah* 54a.

desired to perform the Will of Hashem at every possible opportunity. Being "excused" was not enough for them; they were not content
with the extenuating circumstances. They wanted a part in the mitzvah, whether it was the inauguration of the *Mishkan*, the construc-
tion of the Menorah, or the bringing of the *korban Pesach*. For them,
accepting "no" for an answer was not an easy feat. This is why Aharon
felt distressed, and it is why Hashem, *keviyachol*, "went the extra
mile" to show Moshe how the Menorah should look. Moshe, Aharon,
and the others communicated the will and desire to grow and go
beyond the call of duty, resulting in Hashem reciprocating and allowing them to fulfill their true *ratzon*, desire.

Power of an Individual's Will and Desire

The power of a strong will and desire to grow spiritually is further
illustrated in another episode related in the *pasuk*.

וַיִּשְׁמַע מֹשֶׁה אֶת הָעָם בֹּכֶה לְמִשְׁפְּחֹתָיו אִישׁ לְפֶתַח אָהֳלוֹ וַיִּחַר אַף ה' מְאֹד וּבְעֵינֵי מֹשֶׁה רָע:

Moshe heard the people weeping with their families, each one at the entrance
to his tent. Hashem became very angry, and Moshe considered it evil.
(Bamidbar 11:10)

בכה למשפחותיו: משפחות משפחות נאספים ובוכים לפרסם תרעומתן בגלוי. ורבותינו
אמרו למשפחותיו על עסקי משפחות, על עריות הנאסרות להם.

Weeping with their families — *Families gathered to weep in groups so*
as to publicize their grievance. Our Sages say that the meaning [here of
"their families"] is: "Concerning family matters," that is, they wept because
intramarriage among family members was now forbidden to them (once
the Torah was given).

According to the second opinion cited by Rashi, they were crying concerning family matters, namely, because they were no longer allowed
to marry their family members. Immediate family members were now
forbidden one to another.

A fascinating *Maharal* in his *Gur Aryeh* quoted in the introduction to
Shev Shmat'sa sheds light on this event:

 וישמע העם בוכה למשפחותיו והיינו על עסקי עריות שנאסר להם. והנה בספר גור אריה
פרשת ויגש¹⁰² הקשה כיון דישראל במתן תורה דין גרים היה להם, וכדאיתא ביבמות
דישראל היו צריכין מילה והזאה וטבילה כדין גרים, וקיי"ל גר נושא אחותו משום דגר
שנתגייר כקטן שנולד דמי, ואם כן לאותו הדור היה ראוי להתיר קרובות ערוה. ותירץ דלא
אמרינן גר שנתגייר כקטן שנולד דמי אלא בגר שנתגייר מדעתו וחפצו אז הוא כקטן שנולד,
אבל בשעת מתן תורה שהוכרחו לקבלה שכפה עליהם הר כגיגית, בזה לא הוי כקטן שנולד
ע"ש. לזה בכו למשפחותיהם על עסקי עריות. כיון שהמן הכריחם לקבלת התורה, כמ"ש
אות ח'. על כן נאסרו בקרובותיהם. אבל אם לא היה על ידי הכרח רק ברצון ובבחירה, היו
מותרים בקרובותיהם.

"Moshe heard the nation weeping with their families" (Bamidbar 11:10) — The Sifri says that they were crying about their relatives that were now forbidden to them. The Gur Aryeh on Vayigash raises a question about the basis for this prohibition: "When Yisrael received the Torah, they were in the category of 'new converts,' as the Gemara in Yevamos says, and they required circumcision, sprinkling and immersion just like converts. We know that a convert may marry his biological sister, because "a new convert is like a newborn child [and has no relatives]" — and therefore the B'nei Yisrael should have been permitted to marry their sisters after the Giving of the Torah [unlike what the Sifri says]."

The Maharal answers that we say "a new convert is like a newborn child" only when the convert took on Judaism of his own volition. But when the Torah was given, B'nei Yisrael were forced to accept it, for Hashem "arched the mountain like a barrel over them" — and in such a case, they were not like newborn children.

This is why they cried over the newly forbidden relations, because the manna forced them, as I wrote above in section 8, and they were thus forbidden to their relatives. But if the Torah had been accepted totally willingly, they would have been permitted to them.

(Shev Shmat'sa, Introduction, section 9)

After the Giving of the Torah (when B'nei Yisrael all converted), they might have been considered like newborn children,[103] with all previous family relationships severed and permitting them to marry their sisters. However, the *Gur Aryeh* explains, this Talmudic principle is only applied when the conversion takes place with one's Free Will. It did not

---

102   עה"פ ושאול בן הכנענית מו,י.

103   *Yevamos* 97b.

apply when the Torah was given, because the nation was forced to convert, as the Gemara in *Maseches Shabbos* tells us, [104] "The mountain was raised upon them. and they were given an ultimatum of either accepting the Torah or being buried under it." Given the forced nature of their conversion, they could not intermarry, as the prohibition of *arayos*[105] fully applied to them.

When tapped into, our determination and desire to change that rests deep inside the heart can transform our existence.

Perhaps the lesson derived from this idea is to teach us the power and far-reaching impact of one's own will and desire. Converting to Judaism with the desire to change one's status can actually have the power to render the individual as if he was newly born, with no link to the past. We see again how far an individual's will and yearning for *ruchniyus*, spirituality, can take him — and how much its lack can restrict him. It is not tangible, nor is it necessarily verbalized, but when tapped into, our determination and desire to change which rests deep inside the heart can transform our very existence eternally.

---

104   *Shabbos* 88a.
105   Forbidden intimate relationships.

Shelach

וַיּוֹצִיאוּ דִּבַּת הָאָרֶץ אֲשֶׁר תָּרוּ אוֹתָהּ אֶל בְּנֵי יִשְׂרָאֵל לֵאמֹר הָאָרֶץ
אֲשֶׁר עָבַרְנוּ בָהּ לָתוּר אוֹתָהּ אֶרֶץ אֹכֶלֶת יוֹשְׁבֶיהָ הִוא וְכָל הָעָם
אֲשֶׁר רָאִינוּ בְתוֹכָהּ אַנְשֵׁי מִדּוֹת:

They spread an [evil] report about the land which
they had scouted, telling B'nei Yisrael, "The land we passed
through to explore is a land that consumes its inhabitants
and all the people we saw in it are men of stature."

(Bamidbar 13:32)

Much has been written about the episode of the Spies and their sin. Moshe sent them to scout the land and they were given detailed instructions what to look for and report back. They brought back their findings. What then was their error?

Finding and Uplifting the Spiritual Sparks in the Physical Mundane

Rav Menachem Mendel Schneerson, *zt"l*, the last Lubavitcher Rebbe, explains brilliantly[106] a fundamental idea about *Olam HaZeh*. As long

---

106   *Likutei Sichos* IV, pg. 1043 (Yiddish).

as B'nei Yisrael were in the desert, life was about serving Hashem in a completely controlled spiritual climate, enveloped solely in *ruchniyus*. The manna, Clouds of Glory, and the Well of Miriam were all there to create a utopian environment of total spirituality, satisfying all of the nation's physical needs without any human intervention and rendering the people worthy of receiving the Torah.

The *Meraglim* (Spies) saw the land and understood that upon entering Eretz Yisrael, B'nei Yisrael's role would change dramatically. They would now have to toil on the land, and the scouts were concerned that this would interfere with their ability to dedicate themselves to serving Hashem. They argued that the Land of Eretz Yisrael was an *eretz ocheles yoshvehah, a land that consumes its inhabitants.* That is, the Land would ultimately make its inhabitants one with it, a people of "land," involved in materialistic pursuits. It would thus rob them of the spiritual enclave the *Midbar* offered, which enabled them to be at one with Hashem. They reasoned that being involved with the land and serving Hashem were contradictory ideas with no common ground.

And this is where the *Meraglim* were mistaken. The whole purpose of life in the *Midbar* was to be a preparation. It was a sort of training camp for B'nei Yisrael's mission in the world: to create an environment in which we endeavor to reveal the G-dliness in the non-spiritual. As the *Midrash Tanchuma* says:

בשעה שברא הקדוש ברוך הוא את העולם נתאוה שיהא לו דירה בתחתונים כמו שיש בעליונים.

At the time Hashem created the world He desired a dwelling place for Himself down on earth similar to that in the heavens. (Tanchuma Naso 16)

Hashem created a world in which He wishes that we seek Him out and uncover His holiness down on earth. As the *pasuk* says in *Mishlei,* בְּכָל דְּרָכֶיךָ דָעֵהוּ, in all your paths know Him (*Mishlei* 3:6).

There lives a spark of spiritual essence throughout Hashem's entire Creation, and it is incumbent upon us to expose the hidden Divine Presence that waits to be discovered and made holy.

But the *Meraglim* and the B'nei Yisrael were not satisfied with this approach. They believed that remaining in their current status was far more important than the risk of becoming overpowered by the materialistic pursuit of working and settling the land. Two scouts did not agree; one of them, Calev, spoke out:

וַיַּהַס כָּלֵב אֶת הָעָם אֶל מֹשֶׁה וַיֹּאמֶר עָלֹה נַעֲלֶה וְיָרַשְׁנוּ אֹתָהּ כִּי יָכוֹל נוּכַל לָהּ:

Calev silenced the people to [hear] Moshe, and he said, "We can surely go up and take possession of it, for we can indeed overcome it." (Bamidbar 13:30)

Calev attempted to control the people and calm their concerns by telling them that *ruchniyus* and *gashmiyus* can be partnered together. This is alluded to by his use of the duplicate form: עָלֹה נַעֲלֶה, symbolizing that both *ruchniyus* and *gashmiyus* can be joined as we ascend in our *avodas Hashem*. This is what Hashem intended for us: to find the spiritual sparks in the ordinary by elevating them and giving them a greater and holier purpose than the mundane we see them as, thus giving Him a *dirah batachtonim*, a dwelling place down here in This World.

Back to Mitzrayim?

וַיֹּאמְרוּ אִישׁ אֶל אָחִיו נִתְּנָה רֹאשׁ וְנָשׁוּבָה מִצְרָיְמָה:

They said to each other, "Let us appoint a leader and return to Mitzrayim!" (Bamidbar 14:4)

The story of the *Meraglim* continues: B'nei Yisrael view their situation as hopeless, and conclude that returning to *Mitzrayim* is to be their solution. One could ask: What was it that they sought to gain by returning? If they perceived their situation as intolerable now, would it be any better in *Mitzrayim*? Besides, *Mitzrayim* was completely decimated, with no remnants of the country in which they were enslaved. How would returning to a place in which they had suffered for years benefit them in any way?

Perhaps going back to the physical *Mitzrayim* was never truly suggested. *Mitzrayim*, as its name implies, was about boundaries and narrowness. Egyptian society was based on a hierarchical power structure[107] in which the upper class ruled and dominated the lower classes of society. This represented the inability to go beyond one's immediate environment into which he was born. The culture of *Mitzrayim* had imposed on the nation a perspective of constraints and limitations.

Satisfied and Comfortable with the Status Quo

To this, the people wished to return. They rationalized, "Let us return to the '*Mitzrayim*' which did not require us to think beyond the status quo, which required no movement or growth. We are satisfied with ourselves and comfortable with the present environment of the *Midbar*. We seek no change in our existence and don't want to be bothered with altering our way of life." Being told that entering Eretz Yisrael would allow for an existence of far-greater spiritual heights was not desirable for them, as they enjoyed the narrowness and limits that offered a comfortable way of living, being fed and clothed without any exposure or vulnerability.

This period of time is designed to prepare us for our eventual entry into the world of interplay between ruchniyus and gashmiyus, where the two are merged.

Some are fortunate to experience several years spent protected and hidden away within the four walls of the *Beis Midrash* — the modern day *Midbar* which serves as the foundation for our future spiritual growth. This period of time is designed to prepare us for our eventual entry into the world of interplay between *ruchniyus* and *gashmiyus*, where the two are merged. This is a world of opportunity that allows for the functional application of all those years of preparation. The intended goal is to build up the *gashmiyus* and use it to both sweeten our own *ruchniyus* and, perhaps primarily and even more importantly, bring forth the hidden G-dliness found in this world. Hashem wants to dwell among us, and it is our obligation to make His world holy by elevating and giving spiritual meaning even to the seemingly mundane materialism that we encounter daily.

107   See our discussion of *Parashas Kedoshim* above.

The Piaczner Rebbe Rav Klonoymous Kalmish Shapira, in his sefer *Derech HaMelech*, shares a related idea.

כי איתא מתלמידי הבעש"ט ז"ל, על הפסוק (תהילים קד, כד) מלאה הארץ קנינך — שאנו אומרים לה' ית', שבכל דבר מן העולם יכולים לקנות את ה', עכלה"ק. וזהו אצל כל איש ישראל, רק כל אחד לפי מצבו קונה את ה' ע"י דברי העולם. למשל, האדם שהוא רעב ובאכילתו שבה אליו נפשו. אז אם יתבונן האדם אף מעט — מה היא פעולת התבואה והמאכל בעולם, ולמה נמצאת, אן לה שום תכלית אחר — רק להשיב את נפשו או נפש שאר אדם. ורואה בזה את מפעולות ה' ית', איך שברא כל דבר בחכמה, וזוכר את טובת ה' אשר עליו שברא בריאות רק בשבילו, כדי שיכנס לסעודה מיד, כדאיתא במדרש (ילק"ש בראשית א, טו). וכשהאדם אוכל לשם ה', אז באכילה עצמה, ובחלק הקדושה אשר במאכל שבא עתה בקרבו — נתוסף לו קדושה. ובפרט מי שיודע לכוון כוונות אכילה, כי כל אחד לפי מצבו יכול למצא בספרים קדושים כוונות על כל דבר, אף בדרך הפשוט. ואין קושי עבודת הכוונות, הכוונות עצמם. כי כמו בפשט — יש למוד ללפני למדן, ואף לפני ילד שמתחיל גמרא, כן בענין הכוונות. רק כל הקושי להאדם הוא שיהיה דעתו ולבו קשור תמיד לקדושה.

מי שמרגיל את עצמו כך, מוסיף בכל דבר אכילה קדושה, וכמו שאמר ר"נ לרבא (ב"ק עא:) — "והאי דלאל אמינא לך באורתא, דלא אכלנא בשרא דתורא", וע"י שאכל בשר שור נתוסף לו קדושה ודעת התורהשלא היה לו בערב. כי באמת יש הרבה בחינות בקדושה שצריך האדם להשיג ולקל בכל עת ועונה, אבל יען חשהאדם הוא בגוף, ונמצא בעולם עשיה, לכן מוכרח לקבל זאת ע"י גוף, ע"י הלחם וכדומה, ולא דוקא ע"י אכילה, רק כל שאר דבר.

The students of the Baal Shem Tov, zt"l, state regarding the pasuk, "The earth is filled with Your acquisitions," (Tehillim 104:24) that we tell Hashem, may He be blessed, that in everything in the world we can acquire Hashem.

And that is true of every Jew. But every individual acquires Hashem via the things of the world on his own level.

For instance, a person is hungry and with his eating restores his soul. Then if he contemplates even a little the function of grain and food in the world, and why it exists, [he sees that] it has no other purpose but to restore a person's soul (of himself or of others). And in this he sees the deeds of Hashem, may He be blessed, of how He created everything with wisdom, and he recalls Hashem's goodness to him, that He created food substances only for him, so that he can begin eating immediately (Yalkut Shimoni, Bereishis 1:15)

And when a person eats for the sake of G-d, then with the eating itself, and with the portion of holiness in the food that now enters into him, holiness is added to him. And this is particularly so in the case of a person who knows how to engage in intentions of eating—and everyone on his own level can find "intentions" on everything in the holy books, even on a simple level.

Any difficulty in the service of "intentions" is not in the intentions them-selves, because this is comparable to learning simple [revealed Torah], where the scholar must learn, even before [he teaches] a child who is beginning Gemara. [So here too, one need study and learn the relevant] "intentions." But a person's difficulty is related to the requirement that his mind and heart be constantly connected to holiness.

A person who accustoms himself to that adds holy eating to everything [that he eats]. And as Rav Nachman told Rava (Bava Kama 71b), "I didn't tell you that last evening because we hadn't eaten meat." As a result of eating meat, he gained holiness and knowledge of the Torah that he had not possessed the previous evening.

This is because in truth there are many levels in holiness that a person must achieve and receive at every moment. But since a person is in a body and in the world of "action," he must receive that [holiness] through the body, through bread and the like—not necessarily through eating, but through everything else as well.

> Hashem's entire world is filled with opportunities for us to tap into His holiness.

Again, we are taught that even the seemingly physical mundane activities which we engage in for sustenance has a large spiritual component hidden within. Hashem's entire world is filled with opportunities for us to tap into His holiness.

Korach

וּתְנוּ בָהֵן אֵשׁ וְשִׂימוּ עֲלֵיהֶן קְטֹרֶת לִפְנֵי ה' מָחָר וְהָיָה הָאִישׁ
אֲשֶׁר יִבְחַר ה' הוּא הַקָּדוֹשׁ רַב לָכֶם בְּנֵי לֵוִי:

And put fire into them and place incense upon them before
Hashem tomorrow, and the man whom Hashem chooses —
he is the holy one; you have taken too much upon yourselves,
sons of Levi. (Bamidbar 16:7)

The rebellion of Korach and his followers is ultimately resolved via two supernatural occurrences:

- First, the *ketores* offering of Aharon is consumed by a fire that then consumes the rebellious followers of Korach.
- Second, the opening-up of the ground to swallow Korach and his possessions.

From this incident of the *ketores* we learn several lessons about ill-intentioned individuals, our relationship with them as a group, and how we must respond to their insubordination.

The Ketores' Ingredients

What is the nature of the *ketores* that it was chosen by Moshe as a

213

means to resolve this dispute and put an end to Korach's rebellion? Let us read the words of Rav Meir Simcha M'Dvinsk, the *Meshech Chochmah*, in his commentary to the *haftarah* of *Parashas Devarim*:

לא תוסיפו הביא מנחת שוא קטרת תועבה הוא לי כו' לא אוכל און ועצרה. הענין, דמצאנו
לרז"ל בכריתות כל תענית שאין בה מפושעי ישראל אינו תענית שהרי חלבנה ריחה רע
ומנאן הכתוב עם סממני הקטרת כו', הרי דדבר הפחות בעצמיותו, בכ"ז כשהוא מתערב
באגודה כללית הוא מתבשם ומועיל להוציא ריח ניחוח מן הסממנים האחרים.

You shall no longer bring vain meal-offerings, it is smoke of abomination to Me...I cannot [bear] iniquity with assembly (Yeshayahu 1:13) — The issue here is that we have found in the words of our Sages (Kerisus 6b) that any fast day that does not include the sinners of Klal Yisrael is not a valid fast day, for the chelbenah spice was foul-smelling and nevertheless was included in the spices of the ketores. Thus, something can be of low-level essence, yet still, when it is mixed into a larger union, it becomes improved and even helps to evoke a pleasant fragrance from the other ingredients.

Rav Meir Simcha teaches that the malodorous *chelbenah* (galbanum) spice, which was part of the *ketores*, represents the sinner or lowly individual with no merit to stand on his own. Still, just as the *chelbenah* is a necessary part of the *ketores*, so too the sinner, when joined with the greater *Klal*, becomes part of something much greater and benefits from the others. He quotes the Gemara in *Maseches Kerisus* that teaches that a general day of fasting must include the sinners of Klal Yisrael, just as the foul-smelling *chelbenah* spice was included in the spices of the *ketores*.

Moshe's Strategy to Save Korach

Ketores has an inherent quality to include the sinner and give him a new status, allowing him the opportunity to become inspired by the scent of those surrounding him.

Perhaps we can say that Moshe had a strategy by which to rescue Korach and his followers by planning to have Korach offer the *ketores*. As the Gemara above describes, the *ketores* has an inherent quality to include the sinner and give him a new status, allowing him the opportunity to become inspired by the scent of those surrounding him.

Unfortunately, as the Torah relates, Korach did not grasp the message and the *ketores* did not effect a change in his heart.

The Rambam, in his *Moreh Nevuchim*, explains the practical function the *ketores* served in the Beis HaMikdash when it was brought twice daily:

וכיון שהמקום המקודש נשחטין בו זבחים רבים בכל יום, ומחתכיו בו בשר, ונקטר,ונרחצין בו הקרבים, אין ספק שאלו הניחוהו כפי המצב הזה בלבד היה ריחו כריח בתי המטבחים, ולפיכך ציווה בו בהקטורת: הקטורת פעמים בכל יום בבקר ובין הערבים, כדי לבשם ריחו וריח בגדי כל העובדים שם, כבר ידעת אמרם מיריחו היו מריחין ריח הקטורת, וגם זה ממה שמקיים יראת המקדש. אבל אילו לא היה לו ריח טוב, כל שכן אילו היה ההפך, הייתה ההרגשה הפך הרוממות, כי הנפשות ניחוחת מאוד לריחות הבשמים ונמשכות אליהן, וקצות מן הריחות הרעים ומתרחקות מהם.

Since many korbanos were slaughtered daily in the Beis HaMikdash, the flesh cut in pieces, and the entrails and legs burnt and washed, the smell of the place would undoubtedly have been like the smell of slaughterhouses, if nothing had been done to counteract it. They were therefore commanded to burn incense there twice every day, in the morning and in the evening, in order to give the place and the garments of those who worked there a pleasant odor. There is a well-known saying of our Sages, "In Yericho they could smell the ketores." This provision likewise supported the dignity and awe of the Beis HaMikdash. If there had not been a good smell, let alone if there had been a stench, it would have produced in the minds of the people the reverse of respect, for our heart generally feels elevated in the presence of a good odor and is attracted by it, but it abhors and avoids a bad smell. (Moreh Nevuchim 3:45)

Eliminating a Foul Smell

According to the Rambam, the *ketores* served a simple and straight-forward function: to allow for a pleasant smell in the Beis HaMikdash. Without it, all the sacrifices would have left a foul and unpleasant odor in the Beis HaMikdash — a sacrilege for a place so holy.

Let us suggest the following: Despite the opportunity Korach was given to be included with the rest of Klal Yisrael through the bringing of the *ketores*, he remained obstinate, resolving to continue with his rebellion. He had been given the chance to repent and recognize the power of each individual and his unique, particular role — but he did not latch onto it. There was thus no place for him in the greater Klal Yisrael; his continued presence would have possibly stirred even a greater rebellion among the B'nei Yisrael. Now came the time for this unpleasant odor to be removed. The *korbanos* were holy offerings and were allowed into the holiest of places, even though they had the potential of leaving a repulsive stench — because there was a method to deal with the odor, namely, as the Rambam so beautifully explained, via the *ketores*. This is why the *ketores*, in particular, was used in the process of eliminating Korach and his followers.

Korach failed to recognize the greatness of each individual, regardless of the position of power or leadership role he did or did not possess. Hashem created all of us as equals, each with a particular purpose and function yet still part of one unified unit called Klal Yisrael. Each and every person is invaluable, as we see from the Gemara in *Kerisus* that taught us that excluding sinners from a public fast day actually invalidates the fast day itself.

The World Was Created for Me

Rav Shmuel Brazil, in his work *Beshvili Nivrah Ha'Olam*,[108] presents a beautiful *remez* (allusion) in relation to the *chelbenah* spice. As the Gemara referenced above taught, *chelbenah* represented the lowest members of Klal Yisrael yet was a necessary ingredient in order for the *ketores* to be valid. The Mishnah[109] teaches that one must feel that the world was created for him: חייב לומר בשבילי נברא העולם. The initials of these words spell the word *chelbenah*. The inclusion of this spice in the *ketores* teaches us the importance of valuing our self-worth and believing that, on some level, Hashem created the world solely for each of us. It's not the position we find ourselves in that gives us value and importance; rather, the mere fact that Hashem created us is what authenticates our existence, making us an important link in the chain that connects us to the greater *Klal*.

108   Page 63.
109   *Sanhedrin* 4:5.

Chukas

זֹאת חֻקַּת הַתּוֹרָה אֲשֶׁר צִוָּה ה' לֵאמֹר דַּבֵּר אֶל בְּנֵי יִשְׂרָאֵל וְיִקְחוּ אֵלֶיךָ
פָרָה אֲדֻמָּה תְּמִימָה אֲשֶׁר אֵין בָּהּ מוּם אֲשֶׁר לֹא עָלָה עָלֶיהָ עֹל:

This is the statute of the Torah which Hashem commanded,
saying: Speak to B'nei Yisrael and have them take for you
a perfectly red unblemished cow, upon which no yoke
was placed. (Bamidbar 19:2)

KPTV in Portland, Oregon reported the following story:

A Washington man who recently closed on a home in Northeast Portland was shocked to find that a family had recently moved in and changed the locks. Rod Nylund said he learned about the occupants, whom he assumes are squatters, last week when a contractor he sent to do work at the home called to tell him it was occupied. Nylund called police and confronted the occupants, but said the officer was unable to do anything about it. Nylund said his realtor found out the couple had not only changed the locks, but started utility service at the home in their names. "It's kind of like buying a car and you walk out to get in it and somebody's sitting in there," said Nylund. Nylund's realtor, Kim Spiess, said the home's previous owner has no idea who is currently living in the home, or how they got there. Neighbors, who asked not to be identified, said they noticed the couple had recently moved into the home, which is near NE 170th and Glisan, after it had been standing vacant for several months. Nylund said he has tried to communicate with the occupants, even offering them money to move out, but has had no luck. "These people are pretty sharp," said Nylund. "They turned the power on thirty days prior to moving into it, and they paid the power bill while the home was vacant." Gresham police confirmed that an officer responded to a call for squatters at the residence, but could not provide details on the outcome of the response. The home's occupants answered a knock on the door Thursday, but would not comment about the situation. According to John Henry Hingson, a Portland-area attorney, Nylund will have to go to court to remove the home's current occupants by filing a forcible entry and detainer action. Nylund said he will be contacting his own attorney to try to claim his property.

What do squatters taking up residence in vacant homes have to do with the purification process facilitated by the ashes of the *Parah Adumah*?

The Void When the Neshamah Parts with the Guf

The saintly *Ohr HaChaim*, Rav Chaim Ibn Attar, commenting on the above *pasuk*, offers a fascinating insight into the concept of *taharah* (purity) and *tumah* (impurity), in terms of the *neshamah's* parting from the body:

זאת חקת התורה. צריך לדעת למה כינה למצוה זו שם כללות התורה, שהיה לו לומר זאת חקה וגו' או זאת חקת הטומאה או חקת הטהרה כדרך אומרו (שמות יב) זאת חקת הפסח, ואין לומר שנתכוון להצריך טהרת אפר פרה לעסוק בתורה, כי לא כן מצינו לרז"ל שאמרו

(ברכות כב.) שאדרבא אין דברי תורה מקבלין טומאה, ולכל סברות רז"ל (שם) אפילו להמחמירים בבעלי קריין מטעם שצריך באימה וביראה וכו' מודים בטמאי מת שמותרים בעסק התורה.

ויתבאר הענין על פי מה שאמרו בפרק בתרא דנזיר (סא:) ופסקו רמב"ם בפרק א' מהלכות טומאת מת שאין הכותי נעשה טמא מת, וזה לשונו שאם נגע במת או נשאו או האהיל עליו הרי הוא כמו שלא נגע וא הא למה זה דומה לבהמה שנגעה וכו' עד כאן. והנה ההבדל שבו הורמו עם בני ישראל משאר הגוים הוא באמצעות קבלת התורה שזולת זה הנה זה ככל הגוים בית ישראל, ומעתה טעמנו צוף דבש אמרי אל במה שאמר זאת חקת התורה פירוש חקה זו של הטומאה ותנאי טהרתה תסובב מהתורה, כי על ידי שקבלו התורה נעשו עם בני ישראל דבר שהרוחנים השפלים תאבים להדבק בהם להיותם חטיבה של קדושה עליונה בחייהם גם במותם, בחייהם שבנוגע במת או יאהיל עליו וכדומה תדבק בהם הטומאה שבמת ולא תחפוץ להפרד אם לא בכח גדול אשר חקק ה' במצוה האמורה בענין של פרה אדומה, ובמותם גם כן תתרבה הטומאה כאומרם ז"ל (ב"מ קיד:) בפסוק אדם כי ימות וגו' ישראל מטמאים באהל ואין אומות מטמאין באהל.

וכבר המשלתי במקום אחר ענין זה לב' כלים שהיו אצל בעל הבית אחת מלאה דבש ואחת מלאה זבל ופינה אותם ומיאסים לחוץ מהחדר. אותה שהיתה מלאה דבש מתקבצים לה כל הזבובים והרמשים, ואותה שהיתה מלאה זבל הגם שיכנסו לה קצת מהרמשים לא ישוה לשל דבש, כמו כן אדם מישראל שמת להיותו מלא קדושה המתוקה והעריבה בצאת הנפש ונתרוקן הגוף יתקבצו הקליפות לאין קץ שהם כוחות הטומאה התאבים תמיד להדבק בקדושה ליהנות מהערב, ולזה יטמא באהל ואפילו אלף בתים מקורים ואחת פתוחה לחברתה הטומאה תמלא כל החלל המקורה, מה שאין כן אשר לא מזרע ישראל להיותו מושלל מהקדושה אין כל כך התקבצות הטומאה אלא חלק הממית הנדבק בגוף, ואשר יסובב הכל היא התורה.

Why did the Torah call this single commandment "a statute of the Torah?" The Torah should have written simply "this is a statute etc." Alternatively, the commandment could have commenced with the words, "This is the statute of ritual impurity, etc." We have such an example in Shemos 12:43 where the Torah wrote, "This is the statute of the Paschal sacrifice."

We cannot answer that the Torah wanted to tell us that in order to be able to study Torah, one first had to purify oneself with the ash of the red heifer. This is not only not so, but we have learned in Berachos 22a that "words of Torah are not susceptible to ritual impurity at all." All the opinions offered in the Talmud, including those that are most stringent regarding purification rites needed for men who have experienced seminal discharges, agree that it is permissible to study Torah while ritually impure due to contact with the dead.

We can answer our question by referring to something we have learned in Nazir 61b and which has been ruled on by the Rambam in the first chapter of his treatise of Hilchos Tumas Meis. It is stated there that the concept of ritual purity originating from a dead body and conferring ritual impurity does not apply to [the type of Gentile known in the Talmud as] a Kusi.

The Rambam rules as follows: "If a Kusi touches or carries or tents over [is positioned above] a dead body, it is as if he had never touched that body. The situation is analogous to an animal having touched a dead body: Just as the animal does not become ritually impure thereby, neither does the Kusi."

The Jewish People have been elevated above other nations, in that they have received the Torah, without which the Jews would not be different from any other nation. With this insight, we now taste G-d's words as sweet as honey: When we read, "This is the statute of the Torah," this thus reminds us of the special distinction of the Jewish People: Because we have been given the Torah, contact with the dead confers ritual impurity upon us. Lesser spirits yearn to attach themselves to the Jewish People inasmuch as the latter represents a high level of spirituality not only while alive but even while they are dead. For the sanctity Jews experience during their lives is evident due to the fact that contact with the dead, or even being under the same roof with a dead body, confers ritual impurity on the bodies of living Jews. Were it not for the power of the ash of the Red Heifer with which this legislative act of the Torah has endowed us to help counteract the pull of the impurity associated with a dead body, we would not be able to shake off this attachment of the spiritual residue of the dead…

I have already illustrated this relationship between the B'nei Yisrael and ritual impurity by means of a parable. Let us assume that we have two containers inside a house — one full of honey, the other full of refuse. If both these containers are taken outside, it will be observed that the container full of honey attracts swarms of flies, whereas the number of flies attracted to the container full of refuse is insignificant by comparison. Similarly, when a Jew dies, the fact that he was full of holiness while alive — i.e., he was as sweet as honey — means that he attracts all kinds of spiritual negative elements, seeing the soul has departed from that body. These are the forces of impurity which always attempt to attach themselves to anything sacred, as they wish to benefit from the physical sweetness of holiness. (Ohr HaChaim)

The *Ohr HaChaim* teaches us the significance of our distinction from the other nations of the world, which we possess solely because of the Torah we accepted as a nation. Impure spirits are constantly at work to attach themselves to the sacred *neshamah* of a Jew, and when the *neshamah* departs, it makes way for impurity to be housed within the *guf* — for a void never remains; nature abhors a vacuum. There is either holiness or impurity — and with the occurrence of death, impurity is more able to settle in without a struggle.

Searching for Weakness

Perhaps we can extend this insight to our lifelong struggle with the *yetzer hara* which begins way before the impure spirits appear on the scene. The *yetzer hara* does not rest and is in constant search mode to find an entry point, a breach of some sort where he can plant his seeds of *tumah* and wreak havoc with our souls. He seeks to attach himself to our *neshamos* so that he can inflict us with his impurities and eventually gain complete command over the choices we make. It is imperative for us to be in a continuous state of awareness and vigilance to guard our neshamos. Maintaining a secure *neshamah* means busying ourselves with Torah as an offensive measure. The Torah acts as a seal and shield, not allowing the impurities of the *yetzer hara* to penetrate. As long as we are spiritually alive and not complacent in our commitment to Hashem, the entrance to our *neshamos* is safeguarded and remains pure.

> The yetzer hara does not rest and is in constant search mode to find an entry point, a breach of some sort where he can plant his seeds of tumah and wreak havoc with our souls.

The Gemara in *Maseches Chullin*[110] teaches the concept of אידי דטריד למפלט לא בלע, which means that when something is "engaged" in expelling a substance from within it, it cannot absorb another substance at the same time. The same holds true for our spiritual endeavors. If we are continuously involved with our *avodas Hashem*, we are greatly protected from absorbing the negative influences which target and surround us.

Squatters, too, are on the lookout. They notice changes in neighborhoods. An uncut lawn, lights that are off for extended periods of time, newspapers piled up, no movement around a home. They wait for the right moment and go for their target. Squatters settle down and take

110 *Chullin* 113a; see also *Shulchan Aruch Yoreh Deah*, par. 70.

over, to the extent that the real homeowners are powerless in their quest to remove these individuals.

So is the way of the *yetzer hara*. He waits for the exact moment when we display weakness, and calculates his assault in a devious manner. However, as long as the right protections are in place, we can be assured that we will prevail. If we live and care for our *neshamos*, making it obvious to all that "we" are its owners, we can remain successful in keeping all unwanted guests far away.

Balak

כִּי מֵרֹאשׁ צֻרִים אֶרְאֶנּוּ וּמִגְּבָעוֹת אֲשׁוּרֶנּוּ הֶן עָם לְבָדָד יִשְׁכֹּן
וּבַגּוֹיִם לֹא יִתְחַשָּׁב:

I see this nation from mountain peaks, and I behold them
from hills; a nation that will dwell alone, and will not be
reckoned among the nations. (Bamidbar 23:9)

Rashi comments on these words of Bilam about the B'nei Yisrael's virtues:

כי מראש צרים אראנו: אני מסתכל בראשיתם ובתחלת שרשיהם, ואני רואה אותם
מיוסדים וחזקים כצורים וגבעות הללו ע"י אבות ואמהות.

I see this nation from mountain peaks — I look at their origins and the
beginning of their roots, and I see them established and powerful, like these
mountains and hills, because of their Patriarchs and Matriarchs.

Bilam tells Balak that looking at the B'nei Yisrael's origins, it can be
seen that they are firmly established and well-rooted, as their founding
Fathers and Mothers had strong convictions and were not easily swayed
from their beliefs.

The significance of Bilam's comparing us to a mountain is remarkable
for us, because at times, we tend to drift away from the ways of our
Fathers and Mothers.

223

A Hollowed-Out Stone

The Midrash[111] relates the well-known story of Rabbi Akiva's dramatic turning point which led him to a total life transformation:

מה היה תחילתו של רבי עקיבא אמרו: בן ארבעים שנה היה ולא שנה כלום פעם אחת היה
עומד על פי הבאר אמר, מי חקק אבן זו, אמרו לו, המים שתדיר נופלים עליה בכל יום אמרו
לו, עקיבא אי אתה קורא אבנים שחקו מים (איוב יד, יט) מיד היה רבי עקיבא דן קל וחומר
בעצמו מה רך פסל את הקשה, דברי תורה שקשה כברזל על אחת כמה וכמה שיחקקו
את לבי שהוא בשר ודם. מיד חזר ללמוד תורה הלך הוא ובנו וישבו אצל מלמדי תינוקות
אמר לו, רבי למדני תורה אחז רבי עקיבא בראש הלוח, ובנו בראש הלוח כתב לו אלף בית
ולמדה. אלף תיו ולמדה, תורת כהנים ולמדה היה לומד והולך עד שלמד כל התורה כולה.

What were Rabbi Akiva's beginnings? It is said: Up to the age of forty, he had not yet studied a thing. One time, while standing by the mouth of a well, he inquired, "Who hollowed out this stone?" and was told, "Akiva, haven't you read that 'water wears away stone' (Iyov 14:19)"? — it was water falling upon it constantly, day after day. At that, he asked himself, "If in this case, the soft made an impression on the hard, then how much more so can the Torah — which is hard as iron — make an impression on my heart made of flesh and blood! I will go and study at least one section of Torah."

He went directly to a schoolhouse, and he and his son began reading from a child's tablet. Rabbi Akiva took hold of one end of the tablet, and his son held the other end. The teacher wrote down aleph and beis for him, and he learned them; aleph to tav, and he learned them; the book of Toras Kohanim, and he learned it. He went on studying until he learned the whole Torah. (Avos D'Rabi Nosson)

Rock-Solid Foundations

B'nei Yisrael's foundation is compared to a rock as the *pasuk* above tells us *Merosh Tzurim Erenu*, "I see this nation from mountain peaks," and it was Rabbi Akiva who was inspired by the carving in the rock caused by years of constant and perpetual drips of water. On the one hand, we come from rock-solid foundations based on our unwavering perseverance in maintaining our customs and traditions. But on the other hand, we witness how over time even structures as solid as rock

---

111 *Avos D'Rabi Nosson 6:2.*

can become hollowed-out in a slow and progressive manner, as seen in the rock-water incident observed by Rabbi Akiva.

Our *mesorah* (tradition) is deeply embedded in stone. But just as over time a stone can be weakened and hollowed by the constant flow of water, our traditions, too, if we are not vigilant, can slowly and gradually be chiseled away, unrecognized until it is too late to salvage the remains.

> *Our mesorah (tradition) is deeply embedded in stone. But, just as over time a stone can be weakened and hollowed by the constant flow of water, our traditions, too, can slowly and gradually be chiseled away.*

A friend of mine once related to me that his family has a Pesach custom to cover with a white tablecloth all cabinets and closets holding the *chametz* they sold over Pesach, the purpose being to indicate the cabinets' prohibited status and remind those at home not to mistakenly use their contents. When I questioned this *minhag* and asked why placing a piece of tape or tying its handles shut wouldn't provide the same security, he responded, "I'm not completely sure but my parents and grandparents acted in this way, and it wouldn't be Pesach for us without using the white tablecloths each year."

Securing Our Mesorah

Thus we see the significance of these seemingly simple *minhagim*. They are the rocks, the roots, which kept our forefathers strong throughout the millennia. While halachah may not mandate many of our *minhagim*, they are what prevent the rock from becoming hollowed out, thereby perpetuating our *mesorah*.

Aside from *minhagim*, strict adherence to basic *mitzvos* which are common to us all are important for the bedrock of our *mesorah* to remain secure. Even amongst the non–religious, Yom Kippur once held a prominent place on the calendar; one could barely find a Jew who would not show up in shul at least this once a year, probably fasting as well. This nurtured the starved spark in their soul, though sadly, even this has been slowly deteriorating and disappearing.

A beautiful Midrash provides us with guidance on how to preserve our vital *mesorah* so we are not left just with a hollowed-out rock:

רבי שמואל בר נחמן פתח (תהלים קכא, א): שיר למעלות אשא עיני אל ההרים. אל תקרי
אל ההרים אלא על ההורים – למלפני ולמעבדני.

Rav Shmuel son of Nachman began (quoting Tehillim 121:1), "A song for ascents. I shall raise my eyes to the harim, mountains:" Don't read harim, but rather horim, parents (I shall raise my eyes to the parents) — my instructors and those who conceived me. (Midrash Rabbah, Vayeitzei 68:2)

It's no coincidence that the word for mountains and parents are so closely related. Our parents are referred to as mountains, with rock-like strength. Perhaps the Midrash is teaching us to raise our eyes to our parents and their ways, and there we will find our salvation. At times we look up to Hashem and ask, "From where will our salvation come? How will we survive and get through this difficulty?" The Midrash answers, אל תקרי — don't call out to ההרים, the mountains or to the One above all heights — Hashem — and expect a miracle. The help is at our fingertips and within easy reach; by following and preserving the ways of the *horim*, our parents, the ones who laid the groundwork to keep our future strong, we will find the answer to our troubles. If we slowly abandon the customs of our parents, however, we thus invite new problems into our lives and then wonder why Hashem has forsaken us — while in truth it is our own neglect and lack of resoluteness in the face of the influences of change that eat away at the bedrock that our parents established for us and future generations.

A simple custom disregarded or ignored, chips away and slowly contributes to the erosion of a once strong *mesorah*. It's the little things, the externals, which can go a long way in ensuring that the *Merosh Tzurim*, the mountain tops to which Bilam referred to, remain firm and in place.

Pinchas

יִפְקֹד ה' אֱלֹקֵי הָרוּחֹת לְכָל בָּשָׂר אִישׁ עַל הָעֵדָה:

Let Hashem, the G-d of spirits of all flesh; appoint a man
over the congregation. (Bamidbar 27:16)

Rashi comments on this *pasuk* as follows:

יפקד ה': כיון ששמע משה שאמר לו המקום תן נחלת צלפחד לבנותיו אמר הגיע שעה
שאתבע צרכי שיירשו בני את גדולתי. אמר לו הקב"ה לא כך עלתה במחשבה לפני, כדאי
הוא יהושע ליטול שכר שימושו שלא מש מתוך האהל. וזהו שאמר שלמה (משלי כז, יח)
נוצר תאנה יאכל פריה.

Let Hashem...appoint — *When Moshe heard that the Omnipresent told*
him to give Tzelafchad's inheritance to his daughters, he said, "It is time to
ask for my own needs, that my sons should inherit my high position." G-d said
to him, "This was not My plan. Rather, Yehoshua deserves to be rewarded
for his service, for he "would not depart from the tent." This is what Shlomo
HaMelech meant when he said, "He who guards the fig tree eats its fruit"
(Mishlei, 27:18).

The *pasuk*, according to Rashi, tells of Moshe asking Hashem to
appoint a leader for B'nei Yisrael who will be dedicated and prepared
to make sacrifices on their behalf. Rashi explains Moshe's particular
request: After witnessing the way in which the daughters of Tzlefachad

227

were awarded a plot of land as an inheritance to perpetuate the memory of their father, Moshe, too, took the opportunity to inquire whether his son would be worthy to lead the people into Eretz Yisrael. Hashem responded to Moshe's reasonable request by saying that Yehoshua was more qualified and deserving for the position, given his record of dedication.

An Undesirable Position

Interestingly, we don't find that Moshe greatly valued his high position that he now wished to bequeath to his son. If we look back to when Moshe was first summoned by Hashem to lead the people out of *Mitzrayim*,[112] we will remember that he was hesitant and reluctant to accept the position; only when Hashem promised him that Aharon, his brother, would be his support and assist him did he agree to take it upon himself. Throughout Moshe's tenure as a leader, both in Mitzrayim and in the *Midbar*, there were several times in which he complained[113] of his inadequacy in leading the people and caring for a people undergoing the process of being born into a nation. It should have followed now that Moshe would do anything but consider nominating his own son for this awesome position that caused him so much grief and hardship. Why would he want it for his son?

Furthermore, how many times did Moshe plead with Hashem on behalf of B'nei Yisrael so that they wouldn't be wiped out because of their sins? Surely Moshe knew that the next leader to be appointed could expect to have to deal at some point or other with national complaining or rebelling against Hashem.

The Function and Duty of a Leader

To understand Moshe's efforts on behalf of his son, let us investigate the duty and function of a leader. While many individuals in a leadership role seek to gain and profit materially or otherwise from their

---

112   *Shemos* 3:11.
113   *Devarim* 1:12.

position, true leaders view the very opportunity to serve their people as a true privilege. Rashi on the previous *pasuk*[114] explained how at the time of his death, Moshe put his needs aside and busied himself with the needs of the *Klal* by searching for a suitable leader. A true leader is selfless and looks to serve the people even when it is unpleasant or uncomfortable and, in Moshe's case, even while preparing to part with this world. At times of war, he leads from the front and goes together with his men to fight, putting his life in harm's way.[115] It may have been uncomfortable for Moshe at times, but his position trained him to be completely focused and concerned with the needs of the people. Moshe knew that this quality was developed specifically via his leadership of the nation, and he wanted his son to have the same fortune to reach the point of complete selflessness and devotion to others.

> *A true leader is selfless and looks to serve the people even when it is unpleasant or uncomfortable and, in moshe's case, even while preparing to part with this world.*

Teaching Benefits

There are other advantages to a leader's role, as well. The Gemara[116] teaches:

דאמר ר' חנינא: הרבה למדתי מרבותי ומחברי יותר מרבותי ומתלמידי יותר מכולן.

For Rabbi Chanina said: I have learned much from my teachers, and from my peers more than my teachers, and from my students more than all.

Anyone who has ever been in a position of teaching, whether it be at the school level with young students or as a *kiruv* professional working with those just beginning with their learning, knows that as much as they perceive themselves giving to their students, their students are in some ways giving them much more. When one is charged with

---

114 *Bamidbar* 27:15.
115 Ibid., *pasuk* 17.
116 *Maseches Taanis* 7a.

the responsibility of explaining a difficult concept or with teaching a complex idea, he himself must gain clarity in his own understanding, both by needing to put the idea into actual words and because of the inquiries made by students. This generates enormous growth from the teacher's perspective and the benefits are unparalleled.

Perhaps Moshe Rabbeinu recognized that he had benefited a great deal from being the leader of B'nei Yisrael. While he was the *rebbi* of Klal Yisrael, speaking with Hashem when he pleased, he never lost sight of the great privilege he had merited by being a teacher and thus able to gain so much from his students.

Moshe desired this for his own son. He knew that this opportunity was a one-of-a-kind chance that had lots to offer both in developing one's character by learning to put the needs of the people first and for the actual learning opportunity of *u'mitalmidai yoser mikulam.* These great benefits awaited the next leader that would serve future generations of B'nei Yisrael with humility and an unassuming nature.

Matos

וַיִּקַּח מֹשֶׁה וְאֶלְעָזָר הַכֹּהֵן אֶת הַזָּהָב מֵאֵת שָׂרֵי הָאֲלָפִים וְהַמֵּאוֹת וַיָּבִאוּ
אֹתוֹ אֶל אֹהֶל מוֹעֵד זִכָּרוֹן לִבְנֵי יִשְׂרָאֵל לִפְנֵי ה':

Moshe and Elazar the Kohen took the gold from the
commanders of the thousands and hundreds and brought
it to the Tent of Meeting, as a remembrance for B'nei Yisrael
before Hashem. (Bamidbar 31:54)

The *pasuk* tells of the gold ornaments and jewelry the leaders brought
as a gift from the spoils of war to serve as an atonement[117] for the entire
nation. While the Torah does not reveal what the actual gold was used
for, the Ramban on this *pasuk* discusses its specific use and purpose.

ויבאו אותו אל אהל מועד זכרון לבני ישראל. יראה מזה שעשו מהם כלי שרת ומסרום
לצבור לזכרון לכל בני ישראל שיעשו בהם עבודת ה' לדורות, שאם באו הכלים האלה
לאוצר בית השם היה ראוי שיאמר זכרון להם לפני ה' כי בני ישראל יכלול כל העם והזכרון
בדבר קיים הוא.

"They brought it to the Tent of Meeting, a remembrance for B'nei Yisrael." — It
would appear from this that the donors made Temple vessels [out of the gold]
and gave them over to the general public to serve as a remembrance for all of

---

117 See *Bamidbar* 31:50.

B'nei Yisrael so that they could be used for the Divine service for generations
to come. For if these vessels had merely been brought to the Treasury of the
House of Hashem [to remain there forever], it would have been more fitting
for the Torah to say "a remembrance for them before Hashem," whereas the
words "B'nei Yisrael" includes the entire nation, and remembrance applies to
something that is permanent.

The Ramban teaches that the gold was not simply given to the
Treasury and used to purchase the needs of the *Mishkan* which would
leave no lasting mark. Rather, they were used to make *klei shares*, vessels for the Divine Temple service, which would be used throughout
the generations and serve as a long-standing remembrance for B'nei
Yisrael. Each time the vessels would be used, they would remind those
using them that their leaders had sought to atone for B'nei Yisrael's sins
and therefore made a dedication to the *Mishkan*.

Counteracting Temporary Pleasures

The golden donation made from the spoils of the war with Midian
was specifically used to create service vessels that would be utilized
daily and have an everlasting remembrance. But why was it necessary
to create an item of "permanence" as an atonement for their depraved
worship of *Peor*? If the gold was added to the Treasury and then used to
purchase *korbanos*, would it not have served the same purpose?

Perhaps the dedication of gold which was then turned into permanent
klei shares symbolizes a strong contrast to the sin of which B'nei Yisrael
were guilty. Sexual immorality is the epitome of temporary and fleeting
pleasure with no enduring value. The leaders had in mind to dedicate
something with permanence to counteract the sin which represented
the exact opposite. The *keilim* would now serve as a perpetual reminder
of the dangers of falling for temptation so temporary in nature.

Young people in the workforce today are constantly being reminded
to begin making plans for retirement. They are told that setting aside a
little bit now will go a long way later on, and that taking advantage of
the many tax-free saving incentives should not be underestimated or
overlooked. As time goes on, they find that simply participating in their

employer's 401k plan isn't enough. Financial advisors and investment strategists advise them to diversify their assets into a portfolio with an array of financial products to ensure a safe and prudent investment in the event the economy goes sour. Accountants guide them to benefit from all the tax loopholes available so that they can salvage as much of their income as possible. All this, to guarantee their money is safe and secure so that it can support them through retirement and allow their children an inheritance.

Securing a Spiritual Retirement

Of course, there is another kind of planning for the future that we tend to neglect — our most important investment in ensuring a safe future when we retire from *Olam HaZeh*. Unfortunately, we don't hear of people lining up to be advised by "spiritual accountants" regarding how to accumulate the most "wealth" for the next world. What we should do is sit with calculators and take an account of how many hours of Torah learning we can amass each week; this involves setting for ourselves a schedule of learning. What we should further do is to look at our *mitzvos* as an actual investment that offers dividends and permanent returns. Let our minds be occupied with constant concern of how we will survive in *Olam Haba* after retirement, before it is too late to start saving for that eternal journey.

Let our minds be occupied with constant concern of how we will survive in Olam Haba after retirement, before it is too late to start saving for that eternal journey.

As we navigate this world, we must remind ourselves of its fleeting nature and plan for the infinite existence that awaits us. It is one to which we must arrive with enduring spiritual investments if we wish to support our heavenly retirement in an appropriate manner. The dedication the leaders of B'nei Yisrael made in the Desert signified this *middah* of thinking beyond the temptation of the present moment and building a legacy that is remembered for generations.

Masei

אֵלֶּה מַסְעֵי בְנֵי יִשְׂרָאֵל אֲשֶׁר יָצְאוּ מֵאֶרֶץ מִצְרַיִם לְצִבְאֹתָם
בְּיַד מֹשֶׁה וְאַהֲרֹן:

These are the journeys of the People of Israel who left
the land of Egypt in their legions, under the charge
of Moshe and Aharon. (Bamidbar 33:1)

The *parashah* begins enumerating the journeys the B'nei Yisrael experienced during their years in the desert. The commentators explain that the details of each place are reviewed so that we may appreciate the events which transpired during this tumultuous time in B'nei Yisrael's development as a nation. Furthermore, these journeys serve as a blueprint and guide for our own experiences and travels as we navigate our time spent in *Olam HaZeh*.

Interestingly, the laws of *Arei Miklat*, Cities of Refuge, are also found in this *parashah* of B'nei Yisrael's travels. This is quite appropriate, as the two topics are incredibly interrelated and provide a lesson to help us understand the intricacies of life's challenges.

וְאֵת הֶעָרִים אֲשֶׁר תִּתְּנוּ לַלְוִיִּם אֵת שֵׁשׁ עָרֵי הַמִּקְלָט אֲשֶׁר תִּתְּנוּ לָנֻס שָׁמָּה הָרֹצֵחַ
וַעֲלֵיהֶם תִּתְּנוּ אַרְבָּעִים וּשְׁתַּיִם עִיר:

Among the cities you shall give to the Levites shall be six cities of refuge, which you shall provide [as places] to which a murderer can flee. In addition to them, you shall provide forty-two cities. (Bamidbar 35:6)

As the *pasuk* communicates, much concern was given for unintentional murderers. They were provided with cities to which they could run and take refuge from the relatives seeking revenge. The Gemara[118] tells us that care was taken to ease the accidental killer's escape:

תניא ר' אליעזר בן יעקב אומר מקלט היה כתוב על פרשת דרכים כדי שיכיר הרוצח ויפנה לשם.

It was taught: Rabbi Eliezer ben Yaacov said: A sign with the word "refuge" was posted at every crossing so that the killer should recognize the route to take.

No Signs on the Road

Oddly, no signs were found on the roads directing people to the Beis HaMikdash when they wished to fulfill the mitzvah of being *oleh regel*, going up to Yerushalayim on the Three Festivals. Similarly, we know of no signs posted indicating where to purchase animals for *karbonos* during the Festivals. Would it not have been appropriate to simplify the journeys of those travelling to Yerushalayim just as the unintentional murderer was guided along his way?

Perhaps the Torah is thus enlightening us about our nuanced journey in this world. The *parashah* of *Masei* tells us of the broad challenges and experiences B'nei Yisrael encountered in the desert. We read here of their ups and downs, in which they sometimes soared to spiritual heights and other times fell to the depths of what seemed like a place of no return. Moshe Rabbeinu led them, prayed for them, and helped them return to Hashem. Theirs was a true journey with peaks and valleys, always on a path that required choices to be made and allowed for room to stray from their intended destinations.

How similar is our existence in *Olam HaZeh* to that of B'nei Yisrael in the desert! As they did, we struggle to stay on course — and not always

---

118   *Maseches Makos* 10b.

with clear road signs and directions. Instead, we are given choices to make. We reach a fork in the road and need to decide: Do we turn right, or left? Will we fall into the *yetzer hara's* trap, or stay clear of the rocky and dangerous roads that lie ahead?

The road to success is never a straight line, and getting there requires focus and a strong yearning while being prepared to make sacrifices along the way.

The *oleh regel* on his way to Yerushalayim is analogous to those of us searching for Hashem. We make the long and arduous journey seeking and hoping to grow spiritually so that we can connect ourselves to Hashem and deepen our relationship with Him. There are no clear signs along the way and we are likely to encounter many disturbances and road blocks on our journey. The road to success is never a straight line, and getting there requires focus and a strong yearning while being prepared to make sacrifices along the way.

A Road to Nowhere

The unintentional killer, however, is comparable to a traveler who is lost. His relationship with Hashem is in danger and may be far from repair. He has no desire to grow or bring himself closer to Hashem, and therefore the signs are there to make his destination easily accessible.

This is similar to the idea explained by Rav Yitzchak Meir Alter, the first Gerrer Rebbe regarding the Snake who, after the sin of the Tree of Knowledge, was banished and given his food supply without the need to search and beseech Hashem.

אמרו חכמינו, כי על ידי זה שנתקלל הנחש לאכול רק עפר, הרי תמיד מזונותיו מזומנים לפניו. עולה לגג, מזונותיו עמו. וכן אמרו חכמינו הרואה נחש בחלום פרנסתו מזומנת לו (ברכות נ"ז). קשה איפוא, מה קללה היא זו.

ברם, הקללה היתה בכך, שהורחק כל כך מן הקדושה, עד כדי למנוע ממנו שיצטרך אי פעם לשאת עיניו אל השמים, כדרך ברואים אחרים המחפשים להם מזונותיהם ונושאים לפעמים עיניהם השמימה, לבקש מזונם מאת ד' יתברך, כגון הכפירים שואגים לטרף ולבקש מאל אכלם (תהילים ק"ד כ"א). את קולו של הנחש אין רוצים בכלל לשמוע, בבחינת קח לך את שלך והסתלק מנגד עיני, לבל אראך ולבל אשמעך עוד.

Our Sages said that in being cursed with having to eat only dirt, the Snake's food supply is always in abundance; even if it goes up on a roof, it has what to eat. And our Sages similarly taught: "He who sees a snake in his dream, it means his living (sustenance) is assured" (Berachos 57a). The question is therefore clear: What kind of punishment is this?

The answer is that the Snake was cursed in being distanced from anything having to do with sanctity — to the extent that even the need to ever look heavenward is taken from it. It is not like other creatures that seek their food and sometimes lift their eyes to the heavens to ask Hashem to provide them. For instance, "The young lions roar for their prey, and seek their food from G-d" (Tehillim 104:21). The sound of the Snake's call is not at all desired in the Heavens, as if it were being told, "Take your food and get out of my sight! I don't want to see you or hear you." (Chidushei HaRim, Bereishis)

The idea is, explained by the *Chidushei HaRim* that Hashem is as if saying, "I have no interest in you, so here's your food and get out of My sight." The punishment is being banished from being worthy of having a relationship with Hashem.

The signs were posted for those fleeing to the *Arei Miklat* so that the killer can see what becomes of the person that distances himself from Hashem. When the desire to develop and cultivate a spiritual relationship is non-existent, there is no spiritual purpose or challenge. These are the thoughts the individual should absorb which will hopefully resonate with him while taking refuge as he pleads and seeks to reignite his bond with Hashem.

Devarim

Devarim

וַנִּלְכֹּד אֶת כָּל עָרָיו בָּעֵת הַהִוא וַנַּחֲרֵם אֶת כָּל עִיר מְתִם וְהַנָּשִׁים וְהַטָּף
לֹא הִשְׁאַרְנוּ שָׂרִיד: רַק הַבְּהֵמָה בָּזַזְנוּ לָנוּ וּשְׁלַל הֶעָרִים אֲשֶׁר לָכָדְנוּ:

And we conquered all his cities at that time, and utterly
destroyed every city, the men, women, and the young children;
we left over no survivor: Only the cattle we took for a prey
unto ourselves with the spoil of the cities which we had taken.

(Devarim 2:34–35)

Rashi comments on this recap of Moshe Rabbeinu of the battle
against Sichon:

מְתִם: אנשים. בביזת סיחון נאמר בזזנו לנו לשון ביזה, שהיתה חביבה עליהם ובוזזים איש
לו, וכשבאו לביזת עוג כבר היו שבעים ומלאים והיתה בזויה בעיניהם ומקרעין ומשליכין
בהמה ובגדים ולא נטלו כי אם כסף וזהב. לכך נאמר (דברים ג, ז) בָזזֹנוּ לָנוּ 119 לשון ביזיון.
כך נדרש בספרי בפרשת (במדבר כה, א) וישב ישראל בשטים.

Mesim — [This word means] men. Regarding the spoils taken from Sichon, it
is stated בָּזַזְנוּ לָנוּ, bazaznu lanu, an expression denoting plunder; the loot was
precious to them and every man took freely. When they came to the spoils of
Og, however, they were already satisfied and full, and it was contemptible

---
119 The *pasuk* reads וְכָל הַבְּהֵמָה וּשְׁלַל הֶעָרִים בַּזּוֹנוּ לָנוּ.

in their eyes. They tore into pieces and threw away cattle and garments, and took only the silver and gold. Therefore, it states (Devarim 3:7), בְּזוֹנוּ לָנוּ, ba-zonu lanu, an expression of contempt. So is expounded in the Midrash Sifri, in the chapter, "And Yisrael dwelt in Shittim" (Bamidbar 25:1).

Moshe Rabbeinu reminds B'nei Yisrael of their conquest of the lands of Sichon and Og. Rashi notes the difference between how the spoils were taken from the two cities. With regard to the spoils of Sichon, the Torah uses the term *bazaznu* as in plundering, while at the city of Og, the word *bazonu* — an expression of contempt — is used, since they were already satisfied with the spoils plundered at Sichon and had no need now for the excess cattle and garments.

From Rashi, quoting the *Sifri*, we can extrapolate new meaning for two other sources using similar terminology. Let us begin with a Mishnah in *Pirkei Avos*:

Don't Be Scornful of People

הוא היה אומר, אל תהי בז לכל אדם, ואל תהי מפליג לכל דבר, שאין לך אדם שאין לו שעה ואין לך דבר שאין לו מקום.

He [Ben Azzai] used to say: Do not be scornful [from the root baz] of any person and do not be disdainful of anything, for there is no person without his hour and there is no thing without its place. (Mishnah, Avos 4:3)

The Mishnah's lesson "not to be scornful of any person" may be interpreted as a lesson how to appreciate and respect other people while not taking them for granted. One may rationalize to himself, "I have no use for that person, for what does he have that I can possibly need? He has nothing to offer that can benefit me." This is similar to B'nei Yisrael's attitude regarding the spoils of Og. Being "full and satisfied" with no immediate need can lead one to scorn others and be disrespectful. We must view people not in relation to what they have or how we can benefit from them, but rather recognize that

We must view people not in relation to what they have or how we can benefit from them, but rather recognize that everyone is of significant importance, with something to offer.

everyone is of significant importance, with something to offer — and even if not at the present, perhaps at a future time.

Yerushalayim the Scorned

The second source on which the above Rashi can shed light concerns the prayer that we say on Tisha B'Av. Given that *Parashas Devarim* is always read on the Shabbos before Tisha B'Av, it is interesting to note the connection between the *parashah* and aspects of the *Churban*.[120] The prayer states:

נחם ה' אלקינו את אבלי ציון ואת אבלי ירושלים, ואת העיר האבלה והחרבה והבזויה
והשוממה. האבלה מבלי בניה, והחריבה ממעונותיה, והבזויה מכבודה, והשוממה מאין
יושב ...

Console, Hashem, our G-d, the mourners of Tzion and the mourners of Yerushalayim, and the city that is mournful, ruined, scorned [bezuyah], and desolate: mournful without her children, ruined without her abodes, scorned [bezuyah] without her glory and desolate without inhabitants…(Minchah, Tisha B'Av)

This *tefillah* of *Nachem*, which describes Yerushalayim in ruins, is added to *Minchah* on Tisha B'Av. Many have raised the possibility of changing the wording of this *tefillah*, arguing that when we look around today we see that Yerushalayim is anything but ruined, scorned, or desolate. On the contrary, it is a beautiful city that has been rebuilt and inhabited by Jews. Its beauty and attractiveness are attested to by all its visitors. To this argument, a variety of answers have been offered, including the point that Yerushalayim's Old City is still largely inhabited by non-Jews, and that as long as Hashem's *Shechinah* [Divine Presence] is in *galus*, the city remains in a destroyed state, lacking His full Presence.

According to the above-quoted Rashi, which teaches that *"bazui"* means "scorn resulting from being overly-satisfied," perhaps we can offer a different idea. When we say in *Nachem* that Yerushalayim is *bezuyah* [the feminine form of *bazui*], meaning that it is scorned, we are

120   The destruction of Yerushalayim and the Beis HaMikdash.

referring to a Yerushalayim of which the people feel "full and satisfied;" they experience no void or absence in their lives causing them to yearn for a rebuilt Yerushalayim and the Beis HaMikdash. Yes, even today to a certain extent, the Holy City remains in this state; as written in *Megillas Eichah*;[121] *eichah yashvah badad*, Alas, she sits in solitude, the city is alone with no one yearning and longing for its return.

Yerushalayim is "in ruins" and "desolate" so long as its people and Jews around the world feel satisfied and content with the status quo going about their comfortable lifestyles and don't recognize the incredible void of not having the Beis HaMikdash, a dwelling place for Hashem's Glory and Divine Presence. While Yerushalayim today can be called a contemporary city with beautiful architectural designs, modern-day transportation systems, and an accessible *Kosel* serving as the highlight of anyone's trip to Yerushalayim, it is far from what it once was and will be when the Beis HaMikdash will be rebuilt. Some may be deceived into believing that the Redemption has arrived when contrasting the beauty of Eretz Yisrael today with what it looked like seventy years ago. But, since we remain in *Galus* and still lack the Divine Presence, we need to recognize our loss and yearn for Hashem's ultimate Redemption with a Yerushalayim built up in all its glory.

121   1:1.

Va'Eschanan

כִּי תוֹלִיד בָּנִים וּבְנֵי בָנִים וְנוֹשַׁנְתֶּם בָּאָרֶץ וְהִשְׁחַתֶּם וַעֲשִׂיתֶם פֶּסֶל
תְּמוּנַת כֹּל וַעֲשִׂיתֶם הָרַע בְּעֵינֵי ה' אֱלֹקֶיךָ לְהַכְעִיסוֹ:

When you beget children and children's children, and you will be
long established in the land, and you become corrupt and make
a graven image, the likeness of anything, and do evil in the eyes
of Hashem your G-d, to provoke Him to anger. (Devarim 2:25)

The Gemara[122] teaches that this *pasuk* is symbolic of the *Galus*
following the destruction of the First Beis HaMikdash. It tells us
that during our long and drawn-out *Galus* we might turn away from
Hashem when we become prosperous, successful, and established. So
long as life is going well, we can too easily forget Who it is that makes
it all possible for us; this leads us to take for granted our ability to live
freely. It is a natural tendency for people not to recognize the true
value of what they have until it is taken away from them. The danger
in becoming established and successful — *venoshantem*, you will be
long-established — is the risk of forgetting the value of what we have
and how to appreciate it.

---

122   *Gittin* 88a.

The Merit of Joy

כל המתאבל על ירושלים זוכה ורואה בשמחתה.

All who mourn [the destruction of] Yerushalayim will merit to see it in its joy.
(Taanis 30b)

Some commentators ask why the Gemara chose the words זוכה ורואה בשמחתה, "will merit to see it *in its joy*"? Would it not have been more appropriate to say that one who properly mourned Yerushalayim's destruction זוכה ורואה בבנינה, "will merit to see it *rebuilt*" in its restored, glorious state?

In *Megillas Esther*, we read that after Haman's evil decree was abolished, it was a joyous time for the Jews of Shushan. The Gemara teaches:

ליהודים היתה אורה ושמחה וששון ויקר, אמר רב יהודה: אורה זו תורה, וכן הוא אומר כי נר מצווה ותורה אור שמחה זה יום טוב, וכן הוא אומר ושמחת בחגך; ששון זו מילה, וכן הוא אומר שש אנכי על אמרתך, ויקר אלו תפלין, וכן הוא אומר וראו כל עמי הארץ כי שם ה' נקרא עליך ויראו ממך.

"The Jews had light and gladness and joy and honor" — Rav Yehudah said: "Light" refers to Torah and so it says, "For the commandment is a lamp and Torah is light." "Gladness" is Yom Tov, as written, "You should be glad on your holiday." "Joy" refers to [Bris] Milah, and so it says, "I rejoice over your word." "Honor" refers to Tefillin, as it says, "All the nations of the world will see that the Name of Hashem is called upon and they will be in awe of you." (Megillah 16b)

Appreciating Something after It's Already Gone

Rav Moshe Bamberger, in his *sefer Shiras HaLevi*, asks why the Gemara needed to interpret the actual *mitzvos* to which the *pasuk* was referring. Why did the *pasuk* not write explicitly, "The Jews had Torah, Yom Tov, Milah, and Tefillin"? For what purpose was this concept written in the form of a *remez*, an allusion?

Rav Bamberger explains beautifully that Rashi[123] on the Gemara in *Megillah* comments that Haman's decree prevented all of these *mitzvos* from being performed. When the decree went into effect, the Jews felt a void, and yearned for the pleasure and happiness these *mitzvos*

---

123   *Megillah 16b, s.v. "zu milah."*

provided them — feelings that they had for so long taken for granted. Under Haman's decree, they once again longed for the joy and gladness these *mitzvos* had brought them. The life they had the day before the decree was no longer, and the light of the Torah, the happiness of a *Yom Tov*, and joy of performing *Milah* were now lost. This led them to realize that they had failed to appreciate the true value of what they had had. Once the decree was annulled, however, the light of the *Torah* returned and the happiness and joy of *Yom Tov* and *Milah* were restored. By alluding to this point in the form of words meaning joy and happiness, the *Megillah* is relating to us that more than the *mitzvos* themselves, the Jews now merited their joy and excitement, previously overlooked and undervalued.

> *When the Third Beis HaMikdash is rebuilt, we will once again experience the joy and happiness which was lost with its destruction.*

With this understanding, perhaps we can apply the same idea to mourning over the Beis HaMikdash and then seeing it in its joyous state. When the Third Beis HaMikdash is rebuilt, we will once again experience the joy and happiness which was lost with its destruction. The sins of Klal Yisrael brought about the destruction of the Beis HaMikdash; perhaps if they had recognized and valued the treasure they were at risk of losing, they would have acted differently. After its destruction, they mourned over the loss of joy and happiness the Beis HaMikdash had provided. The Gemara teaches that those who mourn properly will re-experience the precious *simcha* that was felt at the sight of the Beis HaMikdash.

Revitalizing and Invigorating Mitzvos

This is the danger of *venoshantem*, becoming "long-established" and ultimately living by rote. As we become accustomed to the good Hashem provides, and allow it to lose its excitement, we put ourselves at risk of eventually losing it completely. When performing *mitzvos*, it is important from time to time to seek ways to revitalize their performance with a new twist, such as learning the depth of the mitzvah of *tefillin* or *davening* with a new *siddur* thus sparing it from becoming stale and devoid of the potential joy and gladness it carries.

Eikev

וָאֶתְפֹּשׂ בִּשְׁנֵי הַלֻּחֹת וָאַשְׁלִכֵם מֵעַל שְׁתֵּי יָדָי וָאֲשַׁבְּרֵם לְעֵינֵיכֶם:

So I grasped the two Tablets, cast them out of my two hands,
and shattered them before your eyes. (Devarim 9:17)

Parashas Eikev continues with Moshe recounting the sometimes tumultuous events which transpired in the desert, and specifically when he descended the mountain and witnessed B'nei Yisrael serving the *Eigel HaZahav*, the Golden Calf. Not able to withstand the terrible sight of the gravest of sins being committed so soon after *Matan Torah*, Moshe threw the *Luchos* — Tablets of the Law — to the ground and shattered them. He felt that B'nei Yisrael were unfit to receive them.

The *Talmud Yerushalmi* in *Maseches Taanis* lists several opinions describing what occurred with the *Luchos* while in Moshe's grasp.

רבי יוחנן בשם רבי יוסה בר אביי: הלוחות היו מבקשין לפרוח והיה משה תופשן, דכתיב: ואתפוש בשני הלוחות. תני בשם רבי נחמיה: הכתב עצמו פרח. רבי עזרא בשם רבי יהודה בי רבי סימון: הלוחות היו משאוי ארבעים סאה והכתב היה סובלן. כיון שפרח הכתב כבדו על ידיו של משה ונפלו ונשתברו.

Rav Yochanan [said] in the name of Rav Yosah son of Abaye: The Luchos wanted to ascend and Moshe grasped them, as it says, "I grasped the two Luchos." It was taught in the name of Rav Nechemiah: The writing itself ascended. Rav Ezra [said] in the name of Rav Yehudah ben Rav Simon: The

248

Luchos weighed forty se'ah and the letters supported them, but once the letters ascended, the Luchos became too heavy in the hands of Moshe and they fell and shattered. (Talmud Yerushalmi, Taanis 4)

We will yet return to this *Yerushalmi*. Let us first consult the *Midrash Tanchuma*, which teaches an important contrast between the first and second sets of *Luchos* and their respective presentations to B'nei Yisrael:

הלוחות ראשונות על שנתנו בפומבי, לפיכך שלטה בהם עין הרע ונשתברו. וכאן אמר לו הקדוש ברוך הוא, אין לך יפה מן הצניעות, שנאמר, ומה ה' דורש ממך כי אם עשה משפט ואהבת חסד והצנע לכת (מיכה ו ח).

The first set of Luchos, given in a public manner, were therefore susceptible to the evil eye and were shattered. Here [regarding the second set] Hashem said there is nothing more precious than modest behavior, as written (Michah 6:8), "What does Hashem ask of you other than to do justice, loving kindness, and go with modesty." (Midrash Tanchuma, Ki Sisa 31)

The *Midrash* teaches that since the first set of *Luchos* were given with great publicity and fanfare, ultimately, they were destroyed. The second set of *Luchos*, however, which Moshe was commanded to make, was given quietly and in a more private fashion, thereby enabling them to endure and remain safe from devastation. With this lesson, the *Midrash* teaches the importance of *tznius* (modest behavior), and the significant value of leading a quiet life without great fanfare and publicity.

Breaking the Glass

The custom of breaking a glass under the *chuppah* at weddings is well-known, and is brought in the Gemara in *Maseches Berachos* as an example of the concept of *v'gilu bere'adah*,[124] "rejoice with trembling." Even when we are in high spirits and cheerful, the excitement must always be tempered somewhat, lest it lead to light-headedness. The Gemara teaches:

רב אשי עבד הלולא לבריה חזנהו לרבנן דהוו קא בדחי טובא אייתי כסא דזוגיתא חיורתא ותבר קמייהו ואעציבו.

---

124 Tehillim 2:11.

Rav Ashi made a marriage feast for his son. He saw that the rabbis were growing very merry, so he brought a cup of white crystal and broke it before them, and they were saddened. (Berachos 31a)

מכאן נהגו לשבר זכוכית בנישואין.

From here originated the custom to shatter a glass at a wedding. (Tosafos, ibid.)

Rav Hershel Schachter comments[125] in the name of his *rebbi* Rav Yosef Dov Soloveitchik, *zt"l*, who quoted an opinion of the *Geonim* that the reason for breaking the glass under the *chuppah* is to remind us of the *Luchos* that were shattered at Har Sinai — the wedding between Hashem and B'nei Yisrael. It is a reminder for the new couple to lead a life of *tznius*, so that their marriage will thrive and be successful, just as the second *Luchos* were given without fanfare, *b'tzinah,* and remained safe and secure.

A Life of Modesty

Of course, *tznius* is not limited only to appropriate dress and the technical *halachos* of *tznius* outlined in the *Shulchan Aruch*. It rather refers in general to leading a life in which one does not attract attention to him or herself, nor acts in a way which causes heads to turn in their direction.

Perhaps this idea can be further elaborated upon with the help of the *Yerushalmi* cited above. It taught that the letters of the *Luchos* began to ascend because of the sin they were witnessing. This led the *Luchos* to become unbearably heavy and impossible for Moshe to carry, and they fell to the ground in pieces. A life which lacks modest behavior results in a burden too heavy to bear; it is always out in the public eye and does not belong to the private individual any longer, since "living for others" is what drives all his behavior. When we live to impress others or constantly feel the need to be "on the scene," the polar opposite of a modest lifestyle, our lives become lifeless — similar to the set of *Luchos* which lacked its letters for support and fell to the ground.

> *A life which lacks modest behavior results in a burden too heavy to bear.*

---

125   See *Nefesh HaRav*, Rav Hershel Schachter.

Go North and Hide

The *Kli Yakar*, Rav Shlomo Luntschitz, cautions against such behavior in his beautiful comment to a *pasuk* in *Devarim*:

רב לכם סב את ההר הזה (ב,ג): רבים אומרים כי פסוק זה נוקב ויורד עד תהום ויש בו
רמז לשעה ולדורות, ועניין סבוב זה שילכו סחור סחור לכרם ה' צבאות לא יקרבו, כי ימים רבים
לישראל שהיו נדים ונעים סביבו ולא יותן לישראל כח עליהם עד מדרך כף רגל, עד שיבא
מי שנאמר בו ועמדו רגליו ביום ההוא על הר הזיתים (זכריה יד ד) וכל זמן שישראל הול-
כים סחור סחור נאמר להם פנו לכם צפונה ודרשו בזה אם הגיע שעתו של עשו עשו הצפינו
עצמכם (דב"ר א יט).

ועניין הצפנה זו נ"ל, שאם ימצא האיש הישראלי בגלות החל הזה איזו הצלחה זעיר שם, אז
יטמינו ויצפינו הכל בפני עשו כי אין לך אומה שמתקנאת בישראל כמו עשו, כי לדעתם
הכל גזולה בידם מהם מן ברכת יעקב אבינו שלקח ברכותיו של עשו במרמה, וכן יעקב
צוה לבניו למה תתראו (בראשית מב א) פירש רש"י בפני בני ישמעאל ועשו כאילו אתם
שבעים כי שניהם סוברים שיצחק גזל הצלחת ישמעאל, ויעקב גזל הצלחת עשו ע"י הש-
תדלות, ע"כ צוה דוקא על עשו פנו לכם צפונה שלא יתקנא בכם. וזה הפך ממה שישראל
עושין בדורות הללו בארצות אויביהם, כי מי שיש לו מנה זה הוא מראה את עצמו במלבושי
כבוד ובתים ספונים וחשובים כאילו היו לו כמה אלפים ומגרים האומות בעצמם ועוברים
על מה שנאמר פנו לכם צפונה. ומנהג זה הוא ברכת בני עמינו והוא המסבב את כל התלאה
אשר מצאתנו. והמשכילים יבינו ליקח מוסר.

"You have circled this mountain long enough" (Devarim 2:3) — Many say that this pasuk pierces and descends to the depths, alluding to a lesson both for its time and for future generations, as follows:

The matter of this "circling" is that they go round and round the orchard of the Lord of Hosts, but do not approach it itself. That is, Yisrael wanders for many years, not receiving the strength to even "receive a foot-breadth" (pasuk 5) against [their enemies], until the arrival of he about whom it was said, "His feet will stand that day on the Mt. of Olives" (Zechariah 14:4). For as long as Yisrael goes round and round [in the Exile], they are told, "Turn and go northward" (Devarim 2:3), and the Midrash derived, "If Eisav's hour has arrived, hide yourselves" (Devarim Rabbah 1:19); "hide" is from the same root in Hebrew as "north."

And the matter of this "hiding," it appears to me, is as follows: When it happens that a Jewish man finds himself with some small success during this Exile, he should hide it from Eisav [the Christians] — for no nation is as jealous of Yisrael as is Eisav; they feel that we have stolen everything from them, starting from the blessing that Yitzchak gave Yaacov Avinu who deceitfully took it from Eisav. Similarly, Yaacov asked his sons when the famine began,

"Why are you showing off?" (Bereishis 42:1) — and Rashi explains, "Why are you showing off in front of the sons of Yishmael and Eisav, as if you are sated and full."

That is, both Yishmael and Eisav feel that Yitzchak stole Yishmael's success and that Yaacov stole Eisav's success with his efforts. This is why Moshe told Israel to "go north" specifically regarding Eisav (Devarim 2:4) — so that Eisav would not be jealous of them.

And this is the opposite of what Yisrael does nowadays in the lands of their enemies: Whoever has some monetary success shows off with fancy clothes and large paneled houses, as if he has thousands, and this provokes the gentiles against them, thus violating that which Moshe told them to "go and turn northward," i.e., hide yourselves. This custom prevails among many of our compatriots, and it is the reason for all the troubles that befall us. May those who are wise understand and take a lesson. (Kli Yakar, Devarim 2:3)

How relevant are the words of the *Kli Yakar* today. The Torah serves as our guide for living, and in it Moshe commands us to live quietly and modestly, without showing off our successes for all to see and provoking the envy of those amongst whom we live. To flaunt material possessions as if they are the result of our own achievements is also an act of denying Hashem's role in providing us with His kindness.

Re'eh

וּבִשַּׁלְתָּ וְאָכַלְתָּ בַּמָּקוֹם אֲשֶׁר יִבְחַר ה' אֱלֹקֶיךָ בּוֹ וּפָנִיתָ בַבֹּקֶר
וְהָלַכְתָּ לְאֹהָלֶיךָ:

And you shall roast [it] and eat [it] in the place which
Hashem your G-d will choose, and you shall turn away
in the morning and go to your dwellings.

(Devarim 16:7)

The Torah teaches that one who comes to Yerushalayim to bring
a *korban Pesach* should not leave and return home immediately after
eating it, but should rather stay overnight on *Motzaei Yom Tov* until the
second day of Pesach.[126] As Rashi explains:

וּפָנִיתָ בַבֹּקֶר: לבקרו של שני, מלמד שטעון לינה ליל של מוצאי יום טוב.

And you shall turn away in the morning [and go to your dwellings] — *On*
the morning of the second day [of Pesach]. This teaches that [the pilgrim] is
required to remain [in Yerushalayim] overnight immediately following the
Festival.

---

126 The first day of *Chol HaMoed.*

Allowing the Inspiration to Absorb

This is known as the mitzvah of *linah*,[127] remaining overnight after the first day of *Yom Tov*. Many reasons are given for this mitzvah. Most notably, the fifth Gerrer Rebbe, the *Beis Yisrael*, Reb Yisrael Alter, *zt"l*, explains with a beautiful thought based on an idea from Reb Simcha Bunim of Peshischa.[128] The *pasuk* in *Tehillim* says:

ואדם ביקר בל ילין נמשל כבהמות נדמו:

But as for man, in glory he shall not rest; he is likened to the animals.
(Tehillim 49:13)

Reb Simcha Bunim explains: אדם ביקר, When a person merits a moment of *yakar*, glory — an elevated feeling of closeness to Hashem or an occasion of great inspiration in his *avodas Hashem* — but בל ילין, he does not rest, that is, ensure that the experience and passion remain with him for some time, he is נמשל כבהמות נדמו, compared to an animal that only focuses on the here and now, the temporary and short-lived pleasure.

The goal in our *avodas Hashem* is to find ways to internalize and perpetuate the moments of inspiration that arise from time to time, and use them to help us grow and deepen our relationship with Hashem. Accordingly, the *Beis Yisrael* explains, the mitzvah of *linah* after bringing the *korban Pesach* was designed to grant one the opportunity to dwell on and awaken to the spiritual experience of the Festival and allow it to be properly absorbed. Without *linah*, he would leave Yerushalayim quickly and miss out on properly absorbing his *Yom Tov* experience.

Contemplating the Afterlife

With this idea in mind, perhaps we can offer a reason why this *perek* of *Tehillim* was chosen to be recited in a house of mourning at the

---

127 *Pesachim* 95b.

128 ופנית בבקר והלכת לאוהליך וסמך ששת ימים תאכל מצו' הרמז עפ"י פרשיסחא אדם ביקר בל ילין לראות שילין אצלו. וכאן הרמז מפורש ופנית בבקר והלכת לאוהליך אחר לינה הלכת לאוהליך לראות שגם אח"כ יהי' בסדר כדאיתא רמז אחר מתן תורה שובו לכם לאהליכם כו' לראות התנהגות בבית וגם שם כעין ברכה שימשיכו גם באוהליכם אחר שישובו. (בית ישראל, שביעי של פסח).

conclusion of the *davening*. When we are *menachem avel*,[129] our encounter with mourning allows us the temporary
opportunity to think about our time spent in
Olam HaZeh. It triggers us to contemplate
thoughts relating to the afterlife, which we
tend to push aside as they can become too bur-
densome and frightening to deal with. However,
we read in *Koheles*:

We need to grasp the feelings aroused at the house of mourning and put them to work before they are lost.

טוב ללכת אל בית אבל מלכת אל בית משתה באשר הוא סוף כל האדם והחי יתן אל לבו.

It is better to go to a house of mourning than to go to a house of feasting, for that [day of death] is the end of every man, and the living will take it to heart.
(Koheles 7:2)

We must take this to heart, and not allow the inspiration we experience to flash by and be forgotten soon after the short visit ends. It is
for this reason that davening at a house of mourning concludes with
the words:

ואדם ביקר בל ילין נמשל כבהמות נדמו:

As for man, in glory he shall not rest; he is likened to the animals that are silenced.

We need to grasp the feelings aroused at the house of mourning and
put them to work before they are lost. We must take the momentary
inspiration and preserve it for some time such as was done after the
uplifting *oleh regel* experience.

Thus, a simple *nichum avelim* can enrich our spiritual development
for the future and not leave us as an animal, focused on the temporary
pleasure and with no ability to internalize an experience.

---

129 Comforting a mourner.

Shoftim

וְלֹא תָקִים לְךָ מַצֵּבָה אֲשֶׁר שָׂנֵא ה' אֱלֹקֶיךָ:

And do not set up for yourself a monument,
which Hashem your G-d hates. (Devarim 16:22)

The Torah teaches that one may not build a monument created of one single stone to serve Hashem, as this was the practice of idol worshippers in the past to build such structures when serving their gods.

The Danger of Complacency

The *Me'or VaShemesh*, Rav Kalonymus Kalman Halevi Epstein, explains this *pasuk* homiletically with a beautiful lesson relating to our *avodas Hashem*:

כי הנה הגבר אשר הוקם על וקכון לבו בעבודת בוראו ראוי שיעלה במעלות גבוה מעל גבוה ולהוסיף יום יום שכל ואמיץ כח בעבודת השי"ת. אכן האיש אשר ישאר נצב במצב אחד ותפלתו היום כתמול שלשום בלי תוספת זה לאות כי עודנו במדריגה פחותה ולא השיג נעימות אור השי"ת ועבודתו וזהו לא תקים לך מצבה ביאורו שלא תשאר במצב אחד אשר שנא ה' אלקיך כי עבודה כזו בלתי רצויה לפניו יתברך.

A person whose heart is concentrated on developing his avodas Hashem must recognize the importance of adding and growing each day to his avodas Hashem. But he who remains stagnant and inactive, whose davening today is exactly the same as yesterday without any additions, thus shows that he is still at a low level in his service of Hashem and hasn't yet reached the pleasantness of Hashem's light. This is what the Torah alludes to when it teaches not to build a monument for yourself: one should not remain in the same place and situation (matzav, from the same root as matzeivah, one-stone monument) as the previous day, for such behavior is unpleasant before Hashem. (Me'or VaShemesh, Devarim 16:20)

The *Me'or VaShemesh* teaches the significance of daily growth and moving forward in *ruchniyus* and not becoming idle in expanding our spiritual repertoire. One needs to constantly reassess his or her spiritual position in life and seek out ways to strengthen and improve their *davening*, time dedicated to studying Torah, and ways in which they treat others. It is easy to become satisfied with the status quo and become complacent, but contentment in *ruchniyus* leads to downfall, as seen from the following comment by the *Gra*, the *Vilna Gaon*, on this *pasuk*:

אורח חיים למעלה למשכיל למען סור משאול מטה:

The path of life goes upward for the wise, that he may distance himself from the nether-world beneath. (Mishlei 15:24)

The *Vilna Gaon*, Rav Eliyahu of Vilna, in his commentary to *Mishlei*, shares an insightful idea on the following *pasuk*:

> *It is easy to become satisfied with the status quo and become complacent, but contentment in ruchniyus leads to downfall.*

אורח חיים וגו' האדם נקרא הולך שצריך לילך תמיד מדרגא לדרגא ואם לא יעלה למעלה ירד מטה מטה ח"ו כי בלתי אפשר שיעמוד בדרגא חדא וזהו אורח חיים למעלה וגו' למען וגו' כדי שלא יטה לרדת למטה שאולה ומחמת האורח חיים יסור משאול.

Man is called a holech, one who walks, because he must constantly go from one level to the next, and if he isn't elevating himself to greater heights, he will fall deeply, chas v'shalom, since it is not possible to remain constant at one level. This is what the pasuk says, "The path of life goes upward, etc." so that he not stray to fall downward to the abyss; because of his path of life, he will stray from the abyss.

Not to Be Angels

This is one of the differences between a *malach* (angel) and a human being. *Malachim* remain at the level on which they were created, as there is no room or need for them to grow. The opposite is true with humans, who are created with the purpose of moving and progressing, ultimately to leave this world on a loftier level than that which they entered.

The *Gra* teaches us a fascinating lesson about our existence in this world, one which relates to more than just our spiritual growth. Life is like a treadmill, and if we're not constantly moving forward, we will fall behind. There are many forces attempting to pull us off track, and if we aren't vigilant and on-guard, we will lose traction and fall. However, with constant movement and looking for ways to improve ourselves, we are in effect actually working against the force, helping to secure our grip in the climb to spiritual greatness.

Obviously, this task of staying on course is not easy. The *yetzer hara* is constantly at work crafting plans to ensnare us and weaken our ambition, so that we lose our drive to make the right choices. He offers us this rationale, *"What's the purpose in doing the right thing? Even if you're successful in overcoming me today, you'll never be able to outlast me. Tomorrow you will again be faced with a similar situation and will need to make the right choice again. This will go on for days and months; will you really succeed each time? Just give up now!"* And even at times when we are faring well spiritually and in our *avodas Hashem*, the *yetzer hara* is sure to dampen the mood by using this persuasion tactic, *"Does all this hard work and commitment really pay? It's very unlikely that you will last very long on this lofty level, so you might as well give up now and enjoy yourself."*

Battling the *yetzer hara* is not an easy undertaking, but *Chazal* taught that Hashem assists those who seek to purify themselves.[130] We should recognize that while it may seem impossible on our own to maintain the strength needed to overcome the *yetzer's* persuasive arguments, Hashem promises to support us and make it easier to accomplish — as long as we show a commitment and pledge to keep His word.

130 *Yoma* 38b; הבא לטהר מסייעין אותו.

The Satan Attacks from All Sides

We implore Hashem every evening at *Maariv*, in the *Hashkiveinu* blessing, with the following words:

והסר שטן מלפנינו ומאחרינו ...

And remove (the) Satan from before us and from behind us…

What is the significance of the *Satan* being "in front of us" and "behind us" that we pray for his removal? We may perhaps say that we are beseeching Hashem to protect us from both types of the *Satan*'s malicious rationalizations, when he says, "*Regardless, you will eventually fall* **behind**, *so just give up now,*" or when we are at the peak of our *ruchniyus* and he says, "*You won't remain so lofty or* **ahead** *of sin forever, it will simply require too much effort.*" We *daven* for Hashem to prevent the *Satan* from using these arguments which may lead us astray, whether from behind or ahead, and we plead for His assistance as we progress through life hoping to choose our ways correctly.

Ki Seitzei

At the very end of *Parashas Ki Seitzei*, we are once again reminded of the mitzvah to obliterate the name of Amalek. It was he who so impudently attacked B'nei Yisrael immediately after Hashem performed the miraculous events of *Yetzias Mitzrayim* and *Krias Yam Suf*. The *Midrash Tanchuma* describes the extent of this mitzvah:

> רבי לוי בשם רבי אחא ברבי חיננא אומר: כל זמן שזרעו של עמלק בעולם, לא השם שלם,
> ולא הכסא שלם אבד זרעו של עמלק, השם שלם והכסא שלם.
>
> *Rabbi Levi says in the name of Rabbi Acha the son of Rabbi Chanina: As long as the descendants of Amalek exist in this world, Hashem's Name is not complete and His Throne is not complete. [When] the descendants of Amalek are eliminated, His Name is complete and His Throne is complete. (Midrash Tanchuma, Ki Seitzei 11)*

The Descendants of Amalek

The *Midrash* seems to be communicating something specific about Amalek's descendants, for it did not suffice with the word "Amalek," even though it includes his descendants. What are we to understand from the use of the term "the descendants of Amalek"?

260

The *Aish Kodesh*, Rav Klonoymous Kalmish Shapira, *Hy"d*, known as the Piacezner Rebbe, asks this question and offers this incredible insight for an answer:

אין השם שלם ואין הכסא שלם עד שימחה זרעו של עמלק. להבין הלשון זרעו של עמלק, שגם שהראשון היה שמו עמלק וכולם זרעו הם, מכל מקום הוא גם כל האומה נקראת עמלק, כמו שאמר הפסוק בפרשת שלח עמלק יושב בארץ הנגב, וכן בשמואל אגג מלך עמלק, והיה צריך לומר עד שימחה עמלק.

אבל הרמז הוא עד שימחה מה שעמלק זורע, כי גם אחר שימחה עמלק, הזורעים שזרע, ישארו: השבת שמחללים הרבה מישראל רחמנא ליצלן באונם מפני צרותיו של עמלק, ישארו בכמה מהם זמן רב מחולל אצלם, וקדושתו מחוללת, ולא יפחדו כל כך לעשות בו מלאכה כמו עד עתה; הזהירות ממאכלות אסורות לא תהא אצל הרבה מהם כל כך חמורה כמו עד עתה, אם חס וחלילה נכשלים בהם בימי עמלק. והאם אותם בני נעורים שמוכרחים להתבטל מתורה ואינם יודעים בעצמם אם חיים הם מצער וצרות רחמנא ליצלן, ישובו במהרה להכניס את ראשם ורובם לתורה כמאז, גם לאחר שימחה עמלק? אין השם שלם ואין הכסא שלם עד שימחה גם זרעו של עמלק, הזורעים שזרע בנו.

The Midrash says, "Hashem's Name is not complete and His Throne is not complete..." The term "descendants of Amalek" needs to be understood, since the word Amalek refers to the nation of Amalek [and all his descendants] and not just the individual, as seen in Parashas Shelach...and in the book of Shmuel...therefore, why did the Midrash not simply say, "until you obliterate Amalek"?...

[The Midrash] is alluding to the idea [that we cannot stop obliterating Amalek] until that which Amalek planted [zara, from the same root as zera, descendants] is destroyed. This is because even after the nation of Amalek is erased, the seeds he planted still remain. The Shabbos that many in Israel desecrate, may Hashem save us, because of the hardships that Amalek caused us, will remain desecrated among some of them for a long time, and its sanctity will be violated, and they will not fear as strongly to do work on the Shabbos as they had until then. And their caution from forbidden foods will not be as strong among many of them as it was until now, if they, Heaven forbid, had violated this law under Amalek (i.e., were caused to do so under Amalek). And those youths who seem forced to waste time from Torah study, and do not know themselves if they are actually living, due to their sorrow and troubles, may G-d save us — will they quickly return to be head-and-shoulders in Torah as they were before, even after Amalek is erased?

Hashem's Name is not complete and His Throne is not complete until the descendants too are wiped out, that is, the seeds [of evil] that he planted within us. (Aish Kodesh, Parashas Zachor)

The Seeds Planted within Us

The *Aish Kodesh* explains that obliterating Amalek includes not only the physical nation of Amalek, but also that which is weakened and planted within us each time Amalek attacks in the form of the *yetzer hara*. The *Aish Kodesh* elaborates and uses examples of unfortunate Shabbos desecration which took place as a result of us being persecuted, or eating prohibited foods which were consumed when no other options were available and our lives depended on it. What follows is that after Amalek[131] has been removed or the need to desecrate the Shabbos is no longer, those seeds, the behaviors which we accustomed ourselves to have grown to be the norm and those *mitzvos* remain in ruin because of the behaviors that were habituated due to Amalek. These are the seeds which Amalek plants within us, and it is vital that they be uprooted so that they not continue to grow and sprout.

Let us expand upon this idea. We know, as Rashi explains to *Devarim* 25:18, that Amalek was responsible for cooling down the fear and awe that had been widespread among the nations just after *Krias Yam Suf*.

אשר קרך בדרך: לשון מקרה. דבר אחר לשון קרי וטומאה, שהיה מטמאן במשכב זכור. דבר אחר לשון קור וחום, צננך והפשירך מרתיחתך, שהיו כל האומות יראים להלחם בכם ובא זה והתחיל והראה מקום לאחרים. משל לאמבטי רותחת שאין כל בריה יכולה לירד בתוכה, בא בן בליעל אחד קפץ וירד לתוכה. אף על פי שנכוה, הקרה אותה בפני אחרים:

How he happened upon you on the way — An expression denoting a chance occurrence. Alternatively, an expression denoting seminal emission and defilement, because Amalek defiled the Jews by [committing] homosexual acts [with them]. Yet another explanation: an expression denoting heat and cold. He cooled you off and made you [appear] tepid, after you were boiling hot, for the nations were afraid to fight with you, [just as people are afraid to touch something boiling hot]. But this one, [i.e., Amalek] came forward and started and showed the way to others. This can be compared to a bathtub of boiling water into which no living creature could descend. Along came an irresponsible man and jumped headlong into it! Although he scalded himself, he [succeeded to] make others think that it was cooler [than it really was].

---

131 The persecution, or the attack, of the *yetzer hara*.

That is, because of Amalek's audacity in attacking B'nei Yisrael after all the surrounding nations had witnessed Hashem's supremacy, Amalek, in effect, played down all that had occurred. The Torah states about Amalek that he was *"karcha baderech,"* indicating his traits of "cooling down" (*kar*) and of explaining miraculous events as simple occurrences and coincidences (*mikreh*) — both related to *"karcha."* That is, it was his trait not to get excited or inspired by anything and not to take anything too seriously. Perhaps it is this trait that *Amalek* planted within us, or "left with us" and that is imperative for us to uproot. We need to become once again inspired, and refrain from making light of what once may have ignited a spark within us and stirred our souls.

A Strategy of Return

The *Chasam Sofer*, Rav Moshe Sofer, *zt"l*, in his *Toras Moshe*, offers an idea interrelated to the theme of the *Aish Kodesh*. He describes the scheme of the *yetzer hara* and a counter-strategy we can use in turn in our efforts to do *teshuvah*:

כשחוטא ישוב אל ה' בכל לבבו אל יסגף בתעניתו עד קצה האחרון רק ילך ממדריגה
למדריגה וכמו כן כשיצה"ר בא לצדיק ומסיתו לחטוא ג"כ בא אליו מעט מעט היום אומר
לו עשה כך ומחר אומר אומר לו עשה כך ואל יסיתהו פעם אחת להטות מדרך הטובה אל דרך
הרעה כי בוודאי לא ישמע לו ע"כ יבוא אליו מעט מעט וזהו שאמר הכתוב כי תצא למלח־
מה על אויבך פי' על היצה"ר שהוא אויבך ושבית שביו כמו שהוא שב אותך לא בא אצלך
מיד בפעם אחד שהעשה חטא גדול רק מעט מעט כנ"ל כן אם אתה בא אליו לשבותו אל
תבוא אליו עד קצה האחרון בפ"א כי תפסת מרובה לא תפסת כנ"ל שמעתי.

When the sinner returns to Hashem with all his heart, he should not torture himself with fasting to the ultimate degree, but rather should go gradually from one level to the next. The same with the yetzer hara: when it comes to the righteous and tempts him to sin, it too comes slowly and in a progressive manner. One day it tells him commit a given sin, and the next day it says to commit another one; it does not convince him all at once to go astray from the good path to the evil path because [he knows] he won't be heeded. He, therefore, comes very slowly [to go unnoticed].

This is what the pasuk says: "When you will go out to war to fight your enemy" — meaning, the yetzer hara who is your enemy. "And you capture a captive," meaning, just as when he takes you captive [to sin], he does not attempt to lead you to a great sin immediately, but rather very slowly, so too, when you go to take him captive [by returning to Hashem in teshuvah], don't go to the most extreme degree right away, because if you try to grab too much at once you won't be successful. (Toras Moshe, Ki Seitzei)

In an effort to influence us to sin, the yetzer hara makes a quiet entrance, attempting to go unnoticed so that he can quietly implant his ideas in a non-intrusive manner.

The *Chasam Sofer* teaches that we can use the same ploy utilized by the *yetzer hara* to return to *Hashem*. In an effort to influence us to sin, the *yetzer hara* makes a quiet entrance, attempting to go unnoticed so that he can quietly implant his ideas in a non-intrusive manner. These attempts will involve small issues which may pass under the radar as a gray area, meant to manipulate our perspective relating to a particular sin. Once the seed is planted, the *yetzer hara* waits for it to sprout and allows it to work on its own, confident that it will germinate into a progression of *aveiros* that are likely to follow. If he had attempted to assert himself by enticing the individual with a great sin on his first try, this would immediately trigger an alarm within the person, and the *yetzer hara* wouldn't stand a chance. The same is true with *teshuvah*: When it is performed via small steps and minor changes in our behavior, without overwhelming ourselves with an excessive change all at once, we will be more likely to succeed than an attempt at a full-scale transformation.

Using the ideas of the *Aish Kodesh* and the *Chasam Sofer* together, we see that the strategy of "sin seeds," which is the modus operandi used by Amalek, can also be used in battling the *yetzer hara* by planting a small seed of *teshuvah* and then watching it grow into a path to return to Hashem.

Be Extra Vigilant!

וְהָיָה בְּהָנִיחַ ה' אֱלֹקֶיךָ לְךָ מִכָּל אֹיְבֶיךָ מִסָּבִיב בָּאָרֶץ אֲשֶׁר ה' אֱלֹקֶיךָ נֹתֵן לְךָ נַחֲלָה לְרִשְׁתָּהּ תִּמְחֶה אֶת זֵכֶר עֲמָלֵק מִתַּחַת הַשָּׁמָיִם לֹא תִּשְׁכָּח:

[Therefore,] it will be, when Hashem your G-d grants you respite from all your enemies around [you] in the land which Hashem your G-d gives to you

as an inheritance to possess, that you shall obliterate the remembrance of Amalek from beneath the heavens; do not forget. (Devarim 25:19)

Perhaps this *pasuk* is alluding to our dealings with the *yetzer hara* and warning us of a potential vulnerability. *V'hayah b'haniach* — When all is peaceful and calm, when we are relaxed and not vigilant, it is particularly then that the *yetzer hara*, lying in ambush, is waiting to attack, taking advantage of our respite. The *pasuk* then commands, *timcheh es zecher Amalek* — be prepared during these times to be engaged in obliterating the enemy. Just as a seed begins as a small speck and slowly grows, so too is the way of the *yetzer hara*; he begins as a benign character with only a minor presence, makes an increasingly greater impression as he is welcomed, and then catches his prey when we are at rest and off guard.

Ki Savo

וּבָאוּ עָלֶיךָ כָּל הַבְּרָכוֹת הָאֵלֶּה וְהִשִּׂיגֻךָ כִּי תִשְׁמַע בְּקוֹל ה' אֱלֹקֶיךָ:

And all these blessings will come upon you and reach you,

if you obey Hashem your G-d. (Devarim 28:2)

Rav Tzadok HaKohen of Lublin comments on the significance of the word *vehisigucha*, they will reach you, which the *pasuk* here uses when telling of the *berachos* that Hashem will send forth.

> ובברכות כתיב ובאו עליך כל הברכות האלה והשיגוך ואומרים בשם רבינו ר' בונם זצללה"ה
> והשיגוך במקומך היינו שלא תשתנה ע"י הטובות והחסדים והברכות והוא שיהי' אלקים
> ברב חסדך שלא ישכחו כי ה' אלקיך הנותן לך כח לעשות חיל.
>
> *Relating to the blessings (in Parashas Ki Savo), the pasuk says that they will all "come upon you and reach you." It is said in the name of Reb Bunim of holy blessed memory (of Peshischa) that they will "reach you in your place," meaning that you will not change as a result of all the good and kindness and blessings. Rather, it should be that Hashem [remains with you when He provides you] with His abundant kindness, and we should not forget that it is Hashem our G-d Who gives us strength to make wealth. (Pri Tzaddik, Bereishis 13)*

Rav Tzadok explains in the name of his Rebbe that the lesson here is the importance of remaining cognizant of Hashem's kindness when

He bestows His blessing upon us. We must not change; we must always remember that it is Hashem Who is responsible for our success, and that it is brought about by His kindness. When the *pasuk* says "reach you in your place," it means that you will remain with the awareness that Hashem is the provider of all successes.

Hashem's Promise

A similar idea is presented by Rav Mordechai Yosef of Izhbitz in his *Mei HaShiloach* on the above *pasuk*:

ובאו עליך כל הברכות האלה והשיגוך, היינו שלא תשתנה כמו שהיית כי טבע האדם להשתנות בעת שירוח לו ה' וע"ז מבטיח לו הקב"ה כי הטוב שבנפש ישראל לא ישתנה ח"ו משום דבר.

"And all the blessings will come upon you and reach you" —meaning you will not change from whom you were (prior to the blessing). For it is the nature of man to change when Hashem causes him to prosper, and for this, Hashem promises that the good in the soul of a Jew will not change, Heaven forbid, from anything. (Mei HaShiloach)

The Izhbitzer explains that in addition to Hashem bestowing upon us all of these *berachos*, He will also ensure that the blessings do not change the essence of who we are. The nature of success is that at times it has a negative effect on us, causing us to become arrogant in the belief that we alone facilitated our success. We are liable to come to feel superior to others, completely transforming our behavior and interaction with people. Hashem therefore promises that His blessings will reach you in "your place," and that you will remain the same person you were before the blessing arrived.

Later on, the Torah relates a list of curses which will befall B'nei Yisrael in the event that they aren't faithful to Hashem. The *pasuk* says:

וְהָיָה אִם לֹא תִשְׁמַע בְּקוֹל ה' אֱלֹקֶיךָ לִשְׁמֹר לַעֲשׂוֹת אֶת כָּל מִצְוֹתָיו וְחֻקֹּתָיו אֲשֶׁר אָנֹכִי מְצַוְּךָ הַיּוֹם וּבָאוּ עָלֶיךָ כָּל הַקְּלָלוֹת הָאֵלֶּה וְהִשִּׂיגוּךָ:

And it will be, if you do not obey the voice of Hashem your G-d, to observe to fulfill all His commandments and statutes that I command you this day, that all these curses will come upon you and reach (overtake) you. (Devarim 28:15)

Here again, we find the word *vehisigucha*, "they will reach (overtake) you" — but this time with regard to the curses. What is the *pasuk* trying to convey here? Do we really need a promise or guarantee that the curses will reach us?

Do Not Change Your Attitude

Along the lines expressed by the Izhbitzer and Rav Tzadok regarding the blessings, we can suggest the following: The Torah may be teaching us that even if Hashem sends devastating curses our way, we should recognize that they are for our own good — whether it be to help stimulate our spiritual growth, or to cleanse us from past *aveiros*. The Torah tells us that if we perceive the hardship as such, we must not change our attitude toward Hashem by being "upset" with Him or rebelling against Him. We are bidden to accept the curse and look to grow from the experience; we must be satisfied in the knowledge that with this hardship, our sins that may have debased our *neshamah* are being cleansed. The curses should reach us or find us still with steadfast faith in Hashem, and they should leave us the same way without altering our relationship with Him.

The *pasuk* in *Malachi* says:

כִּי אֲנִי ה' לֹא שָׁנִיתִי וְאַתֶּם בְּנֵי יַעֲקֹב לֹא כְלִיתֶם:

For I, Hashem, have not changed; and you, the sons of Yaacov, have not been consumed. (Malachi 3:6)

Homiletically, we can explain this *pasuk* not as Hashem speaking to B'nei Yisrael, but rather the opposite. We are telling Hashem, *"For I, even through all the hardship and adversity experienced, Hashem,* (see that) *I have not changed.* I remain a loyal servant of Yours and my faith has not been lost. I recognize the true intent of Your actions toward me, and I believe that all is ultimately for the good." The *pasuk* concludes with Hashem responding that because of this staunch belief you have in Him, "you, the sons of Yaacov, have

> *The true essence of a Yid is that even in times of pain and anguish, deep down he believes that Hashem has a master plan.*

not been consumed." The true essence of a *Yid* is that even in times of pain and anguish, deep down he believes that Hashem has a master plan. He has *emunah*, belief and faith, that Hashem will get him through the difficult period; he does not abandon his relationship with Hashem and remains with so much more than what was perceived as lost through the suffering.

In the *selichos* designated for *Behab*,[132] we begin with a prayer that Hashem should have mercy on His people that has withstood much suffering and distress:

יִשְׂרָאֵל עַמְּךָ תְּחִנָּה עוֹרְכִים שֶׁהֵם מְצֵרִים וּלְהִוָּשַׁע צְרִיכִים צָרֵיהֶם עֲלֵיהֶם עַל מַאֲרִיכִים כָּל זֹאת הִגִּיעָתַם וְשִׁמְךָ מְבָרְכִים.

Yisrael, Your nation, prepares supplication, because they are distressed and need to be helped. Their oppressors prolong the yoke upon them — all this has befallen them, yet they (continue to) bless Your Name.

This is the fundamental nature of Klal Yisrael, and it lives inside each of us. Throughout all the persecutions and hardships that we have endured, it is Hashem's Name that we continue to bless and it is to Him that we turn in time of need.

---

132 Initials of Monday, Thursday, Monday. The custom to fast on the first Monday, Thursday, and then the following Monday of the Jewish months of Cheshvan and Iyar, shortly following Succos and Pesach.

Nitzavim

אַתֶּם נִצָּבִים הַיּוֹם כֻּלְּכֶם לִפְנֵי ה' אֱלֹקֵיכֶם רָאשֵׁיכֶם שִׁבְטֵיכֶם זִקְנֵיכֶם
וְשֹׁטְרֵיכֶם כֹּל אִישׁ יִשְׂרָאֵל:

You are all standing this day before Hashem your G-d —
the leaders of your tribes, your elders and your officers,
every man of Israel. (Devarim 29:9)

Parashas Nitzavim begins with a continuation of Moshe's last words
to B'nei Yisrael, a series of speeches that detail, inter alia, the importance of adhering to the word of Hashem and recognizing the great
privilege of being part of a nation chosen by Hashem.

Elevating Our Physical Needs

The *Tiferes Shlomo*, Rav Shlomo Hakohen Rabinowitz, *zt"l*, the first
Radomsker Rebbe, explains the opening *pasuk* of the *parashah* as giving
a message about the opportunities to serve Hashem that exist exclusively in This World — *Olam HaZeh* — even though it requires us to be
occupied with basic physical needs:

... אתם נצבים היום כולכם לפני ד' כו'. עפ"י מ"ש בפ' עקב בפ' ואשב בהר ארבעים יום
וארבעים לילה לחם לא אכלתי ומים לא שתיתי על כל חטאתכם כו'. כבר בארנו בפנ'
כי יש לתמוה על התנצלות הזה של משרע"ה שלא אכל ולא שתה מ' יום הלא הי' עומד

270

ומדבר עם השכינה וזה התענוג הוא יותר מכל התענוגים שבעולם ולמה לו לאכילה
ושתי' כלל.

אך הנה העניין סוד כל בריאת העולם רק עבור האדם אשר בחיים חיותו עודנו
בעולם העשי' הגוף עם הנפש יחד והיצר עומד לנגדו ומסיתו והאדם כובש יצרו
ומתגבר עליו לעשות רצון הבורא ב"ה ועובד השי"ת גם ע"י אכילה ושתי' בכוונה
הראוי' וכוונה ועושה יחודים בעולמות העליונים. וז"ש ואתם הדבקים בה' אלקיכם
חיים כלכם היום. פי' רק בעודכם קיימים בחיות הגוף והנפש הוא העת לעשות היחוד
ודביקות בשם הוי'.

*... You are all standing this day before Hashem — Based on what I wrote
in Parashas Eikev (on the pasuk) "I sat on the mountain forty days and
forty nights; bread I did not eat and water I did not drink because of
all your sins." We already explained previously: Why does Moshe see the
need to explain that he did not eat or drink for forty days? After all, he
was speaking and standing with the Shechinah (Divine Presence) — the
greatest pleasure of all the pleasures in the world; why would he need to
eat or drink at all?*

*However, the secret of all of creation is for man and while alive, all his
vitality is in the Olam Ha'Asiyah[133] when his body and soul are together
and the evil inclination (yetzer hara) stands before him to lead him astray
and the person conquers his evil inclination so that he can do the Will of
his Creator, and even while eating and drinking with the right and proper
intentions he facilitates unification with the supernal worlds. And this
is what the pasuk says, "But you who cling to Hashem, your G-d, you are
all alive today" (Devarim 4:4), meaning to say, as long as you are alive
with your body and soul together, that is the time to effect unification
and cling to Hashem.*

Let us explain this Kabbalistic thought. The *Olam Ha'Asiyah* has
much value and benefit and is desirable by Hashem. He created the
world so that we may take His creations and spiritually elevate them
by preventing the *yetzer hara* from controlling us in the way we relate
to them. This opportunity exists only in this world where our souls and
physical bodies are united, facing the challenges put forth by the *yetzer
hara* and successfully overcoming them.

---

133   The *Olam Ha'Asiyah*, World of Making or World of Action, refers to this earth and all earthly
material creation.

The *Tiferes Shlomo* continues:

אבל בג"ע הוא זמן קבלת שכר ותענוג לצדיקים משכר פעולתם בעוה"ז אבל זמן העשי'
חלף ועבר כי המתים חפשי. וז"ש וירא אלקים את כל אשר עשה והנה טוב מאד בעולם
העשי' הוא הטוב בעיניו ית"ש. אבל המלאכים ושרפים שהם בעולם הבריאה אינם חשו־
בים בעיניו כמו האדם. כמ"ש ואביתה תהלה מקרוצי חומר כו' ולזאת צריך האדם לתת
שבח והוד' על כל שעה ורגע שהוא עודנו בחיים ויכול לעשות רצונו ית"ש כי זה כבודו.

Gan Eden is the opportunity for receiving pleasure and reward for the righteous resulting from their earnings in Olam HaZeh, yet the time for performing [good deeds] has passed and is gone; the dead are free [from performing mitzvos]. And this is what the Torah means when describing Creation, "He saw all that he made, and it was very good" — the Olam Ha'Asiyah is that which is good in His eyes. However, the angels and fiery angels which exist in the World of Creation are not as worthy in G-d's eyes as are human beings. As we recite [in our Yom Kippur prayers], "You desire praise from those fashioned of clay." For this, a person must give praise and thanks for every moment he is alive and is able to fulfill the will of Hashem, for this is His honor.

The *Tiferes Shlomo* then continues to explain Moshe Rabbeinu's criticism of B'nei Yisrael and his mention of not eating or drinking for forty days:

וזה שהי' משרע"ה מתנצל על מ' יום שהי' במרום בבחינת מלאך ושרף ובטל ממנו מלחמה
היצר והם היו חסרים ממנין שנותיו וזה הי' מחמת חטאת בנ"י שהי' עומד במרום לבקש
עליהם רחמים. וזה ג"כ הפי' אתם נצבים היום כולכם כו'. ר"ל באותו מעמד ומצב שאתם
בעוה"ז בעולם העשי' הנפש עם הבשר יחד תוכלו לעמוד כלכם לפני ה'. פי' כאשר תעשו
כל מעשיכם בכל צרכי עוה"ז לתכלית המכוון לעבוד הש"י וזה לפני ה' וזה למלאות רצונו
ית"ש.

And regarding the explanation by Moshe Rabbeinu of the forty days he spent in the heavens on the level of an angel [Moshe made a major sacrifice] since it was removed from him the opportunity of battling with his yetzer hara and those (opportunities) were absent from his number of years which was as a result of the B'nei Yisrael's sins since he was up in the heavens pleading for mercy on their behalf. And this is also the explanation of the pasuk, "You are all standing here this day," that is, in the same situation in which you find yourselves in Olam HaZeh, the Olam Ha'Asiyah, with your bodies and souls together; you will be able to stand all of you before Hashem. This means that you should perform all your actions which relate to your worldly needs with the right intentions to serve Hashem, this is what "before Hashem" means — to fulfill the Will of Hashem. (Tiferes Shlomo, Rosh Hashanah)

What an incredible idea! It gives us a new perspective on the seemingly mundane activities with which we involve ourselves on a daily basis; all of our drinking, eating, and other physical behaviors can be revolutionized into spiritual experiences in which we view ourselves as taking some of the material creations which Hashem produced for us and to use as conduits to connect with Him. We have the ability to serve Hashem in this world by directing our intent toward Him, and not allowing the *yetzer hara* to take control over our daily routine activities as we eat, sleep, speak, and even work.

An Equal Opportunity Olam HaZeh

Continuing with the idea of the *Tiferes Shlomo*, perhaps we can explain the opening *pasuk* of our *parashah* in the following way.

אַתֶּם נִצָּבִים הַיּוֹם כֻּלְּכֶם ...

You are all standing this day before Hashem your G-d...

In *Olam HaZeh*, you are all standing here today with equal opportunities to serve *Hashem*. All are given the chance to serve Hashem via simple actions and everyday events. Even those created without the intellectual capabilities to reach lofty levels in Torah understanding can still eat, drink, and care for their physical needs while being performed with holiness and in a manner pleasing to Hashem.

> *All are given the chance to serve Hashem via simple actions and everyday events.*

The *pasuk* continues, however, as follows:

לִפְנֵי ה' אֱלֹהֵיכֶם רָאשֵׁיכֶם שִׁבְטֵיכֶם זִקְנֵיכֶם וְשֹׁטְרֵיכֶם כֹּל אִישׁ יִשְׂרָאֵל

the leaders of your tribes, your elders and your officers, every man of Israel.

When we reach the point in which we leave this world, the *Olam Ha'Asiyah*, and find ourselves *before Hashem*, no longer having the ability to benefit from This World, each person will then be placed individually, categorized by the level of effort and dedication with which they navigated *Olam HaZeh*. Some of them will be "leaders, elders, and officers," since the opportunity to reach our intended spiritual goals no longer exists. Each individual is measured in terms of what he has accomplished. At this point, it is parallel to Moshe Rabbeinu's time spent up in the heavens — where he lacked the opportunity to "eat or drink," with no access to serve Hashem — an opportunity lost forever.

Excellence

To expand this idea further, we can question what it was that Moshe was alluding to with his sacrifice of the forty days spent in the heavens pleading with Hashem on behalf of His People. After a whole life of clinging to Hashem and being the humble servant that he was, was a lost forty days going to make much of a difference in the grand scheme of things?

Rav Moshe Chaim Luzzatto, in his *Mesillas Yesharim*, offers a thought that can answer this question. He exposes the risk of practicing mediocre *avodas Hashem* and highlights the importance and great benefit of not being satisfied with the attitude of "just getting by."

והנה יש מהפתאים המבקשים רק להקל מעליהם, שיאמרו, למה נייגע עצמנו בכל כך חסידות ופרישות, הלא די לנו שלא נהיה מהרשעים הנידונים בגיהנם. אנחנו לא נדחוק עצמנו ליכנס בגן עדן לפני ולפנים. אם לא יהיה לנו חלק גדול, יהיה לנו חלק קטן. אנו די לנו בזה, ולא נכביד על משאנו בעבור זאת.

אמנם שאלה אחת נשאל מהם: היוכלו כל כך על נקלה לסבול בעולם הזה החולף, לראות אחד מחבריהם מכובד ומנושא יותר מהם ומושל עליהם וכל שכן אחד מעבדיהם או מן העניים הנבזים ושפלים בעיניהם ולא יצטערו ולא יהיה דמם רותח בקרבם? לא, ודאי! כי הנה עינינו הרואות: כל עמל האדם, להנשא על כל מי שיוכל ולשים מקומו בין הרמים יותר, כי היא קנאת איש מרעהו. ואם יראה חברו מתרומם והוא נשאר שפל, ודאי שמה שיסבול הוא מה שיוכרח לסבלו, כי לא יוכל למנוע, ולבבו יתעשת בקרבו.

מעתה, אם כך קשה עליהם להיות שפלים מזולתם במעלות המדומות והכוזבות, שאין השפלות בם אלא לפנים, ולא ההנשא אלא שוא ושקר, איך יוכלו לסבול שיראו עצמם שפלים יותר מאותם האנשים עצמם אשר הם עתה שפלים מהם. וזה במקום המעלה האמיתית והיקר הנצחי, שאף על פי שעכשיו אין מכירים אותו ואת ערכו, על כן לא יחושו אליו, אבל בזמנו, ודאי שיכירוהו לאמיתו לצערם ולבשתם, ודאי שלא יהיה להם זה אלא צער גדול ונצחי.

הרי לך, שאין הסבלנות הזה אשר הם דורשים לעצמם להקל מהם חומר העבודה, אלא פיתוי כוזב שמפתה יצרם אותם, ולא דבר אמיתי כלל. וכבר לא היה מקום לפיתוי זה להם לולי היו

רואים אמיתת הענין. אבל לפי שאין מבקשים אותו והולכים ושוגים לרצונם, הנה לא יוסר
מהם פתויים עד הזמן אשר לא יועיל להם, כי לא יהיה עוד בידם לתקן את אשר שחתו.

והוא מה שאמר שלמה המלך עליו השלום (קהלת ט, י) כל אשר תמצא ידך לעשות בכחך
עשה כי אין מעשה וחשבון ודעת וחכמה בשאול אשר אתה הולך שמה. והיינו, כי מה שאין
האדם עושה עד שהכח מסור בידו מבוראו הוא הכח הבחיריי המסור לו כל ימי חייו שהוא
בהם בחיריי ומצוה לעשות, הנה לא יוכל לעשותו עוד בקבר ובשאול, שאין הכח הזה עוד
בידו, כי מי שלא הרבה מעשים טובים בחייו, אי אפשר לו לעשותם אחרי כן. ומי שלא
חשב חשבון מעשיו, לא יהיה לו זמן לחשבו אז. ומי שלא התחכם בעולם הזה, לא יתחכם
בקבר. וזהו שאמר כי אין מעשה וחשבון ודעת וחכמה בשאול אשר אתה הולך שמה.

*There are some fools who seek only to lighten their burden. They say, "Why
weary ourselves with so much Saintliness and Separation? Is it not enough
for us that we will not be numbered among the wicked who are judged in
Gehinnom? We will not force ourselves to enter all the way into Gan Eden.
If we do not have a large portion, we will have a small one. It will be enough
for us. We will not add to our burdens for the sake of greater acquisitions."*

*There is one question that we will ask these people: Could they so easily, in
this transitory world, tolerate the sight of one of their friends being honored,
and elevated above them, and coming to rule over them? Even more so, one
of their servants or one of the paupers who are shameful and lowly in their
eyes? Could they tolerate this without suffering and without their blood
boiling in them? Is there any question that they could not? We witness with
our own eyes all of the labors of a man to elevate himself above everyone he
can and to establish his place among the exalted. This is a man's jealousy of
his neighbor. If he sees his neighbor elevated while he remains low, what he
tolerates will be what he is forced to tolerate because of his inability to alter
the situation, but his heart will brood within him.*

*If it is so difficult, then, for them to abide being on a lower level than others
in respect to qualities whose desirability is elusive and deceitful, qualities in
relation to which a man's being designated as lowly is but a surface judgment,
and his being elevated is vanity and falsity, then how could they tolerate [in
the World to Come] seeing themselves lower than those same persons who
are now lower than they? And this will be in the place of true quality and
everlasting worth, which, though they might not give heart to it now because
of their failure to recognize it and its value, they will certainly recognize in its
time for what it is, to their grief and shame. There is no question that their
suffering will be terrible and interminable.*

*This tolerance, then, that they adopt in order to lighten their burden
is nothing but a deceitful persuasion of their yetzer hara, with no basis*

whatsoever in truth. If they saw the truth, there would be no room for such deception, but because they do not seek it, but walk and stray according to their desires, these persuasions will not leave them until such a time when it will no longer avail them, when it will no longer be in their hands to rebuild what they have destroyed.

As was said by Shlomo HaMelech, peace be upon him (Koheles 9:10), "Whatever your hand finds to do with your strength, do it, for there is no deed, nor account, nor knowledge in the pit to which you are going." That is, what a man does not do while he still has the power that His Creator has given him (the power of choice that is given to him to employ during his lifetime, when he can exercise free will and is commanded to do so) he will not again have the opportunity of doing in the grave and in the pit, for at that time he will no longer possess this power. For one who has not multiplied good deeds in his lifetime will not have the opportunity of performing them afterwards. And one who has not taken an accounting of his deeds will not have time to do so later. And one who has not become wise in this world will not become wise in the grave. This is the intent of the above-cited pasuk, "for there is no deed nor account nor knowledge nor wisdom in the pit to which you are going." (Mesillas Yesharim, chapter 4)[134]

Perhaps this is the message Moshe intended to impart to B'nei Yisrael. Being satisfied with less in *avodas Hashem* is the *yetzer hara's* ploy to outsmart us and deplete us of our motivation. If being average and mediocre is not acceptable for us in other areas of our lives, surely it will bother us to no-end in *Olam Haba*, the World to Come, when there is no opportunity to advance our status and when we are stuck in the back of the room observing others enjoying VIP treatment. Moshe Rabbeinu lived with this idea and wished to use every occasion he encountered to further his growth and bring himself even closer to Hashem.

It wasn't specifically about the amount of time he lost or the service of Hashem that he was missing. Rather, every moment and small opportunity was an occasion to further his responsibility at using the material world as a means to cling to Hashem.

134 Translation from *Mesillas Yesharim*, Torah Classics Library, Feldheim.

Vayeilech

וַיְצַו מֹשֶׁה אוֹתָם לֵאמֹר מִקֵּץ שֶׁבַע שָׁנִים בְּמֹעֵד שְׁנַת הַשְּׁמִטָּה בְּחַג הַסֻּכּוֹת: בְּבוֹא כָל יִשְׂרָאֵל לֵרָאוֹת אֶת פְּנֵי ה' אֱלֹקֶיךָ בַּמָּקוֹם אֲשֶׁר יִבְחָר תִּקְרָא אֶת הַתּוֹרָה הַזֹּאת נֶגֶד כָּל יִשְׂרָאֵל בְּאָזְנֵיהֶם: הַקְהֵל אֶת הָעָם הָאֲנָשִׁים וְהַנָּשִׁים וְהַטַּף וְגֵרְךָ אֲשֶׁר בִּשְׁעָרֶיךָ לְמַעַן יִשְׁמְעוּ וּלְמַעַן יִלְמְדוּ וְיָרְאוּ אֶת ה' אֱלֹקֵיכֶם וְשָׁמְרוּ לַעֲשׂוֹת אֶת כָּל דִּבְרֵי הַתּוֹרָה הַזֹּאת:

Moshe then commanded them, saying, "At the end of [every]
seven years, at an appointed time [after] the year
of Shemittah, in the holiday of Succos.

When all Israel comes to appear before Hashem your G-d, in the
place He will choose, you shall read this Torah before all Israel,
in their ears. Assemble the people the men, the women, and
the children, and your stranger in your cities, in order that they
hear, and in order that they learn and fear Hashem, your G-d,
and they will observe to do all the words of this Torah.

(Devarim 31:10–12)

Moshe commands the mitzvah of *Hakhel* to the B'nei Yisrael. It requires that once every seven years, during the Festival of Succos immediately following the *Shemittah* year, all men, women, and children

277

gather in the Beis HaMikdash to hear the king read sections of *Sefer Devarim*, so that they learn to fear Hashem and observe the Torah.

An Odd Time to Assemble

The *Shem MiShmuel*, Rabbi Shmuel Bornstein, *zt"l*, the Sochatchover Rebbe, asks: The *Shemittah* year was dedicated to learning and reconnecting to Hashem, since all agricultural work was forbidden, naturally allowing for more spiritual undertakings. Why, then, was *Hakhel* held at the end of the year? Would not the beginning of the *Shemittah* year have been a more opportune time to assemble the nation and teach them? This would have given them a whole year to learn and apply the selections read by the king!

מקץ שבע שנים וגו' תקרא את התורה הזאת נגד כל ישראל באזניהם. הקהל את העם וגו'.
הענין מה שהיה המלך קורא את התורה לאחר שנת השמיטה, דלכאורה היה יותר נכון
בתחילת שנת השמיטה שיהיה להם פנאי כל השנה ללמוד.

אך הענין הוא, דהנה יש להבין עיקר ענין הקריאה שהיה המלך קורא למה, דמה חידש להם
המלך בקריאתו התורה, הלא תורה שבכתב כתובה לכל?

אך הענין דהנה ברמב"ם¹³⁵ ז"ל שמלך לבו הוא לב כל ישראל, עד כאן וזאת היתה
הכוונה בקריאת התורה ע"י המלך. מחמת שלבו לב כל קהל ישראל יכנסו דבריו בלב
כל העם בעומק לבם. (וזהי כוונת ירבעם שעשה עגלים ולא הניחם לבוא היינו שהיה
חושש שאם יבואו לירושלים וישמעו הקריאה מרחבעם יכירו וידעו כי לו המלוכה כאשר
דבריו, לירושלים יחדרו לתוך לבות בני ישראל.) ולפי זה יובן איחור הקריאה, שלזה צריכין
מקודם הכנה רבה להכין מקום בלבם לקבל הדברים, ולזה היתה הקריאה לאחר שנת
השמיטה, כי ענין שמיטה פירשו המפרשים שיהיו פנויים ממלאכתם ומעובדת האדמה
להסתכל בתוך עצמם וזאת היתה להם הכנה שיכנסו ויפעלו הדברים בעומק לבם.

"At the end of every seven years, you shall read this Torah before all of Yisrael...Assemble the nation" — The issue [to be understood here] is why the king would read the Torah [to the assembled nation] after the Shemittah year. Seemingly it would have been more appropriate to do so at the start of the Shemittah year, so that there would be time, the entire year, for them to learn.

We must first understand why the king was instructed to read the Torah aloud. What did the king teach them by reading the Torah to them? After all, the Torah was written for all [and they could have read it on their own]!

Rather, this was the intention of having the king read for them: The Rambam

---

135 *Mishneh Torah, Hilchos Melachim 3:6.*

explains that the heart of the king is the heart of the entire Nation of Israel, and therefore his reading the words will cause them to penetrate the depths of their hearts…This is why the reading was delayed [until after the Shemittah year], since for the king's words to properly enter their hearts they first needed to prepare themselves, making room in their hearts to be receptive to what he read. And this is what the Shemittah year was all about, as the commentators explain, that since they were free from working the fields, it gave them time for self-introspection and to prepare themselves so that the king's words would have an impression in the depths of their hearts.

In essence, the *Shem MiShmuel* teaches that the *Shemittah* year, which allowed the farmers time for studying Torah and focusing on self-improvement, made it possible for them to be receptive to the king's words come Succos of the following year. Preparation for *Hakhel* was a prerequisite before the king could read *Sefer Devarim* so that his words would not fall on deaf ears.

This is true of every spiritual endeavor; it can be better appreciated if we first prepare ourselves to be more open to its message and experience.

Preparing for the Experience

The Gemara[136] explains why we wait on Rosh Hashanah until *Mussaf* to blow the shofar, given that we usually try to perform *mitzvos* at the earliest possible opportunity. The Gemara compares shofar blowing to *Hallel*, which is recited as part of the morning *Shacharis*, following the dictum of *zerizim makdimim l'mitzvos*, "the zealous rush to perform *mitzvos*."

מאי שנא שני מתקיע? משום דרוב עם הדרת מלך. אי הכי הלל נמי נימא בשני משום דרוב עם הדרת מלך? אלא מאי שנא הלל דבראשון? משום דזריזין מקדימין למצות. תקיעה נמי נעביד בראשון משום דזריזין מקדימין למצות? אמר רבי יוחנן בשעת גזרת המלכות שנו.

Why is the shofar different in that it is blown during Mussaf? Because of "in a multitude of people is a King's glory" [as more people attend the Mussaf prayer]. If so, Hallel should also be recited then? Rather, Hallel is recited first [at Shacharis] because of the principle, "the zealous rush to perform mitzvos." If so, the shofar should also be blown at Shacharis? Rabbi Yochanan answered, 'This law was taught when the government issued a decree

---

136 *Rosh Hashanah* 32b.

[against blowing the shofar — a decree that was enforced only at the start of the prayers, but not during Mussaf]. (Rosh Hashanah 32b)

A Greater Impact

In addition to the above explanation, perhaps we can suggest another reason for delaying shofar-blowing until *Mussaf*: the much-required preparation needed beforehand so that the message of the shofar can be that much more meaningful to its listeners. Before *Mussaf* of Rosh Hashanah, we have a chance to hear both the Torah reading and the *Haftarah* reading, which provide us with important messages that will help us truly hear the deep calling of the shofar. We read of Sarah Imeinu and Chanah;[137] they were both barren, unable to conceive — yet in their suffering, they turned to Hashem with heartfelt *tefillah*. As the Gemara[138] says, the *Imahos* (Matriarchs) were barren because Hashem desired their *tefillos*. Hashem desires our *teshuvah* too, and wants us to recognize that if we truly repent and return in sincere *tefillah*, He will accept our prayers and grant us life. As we say in *Mussaf* of the *Yomim Noraim*,[139] "You, Hashem, do not desire that the [sinner] die, but rather that he repent from his evil ways and live."[140] On the second day of Rosh Hashanah, too, we read of the *Akeidas Yitzchak* and the dedication and willingness of Avraham and Yitzchak to sacrifice all for the sake of Hashem. Nothing else mattered except for following the Will of Hashem. This, too, is a lesson worthy of hearing prior to the shofar blast.

Finally, then — after reading about the lives of the *Avos* and *Imahos*, our Patriarchs and Matriarchs — the shofar can be blown, as it will have the intended awakening-effect on us to do *teshuvah* and commit ourselves to a more spiritual way of living. The shofar-blowing will have a greater impact on our souls if time is first spent on carving out a place in our hearts to receive its calling.

Preparing ourselves is actually the purpose of our time spent in this world.

---

137   Shmuel HaNavi's mother.
138   *Yevamos* 64.
139   Rosh Hashanah and Yom Kippur.
140   כי לא תחפוץ במות המת, כי אם בשובו מדרכו וחיה.

Throughout life, we may experience hardships and struggles which train us to be attuned to Hashem's deep and personal callings. These allow us to connect with the Divine bandwidth and begin to comprehend the messages of the tests given to us and their significance as opportunities for self-growth.

Another byproduct born of our struggles is the ability to make room within our hearts for others. We must ask:

- Can a person blessed with children fully relate to the suffering of childless couples?
- Can someone comfortably employed and able to support his family understand the dire situation of one who is not?
- Can one who is healthy and strong comprehend the pain of a family whose loved one is battling an illness?
- And, can one who is happily married understand the pain of singles who yearn to share their lives with someone special?

Relating to Others in Pain

Perhaps, via our struggles, Hashem has allowed us a way to more easily relate to others in pain. After we experience challenging times, how much easier is it to then feel for another person who is struggling? How much better can we relate to a person sitting in a hospital bed if we have already been in that situation? The individual who waited several years before getting married can be more sensitive to others who are presently single, because he or she remembers those long and lonely *Shabossim* and *Yamim Tovim*, watching friends move along in the cycle of life while thinking about the frightening possibility of being alone forever. We must use our difficult experiences to ensure that grasping someone else's pain isn't foreign to us and to leave a place in our hearts that can share in another's discomfort.

The objective of *Hakhel* was for all to attend with open hearts, after going through the year-long process of peeling away a thick layer of *gashmiyus* that can accumulate and prevent us from becoming inspired to hear the word of Hashem. After taking some time to renew our souls during *Shemittah*, we can then hear the Divine messages and use our spiritual receptors to comprehend them.

Haazinu

צוּר יְלָדְךָ תֶּשִׁי וַתִּשְׁכַּח אֵל מְחֹלְלֶךָ:

*You forgot the [Mighty] Rock Who bore you; you forgot
the G-d Who delivered you. (Devarim 32:18)*

The Dubno Maggid, Rav Yaacov Krantz, offers a beautiful *mashal*
(parable) on this *pasuk*, which outstandingly describes our shortcomings in disregarding and overlooking Hashem's gracious dealings
with us:

צור ילדך תשי ותשכח אל מחוללך, באור המאמר נראה ע"ד ראובן הי' חייב לשמעון
מנה, ובא ראובן אצל לוי ובקש אותו שיתן לו עצה להפטר מבעל חובו, כי שמעון
נוגש אותו מאד, ויתן לו עצה שיעשה א"ע משוגע, וכאשר יבא שמעון אליך תתחיל
לצפצף ולשרוק ולרקד במחולות, ויעשה כן, ושמעון ראה כי הוא משוגע וירף ידו
ממנו, אח"כ בא ראובן אל לוי ויבקש אותו איזה הלואה על ימים מספר, ויתן לו,
וכאשר הגיע זמן הפרעון בא אליו לתבוע אותו, והוא מתחיל לצפצף כנגדו כאשר
עשה נגד שמעון הנ"ל, וירם עליו מטהו ויכהו מכה רבה ויאמר לו נבל העצה הזאת
הלא אני נתתי לך, וכי בעבורי יעצתי לך כן. הנמשל, כי כבר נתבאר ממעלת השכחה
אשר חנן ה' את האדם, כי אם לא הי' בו טבע השכחה לא היה אדם בונה בית ולא
נשא אשה כו' והאדם הולך עם השכחה הזאת ושוכח את בוראו ומחוללו, ואין נבלה
יותר מזאת, וזהו צור ילדך תשי, ר"ל הוא הוליד אותך בטבע השכחה שתוכל לשכוח
דברים ידועים ובכוונה עשה הקב"ה כן להפיק טובתך קיומך, ואתה עם השכחה הזאת
המוטבע בך תלך ותשכח אל מחוללך.

This pasuk can be understood via the following parable: Reuven owed money to Shimon, and went to Levi and shared his woes with him. "What should I do?" Reuven said. "Shimon is harassing me and demanding payment."

"Listen to me," Levi advised. "When he comes to you, pretend you are insane. Start to dance and sing. When he sees this, he will realize that because of your dire straits you have lost your mind, and he will leave you alone." Reuven liked this idea and followed the advice. When Shimon came to collect his debt, Reuven pretended he was crazy, and Shimon left him alone.

One day, Reuven borrowed money from Levi, and when Levi came to collect, Reuven began to sing and dance as if he were insane. Levi became angered, struck him with his cane, and said to him, "Scoundrel! I'm the one who gave you this idea how to avoid your creditor, and now you're using my advice against me?!"

So, too, this pasuk says, "The Rock Who bore you, you disregarded." Hashem did a kindness with us and gave us the trait of forgetfulness so that we could forget our troubles and difficulties and embark on new projects despite them — and then we "forsake the A-lmighty Who delivered you," using that same trait to forget Hashem![141]

The Gift of Forgetfulness

The *Chovos Halevavos*,[142] Rabbeinu Bachya ibn Paquda explains the value of the great gift of forgetfulness:

ומתועלת השכחה, כי לולא השכחה לא היה נשאר האדם מבלי עצב, ולא היה טורדו ממנו שום דבר משמחת עולם, ולא היה נהנה במה שמשמח אותו, כשהוא זוכר פגעי העולם, ולא היה מקווה מנוחה ממקוה, ולא התעלם ממלוך, הלא תראה איך הושם באדם הזכרון והשכחה, והמה מתחלפים ושונים זה מזה, והושם לו בכל אחד מהם מינים מן התועלות.

Among the benefits of forgetting: Were it not for the ability to forget, no man would ever be free from sorrow. No joyous occasion would dispel his sadness. The events that should bring him joy would give him no pleasure, when he recalled the troubles of life. Even from the realization of his hopes he could not hope to derive rest and peace of mind. He would never refrain from grieving. Thus, you see how memory and forgetfulness, different and contrary to each other as they are, are both benefits bestowed upon man, and each of them has its uses.

---

141 Based on *Diamonds from the Dubno Maggid*, Israel Bookshop Publications.
142 *Shaar HaBechinah*, chapter 5.

If we internalize and are mindful of the words above, we will come to recognize the great treasure we are in possession of. The ability for us to regulate our emotions and feelings play a huge role in our ability to exist amidst the pain and hardship we experience. However, this ability was given to be used in specific instances and surely not to forget Hashem. This would be comparable to someone abusing their privilege of being able to occasionally arrive late at work but then habituates this behavior and becomes a chronic late-comer to work.

> *The ability for us to regulate our emotions and feelings play a huge role in our ability to exist amidst the pain and hardship we experience.*

There Is Nothing in Me That Is Whole

In *Tefillas Zakah*, a prayer said in many communities prior to *Kol Nidrei* on Yom Kippur, we admit our guilt and show remorse in using the gifts Hashem provided us in an ungracious manner:

בראת בי מח ולב ובהם חוש המחשבה לחשוב מחשבות טובות והרהורים טובים ולב להבין דברי קדשך ולהתפלל ולברך כל הברכות במחשבה טהורה. ואני טמאתי אותם בהרהורים ומחשבות זרות. ולא די לי בזה אלא שעל ידי ההרהורים הרעים באתי לידי טומאה פעם ברצון ופעם באונס בטומאה המטמאה את כל הגוף. ומהם בראתי משחיתים ומחבלים הנקראים נגעי בני אדם.

אוי לי כי תחת המחשבות הטובות שיכלתי לברוא על ידי זה מלאכים קדושים שיהיו סנגורים ופרקליטים טובים עלי, תחתיהם בראתי משחיתים לחבל את עצמי כמו שכתוב והוכחתיו בשבט אנשים ובנגעי בני אדם. בראת בי עינים ובהם חוש הראות לראות בהם מה שכתוב בתורה ולקדש אותם בראית כל דברים שבקדושה והזהרת בתורתך ולא תתורו אחרי לבבכם ואחרי עיניכם. אוי לי כי הלכתי אחרי עיני וטמאתי אותם להסתכל בכל דבר טומאה. בראת בי אזנים לשמוע דברי קדושה ודברי תורה. אוי לי כי טמאתי אותם לשמוע דברי נבלה ולשון הרע וכל דברים האסורים. אוי לאזנים שכך שומעות. בראת בי פה ולשון ושיניים וחך וגרון ונתת בהם כח לדבר בהם חמשה מוצאות האותיות הקדושות של אלף בית, אשר בהם בראת שמים וארץ ומלואם, ובהם ארגת תורתך הקדושה, ובכח הדבור הבדלת את האדם מן הבהמה. ואפילו כבהמה לא הייתי כי טמאתי פי בדבור נבלה, בלשון הרע, בשקרים, ליצנות, רכילות, מחלוקת, מלבין פני חברו, מקלל את חברו, מתכבד בקלון חברו, דברי משא ומתן בשבת וביום טוב, בשבועות ונדרים. בראת בי ידים וחוש המישוש לעסוק בהם במצוות. ואני טמאתי אותם במשמושים של אסור להכות באגרוף רשע ולהרים יד להכות בן אדם ולטלטל דברים המוקצים בשבת וביום טוב. בראת בי רגלים להלך בם לכל דבר מצוה. ואני טמאתי אותם ברגלים ממהרות לרוץ לרעה. מששתי את כל איברי ומצאתי אותם בעלי מומין מכף רגלי ועד ראשי אין בי מתום.

You created in me a mind and a heart which contain in them the faculty of thought, to conceive thoughts that are good and musings that are good, and a heart with which to understand Your holy words, and to pray and to recite all the blessings with thought that is pure. But I have contaminated them with musings that are evil and thoughts that are improper. And it is not enough to have done this, but because of the musings that are evil I have come to the emission of semen wastefully, sometimes willfully and sometimes involuntary, causing the contamination of keri that contaminates the entire body. From those thoughts, I have created corrupting spirits and destructive spirits that are called the afflictions of human beings.

Woe to me, for instead of thoughts that are good, that I could have created through them angels that are holy that would have been defenders and advocates for good for myself, in their place I have created destroyers to harm myself, as it is written, "And I shall chastise him with the rod of men and with the afflictions of human beings." You created in me eyes, in which is the faculty of vision, to see through them what is written in the Torah, and to sanctify them through seeing all matters of sanctity. You cautioned in Your Torah, "Do not explore after your heart and after your eyes." Woe to me, for I have gone after my eyes and have contaminated them by staring at all things that are impure. You created in me ears, for hearing words of holiness and words of Torah. Woe to me, for I have contaminated them by listening to words of obscenity, negative gossip, and all sorts of talk that are forbidden. Woe to the ears that such things do hear! You created in me a mouth, a tongue, teeth and a palate and a throat, and placed within them the ability to articulate through them the five sources of sound types of the holy letters of the aleph-beis, with which You created heaven and earth and their fullness, and with which You wove Your Torah that is holy. Through the power of speech, You differentiated man from animal; but even like an animal I have not been, for I have contaminated my mouth with words of obscenity, negative gossip, lies, mockery, tale-bearing, strife, shaming one's fellow man, cursing one's fellow man, glorifying oneself through the embarrassment of one's fellow man, speaking words of business dealings on Shabbos and Yom Tov, and uttering oaths and vows. You created in me hands and the sense of touch, to engage through them in performing mitzvos, but I have contaminated them with touching that which is forbidden, by striking with a fist of wickedness, a hand raising to strike, and moving articles that are muktzeh on Shabbos and Yom Tov. You created in me legs, to walk to all matters of mitzvos, but I have contaminated them, by using them as legs that run to do evil. You created in me a reproductive organ and sealed it with the sign of the holy covenant to be a servant, faithful to Your service, but I have contaminated it by the emission of semen wastefully, by keri contamination, and by improper arousal, not in the performance of a mitzvah. I have examined all my organs and I found them defective, from the sole of my foot to my head there is nothing in me that his whole. (Tefillas Zakah)[143]

What an interesting parallel and so appropriate for this time of year. During these weeks of introspection when we examine our deeds and contemplate areas in which we can improve ourselves, the Torah teaches us not to improperly use that which Hashem has given us and pervert His kindness by using our physical bodies with which He endowed us in a manner antithetical to that which Hashem desires of us.

As we say in *Tefillas Zakah*, "I have examined all my organs and I found them defective,[144] from the sole of my foot to my head there is nothing in me that is whole." Homiletically, the *pasuk* alludes to this by reading it as צור ילדך תשי, "You forgot the [Mighty] Rock Who bore you," followed by ותשכח אל, "and you forgot Hashem," at which point you are left with מחולל, a void and emptiness.[145] When we pervert the use of our organs, and do not use them for what they were created for, they are truly lacking and deficient.

---

143 Artscroll translation.
144 מששתי את כל איברי ומצאתי אותם בעלי מומין מכף רגלי ועד ראשי אין בי מתום.
145 As in חלל in *Shmuel II* 1:19 — הצבי ישראל על במותיך חלל איך נפלו גבורים.

Vezos HaBerachah

וְזֹאת הַבְּרָכָה אֲשֶׁר בֵּרַךְ מֹשֶׁה אִישׁ הָאֱלֹקִים אֶת בְּנֵי יִשְׂרָאֵל לִפְנֵי מוֹתוֹ:

And this is the blessing with which Moshe, the man of
Hashem, blessed the children of Israel [just] before his death.

(Devarim 33:1)

The Midrash teaches:

וזאת הברכה: זהו שאומר הכתוב: רבות בנות עשו חיל ואת עלית על כולנה (משלי לא,כט).
זו ברכתו של משה. שהרי הדורות הראשונים ברכו כל אחד ואחד את דורו, ולא היה בכולם
כברכתו של משה. נח בירך את בניו, היה בה מחלוקת, בירך אחד וקילל אחד, יפת א-להים
ליפת (בראשית ט,כז), ויאמר ארור כנען (שם שם, כה) יצחק בירך ליעקב, היה בה קטטה,
שאמר לעשו: "בא אחיך במרמה" (בראשית כז, לה), וכתיב: "וישטום עשו את יעקב" (שם
שם,מא). יעקב בירך את השבטים היתה בהם קטטה, שאמר לראובן: "פחז כמים" (שם
מט,ד), וכן שמעון ולוי (בראשית מט,ה)...יבוא משה שעינו יפה, ויברך את ישראל, ועליו
אמר שלמה: "טוב עין הוא יבורך" (משלי כב,ט) — אל תקרי יבורך, אלא יברך, זה משה
רבינו שעיניו יפה בברכתו את ישראל.

This is the meaning of the pasuk, "Many daughters have amassed virtues,
but you surpass them all" (Mishlei 31:29). This refers to Moshe's bless-
ing, for earlier generations each blessed his own generation, but none of
them equaled the blessing of Moshe. Noach blessed his son, yet it involved
dispute, for he blessed one of them, yet cursed the other, as it says, "May
G-d expand for Yefes and may He dwell in the tents of Shem; and may
Canaan be a slave to them" (Bereishis 9.27). Yitzchak blessed Yaacov,

but his blessing also caused a quarrel, as it says, "Your brother came in deception…Eisav hated Yaacov" (Bereishis 27:35,41)…Yaacov blessed the tribes, but there was discord among them…Only Moshe of a generous eye could come and bless Israel, as King Shlomo said, "A man of good eye, he shall bless" (Mishlei 22:9)…

The *Midrash* appears to teach us that Moshe Rabbeinu's *berachos* were far superior than those of Noach, Yitzchak, and Yaacov, whose blessings to their children resulted in strife and contention. Yet, if we look at the *pesukim*, Moshe's blessing seems lacking in that it omits Shimon — so how can the Midrash teach that Moshe's blessing *"surpasses them all"*? Can we say that someone was most successful with a particular task if he left out something even while excelling in all else he did complete? If Shimon was excluded, then Moshe's blessing was overall lacking! This Midrash requires an explanation.

The Ramban details at length the intentional sequence of Moshe Rabbeinu dispensing the blessings to the *shevatim*. He then explains why the Tribe of Shimon was omitted:

והנה השאיר שמעון שלא היה שבטו גדול ולא היתה בו ברכת יעקב אביהם מרובה אבל חלקם ביעקב והפיצם בישראל (בראשית מט,ז). והנה יתברכו גם הם מברכת שאר הש־ בטים אשר המה בתוכם.

And the tribe of Shimon was left out, for his tribe was not large, and his blessing from Yaacov their father was not great, but rather he "distributed them in Yaacov and scattered them in Israel" (Bereishis 49:7)— but behold, they will be blessed as well from the blessing of the other tribes. (Ramban)

The Ramban explains Moshe's justification for leaving the tribe of Shimon without a blessing. But the *Midrash* which describes Moshe dispensing his *berachos* as being unique and superior remains unclear.

The Relationship between Completion and Success

Perhaps the Midrash is imparting a lesson about achieving success and completeness in our *avodas Hashem*, service of G-d. Noach, Yitzchak, and Yaacov gave their *berachos*, and these led to a failure of some sort due to the content and mechanics of how the *berachah* was given. Moshe, however, knew Shimon could not be included and left him out completely without even mentioning the name. Yet whatever he did take upon himself to bless was to be complete and that which could not be executed with complete success was omitted.

Reaching a level of *shleimus* (completeness) in our *ruchniyus* does not necessarily mean "reaching the finish line." It is more important that no matter what goal we choose to achieve, we do so with accuracy, precision, and completion. We must strive for mastery in whatever trait we choose to achieve. The objective is not to accomplish everything; rather, whatever field is chosen, it must be done to the best of our abilities, dedication, and perseverance.

> *It is more important that no matter what goal we choose to achieve, we do so with accuracy, precision, and completion.*

Moshe's *berachos* to the tribes "surpassed all," as the Midrash says in its praise, because whichever *berachos* he bestowed, they were complete; none of them resulted in failure.

Realistic Goal Setting

When a company keeps records of its performance and wishes to advertise its success, inevitably it will separate their successes and failures so that it can look more favorable in certain areas in which they particularly excel. Lumping all areas of performance into one category and statistic is liable to put the company at a disadvantage. This can be viewed as a deceptive and misleading tactic to prospective clients and investors as they seek to hide their failures.

The opposite is true with our *ruchniyus*. Here, Hashem judges us according to our efforts. Mastery of a particular *middah* or in the study of Torah isn't the end-goal; rather, the objective is to target a specific task and work at it with exertion and determination. When Moshe dispensed his *berachos* to the *shevatim*, tribes, and left Shimon out, this was a lesson for generations to come to set realistic and definitive goals and perform our best, but not necessarily to conquer it all.

Biographical Sketches of Commentators

Abudraham, Rav David ben Yosef (late 13th-14th century)

Rav David's major work, a guide and commentary on the prayers, has enjoyed much popularity and was reprinted numerous times (first ed. Lisbon, 1489) under the title *Abudraham*. It contains a clear, insightful commentary on the prayers and blessings, a compendium of rituals and customs, a discussion of the obligation of reciting the *Shema*; the laws of prayer; and the various categories of blessings. He introduces his classic work by saying that he perceived the need for a popularly written work that would acquaint the masses with the meaning and laws of the prayers. He succeeded admirably in achieving his goal. His work remains popular both as a galactic source and as a basic text on the prayer book.

The sources used by Rav David include the Babylonian and Jerusalem Talmud, *Geonic* writings, and all the codes down to his own time, both Sephardic and Ashkenazic. To these he has his own comments, sometimes deciding the halachah according to his original explanation. Much of the halachic material of his work is quoted in halachic codes, especially Beis Yosef.

Rav David also composed a running commentary on the Temple *Avodah* liturgy recited on *Yom Kippur*; this was printed as *Tashlum Abudraham* (Berlin, 1900).

Alter, Rav Aryeh Yehuda Leib, the Sfas Emes (1847-1905)

Since his father, Rav Avraham Mordechai, died when he was eight years old, Rav Yehuda Aryeh Leib was raised by his grandfather, the Chidushei Harim. He became Admor of Ger at the age of twenty-three in 1870. On 18 Elul 1901, his wife, Yocheved Rivkah, passed away. He then married Raizel, daughter of Rav Baruch of Gorlitz, the son of the Sanzer Rav. He fathered a total of ten children. Four passed away in childhood and the surviving children were: his eldest son the author of the *Imrei Emes*, Rav Moshe Betzalel, Rav Nechemia of Lodz, and Rav Menachem Mendel of Pavinezh. His two sons-in-law were Rav Yaacov Meir Biderman, *dayan* in Warsaw, and Rav Tzvi Chanoch HaKohen Levine, Rav of Bandin.

Alter, Rav Yisrael, the Beis Yisrael (1895-1977)

The third son Rav Avraham Mordechai, the *Imrei Emes*, he celebrated a double *simchah* on his bar mitzvah, as he became engaged to his cousin, Chaya Sara. They married two years later. In 1940, the *Imrei Emes* escaped the Nazis and reached Eretz Yisrael, along with his sons, Rav Yisrael, Rav Simcha Bunim, and Rav Pinchas Menachem. Tragically, Rav Yisrael's wife, daughter, and son perished, a fact he didn't learn until 1945. He remarried in 1948, but had no children from his second wife. After his father's *petirah*, Rav Yisrael assumed the mantle of leadership as the fourth Rebbe of Ger. For the next twenty-nine years, he rebuilt Ger and was a major force in the Moetzes Gedolei HaTorah of Agudas Yisrael. After his passing, Ger was led by his brother, Rav Simcha Bunim, until his *petirah* in 1992. After that, his other brother, Rav Pinchas Menachem led Ger for four years. Since then, Ger has been led by Rav Yaacov Aryeh, the son of Rav Simcha Bunim.

Alter, Rav Yitzchak Meir, the Chidushei HaRim (1799-1866)

The founder of Gerer dynasty, grandfather of the *Sfas Emes*, Reb Yitzchak Meir was able to trace his lineage back to Rav Meir ben Baruch (the Maharam) of Rottenberg (1215–1293). His mother, Chaya Sarah, was orphaned early in life and was raised by her relative, the Kozhnitzer Maggid. The Maggid had a great influence on Yitzchak Meir during the latter's early years. As he grew, he became a disciple of Rebbi Simcha Bunim of Peshischa and then Rav Menachem Mendel of Kotzk. At the insistence of the Chassidim, the Rim became leader after the death of the Kotzker. At the first Chassidic gathering over which he presided he declared, "Reb Simcha Bunim led with love, and Rav Menachem Mendel with fear. I will lead with Torah!" He had thirteen children and outlived them all, a tremendous personal tragedy. Yet, he accepted it all with love.

Baal HaTurim — Rav Yaacov ben Asher (1340)

Rabbeinu Yaacov ben Asher, the son of the Rosh. *Baal HaTurim* is the commentary on the Torah using *gematria* (number patterns), acrostics, and formations of letters to understanding a *pasuk*. He is also the author of the halachic code known as *Arba Turim* (the Tur). The many commentators on the Tur include those of Rav Yosef Karo (the *Beis Yosef*), Rav Moshe Isserles (*Darchei Moshe*), Rav Yoel Sirkes (the *Beis Chadash*), Rav Yehoshua Falk (*Derishah U'Perishah*), and Rav Yosef Escapa (the *Rosh Yosef*), who deals with only a part of the work. The *Chida* comments that without a proper study of the Tur and its commentaries, one cannot begin to determine halachah.

Bartenura — Rav Ovadia ben Avraham (1440-1516)

Rav Ovadia lived in Italy in the second half of the 15th century and eventually moved to Yerushalayim. He was well known for his role as a Rav in Bartenura, Italy, and for his illuminating *peirush* on the Mishnah. He also wrote *Omer Nekeh*, a supercommentary on Rashi's *peirush* on Chumash. Considered one of the wealthiest men in all of Italy, he settled in Yerushalayim in 1488.

Berlin, Rav Naftali Tzvi Yehuda, the Netziv (1817-1893)

The Netziv was born in Mir, the son-in-law of Rav Isaac, son of Rav Chaim of Volozhin (1749–1821) he married the granddaughter of Rav Chaim Volozhiner when he was fourteen years old. In 1849, upon the *petirah* of Rav Yitzchak, the father-in-law of the Netziv, Rav

Yitzchak was succeeded by his older son-in-law, Rav Eliezer Yitzchak. However, he died five years later, and the Netziv was appointed Rosh Yeshiva, a position he held for forty years. Volozhin was forcibly closed by the Russians in 1893. He wrote *Ha'amek Davar*, a commentary on the Chumash, *Ha'amek She'elah* on the *She'eltos* of Rav Achai Gaon, and *Meishiv Davar*, a collection of his responsa. Among his children were Rabbi Chaim Berlin and Rabbi Meir Bar-Ilan (born to two different mothers).

Bonhart, Reb Simcha Bunim of Peshischa (1765-1827)

Rav Simcha Bunim was one of the key leaders of Chassidic Judaism in Poland. After studying Torah at *yeshivos* in Mattersdorf and Nikolsburg, he was introduced to the world of Chassidism by his father-in-law, and became a *chassid* (follower) of Rabbi Yisrael Hopstein (Maggid of Kozhnitz), and then Rabbi Yaacov Yitzchak of Lublin (*Chozeh*), and the Rabbi Yaacov Yitzchak Rabinowicz (the *Yid HaKadosh)*, the Chassidic leaders of the day. After the death of the *Yid HaKadosh*, most of the *chassidim* followed Rabbi Simcha Bunim as their *rebbe*.

Not wanting to take up a rabbinical position, he supported himself by practicing pharmacy. At a later stage, he became an agent for Temerl Bergson, a wealthy businesswoman who supported many of the *chassidic* leaders during her lifetime.

Among his followers were Rabbi Menachem Mendel of Kotzk (Kotzker Rebbe), the Vurker Rebbe Israel Yitzhak Kalish, Rabbi Yitzchak Meir Alter of Ger (*Chiddushei Harim*), Rabbi Mordechai Yosef Leiner of Izhbitz (*Mei HaShiloach*), Rabbi Yaacov Aryeh of Radzymin and Rav Chanoch Henoch of Alexander.

Borenstein, Rav Shmuel, the Shem MiShmuel (1855-1926)

Rav Shmuel Borenstein, the *Shem MiShmuel* from Sochatchov was born in Kotzk to Rav Avraham Borenstein, the Sochatchover Rebbe and *mechaber* of *Avnei Nezer*. His grandfathers were Rav Nachum Ze'ev of Biala, the *Agudas Eizov* and Rav Menachem Mendel, the Lotzker Rebbe. Rav Shmuel considered Rav Chanoch Henoch of Alexander to be his

Rebbe. After the petira of the Alexander Rebbe in 1870, the *Avnei Nezer* was made Rebbe, and his son followed him as his Rebbe. He was married in 1873, but his wife died in 1901. He remarried in 1903. Rav Shmuel served as maggid shiur in his father's yeshiva in Sochatchov and helped him write *Eglei Tal* on the thirty-nine *melachos* of Shabbos, as well as *Avnei Nezer*. After his father was *niftar* in 1910, the Chassidim crowned Rav Shmuel their Rebbe. His *sefer* contains the thoughts of his famous father. His mother, Sara Tzina Morgenstern, was the daughter of the Kotzker Rebbe, Rabbi Menachem Mendel Morgenstern.

Brazil, Rav Shmuel

Rav Shmuel Brazil is a Rosh HaYeshiva and Rebbi to hundreds of *talmidim*. Rav Shmuel was a *maggid shiur* at Yeshivas Shor Yoshuv for many years before founding Yeshivas Zeev HaTorah in Eretz Yisrael. As a close *talmid* of Rav Shlomo Freifeld he has perpetuated the path of his Rebbi to inspire his *talmidim* with love and warmth. He is best known for his music compositions including the famed Regesh series and is also the author of the *sefarim B'Sharei HaMoadim* and *B'Shvili Nivra Ha'Olam*.

Degel Machaneh Ephraim – Rav Moshe Chaim Ephraim of Sadlikov (1748-1800)

Rav Moshe Chaim Ephraim of Sadlikov, grandson of the Baal Shem Tov, author of *Degel Machaneh Ephraim*. He was born and died in Medzibosh, and his grave is next to that of the Baal Shem Tov. His brother was the famous Reb Baruch of Medzibosh. After the Baal Shem Tov's passing, Moshe Chaim studied under the Maggid of Mezeritch and Rabbi Yaacov Yosef of Polnoye, the author of *Toldos Yaacov Yosef*.

Elyashiv, Rav Yosef Shalom (1910-2012)

Rabbi Elyashiv was the son of Rabbi Avraham Elyashiv (Erener) of Gomel, Belarus, and Chaya Musha, daughter of the kabbalist Rabbi Shlomo Elyashiv (d. 1925) of Shavel, Lithuania. Born in 1910 at Shavel, Yosef Shalom Elyashiv arrived with his parents in Palestine in 1922 at the age of twelve. He was an only child, born to his parents after seventeen years of marriage. Originally his father's surname was Erener, but his father adopted his father-in-law's surname in order to gain a certificate to enter the British Mandate of Palestine. At the suggestion of Chief Rabbi of Palestine, Rav Avraham Yitzchak Kook, Yosef Shalom married Sheina Chaya (d. 1994), a daughter of Rabbi Aryeh Levin. The couple had five sons and seven daughters. Six of their daughters married significant rabbinic figures. One son died of illness as a child, and one daughter was killed in 1948 by Jordanian shelling. Many Ashkenazi Jews regarded him as the *posek hador*, the contemporary leading authority on halachah, or Jewish law. Rav Elyashiv served for twenty-two years as a *dayan* (religious court judge) on the *Beis Din Hagadol* of the *Chief Rabbinate*. He spent most of his days engaged in Talmudical study, and delivered lectures in Talmud and Shulchan Aruch at a local synagogue in the Meah Shearim area in Jerusalem where he lived. He received supplicants from all over the world and answered the most complex *halachic* inquiries.

Epstein, Rav Kalonymus Kalman Halevi, the Maor Vashemesh (1753-1823)

The youngest yet most celebrated of the students of Rabbi Elimelech of Lizhensk, Rabbi Kalonymus Kalman Halevi Epstein was the son of Aaron Halevi Epstein. Young "Kalmish" (as he was known) began his formative years in abject poverty in Neustadt, Poland. Hoping to realize a better life for his wife and ten children, Aaron Epstein moved to the metropolis of Krakow while Kalmish was still but four or five years of age. The story is told that after selling bagels baked in the home of his parents to assist in his family's support, Kalmish would sneak into the Bet Midrash and listen into the Torah sermons given by some of the most illustrious scholars in Krakow, including the famed Rabbi Yitzchak Halevi, Chief Rabbi of Krakow. One day following one of the sermons, Rav Mordechai Gutgold, who was one of the wealthiest Jews in Krakow asked young Kalmish in jest to repeat the profound Torah sermon that he had just heard. After young Kalmish repeated the sermon, indeed, word for word, he was immediately recognized as an extraordinary *iloy* and young prodigy. To the utter delight of little Kalmish's parents, Rav Gutgold undertook to completely support young Kalmish and provide him with the best yeshiva education provided that Rabbi Aaron would agree to the marriage between Kalmish and Rav Gutgold's daughter as soon as Kalmish would reach bar mitzvah. At the age of thirteen, Kalmish married the daughter of Rav Gutgold, Milka Raidel.

Shortly thereafter, having once been present and deeply moved when the famed Hassidic leader Rebbe Elimelech of Lizhensk visited Krakow, Kalmish became determined to study Torah and Chassidus under the direct tutelage of Rebbe Elimelech. His desire to travel to Lizhensk was met with great opposition by his esteemed father-in-law. Despite this opposition and with the encouragement and support of his young wife, Kalmish journeyed to Lizhensk in the hope of having the privilege to study under Rebbe Elimelech. Following his arrival in Lizhensk, Rebbe Elimelech immediately sent young Kalmish for a brief interval to study under the guidance of the famed Rabbi Yechiel Michel of Zlotchov. After less than two weeks at the home of the "Maggid of Zlotchov" Kalmish returned to Lizhensk with a message from the Maggid to Rebbe Elimelech that "you will not find others like Kalmish."

Kalmish then went on to become the closest of all of Rebbe Elimelech's students, as well as Rebbe Elimelech's personal *shamash* or assistant. Recognizing Kalmish's extraordinary aptitude, uncanny abilities and extreme piety, Rebbe Elimelech sent Rebbe Kalmish to assume the mantle of Chassidic leadership of the great city of Krakow.

Counted among the contemporaries of Rebbe Kalmish and fellow leading students of Rebbe Elimelech were the Chozeh of Lublin, the Maggid of Kozhnitz, Rebbe Menachem Mendel of Rimanov and the Apta Rebbe. Although the foregoing were his contemporaries (Rebbe Kalmish being the youngest of all), in his anivus (humility) Rebbe Kalmish referred to all of them as "Rebbe." In fact he called all of the *tzaddikim* of his generation, be they older or younger than he, by the appellation "Rebbe." This was in keeping with the Torah he taught and how he stressed the importance of being close to a Rebbe as a way to elevate oneself in character and Divine service. Rebbe Kalmish lived what he preached and no matter how great he himself was and how all congregated from far and wide to learn from him, he was frequently a guest at the homes of other great *tzaddikim* of his day, including, without limitation, the famed Rabbi Levi Yitzchak of Berditchev, Rabbi Zushe of Annipoli (brother of Rabbi Elimelech of Lizhensk), Rebbe Mendel of Rimanov (his contemporary), and his closest friends, the Chozeh of Lublin and the Apta Rebbe.

Toward the end of his life, Rebbe Kalmish instructed his younger son Rebbe Aharon, to gather together all of his writings and sermons which later was published as the *sefer Maor Vashemesh* — the title by which he became known throughout the succeeding generations. The profound and kabbalistic insights of the *Maor Vashemesh* are studied regularly by Chassidic and non-Chassidic Jews to this very day throughout the world. Many great Chassidic leaders have referred to the *Maor Vashemesh* as the "Shulchan Aruch" of Chassidus. The holy sainted Rebbe Kalmish died on the second day of Rosh Chodesh Tammuz in the year 1825 at the age of seventy-two.

Etlinger, Rav Yaacov Rav, the Aruch LaNer (1808-1871)

Rav Yaacov Etlinger was the great light in Germany as the Reform movement was conquering Europe. He was the linchpin between the old guard and the new guard responsible for saving *Yiddishkeit*. Rav Yaacov was born in 5568/1808 in Germany and spent his youth learning with his father who was the *Rosh Mesivta* of the local *beis medrash*. Afterward he learned by the Rav of the town Rav Asher the son of the *Shaagas Aryeh*. Later he studied under Rav Avraham Bing a *talmid* of Rav Nosson Adler on whose *matzeivah* it is written *"Aluf HaTorah Malach Ha'Elokim"*; a champion of Torah, an angel of Hashem. In his yeshiva Rav Avraham nurtured all the future German *Gedolim* including Rav Nosson Adler of Hanover who later went on to become the Chief Rabbi of Britain. When he was a mere eighteen years old he was invited to Mannheim where he became the *Rosh Mesivta*. Among his *talmidim* included the future savior of German Jewry, Rav Shamshon Refoel Hirsch. Ten years later at age twenty-eight he was appointed to the prestigious position of Rav of Altuna where his predecessors included Rav Yehonoson Eibushitz, Rav Yitzchak Horowitz, and Rav Refoel Hamburger. At this point Rav Yaacov wielded tremendous power as the German authorities recognized his *Beis Din* and the government police force was at his disposal to enforce his judgments. Altuna was the only city in Germany not infected by the Reform movement. It was the last bastion of Torah in Germany. Among his *talmidim* in Altuna included Rav Ezriel Hildesheimer and Rav Meir Lehmann (a.k.a. Marcus Lehmann, author of books for German teenagers still read today). Despite his important position his main occupation was still learning and teaching Torah. He was known to sleep three hours a night and fast many days. His knowledge of Zohar was famous and he gained acclaim as a *mekubal*. He authored a number of famous *sefarim* including *Aruch LaNer* on Shas, *Sheilos U'Teshuvos Binyan Tzion*, and *Bikkurei Yaacov*, which even in his day became famous throughout the world. Rav Chaim Palagi in Turkey and Rabbi Akiva Eiger both wrote comments on this *sefer*. The great *gaon* Rabbi Akiva Eiger wrote in his *sefer* in *Succah*, "Praise to Hashem that I have had the good fortune to think of the same answer…(as the *Bikkurei Yaacov*). He fought the reform movement both in Germany and Hungary and his influence even spread to Eretz Yisrael as he was crowned *"Nasi Eretz Yisrael"* for his active involvement in helping out the *Yishuv*. He was *niftar* the first night of Chanukah 5632/1871 at the age of sixty-three.

Feinstein, Rav Moshe (1895-1986)

Born in Uzda (near Minsk), Belorussia, he was the son of Rav David Feinstein, who was a grandchild of the *Be'er Hagolah*. His mother was Feige Gittel, daughter of Rav Yechiel, *rav* of Kopolia. He joined the yeshiva of Rav Isser Zalman Meltzer in Slutsk at the age of twelve. At the age of sixteen, Rav Moshe completed Shas and Shulchan Aruch. He was rabbi of Luban from 1921 to 1936. He escaped the Stalinist regime in 1936 and settled in New York as Rosh HaYeshiva of Tiferes Yerushalayim. He authored *Igros Moshe*, *Darash Moshe*, and *Dibros Moshe*.

Horowitz, Rav Yeshaya HaLevi, the Shlah HaKadosh (1555-1630)

Known as the *Shlah* after the title of one of his major works *Shnei Luchos HaBris*, was a renowned *halachist*, kabbalist and communal leader. Born in Prague he moved with his father to Poland in his youth, and after building a reputation as an exceptional scholar, he gained a number of positions as head of *batei din* (religious courts) in the area. By 1606 he reached the level of the head of the Frankfurt on the Main *beis din*, one of the most influential of the period.

After the Jews were expelled from there in 1614, he returned to his native Prague, where he remained as a rabbi. In 1621 at the death of his wife, he moved to Eretz Israel, remarried and settled in Jerusalem as one of the heads of the Ashkenazic community there. In 1625, he was captured by the Arab ruler, and ransomed for an exorbitant sum. The *Shlah* died in Tiberius and is buried near the Rambam. During his life, the *Shlah* was a wealthy and active philanthropist, supporting Torah learning especially in Jerusalem. In his many kabbalistic, homiletic, and halachic works, he stressed the joy in every action, and how one should convert the evil inclination into good, two concepts that impacted on Jewish thought through to the eighteenth-century, and greatly influenced the development of the Chassidic movement.

Hutner, Rav Yitzchok (1907-1981)

Rav Hutner was Rosh Yeshivas Rabbeinu Chaim Berlin and author of *Pachad Yitzchak*. His uncle, Rav Benzion Ostrover, had been a disciple of Rav Mendel of Kotzk, and was instrumental in providing his young nephew with a direct link to the world of Chassidus. At the age of fifteen, he went to Slabodka and was directed by the Alter, Rav Nosson Tzvi Finkel. In 1925, he entered the new Slabodka branch in Chevron, where he also met and learned from Rav A. I. Kook. He remained until 1929, after which he returned to his parents in Warsaw. He became a personal tutor for Rav Moshe Soleveichik's son, Aharon. In 1932, he published his *Toras*

HaNazir, a commentary on the Rambam's *Hilchos Nazir*. In 1933, he married Masha Lipshitz and moved to Eretz Yisrael. Despite his great attachment to the Land, they left for America one year later, not to return for thirty years. He built Yeshiva Chaim Berlin to his specifications with his famous blend of Torah philosophies. Among his *talmidim* are Rav Yitzchak Shurin, grandson of Reb Yaakov Kamenetsky. Among his colleagues at Slabodka were Rav Yitzchak HaLevi Ruderman, Rav Reuven Grozovsky, Rav Yaakov Kamenetsky, and Rav Aharon Kotler. In 1949 he began publishing his discourses on morals and ethics which he subtitled, *Divrei Torah B'Inyanei Hilchos Deiyos V'Chovos HaLevavos*. He wrote a profound commentary (*Kovetz He'aros*) on Rabbeinu Hillel on the *Sifra*. His discourses on *Yomim Tovim* and Shabbos (*Pachad Yitzchok*) are collected in seven volumes.

Kagan, Rav Yisrael Meir HaKohen, the Chofetz Chaim (1838-1933)

Rabbi Yisrael Meir HaCohen Kagan was perhaps the greatest Jewish figure and one of the most influential Rabbis in modern Jewish history. He is known popularly as the Chofetz Chaim, after his classic work on guarding one's tongue which he published in 1873 when he was thirty-five. He was recognized as both an outstanding scholar and an extraordinarily righteous man. His impact on Judaism was phenomenal.

The Chofetz Chaim was born in Dzyatlava in 1838 and passed away in Radin in 1933. His many works continue to be widely influential in Jewish life worldwide. When he was ten years old, his father died. His mother moved the family to Vilnius in order to continue her son's education. His mother later remarried and moved to Radin. When Yisrael Meir was seventeen, he married the daughter of his stepfather, and settled in Radin.

The Chofetz Chaim was a modest and humble man. He served as the town rabbi of Radin for a short period. His distaste of the pulpit rabbinate led him to resign from this position. For a while he had a shop selling household provisions, which his wife managed while he supervised the absolute accuracy of the weights and measures, the quality of the merchandise, and the fairness of the prices, to make certain that no one was deceived or overcharged in any way. He spent his days learning Torah and disseminating his knowledge to the common people. He later turned to teaching in order to support himself and his family. From 1864 to 1869 he taught Talmud in Minsk and Washilishok. In 1869, he organized a Yeshiva in Radin. The Yeshiva was a success and grew to world famous prominence. It later became known as "Yeshivas Chofetz Chaim of Radin."

In addition to spreading Torah through his yeshiva, the Chofetz Chaim was very active in Jewish causes. He traveled extensively to encourage the keeping of the mitzvos amongst Jews. He became one of the most influential rabbis within Orthodox Judaism during the late 19th and early 20th century, taking a central leadership role in the World Agudas Yisrael movement in Eastern Europe.

The Chofetz Chaim authored dozens of *sefarim*, all which have been printed and disseminated by the tens of thousands. Most widely acclaimed is his *Mishnah Berurah*, a six volume comprehensive commentary on *Shulchan Aruch Orach Chaim* which has become the final arbiter in halachah. His first book, (published in 1873), deals with the Biblical laws of gossip and slander and which in recent decades has gained worldwide popularity.

Kook, Rav Avraham Yitzchak HaKohen (1865-1935)

The first chief rabbi of what was then Palestine, Rav Kook was perhaps the most misunderstood figure of his time. Born in Latvia of staunch Chassidic and Misnagid stock, he retained throughout his life a unique blend of the mystical and the rational. He was a thorough master of the entire halachic, Midrashic, philosophic, ethical, and kabbalistic literature. He saw the return to Eretz Yisrael as not merely a political phenomenon to save Jews from persecution, but an event of extraordinary historical and theological significance. Rabbi Hutner once said that Rav Kook peered down on our world from great heights and hence his perspective was unique. Above all, Rav Kook pulsated with a sense of the Divine. Though keenly aware of the huge numbers of non-observant

Jews, he had a vision of the repentance of the nation. His concept of repentance envisioned in addition to the repentance of the individual, a repentance of the nation as a whole; a repentance which would be joyous and healing. He refused to reject Jews as long as they identified themselves as Jews. He called for and envisioned a spiritual renaissance where "the ancient would be renewed and the new would be sanctified."

Kotler, Rav Aharon (1892-1962)

The son of Rabbi Shneur Zalman Pines, Rav Aharon was known as the "Sislovitzer Iloy." At fourteen he entered the Slabodka Yeshiva, where he learnt under the Alter and HaRav Moshe Mordechai Epstein. He also heard *shiurim* from Rav Boruch Ber, who had his own yeshiva in one of the suburbs of Slabodka. He married the daughter of Rav Isser Zalman Meltzer, head of the Yeshiva Eitz Chaim in Slutsk, and became his assistant (1914). Even before he was twenty-five years old, he became one of its *roshei yeshiva*. After the yeshiva's forced transfer to Kletsk in Poland due to the Bolshevik takeover and religious persecution (1921), Rav Isser Zalman emigrated to Erez Yisrael, and Rav Kotler directed Eitz Chaim for twenty years. With the Soviet occupation of Poland in 1939, Rav Kotler escaped first to Kobe, Japan, then to the United States (April, 1941). Reb Aharon assumed a leading role in the operations of the Vaad Hatzoloh. Under his leadership, Beth Medrash Govoha opened in a converted house in Lakewood, New Jersey in April 1943, and the yeshiva and *kollel* student body increased from the original fourteen to 140 in 1962, the year of Reb Aharon's *petirah*. Reb Aharon also headed Chinuch Atzmai, the network of Torah day schools in Israel, founded in 1953, and he took over the leadership of Torah U'Mesorah, the American day school movement, after the death of its founder HaRav Shraga Feivel Mendelowitz. He also headed Agudath Israel's Moetzes Gedolei Hatorah.

Krantz, Rav Yaacov, the Dubno Maggid (1741-1804)

Born in a province of Vilna, Yaacov ben Wolf Kranz showed exceptional homiletical and Kabbalistic talents at an early age, and by the age of twenty became the *darshan* of his city. From there he began preaching through the cities around Lublin in Poland, finally settling in Dubno. His reputation as a *maggid* spread, bringing him in contact with the great rabbis of the period, including the Vilna Gaon. The majority of his works were in homiletics, using stories and parables to transmit deeper ethical and moral teachings.

Leiner, Rav Mordecai Yosef of Izhbitz (1800-1878)

Founder of the Chassidic Court at Ishbitz after leading a group of disciples from the court of Rav Menachem Mendel of Kotzk. Born in Tomashov, Poland in 1800, he was a childhood friend of Reb Menachem Mendel Morgenstern, later to become the Kotzker Rebbe, and they studied together in the school of the Chassidic Master, Reb Simcha Bunim of Peshischa. His *sefer*, *Mei HaShiloach*, is considered a fundamental work of Izhbitz and Radziner *chassidus*. Among his *talmidim* were Rav Tzadok HaCohen of Lublin and Rav Leibel Eiger.

Lowe, Rav Yehudah ben Bezalel, the Maharal (1525-1609)

Rav Yehuda Lowe, the Maharal (1525–1609). Born in Posen, Poland, on the night of the Pesach Seder, to a distinguished family of rabbis that traced its ancestry to King David. He was the youngest of four brothers. The Maharal married at the age of thirty-two to Pearl. He had six girls and one boy who was named after the Maharal's father, Betzalel. In 1553 he was elected rabbi of Nikolsburg and the Province of Moravia, where he remained for the following twenty years. In 1573 he moved to Prague, where he opened a yeshiva. In 1592 the Maharal accepted the position of rabbi in Posen, returning to Prague in 1598 to serve as its chief rabbi. The Maharal castigated the educational methods of his day where boys were taught at a very young age and insisted that children must be taught in accordance with their intellectual maturity. One of his leading disciples was Rav Yom Tov Heller, author of the classic Mishnaic commentary, *Tosafos Yom Tov*, who, in his introduction informs us that the Maharal greatly encouraged group study of the Mishnah. At the same time, he was fully conversant with the scientific knowledge of his time as well as friendly with some of the contemporary eminent scientists. His disciple, David Ganz, worked in the observatory of Tycho Brahe, the distinguished astronomer. He was a prolific writer, and his works include: *Tiferes Yisrael,* on the greatness of Torah and mitzvos; *Nesivos Olam,* on ethics; *Be'er Hagolah,* a commentary on rabbinic sayings; *Netzach Yisrael,* on exile and redemption; *Or Chadash,* on the Book of Esther; *Ner Mitzvah,* on Chanukah; *Gevuros Hashem,* on the Exodus; and many others including *Gur Aryeh* on the Torah. Rav Kook stated that the "Maharal was the father of the approach of the Gaon of Vilna on the one hand, and of the father of *Chassidus,* on the other hand." He has been described as a Kabbalist who wrote in philosophic garb.

Luntschitz, Rav Shlomo Ephraim, the Kli Yakar (1550-1619)

Rav Shlomo Ephraim was a Rav and Torah commentator, best known for his Torah commentary *Kli Yakar.* He served as the Rabbi of Prague from 1604–1619. He was born in Lenczyk (also known as Luntschitz) and studied under the *Mahrashal,* Rav Shlomo Luria in Lublin, and subsequently served as *rosh yeshiva* (dean) of the yeshiva in Lvov (Lemberg). In 1604 he was appointed rabbi of Prague, a position he filled until his death. In the introduction of his *Kli Yakar* he relates that the name Shlomo was added to his name during life-threatening illness, a common practice in Judaism.

Luzzatto, Rav Moshe Chaim, the Ramchal (1707-1747)

Author of *Mesilas Yesharim, Derech Hashem, Pischei Chochmah* (138 chapters on the entire scope of the kabbalah in what many authorities consider the most systematic manner ever achieved), and *Daas Tevunos.* Born in Padua, Italy, the Ramchal was a student of Rabbi Yitzchak Lampronti, author of the *Pachad Yitzchak,* the first major Talmudic encyclopedia ever assembled. The novelty of his approach drew opposition from a number of his contemporaries. Partially as a result of this opposition, Luzzatto left his native Italy in 1735 and settled in Amsterdam. In 1743, he traveled to Eretz Israel and settled in Acco. He died in a plague only four years later, along with his wife and his son. The Vilna Gaon declared that the Ramchal had the most profound understanding of *Yiddishkeit* that any mortal human could attain. He furthermore stated that if Luzzatto were alive in his generation, he would go by foot from Vilna to Italy to sit at his feet and learn from him. According to a *mesorah*, the Gaon was going to Eretz Yisrael to be a *talmid* of the Ramchal but then found out that the Ramchal was *niftar* so he returned to Vilna. There is an interesting *mesorah* that the Ramchal was a *gilgul* of Rabbi Akiva. The two are buried right next to each other and the Ramchal was *niftar* when he was forty; it is said to make up for the first forty years of Rabbi Akiva's life, prior to his doing *teshuvah*.

Meshech Chochmah – Rav Meir Simcha HaKohen of Dvinsk (1843-1926)

Rav Meir Simcha was a rabbi and prominent leader of Orthodox Judaism in Eastern Europe in the early twentieth century. He was a *kohen*, and is therefore often referred to as Rav Meir Simcha HaKohen. He is known for his writings on Rambam's Mishneh Torah, which he titled *Ohr Somei'ach*, as well as his *chiddushim* on the Torah, titled *Meshech Chochmah*. In 1906, he was offered the position of rabbi of Jerusalem but bowed to the entreaties of his congregants to remain in Dvinsk.

Ohr HaChaim – Rav Chaim ben Moshe Ibn Attar (1696-1743)

Born into a well-respected family in Sali, Morocco, Rav Chaim spent his early years learning with his grandfather, whose name he shared. Rav Chaim's dream was to go to Israel. With thirty followers he arrived in Israel, four days before Rosh Hashana in 1742 and settled in Acco. Rav Chaim and his students spent Yom Kippur in the cave of Eliyahu HaNavi on Mount Carmel. Purim was spent in Tzfat and Miron, where a great deal of time was spent studying the holy Zohar. On the 15th of Elul of 1743, Rav Chaim finally arrived in Jerusalem with his group. He immediately established a yeshiva called *Knesses Yisrael* and a second, secretive, yeshiva for the study of kabbalah. One of his new students was Rav Chaim Yosef David Azulai, the *Chida*, who at that time was only eighteen years old.

Palagi, Rav Chaim (1788-1858)

Rav of Izmir. Rav Chaim derived much of his Torah knowledge from his grandfather, Rav Raphael Yosef (the *Chikrei Lev*), and together with him, wrote the work, *Semicha L'Chaim*. After his father's *petirah* in 1828, he accepted the positions of *dayan* and *mashgiach ruchani* in the Beis Yaacov Rabi yeshiva. In 1855, he was appointed to the position of *rav hakollel*, the highest rabbinical position in Izmir. During his life, he authored *Kaf HaChaim*, *Moed L'chol Chai*, and at least seventy other *sefarim*. They consist of: twenty-four books on halachah, fifteen on *midrashim* and homiletics, nine on *chiddushim* on Bavli and Yerushalmi, seven on Tanach, five on various other subjects, and three *mussar* works. He also wrote a *sefer* called *Tenufas Chaim*.

Pincus, Rav Shimshon David (1944-2001)

Rav Pincus served as a Rav in Ofakim. In his early years, Rabbi Pincus learned in Yeshivas Beis HaTalmud in New York City under Rabbi Aryeh Leib Malin. Afterwards, he made *aliyah* to Israel to learn in the Brisk Yeshiva under Rabbi Berel Soloveitchik, the son of the Brisker Rav. After his marriage, he lived in B'nei Brak and then in the Negev. At this time, he was the *mashgiach* of the yeshiva in Ofakim. Afterwards, he became the *rosh yeshiva* in Yerucham. At the request of Rabbi Elazar Shach and Rabbi Yaacov Yisrael Kanievsky, Rabbi Pincus accepted the position of Chief Rabbi of Ofakim, where he served for over twenty years. Rabbi Pincus also spoke publicly mostly free of charge all over Israel, America, and South Africa. He used to visit Chile with his parents to strengthen the *kehillah* in Torah and Mussar. Rabbi Pincus and his wife, Chaya had twelve children. His wife administered the religious high school Neve Yocheved for girls in Ofakim. In 2001, at the age of fifty-six, Rabbi Pincus was killed in a car accident, along with his wife and eighteen year old daughter, Miriam. They are buried in Jerusalem.

Rabbeinu Bachaya –
Rav Bachaya ben Yosef ibn Paquda (early 11th century)

Rabbeinu Bachaya lived in Muslim Spain, probably in Saragossa, and served as a judge, but little else is known about his life. He was thoroughly conversant with the entire Biblical and Talmudical literature and was also master of all the knowledge and science of his day.

Though a philosopher in his own right, Rabbi Bachaya's essential contribution is that of the *Chovos HaLevavos*. The first chapter of his work which is devoted to the unity of Hashem employs philosophical arguments which some felt were not readily understandable and was skipped over by many students.

Rabbi Bachaya's work, as indicated by its title, focused on the non-physical obligations of the Jew: the obligations of feeling, heart and mind in contrast to those mitzvos that involve the limbs. Pointing to the neglect of this group of mitzvos, he underscored their critical importance.

Rabbi Bachaya's central focus was on Service of G-d and abiding by His will, and fulfilling the duties of the heart was viewed as the entree to nearness to G-d, the ultimate objective. Understandably, the tenth and last chapter of the book is Love of G-d.

Though emphasizing the importance of rational thought, Rabbi Bachaya's real goal was the experience of G-d. A systematic, carefully constructed work, *Duties of the Heart*, has remained to this day a favorite of serious, sensitive students.

Rabbeinu Yonah – Rabbi Yonah ben Avraham of Gerondi (1180-1263)

Ramban's mother and Rabbeinu Yonah's father were siblings. Many years later, the Ramban's son, Rav Shlomo, married the daughter of Rabbeinu Yonah. Thus, the two great *Rishonim* were related as well as first cousins. He was a student of Rav Shlomo ben Avraham Min HaHar. When King Louis XIV of France, "Saint Louis," burnt all the copies of the Talmud in Paris in the Square of the Louvre, Rabbeinu Yonah, one of the Rambam's main detractors, felt that the events in Paris were a sign that he and the other opponents of the Rambam were seriously wrong. He then composed his work *Shaarei Teshuvah*, in which he outlined the methods of doing *teshuvah*, and he traveled from place to place preaching about the need to back away from matters which cause division among the Jewish People. Among his *talmidim* are the Rashba and Ra'ah. He died in Toledo, Spain.

Rabinowitz, Rav Shlomo HaKohen of Radomsk, the Tiferes Shlomo (1803-1866)

Rav Shlomo studied in the yeshiva of Piotrkow under Rav Abraham Zevi, author of the responsa *Bris Avraham*. His father educated him in Chassidus. In his youth he joined Rav Meir of Apta, leader of the popular trend in Polish Chassidim after the death of the Chozeh ("the Seer") of Lublin. In 1834 Rav Shlomo was appointed Rav of Radomsk, and from 1843 he was accepted as the Chassidic Rebbe. Rav Shlomo's teachings were in the spirit of the popular trend of Polish Chassidism. He engaged in public affairs and worked on behalf of the poor of his town. Rav Shlomo's *sefer Tiferes Shlomo* is considered one of the classic works on Chassidus.

Rabinowitz, Rav Tzadok HaKohen of Lublin (1823-1900)

Rav Tzadok was the author of Pri Tzaddik, Resisei Layla, and other works. The son of Rav Yaacov HaKohen, Rav of Kreisberg, Rav Tzadok studied only the revealed aspects of Torah (halachah and Talmud) until he was twenty-four. Beginning in 1847, he learned only kabbalistic teachings. Rabbi Tzadok became a *chassid* of the Izbitzher Rebbe and a close friend of Rav Yehuda Leib Eiger. Upon the death of Rav Eiger in 1888, he agreed to take over the leadership of the *chassidim*. Rabbi Tzadok was a prolific writer whose works made an enormous impact with their profound thoughts. Besides writing numerous *chiddushim*, he also wrote scholarly essays on astronomy, geometry, and algebra. One of his lone surviving students was Rabbi Michael Mokotovsky, whose son was Rabbi Avraham Eliyahu Mokotovsky, better known by his penname Eliyahu Kitov.

Rambam — Rav Moshe ben Maimon (1135-1204)

Born in Cordova, Spain, the Rambam received his rabbinical instruction at the hands of his father, Maimon. Moshe was only thirteen years old when Cordova fell into the hands of the fanatical Almohades, and Rav Maimon and the other Jews were compelled to choose between Islam and exile. Rav Maimon and his family chose the latter course, and for twelve years led a nomadic life, wandering throughout Spain. In 1160 they settled at Fez, Morocco. In 1165 they went to Acre, to Jerusalem, and then to Fostat (Cairo), where they settled. After the death of Maimon, Moshe's brother David supported the family by trading in precious stones. David perished at sea, and with him was lost not only his own fortune, but large sums that had been entrusted to him by other traders. These events affected Moshe's health, and he went through a long sickness.

After several years of practice, the Rambam's authority in medical matters was firmly established, and he was appointed private physician to Saladin's vizier, who recommended him to the royal family. Between the years 1158 and 1190 the Rambam produced a commentary on the Mishnah, the *Mishneh Torah*, and the philosophical work *Moreh Nevuchim*.

Ramban – Rav Moshe ben Nachman (1194-1270)

Ramban was the foremost *halachist* of his age. Like the Rambam before him, Ramban was a Spaniard who was both a physician and a great Torah scholar. However, unlike the rationalist Rambam, Ramban had a strong mystical bent. His commentaries on the Torah are the first ones to incorporate the mystical teachings of kabbalah.

At the age of sixteen he had mastered the whole Talmud with all its commentaries, and at that early age wrote a defense (*Milchamos Hashem*) of the work of the great codifier and Talmudist, Rabbi Isaac Alfasi, against the attacks of Rabbi Zerachiah Halevi, author of *"Sefer HaMa'or."*

Not wishing to make any profit from the Torah, the Ramban became a practicing physician in his native town. However, he was the communal rabbi of Gerona at the same time, and later became the chief rabbi of the entire province of Catalonia.

For many years the Ramban lived in his native town, supporting himself as a physician, and devoting most of his time to the study of the Talmud and Kabbalah, and to his literary work, writing commentaries on the Talmud. But in his declining days, when he was nearly seventy years old, his quiet life underwent a sudden change. An apostate Jew, masquerading as a devout Catholic, Paulus Christians, had challenged the Jews to a religious disputation. He induced King James I of Aragon to summon the renowned Rabbi of Gerona to a public debate in Barcelona.

Reluctantly, the Ramban journeyed to the king's court at Barcelona. The Ramban easily refuted all the arguments of Paulus, and proved effectively that the Jews were entitled to retain their own beliefs and faith. For four days the public disputation was carried on, and the Ramban's brilliant defense of his faith was too much for his adversaries.

As in the case of the disputation of Rabbi Yechiel of Paris, the enemies of Israel claimed the victory in the debate, spreading malicious propaganda throughout Spain. Indignantly the Ramban published a true account of the debate, and even had it ratified by the king himself. But although he did not publish anything except what he had said at the debate with the king's permission, the Ramban was brought to trial by the influential Dominicans, and was eventually condemned to banishment for "blasphemy."

At the age of seventy-two, the Ramban set out for the Land of Israel, hoping to find peace and solace there. Unfortunately, he found the Holy Land in great desolation; the Jewish communities were scarce and scattered; young and old alike were poor and ignorant of Jewish knowledge. The Ramban at once began a campaign to improve the position of his brethren in the Holy Land, both spiritually and materially. He reorganized the communities, set up schools, rebuilt the synagogues, gave public lectures and discourses. Here he wrote his famous commentary on the Torah, and other works. He sent copies of these to his native land, and he is also credited with having sent a copy of the Zohar from the Land of Israel to Spain, thus being the first to introduce that saintly book to the West.

The Ramban died at the age of seventy-five and was buried in Haifa, near the grave of Rabbi Yechiel of Paris, whose life so resembled his own.

Schick, Rav Yitzchak, the Keren Orah (1788-1851)

Rav Yitzchak Schick was born in Minsk in 1788. His father was HaRav Aharon, a distinguished member of the Minsk *kehillah*, son of HaRav Baruch of Shklov.

Even as youngsters, Reb Yitzchak and his brother Reb Yaacov, author of *Mishkenos Yaacov* and *Kehillas Yaacov*, were noted for their genius in learning. Rav Yaacov was appointed Rav in Davir-Hodrok and published his first work, *Mishkenos Yaacov*, while young. Reb Yitzchak, however, preferred to stay out of the limelight and simply continue his own growth in Torah. Even when times were hard and he could barely support himself, Reb Yitzchak preferred not to become a Rav, but to dedicate himself to working on his *sefarim*.

Later on, Reb Yitzchak and his brother moved to Karlin, where they were supported by the *misnaged* Reb Shaul of Karlin. They both lived there until the end of their days. In Karlin, Reb Yitzchak finished his works on the entire *Seder Kodashim* and on *Masechtos Nedarim*, *Nazir* and *Sotah*. (He had written his *chiddushim* on the other *masechtos* of *Seder Nashim* earlier.) He prepared them for publication and they were printed after his *petirah* by his children. Reb Yitzchak would rise before daybreak to learn *Zohar* and other *sifrei kabbalah*. Later he would learn *Mishnayos*. At daybreak, he would don *tallis* and *tefillin* and *daven Shacharis*. Following *Shacharis*, Reb Yitzchak would deliver a *Gemara shiur* to the *bachurim* in his yeshiva. Then he would return to his private room and put on *Rabbeinu Tam tefillin*, and learn privately until *chatzos*. Whenever he came up with a *chiddush*, he wrote it down, and many of these were published.

After the *petirah* of his brother Rav Yaacov, Reb Yitzchak finally agreed to become Rav in Karlin in his place.

During his tenure as Rav in Karlin, Reb Yitzchak wrote his last *sefer*, *Keren Orah*. His wish was that his *sefarim* be printed and distributed for free in *batei medrash* for *talmidei chachamim*. He expended special effort on *Seder Kodashim*, since this *seder* does not have many of the regular commentaries and it is very hard to comprehend many of its *sugyos*. Reb Yitzchak was *niftar* on 9 Cheshvan 5612/1851, at the age of sixty-four.

Schneerson, Rav Menachem Mendel, the Lubavitcher Rebbe (1902–1994)

Born in in Nikolayev, a town in the southern Ukraine. His father, Rabbi Levi Yitzchak Schneerson, was a renowned scholar, while his mother, Rebbitzen Chana Schneerson, was an aristocratic woman from a prestigious rabbinic family. He had two younger brothers, Dov Ber and Yisrael Aryeh Leib. When Menachem Mendel was five years old, the family moved to Yakaterinoslav, now Dnepropetrovsk, where his father was appointed chief rabbi. From early childhood, Menachem Mendel displayed prodigious mental acuity, leaving school for private tutoring. By the time he reached bar mitzvah, he was considered a Torah prodigy, and during his teenage years, he immersed himself in the intricacies of Torah study. In 1923, he met Rabbi Yosef Yitzchak Schneerson — then the Lubavitcher Rebbe — who drew him into his inner circle giving him various responsibilities; five years later, in Warsaw, he married the Rebbe's second eldest daughter, Chaya Mushka (1901–1988). A short while later, the couple moved to Berlin, where Rabbi Menachem Mendel had already begun studying mathematics and science at the University of Berlin. Because of the Nazi rise, the young rabbi and his wife left Berlin in 1933 for Paris, and he continued his studies at the Sorbonne. Primarily, however, he immersed himself in prayer and religious study, and was referred to by his father-in-law on various matters, including the preparation of Lubavitch publications. He also served as his father-in-law's private secretary and traveled on his behalf to visit various Jewish leaders in Europe.

When the Nazis occupied Paris, the couple was forced to escape the city. On June 23, 1941 they arrived in New York, where Rabbi Yosef Yitzchak Schneerson appointed his son-in-law head of Lubavitch's educational arm, as well as the movements social-service organization and its publishing house.

In 1950, Rabbi Yosef Yitzchak passed away. Although Rabbi Menachem Mendel was the obvious successor, he was initially reluctant to accept the mantle of leadership. A year later he formally assumed the title of Rebbe, explaining to members of the movement that while he would be devoted to his work as leader, each man and women was ultimately responsible for his or her own actions, and for his or her pursuit of G-dliness.

Schwadron, Rav Shalom Mordechai (1913-1997)

Rav Shalom Mordechai Schwadron was a Yerushalmi *maggid* and brother-in-law of Rav Shlomo Zalman Auerbach. He was named for his grandfather, the *Maharsham*, the leading *posek* in Galicia before World War I. He lost his father at age seven, and for a time lived in an orphanage. After his *bar mitzvah* he studied in the Lomzer Yeshiva in Petach Tikvah, and later in the Chevron Yeshiva in Yerushalayim under Rav Yehuda Leib Chasman. After his marriage, he continued his studies in Kollel Ohel Torah. The *kollel's* members included Rav Yosef Shalom Elyashiv and Rav Shmuel Wosner. In addition to his renown as a *maggid*, he published approximately twenty-five of his grandfather's works, as well as *Lev Eliyahu* (of Rav Elya Lopian), and the writings of Rav Chasman, *Ohr Yahel*.

Shapira, Rav Kalonymus Kalman, the Piacezna Rebbe (1889-1943)

He was the author of *Chovas HaTalmidim* and *Aish Kodesh* amongst many other *sefarim*. His father, Rav Elimelech of Grodzisk, was a direct descendant of the Maggid of Kozhnitz and of the Noam Elimelech of Lizhensk. He was named Kalonymus Kalman after his maternal grandfather, the *Maor Vashemesh*. In 1905, Rav Kalonymus Kalman married Rachel Chaya Miriam, the daughter of Rav Yerachmiel Moshe of Kozhnitz. She helped him prepare his *derashos* and *sefarim*, even adding pertinent insights of her own. His works and his guidance showed clear insight and clarity in *chinuch* and psychology. After the Warsaw Ghetto uprising was crushed in Nissan 1943, Rav Kalonymus Kalmish was taken to Treblinka and met his death there on 4 Cheshvan, 1944. His *sefer Aish Kodesh* (Holy Fire), a collection of the sermons he delivered in the Warsaw ghetto was found after the war and sent to Israel to be published.

Shapira, Rav Tzvi Elimelech, the B'nei Yissaschar (1783-1841)

Rabbi Tzvi Elimelech, was born to HaRav Pesach in Yavernik, Galicia. His mother was a niece of Reb Elimelech of Lizhensk, and disciple of the "Seer" of Lublin and of Menachem Mendel of Rimanov. He is best known for his scholarly and mystical work, *B'nei Yissaschar*, which includes a chapter for each month of the year.

Almost immediately, when he learned to read, the signs of his sharp, photographic memory and deep understanding could be seen. He would sit and learn night and day with exceptional diligence until his eyes became weak and his father had to hide all the *sefarim* from him.

In his later years, the B'nei Yissaschar was found *davening* on Yom Kippur all the day's *piyutim* by heart. Upon being asked when and how he learnt them, he smiled ruefully, "When I was little and my father hid from me all the *sefarim* in the house so as to save my eyesight, I found one *sefer* he had overlooked, an old *Yom Kippur Machzor*. Since that was all I had, I learned the whole *machzor* by heart!"

Shmulevitz, Rav Chaim Leib (1902-1979)

Rav Chaim was born in Stutchin, Poland, where his father, Rav Alter Raphael, was Rosh Yeshiva. His mother, Ettel, was the daughter of Rav Yosef Yoizel Horowitz, the Alter of Novardok. In 1920, both of his parents suddenly died, and Reb Chaim was left to care for his younger brother and two younger sisters. When Rav Chaim was twenty-two, Rav Shimon Shkop, Rosh Yeshiva in Grodno invited him to join his yeshiva. Within three years, Chaim was appointed to a lecturing post in the yeshiva. Reb Chaim continued his studies in Mir where the Rosh Yeshiva, Rav Eliezer Yehuda Finkel, chose him as a suitable match for his daughter. With the outbreak of World War II, he remained with the Mirrer Yeshiva in its exile in Shanghai for five years. After the war, he lived for a short while in America. With the establishment of the Mirrer Yeshiva in Yerushalayim, he immigrated to Eretz Yisrael and served as its Rosh Yeshiva. Rav Chaim authored *Sichos Mussar*.

Shternbuch, Rav Moshe

Rav Moshe Shternbuch is the *Ra'avad* of the Eidah HaChareidis in Jerusalem. He resides in Har Nof where he is the rabbi of the Gra Shul, named after the Vilna Gaon of whom he is a direct descendant.

Born in London, England, before World War II he was orphaned by the death of his father at an early age. He attended the Toras Emes yeshiva in Stamford Hill, of which Rabbi Moshe Schneider was the *rosh yeshiva*, before learning in the Brisk Yeshiva. He also studied with Rabbi Bezalel Rakow, later to become the Gateshead Rav. He subsequently took up a position in Johannesburg, South Africa. He was very involved in outreach, including his noted lectures to those in the medical field. Rav Moshe has authored many *sefarim* most notably *Moadim Uzmanim* and *Teshuvos V'Hanhagos*, and *Taam Vodaas*.

Sifsei Chachamim — Rav Shabsi ben Yosef Bass (1641-1718)

The *Sifsei Chachamim* was born in Kalisz, Poland and was the father of Jewish bibliography, and author of the *Sifsei Chachamim*, a super-commentary on Rashi's commentary on the Torah.

After the death of his parents, who were victims of the perse-cutions at Kalisz in 1655, Shabsi ben Yosef went to Prague. His teacher there in the Talmud was Meïr Wärters (d. 1693); and Loeb Shir HaShirim instructed him in singing. He was appointed bass singer in the celebrated Altneuschule of Prague, being called, from his position, "Bass," or "Bassista," or "Meshorer." His leisure time was devoted to literary pursuits, more especially to improving the instruction of the young.

Between 1674 and 1679, Bass traveled through Poland, Germany, and the Dutch Republic, stopping in such cities as Głogów, Kalisz, Krotoszyn, Leszno, Poznań, Worms, and Amsterdam, the centers of Jewish scholarship. He finally settled in Amsterdam in 1679, where he entered into friendly and scholarly relations with the eminent men of the German and the Portuguese-Spanish communities. That city was the center of Jewish printing and publishing, and Bass, becoming thoroughly familiar with the business, resolved to devote himself entirely to issuing Jewish books. With a keen eye for the practical, he perceived that the eastern part of Germany was a suitable place for a Jewish printing establishment. After a residence of five years, he left Amsterdam; going first, it seems, to Vienna, in order to obtain a license from the imperial government. The negotiations between Bass and the magistrates of Breslau occupied nearly four years, and not until 1687 or 1688 did he receive permission to set up a Hebrew printing press.

Thereupon he settled at Dyhernfurth, a small town near Breslau founded shortly before 1663, whose owner, Herr von Glaubitz, glad to have a large establishment on his estate, was very well disposed toward Bass. In order to more easily obtain Jewish workmen, Bass united into a congregation the small band of printers, typesetters, and workmen who had followed him to Dyhernfurth, for whose needs he cared, acquiring as early as 1689 a place for a cemetery.

The first book from Bass's press appeared in the middle of August, 1689, the first customer being, as he had anticipated, a Polish scholar, Rabbi Samuel ben Uri of Waydyslav, whose commentary *Beis Shmuel* on Shulchan Aruch *Even Ha'Ezer*, was printed at Dyhernfurth. The books that followed during the next year were either works of Polish scholars or liturgical collections intended for the use of Polish Jews. Being issued in a correct, neat, and pleasing form, they easily found buyers, especially at the fairs of Breslau, where Bass himself sold his books.

Simon, Rav Baruch

Rabbi Simon is a Rosh Yeshiva at Yeshiva University's affiliated Rabbi Isaac Elchanan Theological Seminary (RIETS). Rabbi Simon is a *talmid* of Rav Hershel Schachter and is known for his extensive *marei mekomos* (source material) for the *shiurim* he delivers. He authored five volumes, named *Imrei Baruch,* on the weekly *parashah* and two other *sefarim,* one on the topic of *Eruvin* and the other on *minhagim.*

Sofer, Rav Avraham Shmuel Binyamin, the K'sav Sofer (1815-1872)

The oldest son of the Chasam Sofer and grandson of Rabbi Akiva Eiger via his mother, Rebbitzen Sorel. After his father's death in 1839, the *Ksav Sofer* succeeded him as Rav and Rosh Yeshiva in Pressburg, at the unusually young age of twenty-four. Before his passing, the Chasam Sofer blessed his son on his deathbed with a *berachah* that contained every verse of *berachah* in Tanach! He served Pressburg for thirty-three years, the exact number of years his father had served before him.

Sofer, Rav Moshe, the Chasam Sofer (1762–1839)

Rav Moshe learned under Rav Nosson Adler of Frankfort and Rav Pinchas Halevi Horowitz, the *Baal Haflaah* (a *talmid* of the Maggid of Mezeritch). He was born in Frankfurt Am Mein. His first position was as a rabbi in Boskovitz in Moravia. He married the daughter of the Rav of Prosnitz and was supported by his brother-in-law, Rav Hirsch. Unfortunately, Rav Hirsch eventually lost all his money, and the *Chasam Sofer* took a position as Rav in the Moravian city of Dresnitz. After five years in Dresnitz, Rav Moshe moved to Mattersdorf. The *Chasam Sofer* was appointed Rav of Pressburg in Tishrei of 1806, and he occupied that position for thirty-three years. After the *petirah* of his first wife, Rav Moshe married the daughter of Rabbi Akiva Eiger. She bore the previously childless *Chasam Sofer* seven daughters and three sons.

Sorotzkin, Rav Zalman (1881–1966)

Also known as the Lutzker Rav, Rav Sorotzkin was a famous Orthodox rabbi who served as the rabbi of Lutsk, Ukraine. Rav Zalman Sorotzkin was born in Žagarinė, Lithuania in 1881. Initially, he studied with his father, Rabbi Ben-Zion Sorotzkin, who was the town's rabbi. He then studied in the yeshivas of Volozhin and Slabodka. Rav Zalman was a son-in-law of the Telzer Rav and Rosh Yeshiva, Rabbi Eliezer Gordon. When Rav Gordon died in 1910, Rav Sorotzkin was offered the position as rabbi and Rosh Yeshiva in Telz. He did not accept the position and was shortly after appointed as Rabbi to Voranava, Belarus (near Vilna). This enabled him to establish a close relationship with Rabbi Chaim Ozer Grodzensky. In Voranava, Rabbi Sorotzkin established a *yeshiva ketanah*. After two years in Voranava, Rabbi Sorotzkin moved to Dziatłava (known as Zhetel or זשעטל in Yiddish), where he served as rabbi for eighteen years. As Zhetel was the birthplace of the Chofetz Chaim, the Chofetz Chaim would affectionately refer to Rabbi Sorotzkin as "my" rav. In 1914, owing to the German invasion, Rabbi Sorotzkin moved to Minsk and became a close friend of the Chazon Ish, who rented a room from Rabbi Sorotzkin. Upon the end of the war, Rabbi Sorotzkin returned to Zhetel. In 1930, he was appointed rabbi in Lutsk, where he remained until World War II. During the early days of the war, when many yeshivas had to relocate, Rav Sorotzkin served as the head of the Vaad HaYeshivos, at the behest of Chaim Ozer Grodzensky. Rav Zalman managed to flee the war and escape to Mandate Palestine.

When the Moetzes Gedolei HaTorah (Council of Torah Sages) of Agudas Yisrael was founded in Israel, Rav Sorotzkin was appointed vice chairman. In 1953, the Chinuch Atzmai was formed and Rav Sorotzkin was chosen to head it.

He died in Israel on June 27, 1966 (9 Tammuz 5726). He is buried on Har HaMenuchos.

Sorotzkin authored the works, *Oznaim LaTorah*, a commentary on the Torah, *Moznaim LaTorah*, on the Jewish festivals, *Sheilos U'Teshuvos Moznaim LaMishpat* and *HaDeah Ve'HaDibur* which is a collection of *derashos*.

He was survived by five sons: Rav Elchonon Sorotzkin, author of *Lemaan Achai v'Rei'ai* and leader of the Chinuch Atzmai; Rav Baruch Sorotzkin, *rosh yeshiva* of the Telz Yeshiva in Cleveland, Ohio; Rav Eliezer Sorotzkin, founder of Kiryat Telz-Stone in Israel; Rav Yisrael Sorotzkin, rosh yeshiva in Lomza and Av Beis Din in Petach Tikvah; and Rav Benzion Sorotzkin, leader of Chinuch Atzmai.

Vilna Gaon – Rav Eliyahu ben Shlomo Zalman (1720-1797)

At the age of seven he gave his first public discourse and displayed a fully developed intellect. By the time he was ten he had advanced to the point where he no longer needed a teacher. At the age of thirty-five he was approached by one of the leading sages of that time, Rabbi Yonason Eybschutz, to act as an intermediary in the conflict between him and another great sage, Rabbi Yaacov Emden. The Gaon's son testified that for fifty years his father did not sleep for more than two hours in a twenty-four hour period. His breadth of knowledge was amazing. He was capable of stating from memory the number of times any sage was mentioned in any particular book of the Talmud. His knowledge of both the revealed and the hidden parts of the Torah was beyond compare. The Gaon considered secular knowledge to be a vital adjunct to Torah study. He was knowledgeable in almost all secular fields and authored books on grammar and mathematics. Among his many writings is *Aderes Eliyahu*, a commentary on Chumash.

Volozhin, Rav Chaim of (1749-1821)

Known as Rav Chaim Volozhiner, he was the most prominent student of the Vilna Gaon. Rav Chaim established the Volozhin Yeshiva in 1803, which was to become the classic model of Lithuanian *yeshivos*. His most famous work was *Nefesh Hachaim*, in which he emphasizes the power of Torah study and fulfillment of *mitzvos* to bring a Jew close to G-d. He also authored *Ruach Chaim*, a commentary on *Pirkei Avos*, and *Nishmas Chaim*, a collection of responsa.

Wolbe, Rav Shlomo (1914-2005)

Born in Berlin, Rav Wolbe's early education was in the Yeshiva of Frankfurt and in Rav Botchko's yeshiva in Montreux, Switzerland. In the 1930s, he spent several years in Mir, where he became a close *talmid* of Rav Yerucham Levovitz and Rav Chatzkal Levenstein. Rav Wolbe spent the war years in Sweden. After the war, Rav Wolbe moved to Petach Tikvah, where he married the daughter of Rav Avraham Grodzensky, Hy"d, the last *mashgiach* of Slabodka. Through her, he became a nephew of Rav Yaakov Kamenetsky, and a brother-in-law of Rav Chaim Kreisworth. In 1948, Rav Wolbe became *mashgiach* at Yeshiva Gedolah of Be'er Yaacov, a position he held for over thirty-five years. Later, he served as *mashgiach* in the Lakewood Yeshiva in Eretz

Yisrael and he opened *Yeshivas Givat Shaul*. Rav Wolbe published his first Hebrew work, *Alei Shur*, to provide today's yeshiva student with a basic guide to assist him to become a *ben Torah*.

Much of the information above was used with permission from Rabbi Kleinman of Timely Messages, a weekly Torah sheet, and from Manny Saltiel, who has compiled an extensive list of yahrzeits and short biographies of great figures.